MW01493633

Urban Youth and Photovoice

Urban Youth and Photovoice

VISUAL ETHNOGRAPHY IN ACTION

Melvin Delgado, Ph.D.
PROFESSOR OF SOCIAL WORK
BOSTON UNIVERSITY SCHOOL OF SOCIAL WORK
BOSTON, MA

OXFORD
UNIVERSITY PRESS

OXFORD
UNIVERSITY PRESS

Oxford University Press is a department of the University of
Oxford. It furthers the University's objective of excellence in research, scholarship,
and education by publishing worldwide.

Oxford   New York
Auckland   Cape Town   Dar es Salaam   Hong Kong   Karachi
Kuala Lumpur   Madrid   Melbourne   Mexico City   Nairobi
New Delhi   Shanghai   Taipei   Toronto

With offices in
Argentina   Austria   Brazil   Chile   Czech Republic   France   Greece
Guatemala   Hungary   Italy   Japan   Poland   Portugal   Singapore
South Korea   Switzerland   Thailand   Turkey   Ukraine   Vietnam

Published in the United States of America by
Oxford University Press
198 Madison Avenue, New York, NY 10016

Cataloging-in-Publication data is on file at the Library of Congress
ISBN 978-0-19-938132-6

9 8 7 6 5 4 3 2 1
Printed in the United States of America
on acid-free paper

This book is dedicated to Denise, Laura, and Barbara, constant sources of inspiration and support.

CONTENTS

SECTION FOUR **Lessons Learned and Future Directions**

Epilogue   217

ACKNOWLEDGMENTS

I wish to acknowledge the following individuals: Christopher Chaplin and Christine Lee (Boston University School of Social Work); Dr. Tina Kruse (Macalester College); Lynne May (East Lansing, Michigan). A special acknowledgement and thank you goes out to Ms. Leah Kriebe for her assistance in obtaining permissions for the use of youth images and narratives, and for her invaluable assistance in providing materials on Camp CAMERA. A thank you also goes to the following youth artists who gratuitously agreed to have their photos and narratives included in this book: Blanca, Brenda, Brittany, Corrina, Dianna, Jennifer, Monica, and Maricella.

Urban Youth and Photovoice

SECTION ONE

Setting the Context

Images convey. The simple and perhaps unequivocal statement becomes much more complex with the addition of a few short words. How do images convey? What do images convey? To whom? In answering these questions, what was originally a simple declarative statement becomes a position; a stance concerning the ways to think about and think with images.

—STANCZAK, 2007a, p. 1

1

Overview

Introduction

The early part of the 21st century brought forth increased excitement and promise for academics and practitioners interested in community practice with a foundation based on social justice principles and an embrace of community participatory actions (Brueggemann, 2013; Burghardt, 2013; Cnaan & Boehm, 2012; Gamble & Weir, 2009; Hardcastle, Powers, & Wenocur, 2011; Sites, Chaskin, & Parks, 2007). The ushering in of innovations in practice resulted in the need for comparable innovations in research. Effective community practice is predicated on the use of research methods that capture conditions and the social determinants surrounding them, and it sets the stage for social change efforts that are embraced by the community (Vaughan, 2014; Wang, 2006).

Research serves the critical dual purposes of generating knowledge and being an integral part of a social intervention. This connection between community participation in research and the social change resulting from it has generated its share of rewards and challenges (Stoecker, 2013). It has also prescribed a role for researchers as discoverers of new knowledge, but with the responsibility of ensuring that this knowledge translates into purposeful social action, particularly in the case of those researchers focusing their efforts on the marginalized of society.

This duality has raised provocative questions about both the objectivity of the research being conducted and the role of researcher as a social activist. Is objectivity possible? Ethnographers and arts-based researchers would argue that it is not. Some would go so far as to say that it is simply an illusion (Goldring, 2010). Although an expansive view of the role of community research is certainly not new, its prominence is unprecedented and it has ushered in what can be considered a "golden age" of community research, even when its "objectivity" is questioned by those who can be categorized as "positivists," as addressed in Chapter 2.

Titchen and Horsfall (2011) consider what creative research is, addressing the question in a manner that resonates with the central thrust of this book:

> What is creative research? Isn't all research creative? Well, yes it is, in the sense that all research is attempting to create new knowledge and understanding, but no, in that it may follow formulaic rather than creative research methodologies and methods. When we research with people and about people interacting in and with their social and life worlds, and when we are also concerned with bringing about change and transformation of self, others, groups, cultures, systems, practices and organisations simultaneously with knowledge creation, then formulaic approaches are unlikely to be sufficient. (p. 35)

"Formulaic" research approaches are problematic, creating a need for creative approaches, and they are far from being transformative or participatory (Boomer & Frost, 2011; Tasker, McLeod-Boyle, & Bridges, 2011; Titchen & Horsfall, 2011).

One of the resulting and promising outcomes for social science and the helping professions has been the development of new methods for engaging marginalized communities in the process of conducting research (most notably, asset, needs, and evaluation) and empowering them to create positive changes within their immediate environment. The prominence of participants and community in the research process has facilitated the introduction of innovative ways of ensuring that the method of inquiry is inclusive and relevant (White & Green, 2012), serving as a backdrop for the emergence and embrace of photovoice.

A number of scholars have taken this charge and produced exciting and important results (H. Jones, 2010). Hannay, Dudley, Milan, and Leibovitz (2013), for example, report on a community assessment project using photovoice and focus groups with a group of Latina adolescents, and on the empowerment and change that resulted from their participation. Booth and Booth (2002) speak to the shift in power that is essential with empowerment and research: "The process challenges the established politics of representation by shifting the means of documenting lives from the powerful to the powerless, the expert to the lay person, the professional to the client, the bureaucrat to the citizen, the observer to the observed" (p. 432).

Booth and Booth (2002) are correct about the challenges that result from a shifting in roles and power. The rewards for participants, their community, and the researcher, however extraordinary, as in the case of photovoice, have increased in prominence, as attested to by Mitchell (2011): "*Doing visual research* offers researchers in the social sciences an innovative orientation to the ways in which visual tools such as photography, video, drawing and objects can be used as modes of inquiry, modes of representation and modes of dissemination in research related to social change" (p. xi). Empowerment can emanate from the arts for those suffering as a result of stigma and marginalization, as in the case of sex workers, for example (Desyllas, 2013).

Photography facilitates depictions of urban public places and place-based communities, as well as the construction of local identity and community building (Loopmans, Cowell, & Oosterlynck, 2012). The close relationship between place and identity is often overlooked, yet it wields such a tremendous influence in shaping perceptions and experiences (Spencer, 2011). Photographing areas of interest and importance allows youth to identify, record, and share with adults in a manner that encourages them to do so in a way that is affirming (Johnson, 2008).

The use of photography for capturing memory is well recognized (Bates, 2010). Kuhn (2007), for example, addresses the importance of cultural memory and the role photography can play in enhancing them:

> Recent years have seen a flowering of research and scholarship on cultural memory across the humanities and social sciences. Among the many facets of this work is a quest to extend and deepen understanding of how personal memory operates in the cultural sphere: its distinguishing features; how, where and when it is produced; how people make use of it in their daily lives; how personal or individual memory connects with shared, public forms of memory; and ultimately, how memory figures in, and even shapes, the social body and social worlds. Personal and family photographs figure importantly in cultural memory, and memory work with photographs offers a particularly productive route to understanding the social and cultural aspects of memory. (p. 283)

Haque and Eng (2011) found that photovoice not only generated dialogue on community concerns and priorities but also resulted in community action. These social change interventions are guided by findings that set the stage for change, empower participants, and also provide tools for those undertaking these change efforts (Delgado & Humm-Delgado, 2013; Teti, Pichon, Kabel, Farnan, & Benson, 2013). This represents a dramatic shift in power for researchers.

These newly acquired "tools" or competencies (agency), in turn, can be transferred to other arenas and change efforts at the community level, and thus enhance a wide variety of community capital (human, economic, political, social, cultural, and physical). Community capacity enhancement has emerged as a form of community practice that captures these efforts at identifying and enhancing capital (Delgado, 1999). These new developments have expanded the options that community groups can use in selecting assessment and intervention methods that best meet their needs, based upon local demographics and socio-ecological considerations, including cultural values.

Visual research methods have grown in importance over the past 30 years or so (Moss, 2008; Patton, Higgs, & Smith, 2011; Reavey, 2011; Thomson, 2008b) and facilitated a shift toward social change resulting from research, though not without engendering considerable debate in the process. There are three prominent ways of categorizing visual research (Spencer, 2011): (1) researcher-found visual data (e.g., murals and graffiti); (2) researcher-created visual data (e.g., drawings, photographs, and videos); and (3) respondent-generated visual data (e.g., photographs and videos). The concept of participatory visual research has emerged to bring together various empowering visual research approaches, including a set of values that have emerged over this period of time (Luttrell & Chalfen, 2010).

The emergence of arts-based methods such as visual ethnography (Mitchell, 2011; Pink, 2007), a qualitative form of community-based participatory research (CBPR), during this time period represents an exciting development that deserves to be highlighted because of its potential for transforming communities, particularly marginalized groups. This trend in using the visual as a new type of knowledge creation emphasizes the role, importance, and grounding of the image in society (Cannuscio et al., 2009; Mitchell, 2011; Thomson, 2008b). Further, engaging in visual research can be fun, and how often can that be said of any form of research (Patton, Higgs, & Smith, 2011).

The subject of image and social research does not get the attention it merits. Self-image is considered the primary mechanism for insight and empowerment (Huss, 2012; Morgan et al., 2010; Phelan & Kinsella, 2011). De Lange and Mitchell (2007) refer to photovoice as a visual methodology for social change. McGregor (2012) refers to the concept of "design for provocation" to help explain the potential of images to provoke change. The importance of sociocultural context is a hallmark of this approach toward research, bringing forth new forms of knowledge to inform research and practice, and creating visual artifacts in the process (Creswell, 2013a; Freedman, Pitner, Powers, & Anderson, 2012; Mejia et al., 2013).

Visual ethnography falls into what Merteus (2010) refers to as a "transformative paradigm": "Paradigms serve as metaphysical frameworks that guide researchers in the identification and clarification of their beliefs with regard to ethics, reality, knowledge, and methodology" (p. 469). Qualitative research brings tremendous advantages to research because it is a multilayered, and nuanced, process lending itself to capturing of people not used to sharing their experiences and perspectives (Bridges & McGee, 2011).

Bearing witness to pain and suffering by capturing the lived experiences that caused these conditions represents one of the noblest goals of research, and arts-based qualitative research offers the greatest potential for this to occur (Rappaport, 2013). Photovoice is arguably one of the most popular forms of arts-based visual ethnography, and like other forms of visual ethnography, it facilitates the development and sharing of a story that previously had been either ignored or rejected (Grieb et al., 2013; Singhal, Rao, & Pant, 2006).

Photovoice as a Discovery and Action Method

Briski and Kauffman's documentary *Born into Brothels*, the 2005 Academy Award winner for best documentary, is arguably the most famous example of photovoice. The film is based on eight children of street workers in Calcutta's red-light district. The children were enlisted to garner support for the project of documenting the lives of these women. They were given cameras and taught to use them so that they could record life as they experienced it, which had been a much overlooked perspective. *Kids with Cameras* (2006) was a follow-up film that focused on the children's progress, and it is also the name of a nonprofit organization that resulted from the project. The power of art, in this case photographs as a basis for inspiring a film, can transform the lives of subjects and artists, and is the basis for photovoice. The popularity of photovoice, however, predates *Born into Brothels* and *Kids with Cameras*.

The origins of any research method seem to be always open for debate, and we can certainly add photovoice to this debate. Paolo Freire's early work with photography in in Lima, Peru, during the early 1970s can be credited as one of the earliest efforts at systematically using participatory photography as a research method (Burke, 2008). There is also little dispute that the popularity of photovoice can be traced to the work done by C. C. Wang and colleagues, and their innovative efforts to more insightfully understand the health status of village women in rural China in the mid-1990s.

The popularity of this method goes beyond academic circles and has found appeal in the national and international popular press, with countless numbers of articles extolling its virtues and its potential for use across groups and geographical settings, including the *New Straits Times*, Malaysia (Chew, 2009); *Sunday Times*, South Africa (Chauke, 2009); *The New Times* (2009); *The International Herald Tribune* (Eckholm, 2005); *South China Morning Post* (2004); *The Washington Post* (Goodman, 2003); and *The Guardian*, London (Gordon, 2002). Needless to say, it is highly unusual to have a research method garner such international public press and support.

Photovoice is an arts-based qualitative research method usually housed within community-based participatory research; photo elicitation, in turn, is a research method that can be part of a wide variety of methodologies, and it can often be confused with photovoice, since both rely on the use of cameras and images: "So, although depictions of these two approaches are sometimes conflated and contested in the literature, we view photoelicitation as a method that can be used in combination with many methodological approaches and photovoice as a methodology for community-based action research" (Phelan & Kinsella, 2011, p. 129). The emphasis that photovoice places on participatory principles and action serves to separate this qualitative research from photo elicitation.

Photovoice, at its most basic level, is the use of photographic equipment, usually digital, to capture a visual image, and then to transform this image into a vehicle for generating information and discussion. Specific images are selected because they lend themselves to use in various venues and exhibitions that can attract large crowds, and thus convey to the broader community important themes and messages (Fleming, Mahoney, Carlson, & Engebretson, 2009).

Radley (2010) argues that images are complex and that there is no one single "voice" that pictures make audible, nor any single image that makes it visible to an audience. The use of photovoice can result in simple or elaborate exhibitions depending upon the goals of the group using this method. Chapter 5 provides a detailed discussion on the subject of photovoice exhibitions.

These exhibits can take place in neighborhood libraries, community centers, houses of worship, nightclubs, schools, museums, governmental buildings, or other such settings. The site is decided on by the group, and the decision takes into account the projected audience. Photovoice is a method that is particularly attractive for community asset or needs assessments that can serve as a basis for creating change at the local level. The method has found increasing use as an evaluation tool (Kramer, Schwartz, Cheadle, & Rauzon, 2012; Sands, Reed, Harper, & Shar, 2009). In essence, its flexibility of use and purpose facilitates how it can be implemented, by different groups of people and under diverse circumstances.

Bessell, Deese, and Medina (2007), for example, illustrate the use of photolanguage (in this case the use of black-and-white photographs) to elicit responses from individuals for use in program evaluation. The use of digital cameras, making the process less expensive than the use of conventional cameras that require film to be processed, has ushered in a high degree of excitement, particularly as technological changes have occurred that make this method more user-friendly and less expensive. The type of camera used is dependent upon the preference of participants, feasibility of use, and budget.

The discussion sessions that transpire in reaction to the photographs can be recorded (on video or audio), and then transcribed for analysis and the creation of a historical record for the organizations sponsoring the project. The use of video recording has not received the attention it deserves. The prospect of capturing reactions and discussion on video introduces an exciting new dimension, although it, too, can raise concerns about youth or adult participants "playing to the camera," which would not be the case when sessions are audiotaped (Haw, 2008). Videovoice can complement photovoice by bringing a different visual method and potential outlet for the photographs and narratives (Thomson & Hall, 2008). This flexibility in how photovoice is used in conjunction with other methods is one of the many attractive aspects of this method.

The combining of these forms of visual research represents an innovative, although technically more demanding, manner of tapping the power of images (Stanczak, 2007b). A number of scholars talk about how images can be seductive and relatively easy to produce, thus giving the impression that they are in fact easy to produce and interpret (Spencer, 2011; Thomson, 2008a). Nothing could be further from the truth, as this book shows. Images represent the tip of an iceberg, so to speak.

Law (2004) raised serious questions about the failings of conventional methods to capture the complexities of an ever-changing society. Photovoice is an attempt to deal with the "mess" associated with complexities. Rabinowitz and

Holt (2013) identified seven reasons why photovoice is such a successful research method: (1) there is an immediacy to the rewards of taking pictures; (2) photography can be fun and an outlet for creativity; (3) photographs of familiar scenes and people can alter perceptions of social and physical context; (4) photography is relatively easy to learn and lends itself to use by a wide range of people; (5) "a picture is worth a thousand words"; (6) photographic images can be understood regardless of language, culture, literacy levels, or other factors; and (7) "policy makers can't deny reality when it's staring them in the face." These reasons for the success of photovoice present a stark contrast with conventional approaches toward community research and illustrate the appeal of photovoice in contrast to conventional, non-arts-based research (Zenkov et al., 2013).

Zuch Mathews, De Koker, Mtshizana, & Mason-Jones (2013) evaluated the success of a three-year photovoice project in South Africa and found it to be successful on multiple levels, allowing participants to shape the results of their labor to different audiences. The long length of this project no doubt provided additional time and effort normally not available in more typical photovoice projects, which can last several months. The power to portray local life and conditions is placed in the hands of local residents, bringing a new dimension to what typically happens with conventional, nonparticipatory research (Downey & Anyaegbunam, 2010). The concept of local solutions to local problems enters my mind, as do the concepts of local research and local participation.

The following description of a photovoice project in San Francisco illustrates a common approach for addressing problems of community health, a very popular topic with this method, as evidenced by the plethora of literature focused on health in a variety of manifestations:

> Residents were provided with disposable cameras and were encouraged to take photographs reflecting their views on family, maternal, and child health assets and concerns in their community, and then participated in group discussions about their photographs. Community events were held to enable participants to educate MCH staff and community leaders . . . The photovoice project provided MCH staff with information to supplement existing quantitative perinatal data and contributed to an understanding of key MCH issues that participating community residents would like to see addressed.
> —WANG & PIES, 2004, p. 95

Hoberecht and Miller-Cribbs (2011) used photovoice to introduce medical school students to community health and participatory research. Another example of health and photovoice is Minnesota's Red River Basin project, which utilized photovoice to have mothers document the effectiveness of an intervention to reduce pesticide exposure among children, along with other health and safety concerns (Stedman, McGovern, Peden-McAlpine, Kingery, & Draeger, 2012).

The potential of photovoice to be used as a discovery method is expanding to reach new groups, geographical areas, and audiences, including in combination with other qualitative research methods to open up new and different perspectives on what constitute knowledge and collaboration with participants. In the process, this method has facilitated and challenged researchers to engage in collaborative partnership with communities through the integration of visual art as a vehicle for social transformation and bridging cultural divides.

Photovoice allows community residents to assume the role of community historians, capturing events and lived experiences that have either gone unrecorded or been given only cursory attention in local media outlets. Community history is often relegated to local media headlines of crimes, fires, and other tragedies, and it thus provides a skewed or stereotypical view of a community. The images and narratives (stories) attached to these images reflect a resident perspective, and a counterbalance that can be tapped by current and future generations.

The concept of "transformation" is ubiquitous to photovoice and other arts-based research methods and will be used extensively throughout this book (Higgs & Titchen, 2011). Therefore, it will be addressed in a more detailed manner in this chapter. Self-referral awareness is synonymous with arts-based research (Franklin, 2013). Boomer and Frost (2011) provide a vivid and detailed description of transformation within a qualitative researchers' perspective, with relevance to co-researchers or partners in this endeavor: "What does transformation look like? In reality this sees us with greater self-awareness. We experience a feeling of being grounded, of knowing where we stand in the world, of being able to handle challenges and also to offer challenge, in a supportive way, to others. We are becoming aware of and learning to articulate how we use our body and our senses, and aesthetics, not only to learn about the world but also to influence the world and to be true to our axiological principles" (p. 288).

Transformation, in essence, represents a dramatic reconfiguration of perception and thought (Gerber et al., 2013). The internal changes resulting from transformative experiences can have a ripple effect throughout the social circle of youth. Transformation can be viewed from a youth, adult researcher, and community perspective. These viewpoints will share both similar and different outcomes or changes.

A Focus on Urban Youth

Photovoice has appeal among all geographical settings, population groups, issues, and concerns. It can be used to focus on conditions of marginality or everyday life. Although the focus of this book will be specifically on urban settings, it is important to note that rural settings, too, have been particularly receptive to this method (Bell, 2008; Bennett & Dearden, 2013; Cooper & Yarbrough, 2010; Downey, Ireson, & Scutchfield, 2009; Leipert & Anderson, 2012; Lopez, Eng, Randall-David, & Robinson, 2005; Panazzola & Leipert, 2013).

Youth in rural areas, too, have been the focus of photovoice and experienced positive outcomes similar to those of their urban counterparts (Downey & Anyaegbunam, 2010; Findholt, Michael, Davis, & Brigotti, 2010; Fresque-Baxter, 2013). Ning (2013) reports on the power of photovoice among Aboriginal youth in Canada. The wide range of youth backgrounds and settings shows why photovoice has a bright future in research concerned with people's well-being and lived experience.

It seems as if there is no youth social-political situation that cannot benefit from the insights gathered through photovoice. Kaplan (2008) notes that "student voice initiatives are sometimes treated and discussed as if they were conducted in a vacuum; such work is always done in highly politicized contexts" (p. 190). Kaplan's observations on power and youth illustrate the value of photovoice as a vehicle for addressing situations that are arduous to put words to, because images facilitate the discussion of power imbalances in the lives of youth. The incorporation of photovoice within youth development projects enhances both the method and overall programming (Delgado, 2006; Kaplan, 2013).

The power of photovoice is also well illustrated in the work reported by Denoi, Doucet, and Kamara (2012). The authors engaged war-affected child soldiers in Sierra Leone, a highly politicized environment and subject, and showed how this experience shaped their postwar lives and efforts at reintegrating back into their communities. The power of photography in showing the danger and horror of war is well recognized. Photovoice, however, brings a depth to the subject that photography by itself does not, by including the perspective, or narrative, as part of the central message. Kaplan's (2013) use of photovoice with the youth of South Central Los Angeles also illustrates the power of this medium to capture and document the hopes and dreams of the participants, as well as the challenges related to power, social class, race/ethnicity, and gender inequality they face in realizing their goals.

Narratives, in turn, are a critical instrument or qualitative method for helping us make better sense of reality, and for helping us to structure and order events (Spencer, 2011). Narratives, or everyday stories of people, can serve as the basis for transformative practice (Ledwith & Springett, 2010). Research and practice are to context what location is to real estate, and context plays an explicit role in giving meaning to images. The narrative associated with the images serves to heighten our understanding and appreciation of how individuals experience social conditions, as expressed in their voices and perceptions (Walker, 2012). "Voice," it should be emphasized, can be articulated or embedded in images and actions (Haw, 2008).

Although photovoice has potential for use across the entire life span, including use with older adults (Bell & Menec, 2013; Fitzpatrick et al., 2012; Rush, Murphy, & Kozak, 2012; Wiersma, 2011; Yankeelov, Faul, D'mbrosio, Collins, & Gordon, 2013), and with groups dealing with a host of oppressive forces, medical issues, and challenges, this method has found a particularly receptive audience among youth (Chonody, Ferman, Amitrani-Welsh, & Martin, 2013; Genoe & Dupuis, 2013; Luttrell, 2010; Owens, Nelson, Perry, & Montgomery-Block, 2010).

Youth have insights into their lives that adults simply do not have, regardless of their sensitivity and caring:

> The use of photovoice recognizes that children and youth may have insights into their own health beliefs and priorities that cannot be known or fully understood by public health professionals without employing empowering and creative techniques to obtain their true perspective. An important goal of using photovoice in health promotion is to have those who may participate in health promotion programs guide the development of these efforts to ensure their saliency and sustainability.
>
> —HENRY, RAMDOTH, WHITE, & MANGROO, 2013, p. 102

In essence, youth are the experts of their lives, and they see the world differently than adults (Burke, 2008).

Researchers need to listen and respond to the perceptions and goals of urban youth for creating transformative community projects (Greene, Burke, & McKenna, 2013). Bharmal et al. (2012), for example, see tremendous value in using photovoice as a research tool to develop greater understanding of how African American males in Los Angeles see their transition to adulthood. Allen (2012) would argue that marginalized youth of color are not the only ones who need more study, with middle-class African American youth, too, being overlooked and benefitting from photovoice.

Photovoice has been called a method for "community listening" because of its ability to penetrate into communities (Aslam, et al., 2013). Lenz and Sangganjananich (2013) see its potential to teach and instill empathy across groups and professions, for example. True, adults were once youths. Much has transpired in society to set the stage for youth experiences being very different from those of their parents. Jones (2009) sums up quite well how structural factors have shaped the social and economic trajectory of certain segments of the youth population: "Youth is a luxury to which the poor have no access" (p. 112). Major structural changes in society have disenfranchised youth from low socioeconomic backgrounds, making achievement of the "American dream" seem just that, a cruel dream that is unachievable.

These youth have constructed a social identity that is responsive to the harsh social reality of their surroundings, and in the process they have also constructed their own language and music, for example, to capture this reality (Allett, 2012; Brader & Luke, 2013; Laughey, 2006; Malbon, 1999). They have a vocabulary that may seem foreign to adults, yet it serves as a bridge between youth from differing cultural backgrounds. Photovoice serves to help capture this reality and conveys concerns and hopes for the future (Harley, 2011).

Drew, Duncan, and Sawyer (2010) identified four key reasons why photovoice has particular appeal for use with youth (complementing the seven reasons given by Rabinowitz and Holt (2013) why photovoice is popular, listed earlier in this chapter): (1) it is an attractive mechanism for recruitment and engendering positive feelings for research; (2) it is different and fun; (3) it serves to promote self-understanding in a highly creative manner; and (4) it facilitates expression, communication, and focus during interviews. Peer learning and self-discovery are essential components of youth photovoice projects, and this process of enlightenment is as important as the final product itself, so to speak (Lico & Luttrell, 2011).

Thackeray and Hunter (2010) address the attractiveness of technology and cell phones among youth, which will be an important theme throughout this book:

> Youth participate in photovoice by uploading pictures of their environment and posting on their SNS [Social Network Site] how that environment impacts their lives. One of the key improvements that mobile technology makes to photovoice is the ability to upload pictures in real time. If the phone has Internet access, the picture could be immediately uploaded to a blog or SNS and the photographer could record his or her impressions instantaneously. It would be more effective for a decision maker to receive a video of cars speeding down the neighborhood street rather than hearing about it anecdotally a few weeks later. (p. 584)

The technological dimensions of photovoice may not be attractive to their parents' generation, yet it is integral to their lives in a way that is second nature to them, making this generation the most technologically savvy generation in history.

Necheles et al. (2007) show the powerful combination of youth technological abilities and social change: "Results were derived from photograph sorting activities, analysis of photograph narratives, and development of advocacy projects. Youth frequently discussed a variety of topics reflected in their pictures that included unhealthy food choices, inducers of stress, friends, emotions, environment, health, and positive aspects of family. The advocacy projects used social marketing strategies, focusing on unhealthy dietary practices and inducers of stress" (p. 2219). Technology and photovoice is a theme that will permeate much of this book in a variety of ways. Not surprisingly, the development of methods that facilitate the integration of technology with social action can find a natural home among youth and other marginalized groups (Escueta & Butterwick, 2012; Wilson et al., 2006).

It is important to note that not all youth will embrace the use of a camera and photovoice, as experienced in Boulder, Colorado:

> Many youth had never used a camera before, and many were hesitant to photograph their homes, saying it was boring or there was nothing to show. YSI staff believed that at the beginning, many youth felt ashamed and did

not realize that other youth lived as they did, or that the project could be an opportunity to say what they wanted to change in their lives. As they worked, they began to express their dreams, including career aspirations and their desire to go to college, to eliminate poverty, and to have greater agency over their lives.

—DERR, CHAWLER, MINTZER, CUSHING, & VAN VLIET, 2013, p. 498

The rewards of photovoice in these instances can be extraordinary if project staff is prepared to invest the time and energy in addressing youth concerns.

Jacquez, Vaughn, and Wagner (2013) concluded, based upon a review of the literature on youth as partners in youth-focused CBPR, that the advantages of involving youth far outweighed the disadvantages:

> Without the voice of youth, research can miss the contextual input necessary to represent the unique youth experience. Unlikely as it may be that adult investigator-driven research accurately captures the youth perspective, it is even less likely that the results of that research will be disseminated to and accepted by youth. By partnering with youth to identify content area, research questions, data collection methods, and appropriate dissemination efforts, researchers significantly increase the chances that research findings will be applicable to children and adolescents living in the real world. (p. 177)

This form of partnership opens up a wide variety of potential collaborations between youth and the organizations that serve them and their community, benefitting all involved parties, and the possibility of using various visual-based methods.

Relationship-building is often one of the immediate benefits of photovoice participation. Intergenerational relationships can result from photovoice projects, representing an unexpected added "bonus" with these types of endeavors (Alcock, Camic, Barker, Haridi, & Raven, 2011). Arredondo et al. (2013) provide an intergenerational example, in this case based in San Diego, of youth using photovoice to make their local park more user-friendly to the community, benefitting them and other community residents.

The advocacy resulting from this youth program resulted in multiple ecological changes: "Removed overgrown plants, relocated storage container, increased park security (i.e., lighting, fencing), improved safety (i.e., covered sewer drain, sand lot removed), enhanced amenities (i.e., drinking fountain, bathroom, benches, tables), improved pedestrian safety in park (i.e., leveled the old and added new walking paths), and improved children's play area (i.e., new play equipment, fencing)." (p. 759).

Derr et al. (2013) argue that intergenerational urban spaces must actively seek to integrate youth perspectives regarding these spaces. The use of photovoice, as well as other arts-based research methods, represents a youth-friendly way of enlisting their views and participation (Woodgate & Leach, 2010). Chio and Fandt (2007) even advocate for the use of photovoice in the classroom to teach about diversity, although it certainly is not limited to this topic and can be an integral part of a service learning curriculum, for example.

Youth benefit from using the photovoice method in creating critical consciousness of their strengths and challenges, and in the process developing a deeper understanding and appreciation of their communities (Gubrium & Torres, 2013; Jain & Cohen, 2013; Wang, 2006). In the case of youth of color, this takes on paramount importance because institutional systems that teach and serve them will not ground their experiences within a social order that is actively ignoring the causes of their disempowerment, which has racism and classism at its core.

Finally, photovoice also can play a significant role in providing youth with leadership opportunities and experiences that can be transferred to other spheres in their lives, and thereby increase both their human capital and the likelihood of civic engagement (Findholt, Michael, & Davis, 2011; Wang, 2006). Civic engagement provides youth with opportunities to engage in the life community organizations and communities (Balsano, 2005; Baker, 2005; Flacks, 2007).

Owens et al. (2010) identified four overarching goals in their project on youth that typify what youth photovoice project goals can encompass: "(1) Gather, document and address youth perspectives on the condition of their lives; (2) Engage youth in creating and sharing their own knowledge about these conditions; (3) Promote youth involvement in civic discussions and decisions throughout the region; and (4) Experiment with and promote use of digital media in order to strengthen *social media capital* among participating youth" (p. 4).

These project goals illustrate the potential range of community-focused activities that can be associated with photovoice, and they are limited only by the imagination of participants and local circumstances and considerations, such as time frames and budgets, for example. This flexibility can also be a challenge or limitation, because it opens up the field so that any form of research involving photographs can be considered arts-based, with little regard to guiding values and principles. In other words, the use of cameras and photographs does not automatically make it a photovoice project. There is a philosophical and value base guiding how a photovoice project unfolds with urban youth, making photovoice much more than the taking of photographs and then talking about it. Art can be a source of knowledge (Eisner, 2008).

Photovoice has also been effectively broadened in scope and used to create community "photo mapping," integrating key concepts of health and place research with urban youth (Dennis, Gaulocher, Carpiano, & Brown, 2009; Woodgate & Leach, 2010). Amsden and VanWynsberghe (2005) undertook a youth community photo-mapping project in Vancouver, Canada. Strack, Magill, and McDonagh (2004) provide another health example of photovoice and youth, in this case involving health promotion. Vaugh, Rojas-Guyler, and Howell (2008) illustrate the use of a photovoice project involving a Latina girls' photography exhibition setting the stage for health interventions.

Dennis et al. (2009) describe a multi-method youth participatory photo-mapping project in Madison, Wisconsin, that utilized digital tools, narrative interviewing, and participatory protocols that resulted in maps that provided direction for youth community-based interventions. Santo, Ferguson, and Trippel (2010), too, report on their multi-method mapping success with youth, and the important role that technology played in sharing their stories through the use of maps, photography, and blogs. Technology-centered methods are particularly attractive to youth since they are often very familiar to this age group, thrusting them into a position of "expert," which is rare from an adult point-of-view (Delgado & Humm-Delgado, 2013; Delgado & Staples, 2007). Youth are further empowered because they possess an expertise that can be taught to others, particularly other youth and adults.

The following description of a North Carolina Latino photovoice project illustrates the potential use of this method for identifying Latino community assets, for example:

> "Over a one-year period, adolescents partnered with public health practitioners and researchers in: generating photo-assignments, taking photographs based on these assignments, using the photographs for photo-discussions, and defining themes based on these photo-discussions. A photograph exhibition and community forum raised awareness among local decision-makers and community members of the issues and assets of Latino adolescents and initiated a process toward change. From the participants' words and photographs emerged contextual descriptions of issues that both challenged and facilitated their adaptation and quality of life in their school and community.
> —STRENG ET AL., 2004, p. 403

Photovoice can be an effective method on its own, or in combination with other qualitative research methods, in helping to identify community assets (Riessman, 2008). Photovoice brings a unique visual perspective that can complement other methods.

Brazg, Bekemeier, Spigner, & Huebner (2010), and Yonas et al. (2009), too, find this method to be appealing for involving youth in community asset and needs assessments because of the technical dimension that it brings to the process, and because of the power it gives these youth to control the message they want to convey to adults and the broader community. Photovoice images and narrative can be distributed through a wide variety of electronic means, including being shown on websites specifically developed by the project (as addressed in Chapter 5), thus expanding the reach of the message that youth want to convey, but also providing challenges associated with ensuring that their images and messages not get compromised.

Schools are popular settings for photovoice projects, although research in this type of setting brings challenges not found in community-centered projects

(Chio & Fandt, 2007; Coronel & Pascual, 2013; Hill, 2013; Mitra, Serrierre, & Kirshner, 2013). Johansen and Le (2012) and Johansen (2012) describe the use of photovoice and involvement of youth in defining what multiculturalism meant to them. These youth translated the pictures and narratives into recommendations for increasing racial understanding in their respective schools.

Zenkov and Harmon (2009), in turn, used photovoice as a visual tool to help urban youth to record their perceptions of the purposes, barriers, and supports for success in school. School-based projects involving photovoice can be used in school-community service learning, thereby minimizing disconnects that often exist between this institution and undervalued communities (Delgado, 2006). Institutions of higher learning, too, are excellent sites for youth photovoice projects. Shell, Ferguson, Hamoline, Shea, & Thomas-Maclean (2009), and Lichty (2013), for example, used photovoice in university classes and extolled its virtues and potential for enhancing teaching in higher education.

Photovoice lends itself to visually capturing the meaning of culture for youth. This cultural context will vary based upon demographic characteristics and local context, and culture in this instance does not limit itself to ethnicity and race, since youth as an age category have a culture, too (Lapalme, Bisset, & Potvin, 2013). For example, Latino youth in urban centers will bring a unique blend of Latino and American cultural views and values based upon how they experience life living in two cultural worlds, and these will differ from the views and values of their older adult counterparts. Photovoice facilitates the identification, capture, and display of these cultural perspectives and nuances, facilitating discussion and increased community awareness of how cultural values and assets can be tapped and mobilized to enhance the community's image (Delgado & Humm-Delgado, 2013).

Photovoice also allows youth to share their experiences with those outside of their community, youth as well as adults, to counteract negative impressions that may exist about them (Walker, 2012). Wilson et al. (2006), for example, in an article examining high school students working with fifth grade community research team members, describe the potential of youth teams to undertake community asset and risk maps by utilizing photovoice, highlighting both sources of youth pride and their concerns. There is no youth setting or youth age group that cannot lend itself to the use of photovoice (Warne, Synder & Gillander Gådin, 2013).

Goals of Photovoice

There certainly is no shortage of goals associated with photovoice. Wang and Burris (1997) identified three overarching goals for photovoice that, not surprisingly, have remained largely unchanged in over 15 years: "(1) to enable people to record and reflect their community's strengths and concerns, (2) to promote critical dialogue and knowledge about important issues through large and small group discussion of photographs, and (3) to reach policymakers" (p. 369). Photovoice also results in participants deriving therapeutic benefits and generating intergenerational relationships (Chauke, 2009; DeCoster & Dickerson, 2014; Prag & Vogel, 2013).

These and other potential goals make photovoice an attractive method for use in community asset assessments, for example, by facilitating the tapping of community concerns through the use of a participatory approach that stresses community assets rather than deficits (Carlson, Engebretson, & Chamberlain, 2006; Wang & Burris, 1997; Wang & Redwood-Jones, 2001). Finally, the comments of Stoecker (2013) about qualitative research benefits also apply to photovoice positively altering relationships between different groups: "A good research process can do more than generate data. In the best case it builds relationships, and in the very best cases it builds relationships across differences. Just like the community suppers get people talking across class and race differences, research can bring perspectives to community issues that people may otherwise dismiss" (p. 54). Vaughan (2010), too, found that youth can use photovoice as a bridge with adults, and particularly with community leaders. Bridging social capital takes on prominence in communities that are fragmented, with youth being isolated from positive adult-youth relationships.

Marginalized groups and communities benefit from having their stories or narratives told to increase positive attention and resources to their communities, and by creating a sense of control over their lives, an increased awareness of the importance of relationships, and their potential to be social change agents (Delgado & Humm-Delgado, 2013; Foster-Fishman, Nowell, Deacon, Nievar, & McNann, 2005; Garcia et al., 2013;). Participation results in a transformative experience, a critical element in any form of participatory democratic-based intervention (Delgado & Staples, 2007; Garcia & Morrell, 2013; Watson & Douglas, 2012).

This transformative experience is then shared with others, thereby being a source of "good" news rather than the usual "bad" news often perpetuated by mainstream media sources concerning marginalized groups and communities: "Unfortunately, marginalized communities cannot expect to see positive media coverage of local events, volunteerism, and indigenous leaders performing important community functions. Thus, any positive community information will need to be generated internally and shared with the outside work" (Delgado & Humm-Delgado, 2013, p. 22). Generating and controlling positive messages to the external community are benefits that photovoice can bring to community groups.

Photovoice as a Qualitative-Participatory Research Method

The popularity of photovoice in large part can be attributed to its novelty, ease of use, and potential use across population groups, goals, budgets, and settings as a vehicle for identifying community assets and increasing community dialogue (Brazg et al., 2010; Castleden, Gacuin & First Nation, 2008; Downey, Ireson & Scutcfield, 2009). This flexibility allows photovoice to be adapted to local goals and circumstances, taking into account the influence of cultural values on how it is conceptualized. McIntyre (2003), for example, used photovoice to capture how women create place and identity within the contexts of everyday life. This method has been used among Latino immigrants to assist with family planning, a group that is not prone to participate in research, and a topic that is taboo, making for a powerful combination of challenges for researchers (Schwartz, Sable, Dannerbeck, & Campbell, 2007). Kelly, Hoehner, Baker, Ramierez, & Brownson (2006), in turn, used photovoice as a tool for promoting physical activity in communities.

Photovoice's popularity is not restricted to the United States. One photovoice project in South Africa sought to promote food security among the poor with HIV/AIDS (Swaans, Broerse, Meincke, Mudhara, & Bunders, 2009). It was used to explore social and environmental change on the Andaman Coast of Thailand (Bennett & Dearden, 2013). Green and Kloos (2009) used photovoice to have youth (ages 12 to 16) document life in a refugee camp in Uganda. Meo (2010) reports on its use among adolescents in Buenos Aires, Argentina, and their exploration of their habitus. Pakistan, too, has witnessed the effective use of photovoice; in this case, capturing the complexities surrounding tuberculosis, including aspects that must be taken into account in developing holistic prevention interventions (Mohammed, Sajum & Khan, 2013).

Halifax, Meeks, and Khander (2008) illustrate the successful use of photovoice in Toronto, Canada, involving health and a homeless group, a population that faces numerous challenges and that we know relatively little about, including their aspirations. Bredeson and Stevens (2013), too, focused their photovoice on the homeless, in this case with families in Minneapolis and St. Paul, Minnesota. Hague and Eng (2011) utilized photovoice to generate community dialogue and action to promote health and well-being in St. James, Canada. Ho, Rochelle, and Yuen (2011) used photovoice among Hong Kong adolescents living in a high poverty area and tapped into their perceptions of their community. Saimon, Choo, and Bulgiba (2013) used photovoice among Malaysian adolescents to generate a better understanding of the forces impeding youth engagement in physical activities. This list of international examples only scratches the surface. It seems that it is safe to say that there is no hemisphere or country that has escaped photovoice.

Not surprisingly, the plethora of scholarly articles on photovoice reflects the popularity of this method since the early 2000s, and this has resulted in at least four comprehensive literature reviews. Catalini and Minkler (2010) concluded, based upon a review of the literature on photovoice, that this method invariably (60 percent) is closely associated with social change efforts following a photovoice activity, facilitating the empowerment of participants. Hergenrather, Rhodes, Cowan, Bardhoshi, and Pula (2009) reviewed the literature on photovoice as a research methodology and concluded that, despite limitations (which will systematically be addressed later on in the book), it holds much promise for facilitating community participation in assessment and bringing about social change.

Kuratani and Lai (2011) concluded in their review of the literature that photovoice supersedes conventional approaches toward facilitating discussion through use of visual means, and that this method enjoys worldwide appeal due to its flexibility, its participatory nature, and its ease in obtaining insights in difficult situations. Lai, Jarus, and Suto (2012) focused on how this method has been used in health research with implications for occupational therapy (OT), and found that the method was very useful for OT.

Finally, Powers and Freedman (2012) focused their literature review using a social justice and environment perspective and found the method held much promise in shaping environmental interventions and policies when viewed from an oppressed groups' perspective. A social justice foundation thrusts this method into creating change for better environments (Moss, 2008). As discussed in Chapter 4, social justice plays a prominent role in shaping urban youth photovoice as conceptualized in this book.

Photovoice, in similar fashion to other arts-based visual ethnographic methods and approaches addressed in this book, seeks to achieve social change goals at a community level through the use of photography and corresponding narrative to bring the pictures and stories to life (Foster-Fishman, Nowell, Deacon, Nievar, & McNann, 2005). Each photograph, whether in color or in black and white, conveys a story or a key point that the photographer wishes to convey to an audience. Collectively, there are themes that emerge that serve as a basis for a holistic picture that serves as a guide to bringing about social change (Haines, Oliffe, Bottorff, & Poland, 2010). A rationale for seeking change emerges from the photographs and accompanying narratives for all to see and understand.

Photography has also found wide acceptance for gender-related projects because of how well it facilitates discourse on painful topics. Frohmann (2005) provides a rationale and vivid description of a photovoice project focused on Mexican and South Asian immigrant women with histories of being battered: "The project is built on the use of participant-generated photographs and photo elicitation interviews as methods for exploring with women, in support group settings, the meanings of violence in their lives and their approaches to creating safer spaces" (p. 1396). Frohmann sees photovoice as a methodological approach with great potential to "amplify the voices of silenced women," thus creating the requisite conditions for community education and social action to occur. These women can find their voices individually and collectively through the use of photographs as vehicles for sharing their experiences (Mejia et al., 2013). Leonard and McKnight (2013), in turn, see tremendous value in this method for use with adolescents.

Sutherland and Cheng (2009) see its value with immigrant women, in this case in small Canadian cities. Duffy (2010), too, sees particular value in using this method with women, in this case lone mothers. Valera, Gallin, Schuk, and Davis (2009) studied low-income women's access to healthy food in New York City and found this method to be an effective way of increasing women's exercise of personal agency. Oliff and Bottorff (2007), in turn, argue that photovoice as a qualitative health method has rarely focused on men's health. They used photovoice to focus on men's health and developed a project titled "Living With My Prostate Cancer." Project participants were asked to mount a photographic exhibition that reflected their experiences and perspectives.

Affleck, Glass, and Macdonald (2012) see value in using photovoice as a way of taping into men's emotional feelings in qualitative health research. Finally, photovoice has been found to be an effective method for HIV prevention interventions involving young African American men having sex with men (Kubicek, Beyer, Weiss, & Kipke, 2012), a highly sensitive topic in the African American community, and a topic requiring creative research methods for interventions to take into account culture, influencing public education, outreach, and culturally competent interventions.

Photography can play a variety of roles in research. Molloy (2007), Peabody (2013), and Russell and Diaz (2013) envision photography and photovoice as a "tool" for social workers to raise awareness about social justice issues and empower undervalued groups in the process. Barnidge et al. (2010) describe the use of "photo elicitation" as a means of increasing community dialogue on community assets, and incorporating these resources into health initiatives. In essence, in many ways we are experiencing the dawn of photography and imagery as qualitative research. Caution is in order: "Imagery is always potentially preyed upon for expedient political uses" (Spencer, 2011, p. 22).

This is not to say that there is mistrust, as is customary with qualitative methods in general: "Qualitative research . . . is frequently mistrusted because it seems to take the user back into the selective perception and value bias from which figures provide an escape. Images (especially photographs and video) appear even more prone to partiality, seen as the obvious victim of unsystematic sampling, subjectivity and the singer point of view" (Walker, Schratz, & Egg, 2008, pp. 164–165). This epistemology will be addressed in greater detail in Chapter 5, illustrating how trust engendering is an essential component of photovoice.

Newbury and Hoskins (2012) see photo elicitation as a method that assists helping professions address needs without losing sight of social justice:

> While it is often a commitment to social justice ideals that bring people to the helping professions as practitioners, our theories and approaches to care are often service-oriented and expert-driven. Such an orientation to helping often focuses more on individual change—that is, changing those who are experiencing difficulties—than it does on systemic or collective change . . . By incorporating photo elicitation into the helping relationship, the social nature of 'social' problems can be acknowledged and attended to, gently

nudging the boundaries of practice in a way that is more contextualized, centering possibilities rather than problems. (p. 20)

Social justice frames these images, which in turn influence practice (Padgett, Smith, Derejko, Henwood, & Tiderington, 2013).

Finally, Rhodes, Hergenrather, Wilkins, and Jolly (2008) see photovoice as a tool for creating knowledge, developing partnerships, and undertaking social change efforts on behalf of people with HIV. A marginalized group, regardless of the source of their marginalization, can benefit from involvement with photovoice because it enhances their understanding of their experiences and creating working relationships and collaborations in the process of self-discovery and enlightening the public (Clark-Ibanez, 2008; Watson & Douglas, 2012).

Photovoice Rewards and Challenges

The benefits of photovoice have been identified throughout this introductory chapter. Photovoice effectively democratizes the research process in a manner that does not exclude residents and, in the case of this book, youth from shaping the key questions that need to be answered and the recommended process of getting the answers (Novak, 2010).

Arts-based qualitative research methods such as photovoice have much in common with what is referred to as "action research": "Action research does bear resemblance to, and frequently draws from the methods of, qualitative research in that both are richly contextualized in the local knowledge of practitioners. Qualitative research is research about practice, not with practitioners. This crucial difference often leaves the work 'inactionable,' that is, not something that practitioners can or even wish to make practical use of" (Huang, 2010, p. 94). Photovoice is a form of action research because the ultimate goal, or outcome, is addressing positive social change.

This new "research and social change tool," in the hands of community residents or groups such as youth, provides a vehicle through which a community can be better understood, both internally and externally (Checkoway & Richards-Schuster, 2012; Delgado, 2006; Strack, Lovelace, Jordan, & Holmes, 2010). It would be a serious mistake to think of an audience for photovoice as strictly external based on the assumption that a community understands how its marginalized subgroups feel and think, and does not need to be educated. Marginalized subgroups in urban communities can also be misunderstood internally, however, with all of the myths and stereotypes society has about these groups, as well as the social consequences inherent in marginalization. Photovoice projects and exhibitions generally have multiple audiences, including reaching out to individuals with similar concerns and problems illustrated in the exhibition, but who have not been able to speak out or seek help because of shame, stigma, or other pressing reasons (Erdner & Magnusson, 2011).

One of the most appealing aspects of this method is its ability to engage residents across the life span, as well as people with various degrees of physical and cognitive abilities (Baker & Wang, 2006; Booth & Booth, 2002; Stegenga & Burks, 2013). Wang (2006), arguably one of the nation's leading experts and proponents of photovoice, has applied this method in numerous studies, and in the process opened the door to other researchers focusing on various marginalized groups. The visual nature of this method has multiple appeals (Pain, 2012), including facilitating rapport building and communications between researcher and participant. It also facilitates articulation of abstract ideas, tacit knowledge, and reflection.

Photovoice has been found to be a particularly viable method for assessing the assets of people with disabilities, since it can be modified to take into account various physical and cognitive challenges (Glover-Graf, 2000; Jurokowski & Paul-Ward, 2007; Jurokowski, Rivera, & Hammel, 2009; Newman, 2010; Schleien, Brake, Miller, & Walton, 2013). The reader may ask how persons that are blind or visually impaired can use photovoice. Although I could not find any literature on the subject, it is possible to pair up with a sighted person, who can take the pictures when directed to. The "go-along" process will be discussed later on in the book and provides opportunities for individuals with severe disabilities to engage this research method.

Photovoice has also been used with homeless people. Wang, Cash, and Powers (2000) describe their effort involving homeless women and men in shelters who photographed their daily existence, documenting their strengths and struggles. Participants, in turn, shared their perspectives in group discussions using photographs that best represented their lives. Photovoice can also be integrated into very creative programs and projects. Thomas and Irwin (2013), in a Canadian project focused on healthy eating and at-risk youth, used photovoice as a critical tool to help these youth advocate for the sustainability of community-based cooking programs being offered for high school credit.

It certainly is tempting to extol only the virtues of photovoice. This method does present a variety of challenges (Drew, Duncan, & Sawyer, 2010), including ethical challenges, which are addressed in greater detail in Chapter 7. A commitment to social justice goals on the part of those in the helping professions facilitates the adoption of photovoice. These professions are expert-driven, emphasizing the importance of formal education and the role of the helper as opposed to collaborator. The perspective of the professional as expert is counter to that which photovoice embraces, resulting in tensions between the researcher and participants.

Mitchell, DeLange, Moletsane, Stuart, and Buthelezi (2005) identified challenges related to technical aspects, documentation and interpretation of findings, ethics, and translating findings into action. Jardine and James (2012) raise challenges related to scheduling, time restrictions for developing group relationships, and consequences related to lost or stolen cameras. Other problem areas include (1) a lack of youth trust in adults; (2) arriving at a consensus on the focus on a photovoice project; (3) obtaining requisite funding and potential conflict; (4) lack of adequate preparation; (5) labor intensity and time limitations; and (6) obtaining parental permission. Some of these challenges are easier to address than others. Trust, for example, is arduous, whereas lack of preparation is easily addressed.

Prins (2010) sees tremendous benefits associated with using photovoice. However, based upon its use in El Salvador, there are potential pitfalls, too. Encountering suspicion, timidity, and fear of ridicule by the community is not uncommon. Prins goes on to note: "Photography is a technology with contradictory potential for social control and surveillance, and for the recovery of marginalized groups' subjugated knowledge. Although participatory has many potential benefits, researchers and educators must also anticipate its unintended consequences, attend to ethical considerations, and recognize how this tool is mediated by the sociocultural setting" (p. 426).

The development of an ethical research vocabulary is one way of helping researcher and participant in negotiating ethical considerations (Aluwihare-Samaranayake, 2012). Context shapes the potential receptivity or resistance to use of this method. These challenges are not insurmountable, but they cannot be ignored if the promise of photovoice is to be realized for use with all population groups, and particularly with urban youth (Mitchell, 2011; Packard, 2008; Taft, 2007).

Book Goals

This book sets out to accomplish five goals: (1) provide a conceptual understanding of visual ethnography and how photovoice is one method of using arts-based visual knowledge as a mechanism for creating awareness and social change; (2) provide an in-depth critique of the rewards and challenges of using photovoice as a mechanism for self-discovery and change; (3) provide a detailed description of the various stages and elements associated with using photovoice with youth; (4) provide extensive case examples of how and why photovoice is a viable method for use in community settings; and (5) draw lessons and recommendations from national and international efforts for using youth-centered photovoice.

Book Outline

This book will consist of eight chapters and an epilogue, which are divided into four sections:

Section 1: **Setting the Context** (3 chapters). This section will introduce various perspectives on qualitative research, ethnography, and arts-based visual methods. In addition, the reader will view these methods, and particularly photovoice, from a youth development perspective.

Section 2: **Photovoice as a Research Method** (4 chapters). Section 2 provides an in-depth understanding of the role and influence of values and principles serving as a foundation for photovoice with youth. In addition, various aspects associated with carrying out a photovoice project will be covered, including how to analyze data, and the consideration of ethics.

Section 3: **Voices from the Field** (1 chapter). This section will integrate theoretical material on photovoice into a live case study of Camp CAMERA (Minneapolis, Minnesota) to illustrate the role of theory and action, with particular attention being paid to the rewards and challenges associated with this form of visual ethnography.

Section 4: **Lessons Learned and Future Directions** (Epilogue).

Conclusion

The world of social research is continually expanding and identifying new and exciting approaches to finding new knowledge and insights into how marginalized individuals encounter and experience challenges in their daily life. An effort to better understand the world of those who are most marginalized in society has necessitated development of innovative ways of gaining new insights. This has thrust researchers into new ways of examining what constitutes knowledge, and highlighted the importance of bringing about change as a result of these new insights.

This chapter provided an overview of the role of the arts, with an emphasis on the visual, and photovoice as tools for discovery and action. Photovoice has a worldwide appeal and offers researchers the potential to apply this method with urban youth, for example. Research without an appreciation of context is research that does not maximize its potential for social good. Urban youth provide a geographic and age-group context for photovoice that has natural appeal. Photovoice must also be grounded within a constellation of perspectives (arts-based, visual ethnography, community-based participatory research [CBPR], and youth-development/youth-led) to maximize its potential for discovery and change, as addressed in the following two chapters.

Photovoice does not belong to any one discipline or profession, and that is the way it should be. It is not owned by the academy or practitioners; it is owned by participants and their community. Photovoice necessitates a multidisciplinary approach that is participatory and empowering, seeking to make a qualitative difference in the lives of those who live on the outskirts of society. It must, in addition, be grounded in the operative reality of residents and not institutions.

Chapter 2 provides an in-depth discussion of arts-based research emphasizing visual ethnography, including how this perspective toward research has shaped community-based participatory research and photovoice. Chapter 3 (youth development/youth-led), in turn, will tie community and qualitative research to youth, illustrating the power and influence of photovoice for achieving social change with urban youth as central characters in these efforts.

2

Arts-Based Social Justice: Research, Education, and Social Action

Introduction

It is appropriate to start this foundation chapter with a story concerning a book I was seeking to get published several years ago. I approached a publisher that I had had experiences with and was asked where the most appropriate home for the proposed book was. In other words, who was the intended audience? I explained that the book had "many homes" because it would have applicability across academic disciplines, and that this was one of the central goals. He then responded that a book with many homes is a book without a place to call home. I think that response is very appropriate in the case of this book, because of the appeal of photovoice across disciplines and helping professions. Arts-based research and practice transcends conventional boundaries of disciplines and professions.

Photovoice has many homes and is best understood and appreciated when it is grounded within a wider context, or umbrella, that brings together various interlocking and complementary disciplines and fields, since this method incorporates elements from multiple fields and perspectives. Having an understanding and appreciation of these many "homes" is important and goes beyond what many would consider an erudite interest, with a very limited academic following.

These streams become important to understand in order to fully appreciate how photovoice has been shaped by historical and current events; further, it helps us better understand what the future may hold in store for this method of research, and the role and shape photovoice will play in shaping fields of practice. Photovoice, in similar fashion to other research methods, is a means to an end, and one that is transformative and social-justice directed, bringing a distinctive perspective to this form of inquiry and practice.

Three major perspectives stand out for their particular relevance and contributions to photovoice: (1) arts-based research (qualitative), education, and social action; (2) visual ethnography, which is a branch of the arts-based field that brings photography as the art form; and (3) community-based participatory research (CBPR), with its emphasis on meaningfully engaging those in all facets of this focus of inquiry at the community level (Hacker, 2013). Common goals and values facilitate these three approaches merging together to inform and shape photovoice, helping to explain the popularity, or draw, of this qualitative method in community-centered research, and opening the door for innovation.

This book brings an added branch, so to speak, because of its emphasis on applying photovoice (a popular form of arts-based visual ethnography) with urban youth, and thus youth development further grounds a geographical and age group in this form of visual research method. The first three of these perspectives will be addressed in this chapter; youth development and photovoice will be addressed in the following chapter. The conceptual foundation of these four perspectives allows the reader to appreciate this universe of inquiry and practice, and it is an expanding one at that, with all of the joy and growing pains associated with a worldwide rapid expansion. Photovoice, it should be emphasized, is not photovoice without a conceptual foundation, set of values, and framework; or, as Phelan and Kinsella (2011) say, it is the equivalent of sailing without a map—or a destination, for that matter. Photovoice creates intellectual space for innovation by extending conventional boundaries and providing qualitative and arts-based researchers with increased options and opportunities for creating new knowledge, transformation, and social change.

This chapter highlights the major dimensions and elements associated with arts-based research, visual ethnography, CBPR, and photovoice, examining the overlap between these perspectives. If there is a contribution to be made by this book, it will be dependent upon how successful the author is in presenting a cogent and coherent portrait of urban youth and photovoice from a youth development perspective. Four streams come together to form a river, as in the case of this book. Each of these streams is formidable onto itself. In combination, it makes for a powerful and seamless river.

Photography as Arts-Based Inquiry and Intervention

In keeping with the river metaphor, arts-based research can be conceptualized as a river with many different tributaries, with a major one being art therapy (Antal, 2013). It should not come as any great surprise to see how an arts-based approach has great appeal for helping professions and academic disciplines, with similar goals helping to shape interventions. Arts-based research has infinite possibilities for significantly changing people's lives (Brown, 2013). This transformative potential can be a powerful impetus to bring academic disciplines and helping professions together in search of a common good.

FIGURE 2.1 Fields Influencing Urban Youth Photovoice

Urban youth photovoice is influenced by a number of prominent fields and approaches. Figure 2.1 presents a basic visual representation of the myriad of influences on urban youth photovoice. These different streams of influence shape how urban youth photovoice is conceptualized. Each of these streams, in turn, consists of multiple elements.

The act of photography, a prominent sector in arts-based research, too, can certainly be viewed through a variety of perspectives, including as a visual art form (Leavy, 2009; Rose, 2012; Stanczak, 2007c). When art is viewed from a sociocultural context and analysis, it becomes a vehicle for meaningfully adding to, or significantly altering, people's lives: "An understanding of the intersection between image production, image-producing technologies and the ethnic, racial, gendered and other elements of the identities of those who use or own them is crucial for a reflexive approach" (Pink, 2007, p. 26).

The power of the photographer undergirds Pink's reflection on photography. The power of manipulating images is inherent in photovoice or any other visual qualitative method: "Try as I might, I can conceive of no photograph that is not manipulated in some way, simply by dint of the many choices that are made between image capture and presentation. Every photograph represents the photographer's choices, hence his interpretation of reality" (Goldstein, 2007, p. 75). The power of historical and cultural text, too, undergirds ethnography (Hammerseley, 1990; H. Jones, 2010; Kuhn, 2007).

In our case, arts-based social justice research, education, and social action represents an attractive "home," or contextualization, for those scholars and practitioners who view research transpiring in a variety of innovative ways, and as a mechanism for redressing the pain and harm perpetrated upon those on the fringes of society because of their demographic profile or belief system (Barone & Fisner, 2012; Garcia & Morrell, 2013; McNiff, 2008; O'Donoghue, 2009). Further, arts-based research and intervention opens up the door for the use of cultural values in shaping how researchers and participants plan their activities to resonate with communities (Leavy, 2009). Arts-based initiatives, in addition, can transpire in a wide variety of "non-arts-based" settings (McNiff, 2013).

No community setting should be exempt from engaging use of the arts for the betterment of the community; even libraries, for example, can be expected to accept this charge:

> One of the hottest terms among public librarians today is "content creation," which involves stuff that library patrons make instead of simply use in a library context. Videos, music, fiction, paintings, 3D printed materials, websites—all these are made in public libraries, and will increase in popularity as more libraries shift from purveyors of content to facilitators of creation. Libraries are becoming "incubators" of art, ideas, economic benefits, and community benefits. . . . A library seething with creative energy can shock some traditionalists, who still see the library as a quiet place to read a book. Yet the mission of many public libraries is not only to inform via printed or multimedia materials but also to connect ideas and people, to build communities, and to offer transformative experiences to all by bridging opportunity divides. In light of the "library=transformation" model, art programs are a natural fit. And art programs require teaching artists to lead them.
>
> —BARNISKIS, 2013, p. 81

Clearly, the research conducted by such a library will look very different from that done by a library with a very narrow mission that eschews social justice and social change themes.

This embrace of a calling to use social research as a means of engaging and working with marginalized groups to achieve social justice highlights how the arts can free the mind, as well as the spirit, by serving as an impetus for social change (Batsleer, 2011; Foster, 2012a). Unfortunately, the typical response when art is mentioned focuses on the aesthetic aspects rather than how it can positively transform a life (Bagnoli, 2012). True, there is an aesthetic aspect to art that can lead to an appreciation of an image solely for its appeal to the eye, for example. That view is very narrow, however, and fails to take into account how art can also be revolutionary in character, bringing the potential for transforming individuals as well as society (Naidus, 2009). Arts-based research has been referred to as subversive research, and we can easily add "political act" to describe this approach to knowledge and social action creation (Rumbold, Fenner, & Brophy-Dixon, 2012).

The parallels between the sciences and the arts may not be readily apparent, yet both emphasize the importance of the process of questioning and knowledge creation (Barone & Eisner, 2012). Arts-based research has expanded our understanding of what constitutes "evidence" or "findings," and even "science," allowing us to appreciate the complexity and multidimensionality of this endeavor to engender new knowledge in ways that can be fun, engaging, awe-inspiring, and transformative (Boydell, Gladstone, Volpe, Allemang, & Stasiulls, 2012; McNiff, 2013b). Sajnani (2012) refers to this form of research as "living inquiry" to capture its transformative potential. Knowledge for the sake of knowledge will not be found in arts-based inquiry and intervention.

The purpose of gaining new knowledge takes on an explicit social mission and sharpens our resolve that knowledge is not politically neutral (H. Jones, 2010; Watts, 2010). Some critics would argue that this approach to research effectively "politicizes" research, rendering it as propaganda. I, and countless others, would argue that research is always political, and that ignoring this is dishonest and unethical. Making the implicit assumptions and values explicit, and acknowledging them, is a step toward moving this field forward by raising consciousness on how oppression manifests itself in visible and invisible ways, and therefore making it easier to detect ways these forces impinge on individual well-being. Making the implicit values explicit allows outsiders to scrutinize the assumptions that have entered into the questions we seek to ask, and the methods we use to arrive at the answers.

For the uninitiated, arts-based interventions (Adams & Goldbard, 2005) and research are not new on the scholarly and research scenes, but rather have a relatively long and distinguished history that has been shaped by the sociopolitical environment and events (Barone & Eisner, 2012; Kossak, 2013; Rolling, 2013). Art therapy has played an influential role in this movement (Antal, 2013). The 1970s, however, are widely considered to be the birth decade of the arts-based research movement using artistic practices to conduct research (Sinner, Leggo, Irwin, Gouzouasis, & Grauer, 2006). This period also witnessed ethnography gaining in prominence, resulting in an emphasis on representation/participation, ethics, relativism, inclusiveness, and subjectivity (J. S. Jones, 2010).

It certainly is no mistake that ethnography places tremendous importance on historical and cultural contextualization. Paris (2011) speaks to the importance of representation and humanizing research with marginalized groups such as youth, and the powerful and transformative role that ethnography, qualitative research, and social language research can play in achieving this goal.

It is no mistake that this decade had as a backdrop a turbulent social context resulting in significant social movements concerning civil rights, women's rights, environmental justice, antiwar, and gay rights, to list but several of the more prominent movements. The importance of using knowledge to alter social conditions influenced numerous academic and helping professions. It is appropriate that a research method that emphasizes context and social justice to the extent that arts-based research has its roots in social-political turmoil.

The attractiveness of arts-based qualitative research addressing health-related subjects increased dramatically during the 1980s as researchers became more successful in obtaining foundation and government funding and publishing their results in scholarly outlets, setting the stage for arts-based research to become part of the constellation of qualitative methods practiced and taught in and out of colleges and universities: "It is in that general context that arts-based research is entering qualitative health research with the aim of being recognized as an innovative, useful, effective, and thus legitimate means of creating and disseminating knowledge" (Lafreniere, Hurlimann, Menuz, & Godard (2013).

Not surprisingly, the three decades since has witnessed an explosion of arts-based inquiry that only promises to continue because it resonates with marginalized communities, thereby meeting pressing sociopolitical needs in a manner that is affirming to those who are on the margins of society. This form of research lends itself to answering questions that do not easily lend themselves to exact measurement or generalizations (McNiff, 2013b). Thus, context meaning is valued over universal meaning (Rollings, 2013).

Barone and Eisner (2012) provide a widely accepted definition of what constitutes arts-based research: "Arts-based research represents an effort to explore the potentialities of an approach to representation that is rooted in aesthetic considerations and that, when it is at its best, culminates in the creation of something close to a work of art" (p. 1). Arts-based research with a social justice focus can be thought of as an umbrella consisting of many spokes that are interconnected. Arts-based research brings an exciting and highly participatory, and innovative, perspective on community research, including introducing nontraditional ways of reporting the results of the research, as addressed in greater detail in Chapter 5.

Numerous scholars posit that the arts lend themselves well to "blended spaces of naturalistic inquiry" (Haywood, 2013, p. 3), facilitating insights into topics that are resistant to typical research approaches. Singh (2011) views the use of the arts as a creation of visual artifacts, or boundary objects, that facilitate the exchange of information that normally would not be sought or captured through conventional means. Visual ethnographers would argue that images have embedded information that can only be successfully accessed by the understanding of the context in which they are based. In the case of photovoice, the photographer acts as a cultural bridge or messenger to convey the central purpose and context of the photo.

A photograph without a context and messenger is but an image in search of a voice. Clearly, a messenger or broker is essential, and that is what photovoice provides. Rose (2012) makes this very point: "Images can present things that words cannot and can therefore be used as evidence to develop and support, or to supplement, written research findings. Nonetheless, images still need to be contextualized by words, and may remain excessively obscure if they are not" (p. 326).

Arts-based research and practice also serves to help those who have been marginalized to reclaim their history and culture, and to use this newfound knowledge as a personal source of strength in seeking social change (Cooper, Nazzari, King, & Pettrgrew, 2013; Garcia, 2012). Art is educational and brings pleasure, but it is also consciousness raising and therapeutic, serving as an impetus for achieving social justice–inspired change for participants and their respective communities (Buffington & Muth, 2011; Walker, 2012).

Arts-based research and practice encompasses an extensive array of methods, and this can be both exciting, inclusive (not everyone is expected to like all forms), and overwhelming at the same time because of the endless possibilities it offers researchers and communities. There are a number of ways of classifying the arts. Davies et al. (2011), for example, examined arts engagement and identified five art forms: (1) performing arts; (2) visual arts, design, and craft; (3) community/cultural festivals, fairs, and events; (4) literature; and (5) online, digital, and electronic arts.

An alternative is the following partial list illustrative of the range of options: *dance* (Boydell, 2011; McEwan, Crouch, Roberson & Fagan, 2013), *drama* (Bresler, 2011; Sinding, Gray, Grassau, Damianakis, & Hampson, 2006), *drawing* (Bagnoli, 2009; Leitch, 2008; Stuckey, 2009), *music* (Brader & Luke, 2013; Springay, Irwin, & Kind, 2005), *painting* (Basto, Warson, & Barbour, 2012; Pedraza, 2010), *sculpture* (Celedonia & Rosenthal, 2011; Hunter & Lewis, 2013), *poetry* (Lafreniere & Cox, 2013), *singing* (Sun, Buys, & Merrick, 2012), *theater and writing* (Linds et al., 2013; MacDonald et al., 2011; Woodson, 2007), and *video and film* (Lally & Sclater, 2013; Schaefer, 2012; Shapiro, Tomasa, & Koff, 2009; Stewart, Riecken, Scott, Tanaka, & Riecken, 2008; Woo, 2008). This list is illustrative of the reach of this field, which is continually expanding and including greater diversity of issue-focused groups and age groups.

Popular theater and poetry may seem odd as forms of arts-based research, for example (Adams & Goldbard, 2005; Naidus, 2009). Popular theater, in similar fashion to other arts-based approaches, has its roots with Paulo Freire's popular education movement (Conrad, 2004). Popular theater has the potential to create insightful knowledge, which may have been deeply buried in the unconscious of the participant due to its association with pain and sorrow, which is then translated into action in pursuit of social justice. Datoo and Chagani (2011), in turn, highlight the important role of participation and creativity in street theater.

Poetry is another example. Foster (2012b) sees the use of poetry as a form of social inquiry that can effectively challenge dominant ideologies of oppressed people and offer alternative discourse, in this case through the written word.

These are two very different forms of arts-based inquiry, and not every participant will find both or either of these approaches to be attractive. It is best to think of arts-based inquiry like a menu at a favorite restaurant, with an extensive number of choices. Researchers, too, have favorite items that they like to eat when going out for a meal. There is a need to match both researcher and participant to arts-based research. When this match occurs, it can be considered magical. The reverse is also true when researchers have to use photovoice but do not feel comfortable with this method, or do not think of themselves as very competent in using it. Participants, too, have their proclivities, and this needs to be taken into account. The matching of method with participant becomes a process of discovery.

Art as a Method by and for the People

Arts-based research can be viewed as an alternative approach with a primary focus on those individuals who are undervalued and stigmatized, and whose experiences and views of solutions are disregarded by those in power. These individuals bring stories about these experiences that may be difficult to capture through conventional means: "As narrative beings, we are surrounded by our own stories and other people's stories. We are not necessarily fully conscious of these stories and they may not even be verbal; moreover, there is never a single version of a story" (Kankanan & Bardy, 2013). The concept of "scholar as activist" has emerged to help capture the duality of those who practice arts-based research (Skinner & Masuda, 2013). Further, arts-based research lends itself to translation of findings, a critical component in creating change from new insights (Parson & Boydell, 2012).

Bagley and Castro-Salazar (2012) view arts-based research as a participatory vehicle for empowering and promoting marginalized groups in society by tapping into their experiences, feelings, and knowledge about oppression and how it is perpetrated by the dominant social order. The arts become a vehicle for sharing these insights with those outside of the group. McNiff (2008) sees arts-based research as the systematic use of the artistic process to alter social conditions.

Finley (2008), in turn, argues that arts-based research is well positioned to give voice to society's marginalized groups and set the requisite stage for social change: "By its integration of multiple methodologies used in the arts with the postmodern ethics of participative, action-oriented, and politically situated perspectives for human social inquiry, arts-based inquiry has the potential to facilitate critical race, indigenous, queer, feminist, and border theories and research methodologies" (p. 71). The influence of feminist theory on photovoice and other visual methods, for example, has a large following (Allmark, 2011; Pinto, Spector,

Rohman, & Gastolomendo, 2013; Wilkins & Liamputtong, 2010). The immediacy of visual image as evidence, for example, thrusts the photographer into an expert role, and probably for one of the very few times in his or her life (Brown & Powell, 2012; Wang & Burris, 1997).

Bell and Desai (2011) make a compelling case for social justice and arts-based research and practice, setting the stage for photovoice: "Social justice practices at their best should also awaken our senses and the ability to imagine alternatives that can sustain the collective work necessary to challenge entrenched patterns and institutions and build a different world" (p. 287). A world that is inclusive and open to actively hearing all voices and not just the voices of the privileged is a goal of arts-based inquiry, with art becoming the vehicle or voice for dissent (Finley, 2011). Art can be used for all forms of community-focused research, including evaluation. Integrating art into evaluation provides researchers with new windows upon which to seek different perspectives, and avenues for participation in helping to shape this form of research and the practice that follows (Kramer et al.,2012; Simons & McCormack, 2007).

Benefits of Arts-Based Research and Practice

It is important in examining the use of arts-based approaches in research that we do not lose sight of the multifaceted obvious, and not so obvious, benefits associated with creative art activities for participants and communities (Schwarzman & Knight, 2005). It is appropriate to start with communities. "Community" is a ubiquitous term that gets used quite freely and is meant to symbolize a context (social relations and institutions) that all researchers understand (Hacker, 2013). That statement simplifies a very complex term that has many different meanings depending upon how community gets defined and operated in the course of research and practice (Chaskin, 2013; Delanty, 2003).

Cleveland (2011) defines the main terms used in the field, and in so doing addresses why arts-based community development, of which research is a part, benefits communities:

> **Community-Based:** Activities created and produced by and with community members that combine significant elements of community access, ownership, authorship, participation, and accountability.
>
> **Arts-Based Community Development (ABCD):** . . . These include arts based activities that:
>
> ¤ EDUCATE and INFORM us about ourselves and the world
> ¤ INSPIRE and MOBILIZE individuals or groups
> ¤ NURTURE and HEAL people and/or communities
> ¤ BUILD and IMPROVE community capacity and/or infrastructure.
> (p. 4)

Cleveland's conceptualization illustrates the potential reach of arts-based projects and why they can play a significant role in the life of communities, including the use of research, as in the case of photovoice.

Communities benefiting from arts-based inquiry and interventions bring an added dimension to the use of photovoice, expanding the reach of this method beyond participants. For example, projects involving communities and universities can create social bridges where none existed prior to the research (Ardoin, Castrechin, & Hofstedt, 2013; Winskie & Murray, 2013). Well-resourced universities are in a position to purchase services, products, and rent spaces in communities, thereby serving to transfer funds (Cameron, Crane, Inge, & Taylor, 2012) and help communities economically. Arts-based resources resulting in public art can also beautify neighborhoods by transforming spaces that were underutilized or blights into attractive and welcoming places and spaces (Delgado, 1999).

From an individual standpoint, participation in the arts has been found to promote personal well-being, quality of life, health, and increased social capital (Bungay & Clift, 2010; Fox, 2013; Erbstein, 2013; Grieb et al., 2013). Participation can also result in increased self-esteem (Syson-Nibbs, Robinson, Cook, & King, 2009). Art can also promote empathy and understanding of the societal forces involved in people's lives (Degarrod, 2013; Potash & Ho, 2011). These benefits are enhanced further when those who are marginalized engage in the arts and discover that they have artistic talents. The discovery of having talent by someone who has been told all of their lives that they are "talentless" is an empowering benefit.

These benefits can be taken further by using the arts to create social change. Urban youth certainly fall into this category (Baldridge, Hill, & Davis, 2011). In addition, the use of the arts in practice and research is not restricted to any one age group (Murray & Crummett, 2010). Artistic abilities are not restricted to the elite. I have always argued that all communities, regardless of their marginalized status, have individuals in their midst who are writers, poets, painters, singers, and so on, but their talent has been overlooked by a society that views them as causalities, at best, and worthless, at worst.

The premise that all members of society have some form of artistic talent, regardless of age, physical and intellectual abilities, and station in life, underpins arts-based research. The embrace of this premise, and the assumptions that underlie it, set the stage for the use of visual arts as a vehicle for personal liberation and community change. Some may argue with the point that "everyone" has some form of artistic talent. I would rather err on the side of "everyone" than run the risk of writing off a segment of the population because some might argue that it is impossible for everyone to have some talent.

Unfortunately, even though there are obvious benefits to using arts-based research in the helping fields, use of this method has found resistance. Colucci (2013), for example, argues that arts-based research has historically had, and continues to experience, resistance from health sciences and represents a counter-movement to the dominance of positivist epistemologies, limiting its use in disciplines such as psychiatry and psychology, for example. Mental health disciplines are uniquely positioned to benefit from arts-based research as evidenced by the popularity of photovoice focused on health and mental health themes (Erdner & Magnusson, 2011).

CBPR and the Arts

CBPR plays a prominent role in how arts-based research is conceptualized and implemented (Yonas et al., 2009). Community-based participatory research, too, can be considered an umbrella, and each spoke represents a different form of research method, with photovoice representing one spoke among many possible art forms (Hacker, 2013; Lavallée, 2009). Further, CBPR is possible with all age groups and people with differing abilities, making this form of research universal and adoptable to different social circumstances and groups (Ardoin et al., 2013).

Westphal and Hirsch (2010) provide an excellent example of how visual ethnography and CBPR can be merged. They developed the concept of *rapid ethnographic inquiry* (REI) as a way of bridging visual ethnography and CBPR. This approach differs from most conventional uses of visual ethnography in that REI is closely aligned with CBPR, it is faster, and it involves more intense data collection. This process was found to facilitate engagement and alignment with communities—in this case it involved Chicago and climate change. Chavez et al. (2004), too, illustrate the use of a multimedia approach in CBPR and youth.

Community researchers can have "good" intentions, but this does not necessarily translate into research that is good for the community: "Research that aims to trouble social, cultural, and economic disparities is usually conducted with the best of socially just intentions. Still, embedded in all research processes is the potential to disrupt and, simultaneously, reproduce mechanisms of power that enable inequalities" (Brann-Barrett, 2009, p. 53). CBPR is intended to increase the likelihood that good research results in good findings and good changes for a community (Jacquez, Vaughn, & Wagner, 2013).

CBPR has been referred to as an alternative philosophy of social research because of its emphasis on taking a position of serving the needs of those who are oppressed (Haw, 2008). The community is the ultimate judge of the outcome, not the researcher. Involving community representatives in all facets of the research helps increase the likelihood that the outcome is what is desired, which is a key recommendation covered in Chapter 5.

The importance of being grounded on the role and prominence of CBPR cannot be overly estimated if photovoice is to achieve its lofty potential with urban youth (Jacquez et al., 2013). CBPR is predicated upon the fundamental belief that all knowledge and observations are value based, making knowledge individualistic (opposite of universal) and subjective, which is the opposite of objective (Durand & Lykes, 2006). Stoecker (2013) stresses the importance of research methods not only uncovering new knowledge, but also serving as the impetus for community change.

Community participatory research can be conceptualized as a process for obtaining new knowledge, but with no concern for community change, and that is not what is sought in this book. This form of research can be conceptualized as the use of new knowledge as the basis for community change (Necheles et al., 2007). Photovoice, as conceptualized in this book, is about the latter. Development of socially just solutions rests upon having the research owned by those facing oppression (Smith, Chambers, & Bratini, 2009). Flicker and Danforth (2013), in addressing HIV and Aboriginal youth in Canada, refer to CBPR and the arts as a way of "decolonizing the research process."

Freire (1982) reflects on CBPR and its transformative power on the community and researcher: "In doing research, I am educating and being educated with the people" (p. 30). This is a guiding principle in CBPR research. Walters et al. (2009) address the role and importance of CBPR principles, illustrating why photovoice has found such a receptive home in this approach:

> Generally accepted CBPR principles recognize the community as a unit of identity and/or analysis; build on the strengths, resiliency, and resources of the community; facilitate co-learning, co-partnering, and community-capacity building throughout all phases of the research project, including dissemination; attempt to strike a balance between research and action; emphasize local relevance and ecological and historical contexts that contribute to multiple determinants; generate systems growth through cyclical and iterative processes; and involve long-term commitment to process and community. (p. 151)

These and countless other authors have set the stage for photovoice to have great potential for engaging communities that historically have not been part of a research undertaking, other than as subjects. The term "subjects" has a very negative ring to it, suggesting that we do things *to* people, as opposed to *with* them. The effectiveness of increasing youth participation does not come without risk, particularly if undertaken in systems that are not used to having youth play meaningful participatory roles, such as schools (Duckett, Kagan, & Sixsmith, 2010; Warne, Synder, & Gillander Gådin, 2013). CBPR is not a panacea and it has never been meant to be viewed as such. Photovoice is also not a panacea. Nevertheless, because change requires contextualized knowledge to inform it, CBPR is an essential element of any solution (Jacquez et al., 2013).

Community-based participatory research is an ever-expanding paradigm that promises to continue to grow in popularity in the foreseeable future, particularly when it involves highly marginalized groups such as youth (Garcia, Minkler, Cardenas, Grills, & Porter, 2014). Visual ethnographic methods lend themselves to CBPR. Chavez et al. (2004), for example, used video as the tool in CBPR. This involved collaboration between researcher and community in all facets of the project—obtaining funding, getting informed consents, writing the script, editing, and music selection. Schreider (2012), in turn, reports on the use of CBPR and a group diagnosed with schizophrenia, and shows how this method can be modified to take into account challenges. If flexible to take physical and intellectual challenges into consideration, this form of research can be quite successful.

Thackeray and Hunter (2010) see the use of photovoice and other types of technology as having tremendous potential for use with youth:

> Technology makes it easy and convenient for youth to participate. It allows for integration of advocacy into their daily route. As a generation who is both comfortable and fluent with using technology, the key for public health is to harness these skills and direct them toward use in health advocacy. Making deliberate efforts to combine technology and youth advocacy will give youth a voice, increase their personal efficacy for participating in advocacy, and impact the social determinants that affect the health status of people in their communities and throughout the world. (p. 589)

Technology, with the requisite supports, can facilitate the integration of the arts into CBPR with youth.

Ethical considerations do not disappear because it is CBPR and the arts. Horowitz, Robinson, and Seifer (2009) warn community-based participatory researchers to balance rigorous research with ethical considerations regarding partners and communities. The ethical principle of "do no harm" takes on prominence when photovoice is used to uncover knowledge that can be particularly painful to participants (Burles, 2010; Neuman, 2007). CBPR with participants with disabilities bring additional challenges, resulting in tension related to competing demands (Aldridge, 2012), as addressed in greater detail in Chapter 7.

Buchanan, Miller, and Wallerstein (2007) note that CBPR lies at the nexus of two major underlying ethical concerns that involve respect for community autonomy and the fair allocation of limited public resources: "Growing use of CBPR raises two new ethical issues that deserve greater public attention: first, the problem of securing informed consent and demonstrating respect for community autonomy when the locus of research shifts from the individual to community level; and second, fair distribution of scarce public resources when practical constraints make the most rigorous research designs for assessing the effects of community interventions virtually impossible" (p. 153). Obtaining informed consent and respecting community autonomy may seem prosaic ethical topics. When placed within a contextual frame, including culture and history, these topics become very difficult to address for the researcher.

Visual Art and Social Justice

The popularity of visual art as a research method is widely recognized (Buckingham, 2009; Mitchell, 2011). The visual arts are home to countless approaches to research and interventions inspired by social justice (McAuliffe, 2012; Sandell & Nightingale, 2012). Boydell et al. (2012) concluded that the most popular art genre for this research is photography, with theater a close second, and other methods such as poetry, dance, and mural art being considerably less popular. Visually based arts are particularly conducive for engendering empathy and helping participants to exercise social justice (Degarrod, 2013; Potash & Ho, 2011).

Arts-based research and practice has an extensive and well-grounded history in seeking new knowledge, insights, and social justice through utilization of participatory research methods, and in disseminating these findings through performances and exhibitions by those who have been marginalized by society. The methods used may seem foreign to many helping professionals and social scientists, although that is changing rapidly, yet the values and goals resonate for academics and practitioners embracing social justice. Photovoice is but one of countless methods that have a home in arts-based social justice research.

Boydell et al. (2012) undertook an extensive review of the literature on arts-based health promotion and arrived at a not so surprising recommendation:

> We suggest that the broadening of qualitative methodologies to include arts-based approaches offers more than simply adjuncts to typical data collection and dissemination approaches, and instead, presents different ways of knowing. We believe that this may be a significant moment in the field in which to question whether or not we are witness to a paradigmatic shift in the ways we approach inquiry into the social world and/or the emergence of an innovative set of techniques that researchers can draw upon to enhance traditional methods of conducting qualitative inquiry.

Expanding the field of qualitative research increases the likelihood of the introduction of innovative approaches that are more capable of integrating cultural values and nuances of new and emerging groups that would not respond well to conventional approaches.

Social justice, as addressed in much greater detail in Chapter 4, can be considered the essential glue that holds together a visual arts-based project. Research is not value-free. Values shape an entire research project, including how the project is conceived and the method selected, the questions we seek to answer, and how we analyze and distribute findings. Weis and Fine (2004), in their book *Working Method: Research and Social Justice*, provide extensive examples of how social justice significantly shapes the entire research undertaking.

Singhal and Rattine-Flaherty's (2009) use of photovoice in Peru is an example of how an embrace of social justice resulted in the development of visual research methods as alternatives to textocentrism, which would have severely limited resident participation in a conventional research project. A vision-based epistemology stresses images (Quinlan, Ruhl, Torrens, & Harter, 2013), which is counter to a prevailing textocentric set of assumptions relying on the written word, which seems to permeate much of the research that is undertaken (Novak, 2010).

Finally, Davey (2010) raises a series of concerns about visual-focused research, in this case that emanating from visual anthropology, which has not been discussed in any prominent manner in the professional literature, but has implications for photovoice and social justice. This shows the dominance of American scholars publishing on this topic, and how this undue influence from a social justice perspective limits our understanding of visual methods. The increased tendency and necessity to have to publish in U.S. journals, even when the primary language of the researcher and their country is not English, limits the range of scholarship on the subject. Relatively easy access to high-cost technology, and how we have been socialized to view visually informed research, further reinforces why no one nation or group of scholars should dominant this research area.

Visual Ethnography as Arts-Based Inquiry

Arts-based research and practice, as earlier portions of this chapter have shown, encompasses all visual forms of arts-based inquiry (Pink, Hubbard, O'Neill, & Radley, 2010). Within this vast arena there are a number of perspectives, one of which is visual ethnography, home to photovoice and other forms. It is important to pause and ground visual ethnography and the many parameters of this emerging field of practice before focusing on photovoice itself.

Photovoice has a prominent place within visual ethnography but it is far from alone in this vast field. J. S. Jones (2010) traces the origins of the term *ethnography* to ancient Greece and the importance of writing about a group of people and their culture. This rather simple description of ethnography, when combined with *visual*, sets the stage for the study of culture through a focus on images. Images are humanly constructed and culturally specific, necessitating interpreting by the individual creating the image (Thomson, 2008a; 2008b). Visual methodologies allow researchers to explore and experiment with new forms of social language (Hernandez-Albujar, 2007).

Harris and Guillemin (2012) highlight the under explored world of the senses in conducting research:

> Within the social sciences there has been an increased interest in the senses. Much of this work has focused on ethnographic methods and has concentrated on research about the senses . . . sensory awareness can enrich interviews by offering a portal to otherwise unexplored illness or health care experiences which are either too difficult to articulate or too intangible to describe. Sensory awareness incorporates not only attentiveness to the research environment but also the utilization of sensory questions or prompts to gain insight into the research experience. (p. 689)

Visual ethnography, as represented by photovoice, opens up a new world for researchers and community activists in search of social justice for marginalized communities and methods that are conducive for capturing their voices (Chew, 2009; Ortega-Alcázar & Dyck, 2012).

Video ethnography, in turn, can be defined as a visual process that captures life as lived through the eyes of an individual or group, who act as writers, editors, and directors of the final product. In essence, they assume all of the major roles in this production. Video ethnography is a tool that can help those who are invisible in society to share their stories and perspectives. Visual ethnography is a research method that holds great appeal when we have a very limited understanding of a particular marginalized group and their perspectives, or voices, which are rarely sought (Harper, 2009).

Visual methods have also been found to show great promise for clarifying contextually influenced concepts that can be used to refine established measures and methods (Keller, Fleury, Perez, Ainsworth, & Vaughan, 2008). A strong argument can be made that effective social change is only possible with well-grounded information (Stoecker, 2013). The new knowledge or insights generated through visual ethnography should be sufficiently valuable so as to identify promising approaches to addressing local issues or concerns, as well potential barriers that must be surmounted to succeed. Photovoice is not a method that has the "luxury" of uncovering new knowledge for the sake of new knowledge (Garvin, 2003). An outcome that betters the life of a group within a community or society must be a driving force in this form of research (Wang, 2006). Social research must ultimately serve a social purpose, and what better purpose than to rectify a social injustice?

Julie S. Jones (2010) listed a series of reasons why ethnography as a research method, and in the case of this book one based on the visual, is predicated upon a set of principles that seek personal transformation and liberation: "A relative stance. A desire to provide a 'thick description' of a social world. An intension to seek ways to 'understand' a social world through immersion (long or short term) in that environment. The importance of historical and cultural contextualization. The intension to present the 'native's point of view'. The stress on ethics, representation, 'voices', power and inclusion. The importance of reflexivity. An awareness of subjectivity" (p. 26). These principles will appear throughout this book.

Lunch and Lunch (2006) provide a good description of participatory video, or what can be referred to as videovoice or video ethnography:

> Participatory Video is a set of techniques to involve a group or community in shaping and creating their own film. The idea behind this is that making a video is easy and accessible, and is a great way of bringing people together to explore issues, voice concerns or simply to be creative and tell stories. This process can be very empowering, enabling a group or community to take

action to solve their own problems and also to communicate their needs and ideas to decision-makers and/or other groups and communities. As such, PV can be a highly effective tool to engage and mobilise marginalised people and to help them implement their own forms of sustainable development based on local needs. (p. 4)

The parallels between video voice and photovoice are quite striking, although these two methods utilize different technology and require different competencies. Further, a photograph, unlike video, is easier and less expensive to achieve and use (Spencer, 2011).

Participatory research methods, as emphasized above, are much more than knowledge creation; they are also an integral part of a social intervention (Villagran, 2011). The concept of activist oriented art applies to how social justice is central to how photovoice is conceptualized (Dewhurst, 2011). Rolling (2013) comments on what results from critical inquiry: "Critical activist inquiry produces resistance narratives—counter-stories to authoritative grand narratives that are critical, indigenous or local, and anti-oppressive" (p. 109). In essence, the goal of achieving positive social change becomes a moral compass, guiding researchers through fog and turbulent seas.

Wee, DePierre, Anthanatten, and Barbour (2013) found visual methods to encourage self-reflection and construction of social meanings. Visual methods lend themselves for use with participants who may be illiterate, or who come from backgrounds where stories or parables are the preferred method for conveying important information. Visual ethnography has provided a conceptual foundation for a wide range of visual ethnographic tools. Literat (2013) and Tay-Lim and Lim (2013), for example advocate for the use of drawing with children and youth as a research method that opens up this process for cultural nuances to emerge and a de-emphasis in linguistic proficiency.

Digital storytelling (Lambert, 2013) and photovoice are arguably two of the most popular ways that visual ethnography has been brought to life in community practice integrating various social justice perspectives. Gubrium and Difulvio (2011), for example, see a merging together of a feminist perspective on knowledge creation and the development of a corresponding narrative approach, in this case digital storytelling, as having the potential for achieving this in community health and social research undertakings.

Visual ethnography can be classified under CBPR along with various other methods for engaging communities. Ethnography is a branch of qualitative research that focuses on culture-sharing groups (Rose, 2012). The power of images is central to this form of research (Huss, 2012): "Indeed, images are a deep and universal psycho-neurological construct though which people process their experiences. Being central to human functioning, images contribute to the individual's ability to remain oriented in the world in light of memories of past experiences and envisioning methods of problem solving based on these images" (p. 1441).

Visual ethnography is also a form of qualitative research, along with other forms such as feminist ethnography, ethnographic novels, life history, confessed ethnography, and auto-ethnography (Creswell, 2013a). One cannot help but think back to C. Wright Mill's (1959) classic work, *The Sociological Imagination*, to conclude that visual ethnography can play an important role in translating "personal troubles" into "public issues" by engendering discussion between urban "insiders" and "outsiders," and setting the foundation for social action to occur (Robinson, 2012).

Qualitative forms of research facilitate the discussion of "private issues" that are arduous to talk about (Hauge, 2013), and this is so important to achieve when addressing those who are undervalued. Visual ethnographic forms, as qualitative research, facilitate in-depth discussion, eliciting both information and what can be described as painful and disturbing affect, some of it being deeply seated.

Prosser and Loxley (2008) argue that visual ethnography represents a viable and attractive alternative to conventional research methods favored in academia: "Simply put visual methods can: provide an alternative to the hegemony of a word and number based academy; slow down observation and encourage deeper and more effective reflection on all things visual and visualisable; and with it enhance our understanding of sensory embodiment and communication, and hence reflect more fully the diversity of human experiences" (p. 4). The academy's strong preference for positivism-based research places academics interested in arts-based research at a distinct disadvantage for career advancement. Arts-based research's search for a prominent place in the academy has made significant strides, but the journey is still long (Smith, 2013).

Digital storytelling is a visual process through which individual stories get captured and transformed to create social change (Gubrium, 2009). The Center for Digital Storytelling (Oakland, California) is widely considered the center of this movement. *Digital ethnography* is a term that can also be found in the literature (Morey, Bengry-Howell, & Griffin, 2012). Digital storytelling allows ordinary people, social activists, and others, to share their stories to a broader audience, including web-based stories, hypertexts, interactive stories, narrative computer games, and film. YouTube, Vimeo, and podcasts, for example, are commonly used venues for the sharing of digital stories.

There is a natural progression that can occur from photovoice to digital storytelling, although this potential is still in its infancy:

> While starting as a mechanism for local community and online exhibition, invariably these PhotoVoice projects have moved to multimedia. While the writing and story work may not be as central to these approaches in making short videos, the emphasis in strong narrative photography accomplishes much more affective impact than the typical digital story. Obviously much

more work can be done to explore the collaboration between photography and the digital storytelling model.

—LAMBERT, 2013, p. 47

Lambert (2013) touches upon the natural bridge between these two methods, and also the challenges.

Digital storytelling and photovoice are two methods that can be used to bring visual ethnography to community practice (Driver, 2007). Gubrium (2009) describes the benefit of participation in this form of research:

> For some participants, the reflexive experience of studying and theorizing the presentation of their experience can prove cathartic, even empowering. Through activities, such as story circles, script revising, digital media construction, and semiprivate and public airings of their stories, participants often gain a sense of ownership of their experiences. For many, maybe for the first time, they have talked openly about an experience previously unarticulated. (p. 190)

Photographs facilitate the capturing of the nuances associated with everyday experiences and activities in a manner that is not labor intensive. Further, it facilitates the identifying and capturing of stressors and important sources of support in the lives of youth that may not seem obvious to their outside world:

> Media production is a way for youth to negotiate mediated ideas, deconstruct cultural messages, and participate in both local and global discourses by authoring and distributing their own media. These are not "frill" skills; they are essential to life-long education . . . Unfortunately, large segments of our youth population fall through the cracks, getting little or no opportunity to acquire this kind of critical literacy or to access the opportunities that art-based media production can offer. Too many young people live in poverty and go without safe shelter or adequate food, let alone computers, cameras, or art supplies.

—LEVY & WEBER, 2011, p. 293

Photographs also lend themselves to exhibitions that can attract large gatherings and media coverage, generating wide attention and excitement. The exhibition itself can be taped for showings at future dates, and individual copies can be given to participants for home use.

The importance of tapping and capturing sincere expression, as in the case of photovoice and other forms of arts-based methods, brings important credibility to a research endeavor, and the quality of this expression, in turn, can result in what Evans and Lowery (2008) refer to as the "elegance to a trust claim" (p. 3). Communicating how to socially navigate difficult terrains and circumstances necessitates the use of creative methods to gain insights, as in the case of photovoice and homelessness, for example (Peterson, Antony, & Thomas (2012). Youth have developed their own "software" that they have tapped in socially navigating their surroundings (Larson, 2011). Arts-based inquiry, ethnography, and CBPR are natural homes for photovoice.

Photovoice as an Educational Tool

The benefits derived from arts-based methods such as photovoice are maximized when they are founded upon a deep contextual understanding of the community. Cleveland (2011) makes this very important point:

> Community art making is necessarily cumbersome, messy, and slow: We have found that one of the most important elements in successful arts-based community development is the understanding that there are no micro-waveable short cuts to participatory art making. Every community's cultural, social, and political ecology is unique. Our research tells us that assumptions and expectations accrued from other sites can inform other programs, but should not drive them. This is not because those experiences are not potentially valuable and informative, but because the time spent learning about a community's culture is an indispensable part of building community trust. (pp. 10–11)

The uniqueness of each community must engender a healthy respect for how photovoice gets conceptualized and implemented, and there is a need to take into account key elements associated with the concept of "community." This does not mean that the issue confronting participants and their community is unique to them, but it does mean that the insights and solutions must conform to the community in which the project is lodged. Experiences with other communities can be introduced and shared in an effort for this group to understand that they are not alone, yet every community is unique, just like every person is unique.

Photovoice From Philosophical Perspectives

Practitioners and academics have every right to ask why they should consider using photovoice in their practice and research with urban youth, and what makes this method particularly appealing to youth. Numerous questions will no doubt follow this fundamental question. Each of these questions is complex and defies simple responses. The questioning process must be encouraged and not just tolerated, even though it is time-consuming and can create uncomfortable discussions. Questions are an integral part of photovoice.

Being a researcher is not antithetical to being creative (Coyle & Olsen, 2011). The "bedrock" of creative research is how it is grounded in the philosophical choices that researchers make (Mockler, 2011). The research paradigm chosen dictates the road taken, along with a host of assumptions or worldviews that will influence what we look for, how we do it, and the language we use. These boundaries, so to speak, shape not only the questions we seek to answer, but also how we relate to those we are asking the questions of.

Photovoice can be grounded within two possible qualitative research paradigms. A critical research paradigm emphasizes participatory democracy, empowerment, and social change action. This paradigm differs from an interpretive qualitative research paradigm, which stresses new understandings and innovations (Titchen & Horsfall, 2011). It may be difficult to neatly separate out these two paradigms, however, because there are elements of both paradigms present with photovoice. The central thrust of photovoice, however, is more clearly centered within a critical research paradigm.

Creswell (2013a) identified four philosophical research assumptions, with each highlighting a different lens, so to speak: (1) ontological—an emphasis in what is the nature of reality? (2) axiological—how do values influence the research process? (3) methodological—what is the language and process of research? and (4) epistemological—what can be considered knowledge? Readers can certainly appreciate how these four philosophical assumptions interrelate to shape the research experience for researchers and their collaborators. Prior (2013) identified five key questions that concretize Crewell's philosophical assumptions: (1) What to know? (2) What is known? (3) What is knowing? (4) Who knows what? (5) How to know?

The subjects of epistemology (the study of knowledge and justified belief) and ontology (the study of the nature of reality), for example, have profound consequences for photovoice and its legitimacy within the scientific community: "Methodologies are highly contingent on epistemological positions, populations, research interests, rapport, and confidentiality, among a host of other concerns" (Stanczak, 2007b, pp. 3–4). Not unexpectedly, there is an intense epistemological debate and methodological uncertainty about how photographic data ("knowledge" or "truth") should be treated in scientific inquiry (Oliffe, Bottorff, Kelly, & Halpin, 2008; Rollings, 2013). Fortunately, an increasing number of scholars have not shied away from addressing this topic, resulting in a growing body of literature on these subjects (Spencer, 2011).

The subject of different types of knowledge will be addressed again in Chapter 4. Prior (2013), in a review of the literature on knowledge, uncovered a wide range of types: procedural knowledge, structural knowledge, domain-specific knowledge, declarative knowledge, situated knowledge, meta-knowledge, concrete knowledge, and strategic knowledge. There are certainly many different forms of knowledge, and there is no one epistemological approach that brings together all forms of knowledge.

The influence and prevalence of the positivistic approach must be acknowledged before moving forward on the assumptions underpinning photovoice. The assumptions shaping positivism are counter to those influencing qualitative research and photovoice (Rolling, 2013): "A philosophy of research establishing that hypothetical assertions can be positively verified through scientific, data-gathering and quantitative analysis" (p. 15). The reader may pose the questions: Doesn't photovoice gather information? Does it not engage in analysis? The answers would be yes, with the assumptions underpinning these answers being dramatically different. The positivist tradition has largely viewed art, as in the case of photography, as emotive and not informative or knowledge creation (Eisner, 2008).

Positivist modes of scientific research have the researcher as disconnected and "objective," making "rational" decisions on the course of the research (Farrugia, 2013). Clearly, this is not what CBPR and arts-based photovoice are premised upon. Mitchell (2008) argues that photovoice is underdeveloped as an innovative epistemological approach. Although that conclusion was made over five years ago, many would argue that it is still in the process of evolving.

The postmodern perspective on knowledge creation, and the assumptions upon which it is based, has spurred the development of innovative qualitative and arts-based research methodologies (Cosgrove & McHugh, 2010; Onwuegbuzie, Leech, & Collins, 2010). Knowledge is socially constructed, and images, too, are socially constructed by individuals or groups of individuals (Thomson, 2008a; 2008b); Finley (2005); Walsh, Rutherford, and Crough (2013) among others, argue that arts-based research is a research method of inquiry with increasing popularity, and has roots in postmodern and participatory types of research.

The postmodern era also has advanced the debate concerning research methods beyond a single method or paradigm to a broadening conceptualization that is more inclusive of other methods that accept or reconcile multiple paradigms or ways of thinking (Rolling, 2013). Qualitative research has had to justify its existence against this backdrop (Loftus, Higgs, & Trede, 2011). There is an international call for integrating various frameworks and perspectives, and positioning research within these new contexts (Trauger & Flur, 2014).

Lavallée (2009) addresses the influential role that epistemology plays in research methods: "The epistemological approach of any research fundamentally shapes a project, beginning with what is deemed worthy of researching, what questions are asked, how they are asked, and how the 'data' are analyzed" (p. 1). Having been involved in numerous discussions, or debates, about "evidence-based" research, I am always fond of asking, "Whose evidence?" This question is not meant to evade an answer but to raise the point that how this question is answered is greatly dependent upon numerous sociopolitical considerations. It is a question of how we come to see what we see. This question shapes a discussion with profound social meaning and implications (Majalhaes, 2010). Hansen-Ketchum and Myrick (2008) point out that there are various "assumptions about reality and knowledge converge to conceive a relationship between the knower and what can be known." (p. 265). These assumptions form the foundation for shaping photovoice research. Viewpoints of realism and relativism wield great influence in shaping epistemological understanding, and influencing the type and use of photo methods in qualitative research.

Reed (2005), in turn, draws on Paulo Freire's epistemology that action and reflection are highly interrelated, with critical consciousness resulting in further action—an idea that is widely recognized and embraced by those who practice photovoice and arts-based research in general: "Praxis requires theorizing in a tripartite interactive model: (a) learning about and applying existing knowledge and theory, (b) enacting that knowledge through action, and (c) reflecting on that action to revise our knowledge and theories which together are the process of theorizing" (p. 89). Praxis is a central theme in arts-based research with a social justice focus, as in the case of youth photovoice.

Photovoice is grounded in the participatory process of collaborative knowledge (Green & Kloos, 2009; Schell, Ferguson, Hamoline, Shea, & Thomas-Maclean, 2009). Further, there is an explicit integration of epistemology and social values (Springett, 2010; Trickett, 2009). Heron (1996) raises a critical point that some would argue strikes at the heart of why methods such as photovoice represent such an important alternative to conventional methods: "To generate knowledge about persons without their full participation in deciding how to generate it, is to misrepresent their personhood and to abuse by neglect their capacity for autonomous intentionally. It is fundamentally unethical" (p. 21).

Participatory action research, too, has required an expanded epistemology, with photovoice finding a promising place within this form of research (Clements, 2012). Nygren and Schmauch (2011) observe that there is a debate within feminist circles concerning whether and how to "develop more inclusive epistemologies and methodologies in order to produce more democratic and liberatory knowledge" (p. 79). A more open and participatory research process creates opportunities for innovation that enhances community capacity and, in the case of youth, is an investment with immediate and future benefits (Greene, 2013).

Arts-Based Research Limitations and Cautions

Not surprisingly, arts-based research has had an uphill battle to be accepted as "legitimate" research in traditional academic circles (Barbour, 2006). To say that arts-based inquiry has a history of being on the margins of social research would be an understatement (McNiff, 2013). Part of this resistance is due largely to academics resisting a shift in paradigms (positivistic) concerning inquiry (Raw, Lewis, Russell, & Mcnaughton, 2012). Borgdorff (2005) acknowledges this debate but also raises the challenges in finding agreement: "If the urgency of an issue can be measured by the ferocity of the debates surrounding it, then the issue of 'research in the arts' is an urgent one. . . . a discussion topic has arisen in recent years that has elements of philosophy (notably epistemology and methods) and of educational politics and strategies. That makes it a hybrid issue, and that does not always promote the clarity of the debate" (p. 1). Debate, I am always very fond of saying, is a critical indicator that those in power feel sufficiently threatened that they can no longer continue to ignore an issue or condition. Debate is a good sign!

Lafrenière and Cox (2013) embrace the importance and popularity of arts-based research this paradigm needs to address shortcomings if it is going to continue its meteoric rise: "The use of artistic forms as an alternative means for representing research findings is gaining acceptance in the research community. There are important yet unresolved, and even contentious, issues arising from these new applications of the arts. These include concerns about the level of expertise required to effectively utilize the arts in research, the appropriateness of various methods of creating artworks and the desirability of identifying criteria for assessing arts-based contributions" (p. 318). "Contentious" issues are always present in social research, although they are not always acknowledged to be present, thereby relegating them to an invisible status.

Mosher (2013), too, notes that arts-based research is very attractive as a means of making science more relevant and accessible to the public, but challenges remain related to making this form of research acceptable to a wider academic audience. Skepticism does not necessarily translate into a dismissed view of the power of the visual: "This is not to say that people who might be skeptical about visual research do not appreciate the power of the image, and are very ready to use it, in promotional activities, in training presentations and even in reporting research (though usually restricted to the role of illustration, or the front cover of the report" (Walker, Schratz, & Egg, 2008, p. 165). Obviously, there is a place for image in research. The question is, can it be prominent or must it be peripheral? Making arts-based research prominent, as in the case of photovoice, means that it will draw increased scrutiny and potential criticism. The field must be prepared to critique and refine this approach (McNiff, 2013).

Spencer (2011), in specifically addressing the benefits of visual research, identified three distinct benefits: (1) it is explicit and immediate while presenting a multisensory response; (2) it can create a vivid and authentic personal narrative; and (3) it provides "thick description," facilitating exploration and understanding of theoretical concepts. Each of these benefits addresses aspects of visual research methods such as photovoice, and stresses use, ability to probe in nonintrusive ways, and contribute to theory development.

Putland (2008) identified the challenges of an evidence-based paradigm being applied to community interventions using arts to address health promotion concerns. The question also emerges as to whether arts-based researchers must be experts in their own art form in addition to research (Woo, 2008). If not, is intent sufficient? The answer to this question is open for debate, and it further complicates the discussion on arts-based research. The fact that there is a debate is significant, because this field of practice is considered important enough not to be ignored. Progress in this field would be very limited without debates about origins, goals, and parameters.

Arts-based research seeks to be inclusive of all forms of artistic expression (McNiff, 2013). Anytime a method seeks to be inclusive of a broad area, questions and issues emerge as to what falls within and outside of its boundaries. This inclusivity, which is a very attractive element, will also bring in academic disciplines and professions (social work being such an example) that will usually not be associated with the arts-based approach. Debates and tension are bound to be a reality.

Conclusion

Qualitative research would certainly not be considered an orphan in the scientific field. It may have an embarrassment of riches because it has numerous homes, with the list ever expanding. As this chapter has highlighted, qualitative research and the arts-based field are closely interconnected, opening up ever-expansive research terrain with CBPR. This partnership facilitates the development of collaborative relationship between researcher and participant that is impossible to achieve in conventional approaches that have the researcher as the "expert," and the participant as the "research subject."

As youth research continues to find favor in the social sciences and arts-based research realms, it creates opportunities for collaborative relationships across a number of social spheres that help to ensure that the research they are part of has relevance in their lives, and in the lives of their loved ones (Brown & Powell, 2012). Youth, as addressed in the next chapter, have their own paradigms that they bring to the field of research, but these can be complementary and enhancing to those covered in this chapter. This means that research methods, including those that are arts-based, must be sufficiently flexible to take into account the influence of the age of participants in the shaping its approach.

3

Youth Development

Introduction

This chapter provides a theoretical grounding on the youth development field and its evolution, including sociopolitical tensions, bringing an added dimension to the discussion that took place in the preceding chapter. This chapter, in addition, provides a rationale for why this book is focusing on urban youth even though one of the primary appeals of photovoice is its universality, and how it can be applied across the life cycle and in various geographic settings, interdisciplinary collaborations, and in combination with other methods. This universal appeal is reflected in the countless number of examples with multiple age groups, nations, settings, and issues addressed in this method. The potential transformative outcomes resulting from youth engaging photovoice as a research method can be viewed as an expanding universe with endless possibilities, and as part of a broader movement of youth as researchers (Checkoway & Richards-Schuster, 2012; Delgado, 2006; Grant, Shimshock, Allen-Meares, Smith, Miller, Hollingsworth, & Shanks, 2009; Phillips, Berg, Rodriguez, & Morgan, 2010).

Youth development is a generic term, similar to *arts-based* or *qualitative research*, for example. How youth development is conceptualized, implemented, and evaluated, is greatly influenced by its sociopolitical premises and emphasis on community context, resulting in various prefixes to this term, particularly "positive" and "youth-led," representing different approaches but also sharing similarities (Benson, Leffert, Scales, & Blyth, 2012; Calvert, Emery, & Kinsey, 2013; Lapalme, Bisset, & Potvin, 2013). A geographical context, too, can be part of a prefix. *Urban* youth development is an example of this.

In the case of this book, youth development is urban in character, with a backdrop of arts, ethnography, and social justice/participatory values, and focused on marginalized youth. Contextualization is not just restricted to better understanding "problems," but is also applicable to understanding resiliency among children and youth, as well as assets within communities (Jain & Cohen,

2013; Ungar, 2007). Much can be learned from how marginalized urban youth are resilient and effective in fighting against marginalization (Wexler, DiFluvio, & Burke, 2013).

Context, in turn, influences the approach used in photovoice as an arts-based visual ethnographic method of research—whether it be "positive youth development," a modified version with a social justice bent, or "youth-led development" with an explicit embrace of social change. The "label" that is used is significant and goes beyond semantics and academic jargon. The "at-risk" label, for example, is ubiquitous when discussing "urban" and other marginalized groups (Kelly, 2007; Riele, 2005). The "at-opportunity" label, stressing current abilities, is not (Futch, 2011). The label that we subscribe to reveals a great deal about our assumptions, values, and goals, and about how we think of photovoice and other visual participatory research methods.

Both positive and youth-led approaches to youth development can use and create positive change with photovoice. How photovoice comes alive will look very different depending upon the approach or school of thought used. This author's preference is for a youth-led approach, because it resonates more closely with how photovoice is viewed by many in the field, and because of the potential to significantly alter the lives of youth and their communities. Nevertheless, photovoice can still be a viable method of inquiry in positive youth development programs that limit youth decision-making powers, and that still have adults wielding significant power in the lives of participants. This author does have a bias, but he also understands the diversity of opinions in the field.

All youth can benefit from participation in youth development initiatives, photovoice or otherwise. Those from affluent backgrounds, as well as those from marginalized ones, can enhance their capacities for caring and competencies, and engage in meaningful civic activities. Yet those youth who are of color, live in economically distressed areas of a city, and have limited options for upward mobility are in greater need for youth development than their counterparts who are white, non-Latino, and living in suburbia or affluent sections of a city.

Urban-focused youth development must be conceptualized as having a social justice foundation, with empowerment being a key element of this conceptualization, because of the socioeconomic circumstances impinging on their lives and neighborhoods:

> [The] social justice youth development (SJYD) model [was] conceptualized to facilitate and enhance urban youth awareness of their personal potential, community responsibility, and broader humanity. The SJYD requires the healing of youth identities by involving them in social justice activities that counter oppressive conditions preventing healthy self-identification. . . . While urban youth engage in social justice activities and become committed agents of change, positive educational and development experiences will emerge.
>
> —CAMMAROTA, 2011, p. 828

Cammarota's embrace of social justice strikes at the heart of the various ways of viewing youth development.

An embrace of social justice, as covered in the next chapter on values and principles, provides a lens through which to view and shape youth projects such as photovoice. The combination of knowledge, skill-building, consciousness-raising, and social action must be present for youth development to take hold and be meaningful among marginalized urban youth (Ross, 2011). The process of engagement and empowerment in youth development is as important as, and some would argue even more important than, the end result, so to speak.

This emphasis on process parallels that of arts-based research, CBPR, and photovoice, in which the nature and extent of participation is of greater importance than the actual exhibition, for example, although that, too, is very important. Youth carrying out a photovoice project reap numerous benefits for themselves and others. The field of youth development has struggled with deciding to what extent social justice and oppression should, or must, be front and center in programming, and to what degree youth participants must be in control of their destines in these programs. These distinctions are fundamentally important in shaping how youth photovoice projects gets planned and implemented.

Youth as a National Resource

There is no disputing that the United States needs to come to grips with how it views youth in general, and urban youth of color in particular. The field of youth development has played a major role in helping communities to rethink how they viewed youth and the role they can play in the life of the community and the institutions in it. This shift in thinking about youth capacity goes beyond semantics and has resulted in very concrete initiatives focused on youth as a group from an assets perspective, including having youth play active and decision-making roles in in all phases of a research project (Delgado, 2006). Youth cannot be passive assets. Their assets must be mobilized or they will be wasted, which is a shame in communities that can benefit from these internal resources.

Youth are assets throughout the world (Aspy et al., 2004; Holland, 2009; Shah, 2011), and any country that neglects this age group is bound to have a very dismal future (Delgado & Humm-Delgado, 2013; Sherman, 2004). Nevertheless, Valaitis (2005) addresses the low status and precarious position youth have in this society: "Youth are among the disenfranchised groups. Adults typically view youth as the cause of community deterioration rather than as a community asset. Youth often feel they have little voice in their communities" (p. 3). Unfortunately, this negative view is all too prevalent and permeates much of the discourse on their potential contributions to communities and society as a whole.

Society can view youth from a variety of vantage points or perspectives with profound implications for their social identity formation (Best, 2011; Jones, 2009). A very common point of view is to use a biological determinism lens: "Today's young people are traditionally understood through biological determinism rooted in psychological and/or physical stages of development. This view typically positions youth in opposition to adulthood whereby young people grow into or toward adulthood or grow out of or away from childhood" (Cerecer, Cahill, & Bradley, 2013, p. 216). Another perspective is to think of youth as "adults in waiting," "not adults, "or "adults-in-the-making." A more positive approach is to view this period of youth as "emerging adulthood" (Flacks, 2007). Youth are in a temporal position that they will eventually grow out of (Raby, 2007). This perspective places youth on an adult trajectory and minimizes their current position in society, and in some cases it pushes them to the margins of society, as with urban youth of color. In essence, they must wait to make their contributions (Brooks, 2013; Raby, 2007).

Thomson (2008a) notes the disempowering consequences of viewing youth as incapable because of their chronological age:

> There is no biological "truth" to suggest that being young equates with nothing to say. As scholars involved in the "new" childhood studies argue, it is a product of our place and times to judge the nature and capabilities of people on the basis of their age. . . . However, despite the evidence that connections between age and the capacity to take responsibility are culturally constructed, we more often than not see children and young people as persons whose views are completely "immature" and not to be taken seriously. (p. 1)

It is interesting to note that older adults, too, are marginalized by equating their age with diminished capabilities, particularly those of color (Delgado, 2014).

A deficit viewpoint (stereotypical view) perspective on represents an all too prevalent perspective in this society (Jones, 2009; Lesko, 2001). This perspective associates youth with "drugs," "sex," "poor impulse control," and "rock and roll." In essence, youth are to be considered hedonist, risk takers, misguided, and a financial drain on society, with no regard for others. In essence, moral panic is associated with this perspective, and nothing positive comes out of such a reaction (Deuchar, 2010; Spencer, 2011). Society is hypervigilante in nature and sees the need to control youth because their immense energy will put them in harm's way. Helping professions, in turn, have been called upon to "help" these youth through various types of interventions without consideration of their marginal status and how that affects their worldview.

Adults typically view themselves as saviors of youth and assume the typical adult roles as mentors, authorities, educators, and counselors. In the case of marginalized urban youth of color, for example, these adults occupy positions of power in their lives and claim to know what is best for them and their future.

In many ways, they become "substitute" parental figures in their lives because there is a basic belief that there are no adults or natural mentors in their immediate circles that can perform this task. Hurd and Zimmerman (2010) address the presence and role that natural mentors (informal support relationships) can have within their social circles at the neighborhood level involving African American youth. In this instance, these natural mentors represent a community asset that gets overlooked in development of programs that target urban youth of color.

The social identity that results from these stereotypical assumptions over a lifetime is negative, with long-term implications for these youth, their families, and the communities they live in (Berlinger, 2013; Taft, 2007). The deleterious repercussions reach far and wide, in the present and into the future. A youth transition to adulthood in a severely compromised state means that they will not be in a position to assume an adult leadership role within their families and communities, because a compromised state will not magically transform them into "competent adults." A cradle-to-grave perspective that outlines how marginalized youth of color are tracked for failure is an example of how a compromised state (socially, educationally, and healthwise) unfolds, with profound and disastrous consequences for these youth (Children's Defense Fund, 2007).

Unfortunately, the only adult sector of society that has a true appreciation and understanding of youth is the marketing sector, or what is commonly referred to as "Madison Avenue." It was estimated that youth aged 8 to 24 years old would spend $211 billion in 2012, and this level of spending does not take into account their influence on parents: "While the purchasing power of today's youth is strong, it is made even stronger when coupled with the influence these kids have on what parents buy. For example, seven-in-ten teens have cell phones (69%) and three-in-ten have smartphones (30%). When it comes to smartphones or cell phones, one-third of teens (34%) say they influence that purchase decision. With over 23 million teens in the United States, that's a lot of influence" (Harris Interactive, 2011). Globally, it was estimated that adolescents spent $819 billion in 2011 (Sommer, 2012), making youth economic influence a worldwide phenomenon.

Youth as a "consumer" group is well understood by adults in marketing. There is a counter-narrative that has been emerging for the past two decades that has youth as assets or national resources, and not just a consumer group (Judd, 2006; Delgado & Zhou, 2008; Kim & Sherman, 2006). This is an exciting development that merges well into ethnography, CBPR, and arts-based research methods such as photovoice, and it bodes well for their communities and society as these youth enter adulthood and are better prepared for the challenges that await them.

A shift in paradigms has youth receiving national and international attention focused on their potential role (assets) as contributors to their communities and society's well-being (Checkoway & Richards-Schuster, 2004; Judd, 2006). The emergence of critical youth studies has played an important role in broadening how society views youth. This school of thought has gathered together activists and scholars alarmed about how society relegates youth to the sidelines and labels them, causing harm and significantly altering their future. This school of thought is critical of adultism, or adult-centered institutions that have embraced the charge of policing "deviant" youth behavior (Cerecer, Cahill, & Bradley, 2013).

Harper (2002) comments typify the emerging viewpoint that youth are a vital national resource:

> Collectively, youth in America represent a power that transcends race, ethnicity, gender, and social and economic status. America's youth are a walking depiction of their worldview externally manifested through clothing, art, attitude, style, movement, music, video, television, film, language, and the World Wide Web. Youth are a big business, and everyone is struggling to get their attention: advertisers, large and small businesses, media conglomerates; the sports, fashion, and entertainment businesses; faith communities; health arenas; schools, community-based organizations, families, and even local, state, and national governments. (p. 2)

This paradigm shift has resulted in communities, particularly those that are urban and undervalued by society, recasting the role youth can play in creating an environment that is conducive to including and respecting all age groups. Youth have not only become visible in a positive manner, but they have also taken on more productive roles, using their talents for the well-being of both their age group and the entire community.

This trend takes on greater significance in the case of youth from immigrant families, since they are able to socially navigate across social arenas that their parents have difficulty navigating (Delgado, Jones, & Rohani, 2005). The adult world is neither simple nor orderly (Larson, 2011). Some cultures, such as those found in East Asia, for example, emphasize the importance of family and community over individual rights (Reisch, Ife, & Weir, 2013). Nevertheless, seeing youth as a community and national stakeholder is certainly a radically different way of viewing them, when they were formerly either invisible or had assumed negative identities, rather than being thought of as a community and national asset (Frank, 2006).

Youth Development

A definition of youth development is in order, since this field, too, is evolving and encompasses a broad arena of practice—to the extent that it covers an ever-expanding area, causing confusion about what constitutes "youth development" and what does not. Further complicating this ability to clearly define boundaries is a dichotomy in the field that has "positive youth development" (PYD) as the major branch of youth development, and the "youth-led" branch, which has many of the same elements as its PYD counterpart, but also a distinct sociopolitical conceptualization that has youth playing leadership roles and embracing a social change agenda (Delgado & Staples, 2007; Delgado & Zhou, 2008).

A basic definition of youth development is therefore in order before addressing the various camps, or schools of thought, on this intervention. Delgado (2002) defines youth development as

> interventions [that] systematically seek to identify and utilize youth capacities and meet youth needs. They actively seek to involve youth as decision makers and tap their creativity, energy, and drive; and they also acknowledge that youth are not superhuman—that they therefore have needs that require a marshaling of resources targeted at youth and at changing environmental circumstances (family and community). Positively changing environments that are toxic and antithetical to youth capacity enhancement requires the use of a wide range of strategies—tailored to fit local circumstances—ranging from advocacy to consciousness raising and political mobilization. (p. 48)

This definition of youth development highlights the dynamic and multifaceted nature of this field, and why social justice and social change should be central to this form of research and practice. This definition, in addition, grounds youth development contextually (culturally and geographically).

A brief historical overview is also in order, since it provides an important sociopolitical context to understand events. The reader is warned that this historical account is one person's version. I believe it was Voltaire who said that "history is the lie we can all agree upon." This statement is quite simple but still quite profound. Any discussion of the history of the United States, for example, will highlight how Voltaire's observation is so poignant. Howard Zinn's (2005) classic *People's History of the United States: 1492 to Present* illustrates how the vantage point of the historian is influenced by whether the perspective of the oppressor or the oppressed is taken.

The Irish folk singer Frank Harte (as quoted in Moloney, 2005) summed up the importance of the idea that where you stand is how you see the world: "Those in power write the history, while those who suffer write the songs." This powerful quote illustrates positions of power and the role of the arts (in this case song) to provide voice, no pun intended, to those who are not allowed to write history. Without this, their perspective is unimportant, at least to those in power.

The field of youth development has evolved since the 1980s and 1990s and has had to struggle with the question of how much social justice and social change should be an integral part of this approach (Delgado & Staples, 2007; Lerner, Lerner, & Benson, 2011; Jenson & Alter, 2013). This early period was called "youth development," and emphasized how adults can help youth enhance their competencies to make the transition to adulthood easier, and also increase their likelihood of success. This field drew practitioners and researchers interested in prevention.

The late 1990s witnessed debates and theoretical developments that caused the field to reconsider its emphasis on context, resulting in an explicit acceptance of how the environment shapes youth expectations and behaviors, as well as their future. Youth in undervalued communities (socially, politically, and economically) could not be made "bullet-proof," regardless of how well programs addressed their individual needs. As a result, it was necessary to also pay attention to the socioecological context in which they lived. Such a shift in thinking necessitated an embrace of, or an emphasis on, social values related to addressing oppression and social justice due to socioeconomic class (classism), gender (sexism), sexual identity (homophobia), and race/ethnicity (racism)—and the how these are manifested in their community (Delgado, 2002).

The emergence of the "community youth development" school of thought represents this shift in context and focus. This shift resulted in youth undertaking projects that addressed oppression in their community, and in the process they also developed social identities and competencies related to key core elements (cognitive, social, physical, moral, and spiritual). It also meant that activities meant to increase their knowledge and skills were grounded within social justice values, as well as the operative reality of the communities in which they lived. Low-income youth of color, for example, could learn histories about their cultural heritage in youth development programs (Delgado, Jones, & Rohani, 2005).

This history was grounded within an oppression lens when addressed in community youth development (CYD) programs. Music and culture, for example, would be learned in CYD programs, but they would be grounded in protest music and how cultural values were assaulted under colonial regimes. Clearly, a positive social identity would emerge that did not blame youth and their families for the social circumstances they found themselves in. In essence, there is no "blaming the victim" in CYD.

The highly politicized and oppression-focused community youth development field caused a backlash from governmental and funding authorities, because youth were staging social protests focused on underfunded and unresponsive schools, police brutality, and other oppressive systems in their lives, and in the lives of their families and neighbors. The field of youth development reached a fork in the road, so to speak: shift course to a less politicized perspective and ensure continued funding from traditional sources, or shift toward a social justice/oppression field of practice. The emergence of "positive youth development" represented a shift back to the more conventional and politically more acceptable forms of practice, although social justice could still play a role, but not a central or defining role. Further, positive youth development emphasizes the importance of adults in this movement, particularly in a role as mentors (Clary & Rhodes, 2006).

There is no disputing that these types of programs can make a positive difference in the lives of youth, though this is not to say that there have been no efforts to reconcile the differences between positive youth development and youth-led development. For example, Ross (2011) stresses the need for a social justice foundation, with a focus on social change efforts, to be an integral part of positive youth development: "Specifically, to affect oppressive community conditions, a blend of PYD's focus on individual skill building, participation, and empowerment—joined with SJYD [social justice youth development] emphasis on community organizing and building youth's self-awareness of how race, class, and other dimensions of power affect their lives on a daily basis—is needed" (p. 681). The concept of "social justice youth development" is meant to bridge these two worlds. There is an understanding about the importance of youth core elements being addressed, but not without a social justice lens to help them see the relevance of activities and programming, and seeking to positively alter their social environment.

Youth-led development became a branch onto itself, although a very small branch dependent upon foundation support, embracing values that parallel those covered in Chapter 4 (empowerment, community participation, leadership development, community investment, utilization of local and self-knowledge, social and economic justice, cultural competence/cultural humility). In turning to youth-led development, the reader will see a distinct shift in thinking and vocabulary. A youth-led definition can be quite simple—it is those interventions that have youth playing central and decision-making roles throughout all facets of an endeavor, and that involve adults only, and when, youth decide. Adults shift roles from mentors to allies. This shift may seem simple in substance but it represents a very dramatic paradigm shift (Delgado & Staples, 2013; Delgado & Zhou, 2008).

Having a youth-led focus means that youth are in charge of all facets of an undertaking, whether research or intervention focused. It does not mean that adults are not in the picture, so to speak. Adult allies are involved if, when, and how youth decide they should be involved (Delgado & Staples, 2007; Larson, Walker, & Pearce, 2005). In essence, youth are the central decision-makers and ultimate authorities of their lives.

White, Shoffner, Johnson, Knowles, & Mills (2012) rightly point out that youth-led research requires adult allies and the investment of their time and talents:

> Youth-led research is not an inexpensive proposition. Youth researchers need adults with the time, talent, and resources to fully invest in youth-led research. The busy lives of youth often parallel the lives of adults. Therefore, the timeframe for planning and conducting research should accommodate the lives of youth as well as adults. Equally important, time should be built into every meeting for socialization including snacks and beverages.

Photovoice must never be thought of as a "cheap" way of doing research. The focus and nature of the projects undertaken in youth development look dramatically different depending upon whether one subscribes to positive youth development or youth-led development.

The context in which we view youth, particularly those who are marginalized, shapes the form of the research and practice that unfolds:

> Research on adolescence has begun to recognize the centrality of ecological context in human development. Ecological approaches, however, need to pay greater attention to the political context of young people's lives, both in terms of how youth interpret their sociopolitical world and how they participate in changing it. Research on youth organizing among African American and Latino youth offers insights about these dimensions of sociopolitical development. Youth organizing enables young people growing up in difficult circumstances to identify the social origins of problems and take action to address those problems. Emerging research suggests that youth organizing has the potential to contribute to youth development, community development, and broader social movements. Youth organizing challenges social constructions of adolescents as apathetic or self-involved and offers an alternative to deficit-based orientations toward youth of color.
> —KIRSHNER & GINWRIGHT, 2012, p. 288

Kirshner and Ginwright effectively tie together youth research, context, and action—and in this case, it involved organizing.

The value of social justice takes on greater prominence in youth-led development initiatives because of how oppressive forces have singled out particular youth because of the color of their skin and economic circumstances. Urban youth use of photovoice to address social justice issues resonates with the history of how photovoice emerged in the academy and the field of practice. It is important to note that social justice as a core value does not stand alone. There are other values that are closely associated with social justice, as addressed in the next chapter.

Core Elements and Social Domains

There is wide interest in understanding better how youth, particularly those living in marginalized communities, are able to succeed despite incredible odds to do so. The concept of "identity capital" has emerged as a key element to capture youth abilities (personal resources) to help them navigate and succeed in society (Jones, 2009). Youth development research and scholarship has identified core elements, social domains, and outcomes for a better understanding of how youth can enhance their likelihood of achieving success through participation in programs and projects. Further, this understanding facilitates an in-depth examination of how benefits from participation in photovoice can be measured across a variety of areas and social domains.

Youth development programs often use service learning as a key mechanism for providing services to communities and as a mechanism for addressing core elements and competencies (Diemer, Voight, & Mark, 2010; Metz, 2014). Service learning also provides communities with an opportunity to see youth in a different light, thereby changing their image. It is also an avenue for bringing adults and youth together in partnership for social action (Arches, 2013; Delgado & Staples, 2007). It has also been found to promote civic engagement in youth (Zaff & Lerner, 2010). This change in image is very important to both youth and the adults in the community.

One popular way of viewing youth involved in positive youth development programs is to emphasize enhancement of what are referred to as the "Five Cs" (Lerner et al. 2005): (1) competence, (2) confidence, (3) connection, (4) character, and (5) caring/compassion. Each of these competencies, alone and in combination with each other, seek to enhance the abilities of youth to socially navigate their way through adolescence.

Some youth development scholars in the field would argue that these five are not of equal importance or equally present in positive youth development programs, particularly those based in inner-cities (Lerner, Alberts, Jelicic, & Smith, 2006). Nevertheless, each of the Five Cs can have various manifestations, depending upon contextual factors. For example, how youth development outcomes get conceptualized and manifested varies across ethnic and racial groups because of the influence of culture and geographical factors (Shek & Ma, 2010).

Five core elements have received a considered amount of attention as manifested through research and scholarship: (1) cognition, (2) emotional, (3) physical, (4) moral, and (5) spiritual. This is an alternative approach to the Five Cs for use in photovoice projects. Each of these core elements have had numerous scholarly articles and books written about, and reviewing them in-depth is clearly beyond the scope of this chapter. Nonetheless, each of these core elements will be examined through the use of photovoice and potential outcomes.

Core elements do not exist in isolation from each other, although an emphasis on particular core elements is often found in youth development programs. Allen, Alaimo, Elam, & Perry (2008) illustrate this in their youth development–focused community gardening program: "Results suggest that the garden programs provided opportunities for constructive activities, contributions to the community, relationship and interpersonal skill development, informal social control, exploring cognitive and behavioral competence, and improved nutrition. Community gardens promoted developmental assets for involved youth while improving their access to and consumption of healthy foods" (p. 418). No one specific activity in a community garden can influence one core element. For the purposes of discussion, each of the core elements will be treated as a separate entity, and of equal importance.

Youth cognition has received considerable attention, particularly from practitioners in the field of education. The Carnegie Council on Adolescent Development (1989), over 25 years ago, identified 15 years of being intellectually reflective as a key characteristic for youth to become effective members of society. Many in the field of youth development may even argue that this is the primary goal of youth development, particularly in cases of marginalized youth with a high likelihood of not achieving in formal educational settings. Supplementing, or even replacing, negative educational institutions can be an explicit or implicit goal of youth development (Dooley & Schreckhise, 2013).

Cognition, it is necessary to pause and note, must not be narrowly defined and needs to be expanded to take into account Gardner's (1983) multiple intelligences (bodily kinesthetic, interpersonal, intrapersonal, musical, and spatial). Social cognition (how we encode, process, and use information about others), for example, is one dimension often associated with youth development programs because of how it touches upon so many areas in their lives, and also because of the role it plays in helping youth socially navigate their surroundings, and particularly their relationships with adults. Cognition's relationship with self-regulation is one dimension of how this core element can influence youth behaviors and academic performance, including learning motivation and performance (Baird, Scott, Dearing, & Hamill, 2009).

When the learning that transpires is practical, and the act of learning is active, this facilitates it being transferred to other situations, and possibly even being fun, making photovoice a tool that is in a propitious position to enhance cognitive development in youth. The technical side of photovoice, as addressed in Chapter 5, opens up possibilities for acquisition of exposure to, and possible mastery of, new technologies (Valaitis, 2005) that youth may not have an opportunity to use, such as the development of Internet sites to display their photographs, for example. Bers's (2012) book *Designing Digital Experiences for Positive Youth Development: From Playpen to Playground"* illustrates the potential of digital landscapes to enhance children and youth development, and in the process make it fun and interesting, in similar fashion to arts-based research.

Emotional core element–related goals represent a dimension of youth development that is multifaceted and can be conceptualized as consisting of nine categories: (1) empathize with others, (2) display appropriate emotions, (3) control anger, (4) identify and label feelings, (5) motivation, (6) inspire hope in oneself and others, (7) delay gratification, (8) establish self-worth, and (9) tolerate frustration. The emotional core element, and its various manifestations, plays an influential role in helping youth confront daily challenges within and outside of their immediate community, making them more confident in their problem-solving. The reader can see the close relationship between social cognition and emotions.

Not surprisingly, a physical core element is highly associated with youth. Youth development programs understand the importance of youth achieving optimal physical health and tapping youth energy and the importance they put on their physical appearance (Coakley, 2011; Fraser-Thomas, Cote, & Deakin, 2005). Access to quality and safe public facilities takes on great prominence in the lives of urban youth (Ries, Yan, & Voorhees, 2011). If these facilities are inaccessible, poorly maintained, or unsafe, their options for physical exercise, particularly group-focused exercise, are severely limited (Delgado, 2013). Youth leadership potential cannot be fulfilled if they are eating poorly or live in an environment detrimental to exercising (Yoshida, Craypo, & Samuels, 2011).

It is also important to note that a great deal of development can transpire while engaging in sporting activities, such as character (Power, Sheehan, McCarthy, & Carnevale, 2010). Activities related to achievement of physical health have evolved to encompass a broader perspective to include other dimensions related to health; hence the emergence of health promotion (Delgado & Zhou, 2008; Duckett, Kagan, & Sixsmith, 2010). Photovoice, as addressed in earlier portions of this book, has certainly found a receptive home in health promotion, as evidenced by the countless number of examples related to health and its various manifestations.

The reader may wonder out loud why morality and spirituality are involved in any discussion of youth development and photovoice, particularly since these two core elements are highly sensitive topics in society. Nevertheless, these two core elements have occupied prominent places in youth development, and programs have been very creative in making them relevant for youth photovoice, particularly when issues of fairness and social justice play such an important role in shaping the reasons a photovoice project is being used. For example, the subject of morality can elicit a wide range of reactions from adults as well as youth. This core element is often associated with "good" and "evil."

This association makes the initial negative response on the part of youth and adults difficult to address. If recast into other forms that make more sense to youth, then a moral core element can play an important role in youth development programs. Goffman (1963) touches upon the bonding that can occur among people with a common challenge, and the stigma that results from it: "Persons who have a particular stigma tend to have similar learning experiences regarding their plight, and similar changes in conception of self—a similar "moral career" that is both cause and effect of commitment to a similar sequence of personal adjustments" (p. 32).

The concept of "code of behavior" also helps to bring this core element to life: "It refers to the appropriateness of specific behaviors in relation to other people and the responsibility one assumes for his actions" (Dreyfus, 1972, p. 68). Travis and Leech (2014), in turn, broaden a moral core element to include community: "A young person's sense of community is especially important for its potential to amplify empowering or risky pathways related to their moral identity and sense of mastery" (p. 18). Issues of fairness and respect are particularly useful ways for morality to enter into discussions and activities with urban youth.

Spirituality and, in some programs, religion have a place in youth development programs (Lerner, Roeser, & Phelps, 2008). Tirri and Quinn (2010) found that religion/spirituality fosters authenticity, which is a one of the key elements associated with purpose in life or meaningfulness to the self and the world beyond the self. Maton and Domingo (2006) focus their attention on positive youth development and religious congregations and faith-based efforts. They see tremendous potential in using a faith-based context for increasing youth volunteerism and instilling a wide range of competencies in youth related to serving others.

A social core element wields considerable influence on how youth define the social and interpersonal goals in their lives. The ability to maintain social relations with different groups, including adults, during a period in their lives when relationships with peers are so important in shaping future relations across age groups, is extremely important for young people. Character attributes, such as empathy, self-discipline, reading social cues, a sense of humor, and many others, illustrate the interrelationship between the social element and the other four core elements.

Core elements, or the Five Cs, need to be conceptualized in a manner that makes them relevant to urban youth and their operative reality. The need to make youth development relevant to urban youth experiences has resulted in efforts to modify and expand on the Five Cs. Travis and Leech (2014), for example, acknowledge the importance of a socioecological context in addressing the developmental needs of African American youth:

> The Five Cs approach certainly has the potential to combat these issues. We must simultaneously acknowledge that the Five Cs occur within an ecological context that may inhibit African American youth's optimal expression of these developmental potentialities. Structural and social realities limit the Five Cs in its current conceptual form from offering a framework that (1) embraces individual and cultural strengths and (2) provides sufficiently specific pathways by which to understand developmental needs and opportunities for African American youth and communities. (pp. 3–4)

As a result, Travis and Leech call for "empowerment-based positive youth development" in order to reintroduce community issues more prominently.

A number of other scholars have raised concerns about how positive youth development's general avoidance of social ecology and issues of oppression, which are particularly salient to urban youth of color and their families. Washington and Johnson (2012), for example, argue that the positive youth development literature rarely addresses ecological factors and concerns that African American youth have, and how the Five Cs are too narrow in scope. Those who subscribe to positive youth development may argue that these topics are subsumed under various competencies. Nevertheless, by not highlighting them, it does raise questions as to the prominence that they occupy in programming.

One can see how a youth development/youth-led field can be a receptive home for photovoice as an arts-based visual ethnographic method that can be used to enhance youth competencies, knowledge, and consciousness, and to create positive social change in an effort to redress the consequences and sources of oppression. Photovoice and urban youth, in similar fashion to any other "tool," is only as good as the person using the tool. When this tool is placed in the hands of competent youth, with a clear agenda of achieving positive changes in their lives, communities, and society, then only "good" can come out of what this tool does.

Core elements, in turn, can be addressed through various social domains or spheres. Four domains have dominated the thinking on youth development: (1) family, (2) peers, (3) schools, and (4) community. Each of these social domains represents an influential sphere in the life of youth, with some spheres playing a more or less prominent role in daily life. Cognitive core elements, for example, may take on greater prominence in school and community, while an emotional core element may take on significance among family and peers. Schools and communities can also be places where health promotion can transpire (Duckett et al., 2010). As the review of photovoice and youth has shown, these social domains lend themselves to the use of photovoice, with some domains, such as schools, being more challenging than the others, such as family, peers, and community. This does not mean that we should eschew school settings, but it does put researchers on notice that additional time and political acumen will be required to successfully navigate them. It also gives adults an appreciation for what youth must content with in their daily lived experiences within these institutions.

Urban Youth Research and Photovoice

It is appropriate to start this section with an example of youth research that draws a distinction between youth as collaborators and youth as leaders, setting a backdrop for the use of photovoice by youth. Kellett (2010) draws an important distinction between children/youth undertaking research with adults, and initiating and carrying out the research themselves, which illustrates a fundamental difference between positive youth development and youth-led development:

> The concept of children as researchers has gained credence in response to changing perspectives on their status in society, recognition of their role as consumers and increased attention to children's rights. While this has led to greater involvement of children as participant and co-researchers, research *led by* children—research they design, carry out and disseminate themselves with adult support rather than adult management—is still relatively rare. Children designing and leading their own research opens up new protagonist frontiers. Children are party to the subculture of childhood which gives

them a unique "insider" perspective critical to our understanding of their worlds. Child-to-child enquiry generates different data from adult-to-child enquiry because children observe with different eyes, ask different questions and communicate in fundamentally different ways. (p. 195)

Kellett's distinction between youth as participants and youth leading research illustrates the interplay of key values, premises, and assumptions, and potential outcomes of the research. Clearly, the setting in which the research transpires wields tremendous influence on whether those in autority can tolerate a research project involving youth playing leadership roles. Mind you, my position is that I prefer having youth leading with adults assisting as needed. If it was a question of not being able to conduct the research with youth as leaders but being able to do so with youth participants, I would go ahead and still undertake the project.

Having youth initiate and/or participate in research, including using photovoice projects as vehicles for inquiry, is not new. The popularity of youth as researchers can be found in the proliferation of scholarship as a subject. Thomson's (2008b) edited book *Doing Visual Research with Children and Young People* is an example of how youth research, in this case visually focused research, is drawing scholarly attention.

Nevertheless, it is important to take a moment and contextual or ground youth as researchers from a historical perspective. The 1970s represent a watershed moment in having youth fulfill the role of researcher (Delgado & Staples, 2007). The 1980s witnessed a dramatic shift in thinking about youth researchers, as evidenced by the number of scholarly publications on the subject (Heath & Walker, 2012a). No longer was it research being done on youth; this decade shifted youth from subjects to active participants and decision-makers in the research process (Sharpe, 2012).

There was a realization that youth possessed insights that increased the likelihood that research seeking new insights into youth experiences would benefit from having the "experts," meaning youth themselves, playing pivotal roles throughout the research process (Delgado, 2006; Ozar, Ritterman, & Wanis, 2010). Further, as Schubotz (2012) notes, youth participation and leadership in research undertakings should never be viewed as a favor that adults do for them and consideredto be "cute": "The involvement of young people as peer researchers in social research should primarily be informed by the attempt to produce qualitatively better research . . . there is no doubt that young peer researchers can help us design better research instruments and help us get access to hard-to-reach groups of people and information" (p. 107).

This attempt to produce more informed research has expanded the parameters to include very young children. Clark (2010) demonstrates that even young children under the age of six, although not without challenges, can engage in the research enterprise. Further, there is the question of whether a new category specifically focused on young children is advisable, and whether the lessons learned in making adjustments for their age can also have implications for adults engaging in research:

> One question that arises is whether there should be a category of participatory research methods that are adopted solely with young children? There appear to be new possibilities for inter-generational and professional/lay communication that the use of participatory, visual methods with young children has facilitated. However, . . . one of the catalysts for these methods came from research and development projects with adults using techniques used in participatory rural appraisal programmes. Perhaps some of the adaptations made to these methods whilst working with young children can now be reapplied to adults to make certain "voices" more visible. (p. 112)

Haw (2008) talks about four methodological issues related to video and giving voice to those who are not listened to, and they have applicability to photovoice: (1) relational (importance of an authentic and trusting relationship between researcher and participant), (2) technical, (3) creative, and (4) potential for achieving positive social change. Each of these issues of methodological dimensions stresses unique challenges and rewards, but, in combination with each other, they highlight the importance of researchers being highly attuned to youth vulnerabilities related to these methodological issues.

Cameron and Theron (2011) articulate a powerful rationale for engaging youth in research that eventually results in programming with relevance to their lives: "Our research with adolescents highlights the necessity of projecting the voices of youth in order to come to understand and share their experiences fully. . . . Teenagers have powerful statements to make about their own situations. Their narratives are powerful: They are insightful; they are veridical; they are deeply engaging; and, most importantly, youths have stories that can inform theory and practice" (p. 205). Cameron and Theron provide an emotionally moving rationale that, on the surface, is far from radical, and can easily apply to any group. When applied to youth, however, it is very radical, and that says a great deal about their secondary status in society.

Youth participation in CBPR, for example, has been found to benefit youth in very personal ways, including development of sociopolitical skills, motivation to change their school and community, and connectedness to their neighborhood (Nation et al., 2010; Ozar & Douglas, 2012; Rudkin & Davis, 2007). Equally importantly, the images resulting from photovoice are resistant to the typical discounting undertaken by power structures and adults (Streng et al., 2004), creating a cultural artifact as a mechanism to fight marginalization. This cultural artifact can take various manifestations as addressed in Chapter 5.

A number of scholars have developed typologies to classify different levels of youth participation and empowerment in research projects. These typologies go by a variety of different names, but they all seek to help practitioners think about the degree of decision-making, or power, that youth will have in planning and carrying out their research, and also what role adults will play. These typologies generally range from youth having minimal, or no, power, at one end of the continuum, to youth having ultimate power, at the opposite end of the continuum. The following two examples illustrate this conception of youth decision-making and roles.

Schubotz (2012) adapted Hart's (1992) eight-step ladder of youth participation in participatory research, providing a useful way of categorizing different levels of youth participation by identifying five different ways they can engage in research with varying degrees of power and influence:

1. *Being informed.* This level of participation, of just being informed about research, typifies how conventional research usually views youth as subjects.
2. *Expressing a view.* At this level, youth are turned to for advice, which may or may not be followed, and adults make this determination.
3. Influencing decision-making. Here youth have an active role that influences decisions and outcomes, but adults are still the ultimate deciders.
4. *Deciding partners.* Youth are considered co-investigators at this participation level, and they make joint decisions with adult researchers.
5. *Main deciders (leaders).* In this approach, youth are in positions of sole authority and make final decisions, although adults can be tapped for advice and consultation.

Each rung in this "ladder" of participation dictates the degree of power youth have in shaping and leading a research endeavor, and each determines the nature and extent of adult involvement. Positive youth development generally subscribes to steps 2 and 3 and youth-led development can be either step 4 or step 5. Both positive and youth-led developments are in agreement that step 1 is antithetical to their central mission. How youth development unfolds is dramatically different if one subscribes to positive youth development or youth-led development.

Wong, Zimmerman, and Parker (2010), in turn, developed a typology of youth participation that integrates empowerment, and it, too, consists of five levels:

1. *Vessel.* At this first level, adults provide guidance, mentoring, or education, since youth are seen ans an "empty vessel" to be filled.
2. *Symbolic.* This level is one of tokenism, with adults dictating all major facets of the research.
3. *Pluralistic.* Youth and adults serve as co-collaborators and equal partners throughout all facets of the research at this level.
4. *Independent.* Youth are now left on their own, without adult involvement.
5. *Autonomous.* At this final level, youth create their own spaces, but the potential still exists for adult involvement.

This typology shares many similarities with Schubutz's. Readers may have their own typology in helping to conceptualize how youth participation in research can be implemented to take into account local circumstances and goals.

One of the positive outcomes of youth participation in research has been the changes that have resulted in seeking to introduce new methods. The motivation for using research methods, such as photovoice and other qualitative arts-based approaches with youth, is the desire to gain knowledge that was previously either overlooked or too difficult to obtain using conventional methods (Heath & Walker, 2012b): "[O]ne of the important catalysts for methodological innovation and experimentation has been a desire to hone the methods used by youth researchers for capturing the complexities of young people's life, particularly those relating to relatively new or rediscovered areas of enquiry" (p. 252). Necessity is the mother of invention in youth research!

Benefits and Challenges

Any social intervention or paradigm brings inherent benefits and challenges, and youth photovoice is not an exception. The benefits, I and others would argue, far outweigh the challenges or limitations. Identifying these benefits and challenges serves to maximize the potential of the former, and to possibly minimize the consequences of the latter, for researchers and practitioners. Youth ask different questions than adults, and this is based upon their position in society. Their priorities also differ from those of adults (Kellett, 2005).

Schubotz (2012) raises a critical concern faced by those researchers who propose a shift in roles to involve youth as peers in the research process: "Involving young people as peer researchers challenges us methodologically and epistemologically. It challenges our views on how we generate knowledge, to what extent we trust accepted and tested methodologies and our willingness to develop and apply new innovative ways of collecting data" (p. 101). In essence, the shift in roles is much more than a theoretical or abstract position; it represents a dramatic change in power and decision-making.

Further, the benefits of bringing together the power of youth development and photovoice go far beyond the immediate gains, with long-term ramifications for how youth participants develop a sense of belonging and capabilities: "Youth photography programs take a strength-based approach, providing participants with the opportunity to build upon their individual and community assets, to become activists and active contributors to their social world, to explore freely and in innovative ways, and validity, to develop a stronger future orientation, sense of cohesion, efficacy, and sense of meaning" (Kia-Keating, 2009, p. 386). Resources invested in youth today will bring significant future payouts for their family, community, and society. Taking a capital perspective, photovoice and youth translates into human, social, economic, and cultural capital gains.

Arts-based visual ethnography opens up previously untapped areas of enhancing youth competencies. White et al. (2012) draw an important analogy between youth-led research and drama, a very popular arts-based activity: "The roles played by youth conducting research are similar to actors in a play. . . . Success in research and evaluation, as on stage, is the result of repeated rehearsals, multiple performances, and receptive audiences. Intentional training in youth-led research, clearly defined leadership roles, and manageable timelines should be facilitated, accepted, and established to accommodate the busy lives of youth."

Wexler, Gurium, Griffin, and DiFulvio (2013), for example, used digital storytelling involving video, photos, music, and voice in northwest Alaskan youth to create "hope kits" as a central part of a positive youth development program for suicide prevention. The vast majority of the efforts using photovoice, either explicitly or implicitly, are based upon a youth development foundation. Youth development, in similar fashion to the arts-based movement, has witnessed a dramatic expansion nationally and internationally, opening up opportunities for the introduction of innovative methods of engagement and ways of capturing the lived experience.

Jones (2009) argues that there is a desperate need to find new ways of thinking about youth: "If we want to understand youth and engage in debates about young people, we need to build a new conceptual framework from the ashes of old ones" (p. 164). There is no question that urban youth development and photovoice will have a prominent place at the table of discussion concerning a new or emerging paradigm on urban youth. Riele (2010), for example, puts forth the concept of hope (a positive culture, a focus on possibility, a community of hope, and critical reflection) as a means of introducing a new way of thinking about marginalized youth and success in a hostile social environment.

One cannot help but revert back to Erving Goffman's (1963) classic book *Stigma: Notes on the Management of Spoiled Identity* when thinking about the potential of photovoice to help urban youth with "spoiled identities" to create new and more positive identities. Goffman comments on the power of society and its institutions to shape identities:

> Society establishes the means of categorizing persons and the complement of attributes felt to be ordinary and natural for members of each of these categories. Social settings establish the categories of persons likely to be encountered there. The routines of social intercourse in established settings allow us to deal with anticipated others without special attention or thought. When a stranger comes into our presence, then first appearances are likely to enable us to anticipate his category and attributes, his "social identity." (p. 2)

If these individuals possess a spoiled identity (stigma), as in the case of urban youth of color, their ability to successfully socially navigate society is severely compromised. Adolescents with HIV and young African American men who have sex with men are cases in point. Fielden, Chapman, and Cadell (2011) address adolescents with HIV and the role of stigma in creating silence, secrets, and sanctioned spaces (physical and social). Radcliffe et al. (2010), in turn, speak to the multiple forms of stigma faced by young African American men who have sex with men. Learning how to respond to and manage responses to their identities becomes very important for youth (O'Brien, 2011). The benefits of qualitative methods such as photovoice are multifaceted, including discovery of unnamed processes (Ungar, 2007). Photovoice provides a window into their obvious and not so obvious challenges (Heery, 2013).

Strack, Magill, and McDonagh (2004) see the value of photovoice as a strategy for engaging youth to develop competencies and positive identities:

> A process such as photovoice provides youth the opportunity to develop their personal and social identities and can be instrumental in building social competency. Youth should and need to be given the opportunity to build and confirm their abilities, to comment on their experiences and insights, and to develop a social morality for becoming a positive agent within their communities and society. (p. 49)

Providing opportunities or the space for youth to explore their abilities seems like a noble goal. There are very few spaces where youth in general, and youth of color in particular, can engage in this exploration.

Social identities that are affirming and restore cultural pride wield great influence on how urban youth view themselves, their families, and their communities. A counter-narrative is essential to undo the harm that has been perpetuated by a society that is adultist, sexist, racist, ableist, and classist, for example (Delgado & Staples, 2007). The interplay of these forces requires bold initiatives and new ways of engaging these youth and their world, because they must play a central and leading role in the solutions. These solutions must start with a deep and profound understanding of these youth, and that is why photovoice holds so much promise.

Langhout and Thomas (2010), in their introduction to a special issue of the *American Journal of Community Psychology* on participatory action research with children and adolescents, stress the interconnectedness of knowledge and action (solutions):

> Research that affects children can be further reinvigorated by reconceptualizing the research process as an intervention in and of itself, where children learn skills through guided participation and active engagement. In other words, research and intervention are not separate steps, but rather are the components of praxis, or an embodied theory, with an agenda of creating conditions that facilitate individual and group empowerment, as well as social change. Using the theoretical framework of participatory action research with children has the potential to strengthen research findings, interventions, and social action. (p. 60)

Langhout and Thomas stress the importance of praxis, which makes the research process much more meaningful for youth, since it is not an exercise but can have real and concrete outcomes for their lives.

Finally, the value and goal of actively seeking to tap youth voices is operative in all projects with youth as co-researchers. Tapping youth voices is a key goal in photovoice. Accomplishing this goal is far more complex than it appears on the surface, because there are at least three perspectives, or meanings, of what is meant by "voices." Britzman (1989), almost 25 years ago, addressed this complexity: "The concept of voice spans literal, metaphorical and political terrains: in the literal sense, voice represents the speech and perspective of the speaker; metaphorically, voice spans inflection, tone, accent, style and the qualities and feelings conveyed by the speaker's words; and politically, a construct of voice attests to the right of speaking and being represented" (p. 146). When discussing youth voices, in the case of arts-based visual methods, "voice" represents all three views, with an emphasis on the political.

Conclusion

This chapter has outlined the core elements, domains, and considerations associated with research involving youth, and explored why arts-based visual methods can converge together with youth development and set a foundation youth photovoice within an urban context. The appeal of research and interventions focused on youth development is well founded, with a strong conceptual base and extensive empirical data substantiating its usefulness for engaging urban youth from marginalized existences. There is no denying that urban youth have not had the opportunities that their white affluent counterparts have had during their childhood. The systems in place that focus on them have failed them, and even perpetrated harm.

The field of youth development, too, has evolved since the 1990s; it has had to struggle with issues of identity and direction, and with the extent to which social justice values will shape its focus. Its parallels with arts-based research and CBPR are quite striking and indicative of vibrant fields with important social messages and consequences. Participatory research has been called the "new orthodoxy" in youth research (Heath & Walker, 2012c). A field that is not experiencing debates and tensions is a field with little or no significance and vibrancy. Photovoice has a central role to play in this youth field and, depending upon the definition of youth development, it can play varying roles in achieving personal and community transformation.

The introduction of photovoice to the youth development field also brings with it inherent tensions concerning who is ultimately in charge of the process, and to what extent will adults play a prominent or secondary/axillary role in shaping projects that are focused on youth. The answers to these two questions have a profound influence on how a photovoice projects unfolds, and on the outcomes that we can reasonably expect for youth and their communities. Values and principles were integrated throughout this chapter, and they will be the focus of the next chapter, which sets a values foundation for using photovoice by integrating a variety of fields, philosophies, and approaches into urban youth photovoice. Values and principles will answer the questions of ultimate power, control, and benefits.

Photovoice as a Research Method

Choosing a research methodology means developing a research question and the tools to generate evidence for its answers; both of these should be consistent with a theoretical frame. There are, of course, a very large number of philosophical, theoretical and conceptual discussions of visuality and images.

—ROSE, 2012, p. 1

4

Values and Principles Guiding Photovoice

Introduction

Community-focused participatory research and interventions such as photovoice are guided through an implicit or explicit embrace of values that shape how they get conceptualized, how they get implemented, and the goals that they subscribe to (Brydon-Miller, 2012). Unfortunately, it is rare for the values guiding interventions, research-focused or otherwise, to be made explicit for discussion or debate. Yet no intervention is value-free, and it is important to acknowledge that in this book on photovoice. Values are predicated upon assumptions and biases, and that is human nature. Research, it must be remembered, is also value-laden.

Principles, in turn, flow from values and provide practitioners with a way of combining them with theory and translating them to real-life situations—serving as a practical guide, so to speak (Parrott, 2010). Principles help researchers navigate their way through difficult and ethically challenging situations. The importance of values and principles is such that it warrants specific attention for fear that they will be overlooked in the course of planning and implementing a photovoice project. Uplifting values and principles for discussion, or even debates, helps researchers identify potential barriers to carrying out a project and possible areas of ethical tensions.

Photovoice is predicated upon an almost universal set of values and principles that have guided its use with a wide range of populations, settings, and issues (Richter, 2011). These values and principles can also be found in other forms of arts-based inquiry, CBPR, and youth development, with the youth-led projects, in particular, emphasizing social justice and empowerment. The convergence of a common set of values and principles is extremely powerful and a key reason why youth photovoice has so much promise, and can easily have an entire set of books devoted to them.

Furthermore, the role and importance of values and principles must not be overlooked if the social sciences and practice are going to make a significant difference in the lives of marginalized communities, and if several disciplines and helping professions are to converge in shaping a comprehensive research agenda involving photovoice. Values and principles also serve an important function by serving as a bridge between social sciences and practice, and this bridge is essential in order to establish a foundation for research methods (Hacker, 2013).

Lundy (2007) identified four key values in responding to Article 12 of the United Nations Conventions on the Rights of the Child that have direct relevance to youth photovoice, with each of these values influencing a specific aspect of well-being and shaping the role that children and youth can be expected to play in bringing these values to fruition: "(1) 'Space' in terms of creating opportunities for children to express their views; (2) 'Voice' in terms of facilitating the expression of these views; (3) 'Audience' in terms of actively listening to these views; and (4) 'Influence' in terms of responding appropriately to these views" (p. 933).

Each of these values contextualizes the multifaceted nature of youth participation, highlighting how research, in the case of photovoice, must take them into account if it is going to be relevant for urban youth. Youth are not interested in being window dressing or occupying a seat of tokenism at the table, but that, unfortunately, is the prevailing thought among many adults on how they should participate. Youth are not interested in setting the table, nor are they interested in cleaning the table. They are interested in having a seat of prominence at the table. Photovoice has the potential of creating "space," "voice," "audience," and "influence." It is important to stress that youth are the experts on their own lives, and it would be unthinkable and unethical for them to be discussed at the table but not be at the table to direct the conversation.

Fortunately, community practitioners and researchers have a wide array of methods at their disposal when considering a qualitative research project involving youth. Qualitative research is considered a "youth-friendly" method: "Qualitative research is often considered particularly appropriate for youth research. Its open-ended and flexible nature is seen as offering an opportunity for young people's voices to be heard more clearly, and in some cases, for them to assume more control of the research process than is possible when using other methods" (Brooks, 2013, p. 183). Qualitative research's emphasis on giving voice to those who have not been heard makes it particularly appealing in the case of urban youth.

The question of when photovoice makes sense as the most appropriate method is closely tied to goals, a set of values adhered to, and sociopolitical assessment of what is most needed. The answer to this question will go a long way toward helping researchers clarify why photovoice is the preferred arts-based research method, and what their ultimate goals are. Although these and many other questions may appear on the surface to be quite straightforward, that is not the case, as addressed in the next chapter.

As noted in Chapter 1, Wang and Burris (1997) identified three overarching goals for photovoice that have served as the basis for guiding numerous photovoice projects and withstood the test of time. Shimshock (2008), however, went on to identify seven goals that more explicitly elucidate the values serving as a foundation for photovoice as a research and intervention method: (1) to meaningfully engage a community, (2) to discover or go deeper into a community, (3) to engage in community capacity enhancement (4) to create social change. (5) to communicate an issue within and outside of the community; (6) to create alliances and collaborations, and (7) to empower groups and community. These seven goals are overarching and highly interrelated, providing a holistic or comprehensive, view of the multifaceted purpose behind photovoice. Each of these values goes on to influence a specific aspect of photovoice and can be thought of as its DNA.

This chapter emphasizes seven key values that underlie the goals identified by Shimshock (2009), because these values introduce a community capacity enhancement perspective (Delgado, 1999), which resonates with the central thrust of this book. These values are (1) empowerment, (2) community participation, (3) leadership development, (4) community investment, (5) utilization of local knowledge and self-knowledge, (6) social and economic justice, and (7) cultural competence/cultural humility. These seven values are highly interconnected, and none will be "new" to the reader because of how they have been weaved into the first three chapters of this book.

This is not to say that researchers may not have preferences for one value over another, or that some values may prove more challenging based upon the institution sponsoring the research and the trust levels of the community where photovoice will transpire. In order to maximize the potential of youth photovoice, all seven values must be operative. The more explicit and detailed these values are made through principles, the easier it will be to explain and implement photovoice. In essence, there should be no mystery on any aspect of photovoice. Making these values explicit also serves to minimize ethical dilemmas.

Seven Overarching Values

Bryden-Miller, Greenwood, and Maguire's (2003) definition of action research captures well the values and principles that shape youth photovoice in this book, and will be addressed specifically in this chapter: "A respect for people and for the knowledge and experience they bring to the research process, a belief in the ability of democratic processes to achieve positive social change, and a commitment to action, these are the basic values which underlie our common practice as action researchers" (p. 15). It should not come as a surprise to the reader that youth photovoice has much in common with action research.

The seven values listed above, and enumerated below, are of equal importance and will be the foundation for the nine principles that will follow later on in this chapter. These values are not presented in any order of importance, since they are to be considered of equal importance. Each of these values necessitates a book onto itself. These values, and the principles that follow, are addressed in a manner that provides sufficient information to develop an understanding and appreciation of what they mean and how they are manifested in a photovoice project. The level of attention or detail may not be sufficient for some readers.

EMPOWERMENT

It is appropriate to start this section on values with a value that seems to be a part of any community-focused initiative, whether research-based or practice-based, and that is empowerment. Its universality complements the universality of photovoice. Empowerment is a concept that has a long tradition within the social sciences and helping professions, with missions of specifically helping to redress the deleterious consequences for groups on the socioeconomic margins of society. It seems almost impossible to go through a day without this concept appearing in some public or scholarly form for those practicing in those disciplines and helping professions. Consequently, extra attention will be paid to this value in comparison with the other six covered in this chapter.

Unsurprisingly, a popular concept such as empowerment will have many different definitions, or homes, with each one stressing a particular aspect of the goal, process, philosophy, or practice. I will not make an effort to reconcile these various perspectives and definitions on empowerment. I have a favorite definition of empowerment that was developed by a pioneer on this topic (Barbara Bryant Solomon) and has withstood the test of time. Solomon (1976) defines empowerment as "a process whereby the social worker [researcher] engages in a set of activities with the client [participant] that aim to reduce the powerlessness that has been created by negative valuations based on membership in a stigmatized group" (p. 19). This definition, written almost 40 years ago, is widely considered to be the first effort at defining this concept, and the definitions that have followed have not differed from it significantly.

This definition, although originally directed at social workers, is applicable in this instance concerning youth photovoice, and it highlights the importance of process, social justice (although it does not specifically use those terms), and membership in a stigmatized group. In the case of urban youth, it means that youth, depending upon their backgrounds, have multiple identities and multiple reasons for being stigmatized, including age, ethnic/racial background, socioeconomic class, and place of residence. In the case of girls, gender must be added to this list. In the case of LGBT, sexual identity becomes another reason for being stigmatized (Jones, 2009).

The road or transition to adulthood involves different "highways" and " exits" depending upon the racial and socioeconomic class composition of youth. Those from marginalized backgrounds have a quick exit toward a life with minimal chances of success and a high likelihood of life in highly structured and monitored existences, such as prisons (Delgado, 2013). Youth, for example, represent an age group that shift from private dependency to public dependency, and all the stigma and socioeconomic consequences associated with this existence (Goffman, 1963; Jones, 2009).

The context in which empowerment occurs cannot be easily dismissed because of how environmental context shapes its definition and manifestations: "youth empowerment is a context dependent process that requires attention to a multiplicity of factors that influence possibilities for empowerment via second order change." (Kohfeldt, Chhun, Grace, & Langhout, 2011, p. 28) Not surprisingly, empowerment is a value that very few people would have a hard time dismissing as worthless, regardless of where they are on the political spectrum. The "devil" is in the details. I am very fond of saying that the Reverend Jesse Jackson and the late Senator Jesse Helm (R–NC) both exposed the virtues of empowerment. Upon closer examination of the details, there were two very different visions of what empowerment meant to them, with dramatically different consequences for marginalized people in this country.

The social context of empowerment is influenced by who is defining it (Dupuis & Mann-Feder, 2013). Invariably, empowerment is defined from an adult perspective and imposed on youth. Empowerment is not a universal concept that is exempt from contextual influences such as age, for example. Indeed, nothing could be further from the truth, since research has shown that youth's vision and experiences can be dramatically different from those of their adult counterparts. Youth perspectives on empowerment will have a vantage point that is different from that of an adult, since their view of the universe is different. For example, most of the literature on youth empowerment examines youth-adult relationships, neglecting to examine the broader context in which these relationships function (Kohfeldt et al., 2011). The differences in this case will be manifested in subtle and not so subtle ways.

As a result of differences in age and experiences, there are many different elements and ways that empowerment can transpire, particularly with urban youth (Ozar & Schotland, 2011; Stanton-Salazar, 2011). Russell, Muraco, Subramanian, and Laub (2009), for example, examined how youth leaders in gay-straight high school alliances defined empowerment and the different elements that comprised their views. Youth identified three interrelated dimensions of empowerment: personal empowerment, relational empowerment, and strategic empowerment through acquiring and using knowledge. Each of these manifestations of empowerment addresses a different sphere of influence in their lives.

Christens, Peterson, and Speer (2011) specifically examined whether there is a reciprocal (bidirectional) relationship between youth community participation and psychological empowerment, and they found that community participation did influence future psychological empowerment. Participation in community life translates into experience (knowledge and skill-set acquisition), which, in turn, better prepares youth for future participation, and thereby empowers them in this journey. Civic engagement is one popular way of conceptualizing youth participation, and it is a theme in youth development programming.

Finally, empowerment is related to many other values, such as self-determination and self-efficacy, which will be addressed in the next section of this chapter. Morton and Montgomery (2011) undertook a review of the literature of experimental or quasi-experimental studies on youth empowerment programs and found insufficient evidence to substantiate that these programs had a positive impact on self-efficacy and self-esteem. Some scholars would argue that any study of youth empowerment must introduce qualitative methods and take into account how youth perceive empowerment, rather than rely on adult interpretations of what constitutes youth empowerment. Mohajer and Earnest (2009), for example, undertook a review of the literature on global adolescent empowerment programs and found that most of them did not fully integrate empowerment as proposed by Freire—a key value in any form of meaningful empowerment.

Do practitioners and researchers differentiate empowerment from the other values addressed in this section? Not easily. When this value is the focus of attention, it means that ownership of the findings and the resulting social change will be in the hands of participants and their community, and that there is a conscious effort for this to transpire. If the answer is a resounding yes, then empowerment is the result. In essence, youth photovoice does not relegate empowerment to a secondary goal, and if it happens in the course of a project, that is good.

The universality of empowerment does have a qualifier. It is important to end this section on empowerment with a cautionary note concerning youth from families that subscribe to very traditional values on how youth are viewed within the family and community. There are ethnic and racial groups, particularly newcomers to this country, that have cultural values that urge their children to do well in this society, but there are conditions that must be met.

Among these groups there is a strong and, some would argue, rigid hierarchy based on age or seniority, and children still occupy secondary roles within the family. They are not, therefore, expected to exercise the newly discovered rights that are associated with empowerment: "It was important for us to negotiate a fine balance between understanding that the community frequently made decisions on behalf of young people, while still respecting young people's autonomy and capacity to make informed decisions themselves" (Jeanes & Kay, 2013, p. 23). The context in which empowerment is viewed cannot be ignored. If it is, youth will not be allowed to participate for fear that participation will result in the undermining of adult authority within the home, or in a house of worship, in cases where their religion, too, relegates youth to secondary status.

COMMUNITY PARTICIPATION

In many circles, community participation is considered a buzzword that few would argue against, but that very few really embrace in its purest form. It is a concept that is not new, with many practitioners and academics tracing its modern-day origins to the early 1960s and the Great Society programs that stressed this form of participation. The following questions, posed by Leadbeater et al. (2006), illustrate the complexity associated with implementing community participation in community research such as photovoice: (1) How is the community defined (psychologically, ethnic/racial/class, geographically, concentration of facilities)? (2) Who is defining the community? (3) Who actually represents the community?

Community participation can mean many different things to many different people, depending upon the context in which it is discussed (Boote, Baird, & Beecroft, 2010; Greene, 2013; Woodgate, Edwards, & Ripat, 2012). Youth in schools, for example, exercise very little control or participation in decision-making, even though they spend a significant part of their lives in this system. Youth development is rarely practiced in school settings during regular school hours. After-school programs are a rare exception.

The belief that urban communities and groups, such as youth are not capable of understanding their predicament or situation, and also cannot help themselves, is a myth (Harris, Wyn, & Younes, 2010). It is what is called an "urban myth." This stance is not only disrespectful, but also unethical. Not giving urban communities, and in this case youth, this respect is a fundamental flaw that shows how many in the social sciences and helping professions simply cannot understand this fundamental value. Nevertheless, this is an enduring myth that refuses to die, even in the face of research showing youth as caring and action oriented (Wearing, 2011). As a consequence, we as professionals must do *for*, as opposed to *with*, communities (Ahmed & Palermo, 2010; Meenai, 2008). This distinction may seem to be merely semantics, but there is a profound difference between planning *for* and planning *with* (Leung, Yen, & Minkler, 2004).

Community participation means much more than giving a community the opportunity to participate. The value of community participation is much more profound. Having community participation translates into having a community own both the process and the outcome of a photovoice undertaking. This value translates into identifying ownership of photovoice, with the lessons and the products resulting from the research resting with the participants and their community. Ownership and participation go hand-in-hand, and empowerment is not possible otherwise (Meenai, 2008).

Head (2011) addressed the question of whether or not young people should be asked their opinions, and he identified three key reasons for doing so:

> First is the argument that young people have the *right* to be nurtured, protected and treated with respect, and where appropriate be involved and consulted. Secondly, it is argued that *improvement of services* for young people requires their views and interests to be well articulated and represented. Thirdly, it is asserted that there are *developmental* benefits arising from participation, for both the individuals themselves and for civil society as a whole. (p. 541)

The human rights principle of participation is applicable to youth, too.

Tapping youth voices increases the likelihood of uncovering alternative knowledge or layers of information (Goodwin & Young, 2013). Much can be gained by tapping youth opinions and experiences that benefit youth, their families, their communities, and society in general (Serido, Borden, & Perkins, 2009). Asking youth their opinions illustrates both the process of and challenges associated with this goal.

We, as adult researchers, can view our role as facilitators in the discovery process. True, we benefit from participation in both instrumental ways (funding, publications, career advancement) and expressive ways (feelings of worth and satisfaction that our work has meaningful outcomes for population groups we care about). What we gain is secondary to the the gains of participants and their community, however. This may seem obvious. As addressed in Chapter 7, the question of who owns the "rights" to this project will dictate how, and to whom, the results are distributed, raising important ethical issues and tensions for researchers.

There is no universal definition of what constitutes youth participation, and until we make significant progress in defining this subject, advancement in operationalizing youth participation for research and practice, both as a value and a strategy, will be limited (Checkoway, 2011; Checkoway & Aldana, 2013). A universal definition, as much as it is possible in the social sciences, represents a goal or quest, even though it is an impossible goal, but one that is worth pursuing and discussing at length.

Checkoway and Aldana (2013) address the topic of civic engagement and youth and propose a framework that conceptualizes participation along a four-perspective scale: (1) citizen participation (formal engagement in institutions), (2) grassroots organizing (social-political groups), (3) intergroup dialogue (engagement in decisions related to systems and oppression), and (4) sociopolitical development (participation in institutional systems but addressing inequalities). Youth can participate in permutations and combinations of these forms of civic engagement, and local circumstances will dictate how each of these four perspectives get conceptualized and acted upon.

The value of community participation can mean many different things, depending upon the political perspective of the researcher. It can mean token representation to give the illusion of democratic participation, and it can go so far as to place the power of decision-making in the hands of youth. Yet there will be minimal or no argument that democracy is predicated upon "meaningful participation." Of course, the meaning of participation is in the eye of the beholder. How youth view this meaning will no doubt differ significantly from how adults view it. Youth civic engagement has tremendous promise (Jones, 2009). It takes on even greater significance when youth are involved at a very early age, and it increases the likelihood of civic participation as they age (Fredricks & Eccles, 2010; Serido, Borden, & Perkins, 2009).

A goal of social inclusion helps ensure development of self-confidence in youth (Wearing, 2011).

LEADERSHIP DEVELOPMENT

The well-known axiom that "youth are our future leaders" comes to mind when the value of leadership development emerges in conversations regarding community research and practice (Christens & Dolan, 2010). Few people would take issue with that statement. It does not take a genius to understand the value of investing in human development from the beginning, rather than waiting until that human being comes of age and represents a safety threat.

This axiom simply disappears the moment that most forms of community research are discussed. In essence, if a value cannot be translated into practice, it simply is not real. Leadership development and photovoice must come together in a manner that takes into account participant abilities at the start of a project, with the goal that their potential increases as the project unfolds. Adults grow with experience, and so do youth. Leadership, too, can be viewed experientially, with opportunities to grow in this realm being made available to participants.

The importance of developing indigenous leadership is a critical value in community capacity–enhancing research and practice, and nowhere is this as important as when discussing marginalized youth and photovoice. Leadership development is closely tied to community development (Meenai, 2008). Many of the leading thinkers in the youth development field have embraced this value (Checkoway & Aldana, 2013; Christens & Dolan, 2010; Morrison & Arthur, 2013) because of their awareness of how indigenous leadership has the potential for transforming a community and serving and inspiring future generations to serve their community. Youth are no exception, because their age group is worthy of having indigenous leadership rather than relying upon traditional adult leadership. Youth leaders bring a perspective and understanding that can only be obtained by being part of this age group. This authenticity, in turn, engenders trust, an essential element in any leadership model.

Youth do have leadership abilities, particularly if leadership is not defined in a hierarchical manner and instead is conceived as qualities that can be emphasized and deemphasized as situations warrant. It is critical that youth voices on what constitutes leadership and for what purposes it must it be exercised, be heard (Dempster, Stevens, & Keeffe, 2011; Emery & Flores, 2006; Waasdrop, Baker, Paskewich, & Leff, 2013). Freire found photography to be a useful tool for developing critical dialogue (Burke, 2008). Furman (2012) put forth a conceptual framework for social justice leadership as praxis (Freireian sense) that brings together youth programming, research/action and consciousness raising, lending itself to youth photovoice projects.

Griebling, Vaughn, Howell, Ramstetter, and Dole (2013) tie the use of photography and praxis and describe why the power of image, in this a photograph, can be the impetus for action:

> An ultimate goal of some research is to create awareness of a social problem and be a catalyst for action. Social action on a basic level implies an ownership of the issue at hand by those individuals and communities who are participating in the research. As voices emerge in this research, so does a more representative view of individuals' or community's strengths and concerns. Photography is one method that can drive this movement. Photographic methods used in a participatory fashion allow for active reflection and identification of individual and community strengths and challenges. It is through identification of strengths that people can begin to address the challenges that have contributed to the muting of voice. Movement from passive to active voice through photography provides a vehicle for the expression and action of their concerns. (p. 17)

The development of indigenous leadership in urban communities takes on greater urgency in light of demographic shifts that reflect a changing urban scene, making urban communities increasingly both populations of color and younger populations (Gooden & Dantley, 2012). The "browning" of America is no longer a theory; it has become reality now and will continue to expand for the foreseeable future. This demographic shift is projected to continue to increase in the next forty years, making this nation and its cities that much more browner and younger.

COMMUNITY INVESTMENT

The value underpinning community investment and photovoice will seem quite obvious to anyone who has practiced or done research in marginalized communities. One cannot help but see the tremendous needs in marginalized urban communities, for example. This value is often absent when discussing most forms of community research, quantitative as well as qualitative. Research can play an important role in generating knowledge and bringing attention to urban needs. However, knowledge and attention are not sufficient.

Conventional approaches to community research generally include the researcher and his or her team, which increasingly consists of outsiders, with a few entry-level positions set aside for residents. This "tokenism" is offensive, to say the least, and fails to emphasize the need and importance of investing in a community. Researchers and their teams figuratively parachute into a community, and upon completion of their "mission" they are retrieved back to their organizations, such as universities, to complete their data analysis and the writing of scholarly articles and books. Obviously, this is not how photovoice projects are typically conceptualized as unfolding.

Nevertheless, community investment is a value that must be made explicit. Community investment and development are closely tied to social justice (Checkoway, 2013). Community investment can cover a wide range of types. Four types stand out in importance: (A) financial resources, (B) access to higher educational institutional resources, (C) brokering external contacts, and (D) hiring local residents. These are some of the most obvious ways for community investment to transpire. Each of these viewpoints provides researchers with a way of investing resources, time, and energy, with community-wide benefits.

Financial Resources

Photovoice projects with external funding are in a position to help circulate funds within the community they are based in. This necessitates a conscious decision that every effort be made to purchase products and services locally, in an effort to help the community from a financial perspective. This value stance will be addressed again in the next chapter, for it is of sufficient importance to warrant its own attention and section. It is surprising how infrequently this position comes up in discussions of how to "help" communities, yet it has incredible instrumental and expressive benefits.

Circumstances will vary from photovoice project to photovoice project. Recirculating funds within the community can transpire in a variety of obvious, and sometimes not so obvious, ways. Food and equipment used in photovoice can be supplied by local merchants; transportation services, too, can be contracted for locally. Space, where there are funds to pay for it, can be rented locally. I have, for example, even gone to the extent of purchasing gasoline for my travel to and from the sites locally. Takeout dinner for my family is also purchased locally. In essence, we can be very creative in thinking about ways of funneling funds to local establishments, thereby infusing badly needed money into community circulation.

Access to Higher Education Institutional Resources

There is probably little disputing that the vast amount of research conducted in communities originates in institutions of higher learning. These institutions are rarely located within these communities, and they may not see the importance of providing access to their resources for residents. Recent examples of how institutions of higher learning can positively impact local communities have shown the potential these institutions have to shape their surroundings (Ross, 2013).

Academic-based researchers are in a position to use their institutional base to broker resources and access for communities that do not have social capital to gain access to these resources (Grieb et al., 2013). This access can manifest itself in a variety of ways. The possibility of opening up the institution for community activities requiring large spaces, such as festivities or graduations represents one way of breaking down institutional barriers between universities and communities.

Universities are also in a position to provide consultation and advice to local businesses (Delgado, 2012), as well as interns with the skill sets needed by community institutions. They can also help communities share their stories of success and challenges with the outside world. We often think of resources as financial. Nevertheless, broadening our concept can introduce creative ways of helping communities establish contacts that can have immediate as well as long-term benefits.

Brokering External Contacts

Connecting youth with outside actors and institutions brings potential for positive and negative consequences. Marginalized communities consistently find themselves in isolation and without access to people in authority or government, key external institutions, and major funding sources. This lack of access severely limits their abilities to form partnerships and help shape external images of their community. The brokering of potential external relationships can be viewed as an important objective in carrying out a photovoice project (Pyne, Scott, & Long, 2013).

Making a conscious effort to engage external entities to facilitate a youth photovoice project enhances the likelihood of these supports or contacts being there when a change effort is to be initiated. Researchers must be keenly aware of potential efforts on the part of these external sources to shape photovoice initiatives that can severely compromise the goals of the research. Further, these potential relationships will need to overcome feelings of mistrust on both sides. Nevertheless, if successful, the impact of photovoice will go far beyond that of a typical community research project.

Hiring Local Residents

Investment in local communities through a conscious effort of employing residents is a direct and indirect investment that generates multiple gains (Greene, 2013). Development of human capital can certainly be a secondary goal of externally funded youth photovoice projects because the training, consultation, and supervision that transpires enhances resident capacities. Youth are seen through a different light, so to speak, when they can be put into positions of authority. The power of being a role model benefits youth participants and the community as a whole.

The circulation of money in the community helps local businesses, for example. Providing employment opportunities for individuals with inherent abilities to engage in photovoice research can serve to generate a cadre of community researchers who can be tapped in future research, as well as circulate money in the community. When these researchers are young, the return on investment can be a long-term one. Furthermore, employing community residents represents a viable strategy for communities to maintain control over research and interventions (Smith and Blumenthal, 2012).

UTILIZATION OF LOCAL KNOWLEDGE AND SELF-KNOWLEDGE

"Knowledge is power" is a phrase that is well recognized by community practitioners and researchers. What knowledge is called when it is rooted in community insights and experiences will vary. Terms such as *community knowledge, local knowledge, contextual knowledge, indigenous knowledge, experiential knowledge,* and *self-knowledge* can all be found in the literature and are essentially interchangeable (Delgado & Humm-Delgado, 2013). Thus the concept of knowledge originating outside of academic or expert circles is widely acknowledged, attesting to its importance.

The power of self-knowledge has the potential of unleashing transformative forces at the individual and collective level:

> Expressing oneself through art is no panacea for social ills but it can sometimes act as a political gesture or call to action. The transformative and emancipatory practice of producing meaningful media with the intent to examine and articulate one's situation inspires self-knowledge. Self-knowledge is power; sharing self-knowledge is empowering. When self-study reveals the connections between personal experience and social action and encourages others to look critically, it becomes a form of critical pedagogy and activism.
> —LEVY & WEBER, 2011, p. 307

Community-focused researchers wear many different hats in the course of carrying out their research. The hats of "teacher" and "facilitator" take on prominence in youth photovoice because of their lifelong implications.

Self-knowledge may be present but go unrecognized, and thereby not valued or tapped in the development of consciousness about social conditions (Diemer & Cheng-Hsien, 2011). The role of the researcher becomes one of helping participants to discover this knowledge and insight (Montoya & Kent, 2011). This may be quite a challenge for individuals who have a history of being told by society and its institutions that they do not possess knowledge of any significance, but must instead rely upon outsiders and professionals to aid them in finding solutions. The development of research methods such as photovoice, which uses imagery to provoke a journey of enlightenment, is intended to facilitate uncovering new insights that normally would go unnoticed.

Delgado and Humm-Delgado (2013) address why self-knowledge and local knowledge among youth must be tapped:

> They possess self-knowledge and local, "contextualized intelligence," knowledge that often gets overlooked by adults. Youth are able to ground their concerns and experiences in a manner that escapes most adult comprehension of their lives. In essence, youth are the best experts of their lives and the neighborhoods in which they live. We as adults are not the sole possessors of "knowledge." This informal expertize is best conceptualized as a form of a community quilt, requiring many different pieces of fabric of various shapes,

texture, and colors, to make a quilt. Youth have their contribution to make to this knowledge quilt, and their contribution is no less valuable than that of their adult counterparts. (p. 197)

The quilt metaphor highlights that knowledge is neither static nor universal, so that the contributions of many are necessary, as in the case of a community knowledge quilt. Rodriguez (2011) has used a "mosaic quilt" metaphor to talk about how youth photovoice can enhance youth knowledge of diversity.

Self-knowledge is closely related to empowerment for youth. Pritzker, LaChapelle, and Tatum's (2012) work with Latino adolescents found that their participation led to their empowerment. Gant et al. (2009), too, found tremendous transformative potential in using photovoice as a means of empowering urban youth and creating social change. Youth empowerment is an essential element of creativity, photography, and social action (Gosessling & Doyle, 2009).

SOCIAL JUSTICE

The topic of social justice in the lives of marginalized urban youth of color is one that permeates their daily existence, as they are constantly reminded that they are second-class, if not third-class, citizens because of their age (Fisher, Busch-Rossnagel, Jopp, & Brown, 2012). They occupy a low social-status position in this society, and within their own communities, too, making issues of fairness that much more important in their lives. It is hard enough to fight for their voices to be heard outside of their community, but having to do so within their immediate world adds insult to injury for millions of young people.

The importance of social justice in the social sciences and helping professions has resulted in numerous definitions. Weil (2004) provides a useful one: "[Social justice] essentially means fairness. As social refers to our human relations and interconnectedness in society, social justice implies commitment to fairness in our dealings with each other in the major aspects of our lives—the political, economic, social and civic realms" (p. 8). It is important that social justice be thought of in a way that makes sense to youth, including the use of vocabulary that resonates and takes into account cultural and local circumstances. "Fairness" is a popular way that youth operationalize such a difficult concept, as noted in the discussion of core elements and youth development in the previous chapter (Ginwright, Noguera, & Cammarota, 2006).

The subject of social justice has been addressed throughout the early parts of this book, and it will continue to permeate the rest of this book for very clear and justifiable reasons. Social justice provides a frame through which to study the interactions of economic, political, and sociohistorical issues and events, and how they have impacted the lives of urban youth of color (Shin et al., 2010). This contextual grounding makes social justice explicit in photovoice regarding age, and it brings a dimension to the discussion of this topic that does not receive the attention it deserves, particularly among quantitative researchers.

CULTURAL COMPETENCY/CULTURAL HUMILITY

It would be unthinkable and unethical to conduct a youth photovoice project and not take into account the subject of cultural competency and cultural humility. Ethnography concerns itself with developing a richer and deeper understanding of how a group thinks and acts. It only stands to reason that the seventh and final value addressed in this section focuses on culture.

The reader will probably think that this section will go forth and focus on culture from a traditional point of view, with a discussion of ethnicity and race and how culture is viewed from this perspective. True, we will discuss cultural values, traditions, and perspectives from this point of view. But we need to pause and broaden the discussion to include youth culture, too (Jones, 2009). In essence, the construct of culture can be quite all-encompassing (Raby, 2007), accentuating an insider-outsider status for researchers (Taft, 2007).

Adult researchers must avoid a trip down memory lane when they engage in youth photovoice, because memories can be filled with contradictions for researchers. Biklen (2007) addresses this important point and stresses the importance for researchers, in this case ethnographers who focus their research on youth, to not impose their experiences and perspectives on youth. In essence, we need to guard against letting these memories compromise the perspectives and experiences of youth photovoice participants.

A focus on urban youth automatically brings to the forefront the importance of cultural competence/cultural humility as a core value. U.S. urban centers are highly diverse, and they are becoming even more diverse as they attract newcomers to this country and continue to play a pivotal role as ports of entry. The youthfulness of people of color as a population group takes on prominence in the case of culture. "Youth culture," as a result, needs to be added to a cultural competence/cultural humility value.

It is necessary to pause and note that "youth culture" is a broad generalization that, upon closer scrutiny, consists of numerous subcultures, further challenging a monolithic view of youth, regardless of their ethnic, racial, or socioeconomic class, their sexual identity, and their abilities (Allett, 2012; Blackman & Commane, 2012; Morey, Bengry-Howell & Griffin, 2010). These subcultures take into account key sociodemographic, acculturation, and geographic factors, such as urban versus rural, for example. Age, ethnicity, race, gender, sexual identity, and socioeconomic status, among many other factors, for example, all reside within a cultural construct: "It is time therefore to begin to get beyond misleading images and understand how complex identities are constructed. How much freedom do young people have to define their self-identities and act according to them?" (Jones, 2009, p. 60). Researcher sensitivity and ability to breach dynamics of similarity, differences, and power also serves to confront issues related to ageism and racism (Taft, 2007).

Context wields influence as to which dimension of culture takes prominence at a particular moment in time. It is best to think of cultural dimensions as foreground and background. There are instances where either ethnicity or gender wields the greatest influence. A change of scenes will result in socioeconomic class taking prominence: "However, in analyzing age as a significant axis of power and difference, we must also be conscious of how it intersects in unique ways with gender, race, class, sexuality, and ability" (Taft, 2007, p. 203).

In the case of the author of this book, being Puerto Rican may be the dominant factor in an interaction. A change in context, occupation, or gender might be the most influential factor in facilitating a working relationship. In my work with youth across the United States, being an adult can be a major stumbling block to a positive working relationship. Being of the same ethnic and socioeconomic background and having language competencies (Spanish) may mitigate the influence of age and occupation.

Raby (2007) addresses this point in background of the researcher: "Age is a salient feature of insider-outsider distinctions, but it is at the same time intersected by other identifications that may provide points for connection across age" (p. 55). Local circumstances will go a long way toward dictating the level of trust youth have in adults, and being of the same ethnic and racial background is not an automatic ticket to the existence of trust and willingness to work, yet there is no denying that it can certainly help.

Baszile (2009) notes that hip-hop culture has been viewed as a window into youth culture to be inform educators. Hip-hop culture can also be viewed as a way of critically understanding "hip hop's curricular dimensions; that is, what hip hop might teach educators not only about the way in which the last three generations of young urban dwellers negotiate identity and difference across cycles of urban blight and ongoing educational disenfranchisement but also about the limitations and possibilities of our work as educators" (p. 6). Irizarry (2009) takes a similar stance regarding the role of hip-hop as a "fund of knowledge" for learning and using urban youth culture to inform adults in teaching and other positions where they come into contact with urban youth.

In turning to cultural competence, it is understood that age needs to be factored into any discussion of competence or cultural humility, which for some readers may be a totally new term and will be addressed later on in this section. Every profession has addressed cultural competence and arrived at a definition from its own vantage point. Social work, too, has done this: "Cultural competence refers to the process by which individuals and systems respond respectfully and effectively to people of all cultures, languages, classes, races, ethnic backgrounds, religions, and other diversity factors in a manner that recognizes, affirms, and values the worth of individuals, families and communities and protects and preserves the dignity of each" (National Association of Social Workers, 2000, p. 61). This definition of cultural competence translates into "a set of congruent behaviors, attitudes, and policies that come together in a system or agency or among professionals and enable the system, agency, or professionals to work effectively in cross-cultural situations" (p. 61). Both practitioners and academics must contend with making this definition operative. This definition brings challenges for use in youth photovoice. For example, this definition is apolitical and does not challenge the power structure, which is needed in youth photovoice (Ridenour, 2012). Cultural competence, at least in how it is envisioned in this book, incorporates a social justice lens and an acknowledgement of how oppression influences social identity and opportunities for achieving well-being in society.

The concept of cultural humility has emerged to address a key element that is often stressed in most definitions of cultural competence; namely, is it possible to be truly culturally competent in a cultural system that is not ones' own? Tervalon and Murry-Garcia (1998) addressed this key point over 15 years ago when they said that cultural humility is a "process that requires humility in . . . [bringing] into check the power imbalances that exist in the dynamics between [researchers and respondents]" (p. 118). Cultural competency is best thought of as a journey and not a destination.

Taking a cultural humility perspective acknowledges that someone who is middle-aged, for example, cannot possibly be culturally competent to know what a 14-year-old African American youth in the South Bronx, New York, is facing. It does not mean that this adult cannot be empathetic. It does mean that he understands how much he must rely upon that 14-year-old to develop an in-depth appreciation of his or her social circumstances, dreams, and fears. Engaging youth within community settings is one way of minimizing power differences and signifying a cultural humility understanding (Marshall & Shepard, 2006). In essence, a cultural humility perspective means that researchers, as in the case of photovoice, must be humble in knowing what they know.

Nine Guiding Principles

Some readers may be satisfied with the seven overarching values covered in the previous section, and may ask why principles are necessary if we have goals. I always like to think about goals as vague and inspirational statements of what we hope to accomplish. For some, goals are meant to be unattainable, or what I like to call "the impossible dream." Others, however, do not like the idea of having goals that are impossible to achieve. Readers will have to decide for themselves which school of thought they fall into. Neither is wrong.

Principles, on the other hand, are kindred spirits to objectives, which are clear, measurable statements of what you hope to accomplish by a given point in time. In other words, goals inspire, but objectives bring you back to earth, so to speak. Principles represent a critical step in helping researchers achieve their goals (Underwood, Mayeux, Risser, & Harper, 2006). Some would refer to principles as guides or strong suggestions of how best to proceed with a community intervention such as photovoice. The nine principles that follow represent a bridge between values and practice, helping researchers "concretize" values.

Some of these principles overlap, yet each brings a focus that is distinctive on its own. At the same time, the boundaries between different principles can be quite mutable. Urban youth photovoice pushes the boundaries of qualitative research. Horsfall and Higgs (2011) identified five key features associated with boundaries, and these are highly applicable to this form of arts-based research: (1) boundaries are not fixed or rigid; (2) they represent spaces where new collaborations can evolve; (3) they can facilitate differences of perspective without causing tension; (4) boundaries, if one is not careful, can cause divisiveness and destruction; and (5) they can cause anxiety when conventional lines are breached.

The will and ability to help themselves. Self-determination and a willingness to chart a community's destiny is an important principle. No community (or nation, for that matter) wants to be a position where it is totally dependent upon the will of others to dictate what its future entails. Youth are certainly no different in this regard. This does not mean that assistance given in the spirit of partnership and collaboration is not welcomed, because it is. Taking the political stance that urban youth and their communities just want to be left alone is not what this principle means. That is the equivalent of saying they must pick themselves up by their own bootstraps, or of blaming them for the situation they were put in.

Self-determination is a cornerstone of photovoice, and this value needs to permeate all aspects of this type of project. A fundamental belief that communities, regardless of their socioeconomic status, have the desire and ability to shape their own destinies if provided with the opportunity and support is at the heart of what this country professes to believe. This is not to say that communities with histories of being devalued must pull themselves up by their bootstraps without any external supports. This principle is not meant to be an opportunity for society to blame the victim.

This principle provides researchers with a moral compass to help them navigate their way through decisions. This is accomplished by having researchers ask two questions: What does the community want, and how does it want to play a role? The answers will never be simple, because communities are not monolithic in compositions, values, and thoughts. I would rather be accused of spending too much time and effort at arriving at answers to these two questions than be accused of running roughshod over communities because they are not capable of thinking or knowing what is best for them.

Setting aside the necessary time to arrive at the answers to these questions is a crucial initial step in uncovering the will and identifying the ability of youth and their communities to help themselves (Hacker, 2013). This principle or belief conveys to youth that they are important enough and knowledgeable enough to understand their situation and craft a solution to their circumstances. It does not mean that adults cannot assist them in this journey. Assisting is not the same as leading to awareness and solutions.

Youth and their community know what is best for their advancement. A detailed description of informal knowledge does not need to be repeated here, because it was covered in some degree of depth in the previous section. It is necessary to elaborate on several aspects of informal knowledge as a means of facilitating its transition to photovoice. Chin's (2007), observations, though addressed to anthropologists, are equally applicable to other academic disciplines and helping professions:

> For me, the apparent inability of many to think of children as competent, thinking, aware beings is key to understanding the problems we face in creating an anthropology of children and, more specifically, an anthropology (and body of social theory more generally) that *takes children seriously.* Here I mean not the *idea* or theory of children, but children themselves. (p. 270)

An embrace of the fundamental premise that youth are the best judges of their lives (Gertler, 2003) translates into them having decision-making powers over how to express their experiences, dreams, and concerns (Smith, Bratini, & Appio, 2012), and to do so in a manner that best captures their intents. This does not mean that youth cannot tap the knowledge and resources that adults possess (Delgado & Staples, 2007). Adults can become allies, as can other groups. Youth decide whom they want as "consultants," and when they want them. That is decision-making power, and it is a key principle in youth photovoice.

Ownership of how best to use photovoice to assess internal assets rests within, rather than outside, the community. Direction and ownership of an urban youth photovoice project must never be questioned, although it may seem obvious. Youth photovoice rests in the hands of youth participants and any effort to wrestle control away from them represents a violation of this principle (Ozar, Newlan, Douglas, & Hubbard, 2013). Youth insights and experiences will shape how photovoice comes alive, and it is their expertise that must be acknowledged and tapped.

Mind you, adults may have the best of intensions in "helping" youth avoid setbacks. It is important to remember that much can be learned from success, but even more can be learned from failure. Learning from failure is an excellent skill to possess. I am fond of saying that I have learned more from my failures than from my successes. Both are essential of life.

Partnerships and collaborations between residents and community practitioners are the preferred route for any photovoice assessment, with assessment being planned with, rather than for, the community. It is simply unimaginable to think that any form of arts-based visual research is not participatory and collaborative (Moss, 2008; Pink, 2007; Thomson, 2008a). Few practitioners would argue against the development of partnerships or collaborations in service to communities (Hacker, 2013). That goal is easier said than done within the academic institutions I have been a part of. A conscious effort to create sustaining partnerships that will continue to exist and thrive after a photovoice project has been completed is a worthwhile principle that can result in new and lasting relationships (Leadbeater et al., 2006).

Pink's (2007) analysis, although referring specifically to film, is also applicable to other visual arts–based methods, including photovoice: "It is not simply the final product film document that is important but rather the collaborative processes by which it is produced: it is through these processes that both new levels of engagement in thematic issues and of self-awareness are achieved by participants and ethnographic knowledge is produced" (p. 112). The benefits of collaboration and participation go beyond the product and new insights Leung, Yen, & Minkler, 2004; Horowitz, Robsinson, & Seifer, 2009). They also result in new relationships that can transcend participation in photovoice to encompass other projects and the involvement of new participants.

Reliance and use of community assets in one area will translate into other facets of the community, often creating a synergistic effect. The reasoning upon which this principle is based is the fundamental belief that tapping strengths or assets creates a ripple effect that reverberates throughout the community, particularly in cases where the community is marginalized and geographically segregated (Hacker, 2013). A photovoice project has the opportunity to spark other projects, photovoice and otherwise, that can benefit specific groups within the community, as well as the community as a whole.

Although much of the initial motivation for the use of photovoice with urban youth has to do with the low regard that society holds for them, and with the consequences that are associated with having a secondary status, community assets will emerge in the course of a project (Ungar, 2011). All communities possess assets. Undervalued communities will not have these assets acknowledged by external forces, and they may even be unaware of these assets internally (Delgado & Humm-Delgado, 2013). It is incumbent upon those initiating a photovoice project to purposefully create an environment and conditions that can lead to other members of the community to engage in capacity-enhancement projects. Photovoice must operate on the principle that the benefits of participation can extend beyond those who are integral to the project, and that other groups within the community can derive benefits, too.

Photovoice assessments must be inclusive rather than exclusive of community participation parameters and must not reinforce biases between and within groups. Ethnography, like other qualitative participatory research methods, also stresses the need for inclusion (J. S. Jones, 2010). The principle of inclusion, and the values it is based upon, takes on greater significance when a photovoice project is focused on a group that has been marginalized and excluded from defining the issues that affect its members, who have had "spoiled identities" compromise their well-being (Goffman, 1963; Ollerton & Kelshaw, 2011). In the case of youth, it is based upon their age. In the case of urban youth, we must add race/ethnicity, social class, sexual identity, documented status, gender, and abilities.

In an effort to be inclusive, it is important that researchers differentiate between key informants and community residents (McKenna, Iwasaki, Stewart, & Main, 2011). Key informants can be residents. These individuals typically occupy the role of stakeholders, and they may hold prominent positions within community organizations. They are often turned to for their opinions. Community residents may rarely be turned to for their opinions, yet they possess important knowledge that must be tapped. When turning to key informants, it is essential that the rationale for their selection be explicit. Mind you, these opinions can be very important. It is essential to broaden our understanding of community input to include non-stakeholders.

The reader may argue that a youth photovoice project focused on lesbian, gay, bisexual, and transsexual identity is sufficiently inclusive. There are youth who fall into these categories but may also be undocumented, or may have some intellectual or physical challenge. Careful thought needs to go into who is being selected for inclusion and who is being excluded (New Zealand Ministry of Health, 2012). This decision must be conscious and the group must be able to defend their decisions publicly. This will take on significance in cases where the number of applicants far exceeds the number of positions.

Goldbring (2010) uses the term "gently elevating the quite voices" (p. 132), and this idea has much relevance in regard to this principle. Estrada and Hondagneu-Sotelo's (2010) study of Latino immigrant youth street vendors in Los Angeles illustrates the importance of inclusion and countering stigma and spoiled identities. These youth earn a living in an occupation that is not held in high regard by other youth in the community. Nevertheless, they manage to build affirming identities. Inclusion of youth such as these must be a goal of photovoice whenever possible, because communities consist of all types of individuals and are not monolithic in composition.

Youth participation can result in changes at multiple levels, including at the social policy level (Hannay, Dudley, Milan, & Leibavitz, 2013; Sullivan et al., 2010). Conner, Zaino, and Scarola (2013), for example, show how youth efforts at social change can be possible at policy levels, as in the case of Philadelphia's public schools. Youth there were able to increase accountability, increase the role of student voice, shape agendas, and find a place at the table as significant players. Increasing youth participation changes the power relationships with adults in authority.

Photovoice must not be expected to conform to predictable timetables and themes, because each project is unique to the community being assessed, although assessments may share a core of similarities among communities. Youth photovoice projects, like other types of photovoice projects, must be thought of as unique. In essence, photovoice marches to the beat of its own drummer. Each project may not neatly conform in substance and time frame to other photovoice projects reported in the literature. This principle can be quite challenging when funding sources have preexisting expectations of what a photovoice should look like, or strict timelines or benchmarks that seek to make photovoice projects conform to a preexisting timetable.

The necessity to develop urban youth photovoice projects that reflect the unique characteristics, history, circumstances, goals, and concerns of a community is a principle that few researchers would argue about. This does not mean that the issue that is the focus of a photovoice project is unique in all aspects to a particularly community. Oppression exists in marginalized communities, and how it gets manifested may differ from place to place, at least on the surface. Taking a broad view will illustrate how institutions that are supposed to serve all residents equally do not always do so.

Photovoice findings must be exhibited and distributed in a manner that reflects culture- and community-specific preferences for communication. Photovoice puts power in the hands of marginalized groups to "reproduce and understand their world as opposed to the dominant representations depicted in the mass media" (Barnes, Taylor-Brown, & Wiener, 1997). Although this quote is over 15 years old, it is still relevant today. It stands to reason that the findings of a youth photovoice project must reflect their preferences for dissemination, and this can occur in rather "unconventional" ways to take into account youth-specific venues, for example.

Hammersley (1990), although specifically making reference to the purpose of ethnography, stresses that one of the central purposes is to give new insights: "The purpose of ethnographic analysis is to produce sensitizing concepts and models that allow people to see events in new ways. The value of these models is to be judged by others in terms of how useful they find them" (p. 15). Youth photovoice participants are not always interested in developing new models. They are interested in creating new insights to spur action. New models can result that are secondary to the primary goals of achieving new insights and change.

The final cultural exhibit of the photographs must take place in a setting that opens them up to maximum exposure while also keeping the target audience in mind. A key challenge faced by many youth photovoice projects is determining the target audience as specifically as possible. There will be periods in the discussion of this topic when a group will express the wish to open up the exhibit to as many people as possible. There is a natural tension in trying to reconcile these two goals—a specific versus a general audience.

It is important to emphasize that there are no absolute right or wrong answers. The group will need to decide who is it that they want to have attend that at the end of the day. Getting at the answer to this question will help the group determine how specific or broad the audience should be. It will help guide participants and aid in crafting culturally relevant messaging and outreach, along with the most appropriate forum for getting this information out to the right audience. Social media such as Facebook and Twitter, for example, may work well in reaching a youthful audience, but they will not be successful in reaching older adults. That audience may require highly targeted outreach and a much more personalized invitation.

Many things can go wrong in mounting an exhibition. However, if I am forced to select what is probably the worst, it would be for the exhibition to be boycotted or simply ignored. That would be a divesting conclusion to a long and arduous process. The reader may argue that the worst outcome could be acrimony and division resulting from the exhibition. The debate that ensues shows serious reflection and thought on the part of the audience, and such an outcome can still be viewed in a positive light.

Having an exhibition boycotted because of its controversial content, or, even worse, simply ignored, with minimal attendance and no media coverage, can have a long-lasting impact on the participants. As Haw (2008 notes, "the converse of having a 'voice' is being silenced, and a key part of the discussion around 'voice' is to examine and challenge the processes "silencing' different groups of young people" (p. 206). Silencing young people as they consciously seek to have their voices heard is tragic and cruel.

The location of the exhibition, which will be addressed in much greater detail in the following chapter, must be viewed positively within a community. Some practitioners may think that city hall may be a good site. That may be the case in urban communities, where city hall is viewed well by the community. If city hall has a reputation for exclusion and scapegoating a community, then it will not be a good exhibition hall and will undermine the central goals of an exhibit. The community will simply stay away, even though the content of the exhibit is of great importance to them.

Besides location, it is necessary to think through carefully how to make an audience feel as if they are an integral part of the exhibit and that they can feel safe, particularly in cases where the photovoice project raises internal issues within the community. Decisions on music, for example, take on prominence and must be culturally conducive for the reflection and conversation that is integral to the images and narratives being shown. Yet the central focus of the exhibit dictates this choice, and there will be circumstances where music may be loud and not conducive for reflection and conversation.

Photovoice must seek to maximize external financial, political, and emotional investment in the community. The reader may recall the discussion in the previous section on the value of community investment, which emphasized financial resources. This principle will only be touched upon here because of the level of detail provided earlier. Investment in communities, particularly its youth, can occur in instrumental (concrete), expressive (psychological), and informational ways. There is a great deal of flexibility in how investment in youth can transpire, allowing researchers to take into account local circumstances as well as the resources at their disposal. It is also important to point out that this investment can help the parents of youth, and indirectly help youth themselves.

Every effort must be made to help broker connections between the community and external institutions in an effort to bridge divides and establish a solid foundation for future initiatives and exchanges. The creation of bonding social capital brings with it connections that either never existed or, if they did, existed in a precarious manner. These relationships will continue to exist even upon completion of the photovoice project. This principle, for example, can translate into facilitating positive news coverage of the photovoice exhibition, opening spaces for the community to gather, facilitating university-community partnerships that are true partnerships, offering scholarships for gym participation on campus, internships, and technical advice to local for-profit and non-profit groups. The possibilities are endless and take on even greater significant for youth who will grow up and stay in their communities. Investment can take many forms and it is only limited by our imagination and commitment to youth and their communities.

Conclusion

The axiological assumption identified in Chapter 2 raises provocative questions pertaining to what role values play in shaping research. These values, in turn, translate into questions about how the researcher goes about acknowledging and addressing his or her biases (Creswell, 2013a). Youth are not value-free. They, too, must be prepared to examine what values they subscribe to, and to discuss how these values shape their views of research and photovoice. Engaging youth participants as equal collaborators, if not outright leaders, will help minimize the undue influence of implicit values on the research process. This chapter has identified seven values and an accompanying nine principles that can serve as guides in the selection and use of photovoice involving urban youth.

Each of these core values and principles shapes an aspect of urban youth photovoice. The totality of these values and principles far outweighs any one in particular. The whole, in this case, is far greater than the individual parts and represents a stance and worldview of how photovoice must be conceptualized to maximize its potential for achieving positive change in the lives of youth. It is obvious that these values and principles can be conceptualized and carried out differently depending upon the context in which they are viewed. Nevertheless, even though there is sufficient "wiggle-room" in them, they represent an important step toward bringing a coherent vision of photovoice and its use with urban youth.

5

Conducting a Photovoice Project

Introduction

This chapter presents a challenge of balance: providing sufficient information to carry out a photovoice project, but not so much information that the reader will be drowned in detail. In addition, it is essential to continue to ground the nuts and bolts of photovoice within a theoretical base to help those carrying out the project grasp the significance of their actions across the entire spectrum. The previous four chapters have provided a foundation as to why arts-based visual ethnography, photovoice, youth development, and social justice/participatory values make this method particularly attractive for use with urban youth, including challenges inherent in this form of research.

These chapters laid out a conceptual foundation and provided a perspective on how urban youth photovoice must take shape if this research method is to achieve its transformative potential at the individual and community level. This chapter will be devoted to providing the very practical information and considerations to help the reader think about all of the critical facets of photovoice, including how a theoretical framework that consists of analytical and interactional (political) aspects facilitates its use across different settings and with different urban youth groups.

Those individuals and organizations carrying out a photovoice project will undoubtedly encounter aspects of this research method that they will find particularly appealing and rewarding, and that they may well be familiar with. They will also encounter aspects that are unappealing, challenging, and totally new, including new forms and types of collaborations and the challenges and ethical dilemmas associated with these partnerships. This is natural and to be expected. The more these new experiences are made explicit, the higher the likelihood that researchers will be prepared to address them in a professional and ethical manner, although no researcher, regardless of how *conscientious*, can be completely prepared.

This is important to keep in mind, because every effort should be made to develop collaborations between individuals and organizations as a way of building upon the strengths and proclivities of those undertaking this form of research (Harper, 2009; Tobias, Richmond, & Luginaah, 2013). These collaborations, in turn, can bear fruit after the completion of the photovoice project by establishing working relationships that can result in future endeavors. The best examples of photovoice are those that result in the establishment of new relationships or that cement relationships that currently exist. Nevertheless, while everyone seems to talk about establishing collaborations, including funders, it is arduous to accomplish them.

Photovoice Project Framework

The professional literature has experienced a dramatic increase in publications on CBPR, as this method has started to enjoy worldwide appeal and across age groups. Publication gaps remain between CBPR, particularly when focused on youth, and other interventional research methods (De la Nueces, Hacker, DiGirolamo, & Hicks, 2012), making CBPR seem out of the mainstream of "conventional" community research. The fact that CBPR "stands out" can be a key factor in causing difficulty, or challenges, in getting results of the research accepted by policy authorities when it comes time to present findings and initiate a social change effort (Hannay, Dudley, Milan, & Leibovitz, 2013; Mantoura & Potvin, 2013; Wright, Roche, von Unger, Block, & Gardner, 2010). Although impressive progress has been accomplished in bringing CBPR to the forefront, much work remains to be done, including attention to ethical challenges.

It is essential that researchers undertaking a photovoice project adopt a framework to conceptualize and implement the project (Ahmed & Palermo, 2010; Beh, Bruyere, & Lolosoli, 2013). The structure and process of establishing an urban youth photovoice project consists of multiple stages, with each stage necessitating certain resources, time, and criteria for determining the success of the individual stage. Political considerations also come into play. Breaking this process down into distinct steps or stages not only demystifies photovoice, it also allows each phase to receive its due attention, minimizing the possibility that critical considerations and actions will be overlooked.

Booth and Booth (2002), well over a decade ago, proposed a seven-step process for photovoice research that still has applicability today: (1) establish goals and central questions; (2) recruit participants and obtain informed consent; (3) distribute cameras and provide training; (4) take photographs; (5) ground photographs through participants sharing their photos and explaining their meaning; (6) code themes or identify a message for your potential audience; and (7) incorporate key findings into broader research in the case of mixed-methods.

These seven stages help breakdown a photovoice project into manageable steps to facilitate its implementation.

This book presents a nine-stage framework to better illustrate the structure and process that increases the odds of success for a youth photovoice project:

1. Pre-project considerations, including the creation of a project advisory committee and preliminary fieldwork
2. Selection of project participants and leadership
3. Training and ongoing support, including the necessary management and care of equipment and approaches towards photography
4. Assessment (needs and assets) of goals
5. Planning, scheduling, and implementation
6. Selection of images and narratives
7. Cultural final portrait/exhibition
8. Project evaluation
9. Post-photovoice social change action selection

Each stage must be viewed from an analytical (theory) and interactional (political) perspective in order to ensure that what may seem practical has a strong theoretical and interactional (political) rationale, rather than being the easiest way to cut corners, so to speak. Theory has a very important role to play in helping to guide arts-based researchers. Theory is important because "we must guard against unintended consequences that can create or sustain injustices and power imbalances and must strengthen forces that can promote social transformation to a more just society and societal processes" (Reed, 2005, p. 87). Politics must also be acknowledged, and the influence that it wields in creating or sustaining injustice and power imbalances.

Each of the stages of a photovoice project brings its own set of major activities, challenges, and rewards, and each is important onto itself and is no more, or less, important than the stage that preceded it. It is not advisable to take shortcuts or simply skip a phase to save time and money. Each stage, as already noted, has two important dimensions: (1) analytical (theory) and (2) interactional (political). Each of these dimensions interacts with each other and must be carefully considered. To examine theory without considering politics is not recommended; to view photovoice from a strictly political perspective without regard to theory, too, is not recommended. Analytical and interactional aspects of photovoice go hand-in-hand.

PRE-PROJECT CONSIDERATIONS

The pre-project consideration phase can be conceptualized as the "silent" phase of a fundraising campaign, or that part of an iceberg that exists below the water. The actual photo-taking and the activities that follow can be thought of as the "active" part of a campaign, or that part of the iceberg that exists above the water (in essence, what actually gets to be seen by audiences).

Most research and practice frameworks may simply incorporate the pre-project consideration phase into other initial phases, or simply not highlight the multiple aspects associated with establishing a photovoice project. At the risk of using another metaphor, this phase is the foundation for the house; it is very easy to take it for granted, because we have a difficult time seeing it, yet it is critical to the longevity and well-being of both a house and, in the case of this book, a photovoice project.

For our purposes, several key elements of pre-project considerations will be addressed, although the reader may have others that they would add: (A) establishment of an advisory committee; (B) selection of facilitator/co-facilitator; (C) securing funding; (D) selection of project location within a community; (E) affirmation of key values and principles; and (F) project length. Each of these elements, or facets, will be treated independently of each other, although in reality there is considerable overlap between them.

Depending upon local circumstances, each of these facets may require more, or less, time and attention. In addition, each of these facets will consist of analytical (theoretical) and interactional (political) dimensions, as addressed in the following sections. Those involved in photovoice projects never have the luxury of only worrying about theory or politics, since both must be taken into account in order to help increase the likelihood of success (Blackman & Commane, 2012). Being able to address analytical and interactional considerations in everyday language may prove to be a challenge, but it is one that must be surmounted if a youth photovoice project is to succeed. Language plays such an influential role in facilitating relationship building and establishing trust.

Establishment of an Advisory Committee

Advisory committees can play an influential role in the life of a project, whether research or practice focused (Boote, Baird, & Beecroft, 2010; Chouinard & Cousins, 2009). It should not come as any great surprise that I am a big proponent of the establishment of a photovoice advisory committee, since it is an invaluable resource that can be tapped throughout all phases of a project, and it requires minimal outlay of funding, although it is labor intensive. This labor intensity should not scare off researchers, because all arts-based research methods are labor intensive.

Newman et al. (2011), in their review of best practices with community boards and CBPR, concluded that these bodies can be extremely helpful in all facets of a research project and, as a result, are highly recommended for community research projects such as photovoice. Quinn (2004), and Shore et al. (2004) envision community advisory boards playing an active role in helping to ensure that community research is ethical, for example.

Although the establishment of an advisory committee may appear at first to be a labor-intensive project that adds yet another layer to a process that is complicated, it is time and effort that is well invested, because if serious thought goes into its role and composition, an advisory committee will help in averting or minimizing obstacles throughout all facets of the project (Pinto, Spector, Rohman, & Gastolomendo, 2013). Photovoice projects, regardless of the characteristics of the group undertaking it, work best when they seek to widen the net of inclusion rather than focus on a select group.

In addition, use of community advisory committees has been found to facilitate the translation of research by community organizations, making research that much more attractive to these organizations and the groups that they serve (Fraser & al Sayah, 2011; Wilson, Lavis, Travers, & Rourke, 2010). In essence, it increases the relevance of research for communities, making their investment of time and effort worthwhile, because the return on investment directly benefits them. Further, committee members are in a position to inform and elicit support from the community, and to act as project ambassadors to explain the process and goals of photovoice.

This task takes on greater significance in situations where there is a tremendous distrust of outsiders: "Negative perceptions of research and researchers have led some community leaders to decline to work with researchers and public health workers on so-called 'helicopter projects', or 'drive-by research'. Researchers are naturally loath to share ideas and strategies with colleagues they do not trust" (Horowitz, Robinson, & Seifer, p. 2639). Community distrust of "research" is understandable, and labeling research as "community research" does not automatically mean that researchers will be greeted with open arms (Hacker, 2013).

A number of scholars have studied the role of advisory committees in carrying out community research. Slade et al. (2010), for example, based on their extensive study of advisory committees and public involvement, identified six areas of recommendation that must be taken into account in the development of advisory committees, which will be incorporated in this section:

First, have a clear rationale for each advisory committee expressed as terms of reference, and consider the best balance between committees and individual consultation with experts. Second, an early concern of committees is inter-committee communication, so consider cross-representation and copying minutes between committees. Third, match the scope of advisory committees to the study, with a less complex advisory structure for studies with more finalised designs. Fourth, public involvement has a mixed impact, and relies on relationships of trust, which take time to develop. Fifth, carefully consider the match between the scientific paradigm applied in the study and the contribution of different types of knowledge and expertise, and how this will impact on possibilities for taking on advice. Finally, responding to recommendations uses up research team resources, and the costs can be reduced by using the three implementation criteria. (p. 323)

Newman et al. (2011), too, address the role and composition of community advisory committees and make a series of recommendations:

> To select appropriate board members, specific inclusion criteria should be established that reflect the goals of the research and the intended functions and purpose of the CAB [community advisory board). . . . The intended outcomes of the study facilitate determining what type of person (e.g., service provider, consumer, community leader) or agency is represented on the CAB. . . . New partnerships are often encouraged to start small and to involve a few community-based organizations that are highly regarded by community members. (p. 3)

The recommendations of Slate et al. (2010) and Newman et al. (2011) provide a sociopolitical and multifaceted perspective on advisory committees in order to appreciate more fully their potential contributions to a research project. The benefits of an advisory committee on youth photovoice, if careful thought is given to its creation and role, can be invaluable throughout all facets of a project, particularly those regarding external relations and even ethical dilemmas that are inherent in this type of arts-based research. It is important to keep in mind that we should not approach these committees from a "cookie-cutter" perspective, since each brings unique qualities into consideration. Nevertheless, the central thrust and goals of photovoice advisory committees have universal appeals.

The advisory committee is in a propitious position to help select a co-facilitator if the facilitator is not from the community, which is usually the case. This task is extremely important for the future of the project. In addition, having the committee assist in the screening and selection of the co-facilitator brings the political backing of the community into the selection process, and conveys to the eventual co-facilitator and community at large that the photovoice project is respectful of the community and accountable to it as well.

Finally, the committee can also assist in making key decisions concerning the physical location of the project, the ideal timing and place for the final photographic exhibition, where services and products should be purchased, and the allocation of project resources in cases where there is external funding. These decisions will be covered later on in this and the remaining chapters.

IDEAL NUMBER OF MEMBERS

How many members should be a part of an advisory committee? The answer to this question is that it depends. The size of a committee is as important as its composition and determined by the role it is expected to play. Making the committee large brings with it challenges; making the committee too small, in turn, also brings challenges. There are countless activities and considerations at play in arriving at the "ideal" number of members. My experience is that eight is the ideal number. This number provides the project with a sufficient resource base upon which to draw throughout all facets of a photovoice project, and it also takes into account group processes (deliberations and trust building), scheduling, and communication aspects so that they do not become overly burdensome.

The importance of establishing trust among members cannot be overly emphasized, and this can be facilitated when the group is sufficiently small to allow more in-depth exchanges (Parkins, 2010). A small group also facilitates the use of trust-building exercises. Trust is a concept that practitioners and researchers understand, and the absence of trust will compromise any community-based initiative and result in conflict, which, if it goes unresolved, will undermine the likelihood of success (Seifer & Sisco, 2006; White-Cooper, Dawkins, Kamin, & Anderson, 2007). Community advisory committees must not be glamorized. These entities bring all of the foibles and trials and tribulations associated with group entities. In essence, they are political entities regardless of how noble their intensions. Nevertheless, they are often overlooked in the crafting of a photovoice project or other types of arts-based qualitative research.

LEGITIMACY OF MEMBERS

It is important to think of photovoice as a community-based research project, and as with any community-based project, sociopolitical considerations must enter into the decision as to who should be on an advisory committee. The committee composition must reflect the community of interest. If this does not occur, the findings and the change that is supposed to occur will be considered illegitimate by the community. The question of who should be a member of the committee thus takes on great significance.

Rein (1977) developed the concept of legitimacy to analyze the question of representation, and identified four types of legitimacy that have great relevance for aiding in the development of an advisory committee, formal, institutional, ethical, and consumer. Formal expertise refers to knowledge obtained through formal education and training and is usually associated with academic degrees. Institutional legitimacy seeks to capture the power and influence that an organization has within a community. Ethical legitimacy captures two potential sources of legitimacy—formal, which is represented by professional credentials and professional review boards such as the American Medical Association, National Association of Social Work, and American Bar Association, to list three. Unethical behavior on the part of doctors, social workers, and lawyers can be brought before these boards for review and possible disciplinary actions. The second type of ethical legitimacy refers to the power that community leaders (formal and informal) bring because of the high esteem residents have for them. When they speak, people listen. Finally, consumer legitimacy is captured by the phrase "represent the people."

Each of these forms of legitimacy brings a perspective of support or power that must be taken into account if a project is to enjoy widespread community respect. Ideally, a photovoice project must actively seek to have all four types of legitimacy represented among its members. Having all four types helps ensure that input is sought from key perspectives in the community. Some members may bring multiple forms of legitimacy, maximizing the contributions as members. A well-respected member of a local house of worship, for example, may bring institutional and ethical legitimacy. In addition, this person may also represent the racial and ethnic demographics of the community. A youth member may bring experiential expertise by having been a part of a previous photovoice project, and as a member of the community's youth community, this person will bring consumer legitimacy to the table. It is important to remember that young people eventually enter adulthood. Having a cadre of young adults helping upcoming generations is a value that must not be lost in discussions of legitimacy.

These considerations take on greater prominence when collaborations with community-based organizations are expected to play a meaningful role in implementing the research, and to assisting in carrying out the social action that can result from the process, and the findings of the research (Bogart & Vyeda, 2009; D'Alonzo, 2010; Wallerstein & Duran, 2006). The "legitimacy" of the photovoice project must withstand the potential criticism and backlash that can result. The composition of the advisory committee will require careful thought and deliberation and should not consist simply of those who have the time and are willing to participate (Roholt & Mueller, 2013). A photovoice advisory committee must be conceptualized as an orchestra—only one pianist, and not two; two violinists instead of one, and so on. Too many of one type of instrument limits the musical scores that can be played.

ROLE OF COMMITTEE

Advisory committees have a viable role to play in photovoice. Mattessich (2012) specifically addresses the role of advisory committees in contract and grant-funded research, and identifies five critical sociopolitical functions served by this entity: stakeholder engagement, maximizing external credibility, political conciliation, promotion of methodological integrity, and promotion of use. Although there are technical or scientific aspects related to committee membership, the explicit understanding of the role of political (interactional) influence is undeniable, and is also applicable to photovoice projects, as addressed in the following section (Groundwater-Smith, 2011).

Having a framework of the different phases or stages of a photovoice project will aid in helping the advisory committee think through all of the necessary process and technical aspects that will be carried out, including when they will occur. Having this grounding also serves to help assure committee members of how the different stages of a project are interrelated, and to assign timelines to help them assess progress. For the well-initiated, this recommendation may seem to be common sense. For the uninitiated, it will be a very different way of looking of this type of experience. This experience, incidentally, can result in knowledge and skill set gains that are highly transferable to other spheres of life, such as school and community (Roholt & Mueller, 2013).

SOCIOCULTURAL FACTORS

Photovoice advisory committees must reflect the sociocultural characteristics of the community they are wishing to learn more about. Factors such as gender, common interest, identity (racial, ethnic, and sexual), illness experience, history, language, and culture will enter into decisions as to the composition of the committee (Newman et al., 2011; Richardson, Sinclair, Reed, & Parkins, 2011). Mahalingam and Rabelo (2013) argue that our knowledge of newcomer communities is reductionist, stereotypical, simplistic, and predicated on cultural deficit models, necessitating the use of research. A community of newcomers who are unauthorized, for example, will generate sociopolitical concerns, such as arrest and deportation and an inability to go to authorities when they are exploited, which that a community of similar ethnic and racial background who are citizens or residents with appropriate documentation do not have to face.

A community of unauthorized newcomers from El Salvador, for example, within a Puerto Rican or Dominican community, may not be receptive to youth from these communities undertaking research focused on them. True, they are Latino and speak Spanish, and may even share many cultural values, but this may not be sufficient to break down barriers of trust. Ideally, such a youth photovoice project focused on El Salvadorans will consist predominantly of youth from this background, depending upon the goals. If the goal is to address tensions between newcomers and those already established in the community, then a team of youth representatives from all three Latino groups will be in order. Suffice it to say that being "Latino" is too general a demographic characteristic.

Sensitivity to local political tensions must be taken into account, and this will prove a particularly challenging task for facilitators, particularly those that do not consider themselves "political" by nature. The timing of a photovoice project faces all of the challenges associated with community research. Nevertheless, photovoice faces additional challenges because of the emphasis on images. Photographs take on added sensitivity when a community feels itself to be under scrutiny or fire by outside forces, causing fear and resentment because of local tensions (Delgado, 2006).

Selection of Facilitator/Co-Facilitator

Photovoice is heavily dependent upon process playing an influential role throughout all facets of a project. It only stands to reason that the facilitator(s) will play a critical role in helping to ensure that the trials and tribulations related to community research be addressed in a timely, professional, and sensitive manner, since a major part of the transformation participants will experience will be related to emotional insights and growth. Facilitators are not "therapists" in the conventional sense of the word, but they will be called upon to be therapeutic, and they must possess excellent listening skills, extensive knowledge of local resources, and patience.

If the facilitator of a project is a professional practitioner or academic, it is strongly recommended that a co-facilitator be selected that represents the characteristics of the group undertaking the photovoice project. Co-facilitators of different gender and ethnicity/race bring an added benefit by providing the group with role modeling of anti-oppressive behavior (Garcia, Lindgren, & Pintor, 2011). In the case of this book, the co-facilitator must be a youth member of the community who is widely respected and has a reputation for fairness. In addition, it is also recommended that the youth co-facilitator selection process take into account gender, ethnicity/race, place of residence, and communication/group facilitation skills.

Robinson (2011) raises a cautionary flag when a visual method attempting to give voice to a group relies solely on a facilitator from outside the group:

> Whilst the artefactness of participatory outputs may provide a link to the subject and directly deliver resident or participant voice and views, it can also, quietly, act to mask the role of the facilitator or researcher. Such work is often engaging and appealing and far more likely to be seen as authentic and "honest" by the viewer who is encouraged by both content and aesthetic to take it at face value. This aspect perhaps tempts us to lower our guard in terms of our otherwise increased skepticism regarding photographic truth and authenticity. Such work might just as easily mislead as inform the viewer and disenfranchise as empower the subject. (p. 131)

An indigenous co-facilitator serves to mitigate unconscious efforts at misleading a group.

Photovoice is considered a labor-intensive and highly complex method when compared to other research methods, requiring the facilitator to have an in-depth appreciation of the culture of the group undertaking these types of research projects, which must be taken into account if a project is to have a high likelihood of success (Creswell, 2013a; Meo, 2010). Furthermore, photovoice is a highly contextualized research method that must be attuned to the nuances, history, and circumstances at the local level where the project will be implemented, if the results and the change effort that follows are to be relevant to the community (Duffy, 2012; Rosen, Goodkind, & Smith, 2011; Stevens, 2010). The value of having at least one co-facilitator from the community is undeniable.

It is true that having co-facilitators requires an expenditure of additional time. Having co-facilitators also allows a sharing of the workload, however, which will be considerable during certain critical periods in the life cycle of a photovoice undertaking. Co-facilitators, for example, can divide the workload to take into consideration competencies that may be complementary. In addition, co-facilitators must have a solid working relationship, because they will "model" for the group how differences of opinion can be communicated and navigated.

Powers, Freedman, and Pitner (2012) have published a facilitator's manual to help organizations thinking about using photovoice. It outlines key procedures and considerations for this method. Shimshock (2008), too, has produced an excellent and detailed manual. The skill sets of the facilitators must encompass a wide variety beyond the technical skills associated with photography. As noted above, communication skills, verbal and written, and an understanding of cultural values take on importance because of their role both within and outside of the project.

In addition, group skills that facilitate processing of emotionally laden content within a group, as well as task-oriented skills, help the group progress in achieving the multiple tasks related to launching a photovoice project. Lorenz's (n.d.) description of some of the challenges a facilitator experienced highlights why these group skills are necessary:

> It was challenging to design and lead a photovoice project for the first time with a group of girls who did not get along very well. They were resentful if any of the cameras differed. They got bored filing their photos. Some kept their notebooks in perfect condition; others lost them. Some had lots of good ideas of things to photograph in the community; others focused on their home, family, and friends. Sometimes they waxed enthusiastic; other times they seemed to barely drag themselves to the session. At times I despaired of reaching our goal, though in the end, we did and with resounding success.

Lorenz paints a very realistic picture of some of the challenges that facilitators face in conducting a photovoice project. It is important to remember that youth participants are human beings, and it is necessary to not romanticize them, because that is condescending and unrealistic. This does not mean that there are not periods of joy, elation, and fun. Facilitator group skills will not be tested during these periods (Alderson & Morrow, 2011). They will be tested as the project unfolds and the hard work begins to take its toll on participants. It is important to help participants understand that the project will have its ups and downs.

Curry-Stevens (2012) addresses the issue of power of those who embrace CBPR, and her conclusions have applicability to power and photovoice:

> Those of us engaged in CBPR tend to be at the margins of our professions, tending to be lesser funded than those working within traditional paradigms (although currently in an expansion phase), and accustomed to a marginal stature due to our epistemological beliefs in the subjectivity of research practice and world views that are conflict driven (for what else would explain the excessive social and economic divides between the academy and the community?). We perceive ourselves as allies to communities that struggle with various forms of oppression, and have typically engaged in such work before

entering academic life. Integral to such a stance, however, is a position that is inclined to position ourselves as innocent to relations of domination. (p. 100)

Co-facilitators must possess certain knowledge, skills, language competencies, and personal qualities to maximize the potential of photovoice for participants. Garcia, Lindgren, and Pintor (2011) identified six qualities that are essential, in this case for those leading girls' groups, but also applicable for other types of groups; co-facilitators should be (1) respectful and patient, (2) trustworthy and caring, (3) engaging and relevant; (4) flexible, (5) role-modeling, and (6) self-aware. These qualities reflect how co-facilitators may wear different "hats," and they do not have to all wear the same hats to make a successful team.

It is highly recommended that the co-facilitators have equal decision-making power. This takes on even greater significance when one is an academic or professional and another represents the group or community that is the focus of the project. Expertise legitimacy can be educational and experiential. Shared decision-making power must be explicit, with the members of the advisory committee having an understanding of this decision. Time and effort must be set aside for the co-facilitators to plan and implement a photovoice project.

Securing Funding

The subject of money is certainly one that requires considerable thought. Ideally, an advisory committee will be formed and play an active and meaningful role in helping to secure the necessary funding for a photovoice project. Invariably, the researcher seeks and obtains funding and then forms an advisory committee to help implement the project. This can result in the researcher conceptualizing the project and the advisory committee helping to implement it. The advisory committee is almost an afterthought in the seeking of funding (Vissing, 2007).

It is highly encouraged, if at all possible, to include the advisory committee in determining the types of funding and the sources for securing funding. Involving them in this task is highly unusual. This is probably the result of an interplay of various factors, with assumptions that they have very little information to add on sources of funding and and lack of time because of deadlines being the two most prevalent reasons. If at all possible, involving them in this task translates into a sharing of power and increasing their ownership of this important task.

Lack of external funding should not be viewed as making a photovoice project impossible (Day, 2011). It does free the project up from having to respond to external funding pressures in shaping how a project unfolds. Creativity and collaboration can result in local contributions, in-kind services, and greater community ownership of the project and the social change efforts that follow. Youth photovoice can be quite elaborate or simple depending local circumstances, including funding.

Selection of Project Location Within a Community

The physical location of the project, or its "home base," is to be carefully thought out, because that establishment will become part of the "face" of the photovoice project. If the institution has a positive reputation within the community, it brings institutional legitimacy, making the results of the project that much more easily acceptable both within and outside of the community. The advisory committee is in an excellent position to recommend community institutions, as well as political negotiations as needed.

These institutions do not have to be nonprofits. An institution such as a well-known and respected restaurant, for example, may be ideal. Conversely, a house of worship with a reputation for being progressive and championing community causes can also be an excellent community institution to house the project. There certainly is room for innovation concerning the setting for the exhibit, although libraries are very popular settings (Lorenz & Kolb, 2009).

An England-based photovoice project on alcohol exhibited its photographs in a local nightclub (Public Health England, 2009). A photovoice project on domestic workers in Salvador, Brazil, was exhibited in an exclusive exhibition space (Cornwall, Capibaribe, & Gonçalves, 2010). The organization sponsoring the project must be accessible along psychologically (residents feel comfortable visiting), culturally (individuals who work there represent the same background as the community), geographically and physically (accessibility), and operationally (the hours and days it is open are not restrictive). These four dimensions of accessibility are required to ensure that the exhibition does not present barriers to attendees.

Affirmation of Key Values and Principles

An understanding and embrace of values and principles guiding the photovoice project will go a long way towards facilitating the implementation of all facets of the project. The values and principles specifically outlined in Chapter 4, and touched upon in other sections of this book, are an example of those that are typically found in other forms of community participatory research. Publically acknowledging these values to projects participants and communities is one step in the direction of a photovoice project being taken seriously, and in separating out such a project from "business as usual" regarding community-based research.

Project Length

The length of time devoted to a photovoice project can vary considerably, depending upon the goals of a project, number of participants, experiences with photovoice, budget, and the commitment made by the participants. A project can be labor intensive and operate within a short time frame; it can also span months or years. A project with a limited time frame may be the result of a community event or incident, for which a response that is timely is in order. A long-term project brings the potential of major change, but it also has the potential to lose many participants. In essence, the goals of the photovoice project should dictate its length.

The reader may ask why "rush" a photovoice project, since reflection and transformation often require time and space, and do not necessarily proceed in a linear fashion. A short project period facilitates marshaling of participants and communities for a concentrated effort. That brings excitement and a clearer sense of purpose to the project, minimizing distractions. Circumstances leading to a youth photovoice project may dictate a longer period of time, however, which may involve months. This extended period of time, in turn, allows for a more deliberate pace, more ambitious goals, and the introduction of activities in a manner that conforms more to group process considerations. An extended period of multiple months can also experience dropouts, distractions, and even slippage of goals

SELECTION OF PROJECT PARTICIPANTS

This phase of a photovoice project may well be considered the heart and soul of the project, and it brings a great deal of excitement and energy. After all, photovoice participants are induced to generate information and insights from their own perspective. It is best to think of this phase as consisting of four elements:

1. Characteristics of participants—in essence, whose perspective is being sought?
2. A culturally appropriate process for recruiting participants.
3. A process for screening, interviewing, and selecting participants.
4. Administrative functions related to the review and signing of consent and rights of participants forms, and determination of payment for participating.

Characteristics of Participants

The goals of the photovoice project will dictate who the participants will be, or who are the most likely to benefit from participation. The "who" question goes beyond demographic factors and must encompass personality factors that may be more challenging to discern, yet can play a critical role in increasing the likelihood of success for a project. The perspective and experiences of participants will shape how a project unfolds and the final outcome and benefits. The characteristics and experiences of the participants cannot be left to chance.

Ideally, participants and co-facilitators must share the same sociodemographic profile as the group or community they are researching. Participants must be prepared to tackle situations that are highly ambiguous. One of the key characteristics or traits in the selection process must be an ability to tolerate ambiguity. What does this mean? Simply stated, participants who require highly detailed directions, are impatient with indecisions, are rigid, and lack of patience overall will likely have a difficult time feeling fulfilled by a photovoice. Arts-based researchers must be open to uncertainty and ambiguity (Sajnani, 2012). They do not subscribe to, or advocate, a set of methods for conducting research, thereby providing space for the introduction of new approaches towards answering research questions (McNiff, 2013b).

A Process for Recruiting Participants

The appeal of photovoice is that it can be perceived as different, challenging, and fun by youth. Further, the use of technology and photography makes it easier to recruit youth (Drew, Duncan, & Sawyer, 2010). The process of recruiting youth lends itself to a wide range of recruitment approaches. The advisory committee can recommend ways and places that can bring in potential participants with characteristics and considerations that will aid the project's goals.

Various local media markets can be tapped to get the word out in a community (Morgan et al., 2010). Local (social-cultural-political) circumstances should dictate the most effective sources and approaches, and every effort should be made to have a recruitment strategy that is personal and emphasizes person-to-person contact. Use of local nontraditional settings and places, where youth with particular characteristics congregate, are examples of ideal places. This phase may be labor intensive, particularly if extra time is taken to describe a photovoice project in greater detail than what is customarily found on a flyer, for example. Nevertheless, this time and labor is well invested, and facilitates the process of screening and selecting participants, as well as informing the community at large about the effort.

A Process for Screening, Interviewing, and Selection

Getting a group of potential participants sufficiently large in numbers to implement selection criteria is but the first step in this process. The recruitment process will be facilitated greatly if participants can be paid for their involvement. This is particularly important in the case of youth from low-income/low-wealth communities, since many cannot afford to volunteer after school (Jansson et al., 2006):" Remuneration provides an explicit recognition of youth as experts or quasi-consultants as well as an incentive and sign of appreciation" (p. 66). Payment can take various forms. Money can be a powerful inducement and does not take away from the central goals of the project. Payment does introduce potential ethical dilemmas, however, as addressed in Chapter 7. Relying solely upon participants who can afford to get involved or volunteer also raises ethical questions.

Depending upon the initial number of inquiries, it is recommended that the screening process consist of three stages: (1) initial telephone screening, (2) a group interview, and (3) a follow-up individual interview. This does not mean that the selection process may not require additional material to enter deliberations. Depending upon the formality of the selection, this process can take on elements of an application for employment. Porter et al. (2010), for example, required a short essay describing the reasons why youth, in this case students, wanted to participate. References may also be required. These can be quite formal, requiring a written response, and the process can occur over the telephone or in person.

Schubotz (2012) suggests a two-prong selection process whereby all applicants that meet the initial screening criteria attend a training session on photovoice. At the conclusion, assuming none or few of the attendees dropped out, all participants who have successfully completed the training receive a certificate of achievement. Those who are not chosen can be eligible and have priority for future projects. Some may not like this method because there are "winners" and "losers," and the process may lead to hurt feelings. Nevertheless, this approach is presented in the hopes of opening up the screening process to new models.

The group screening interview not only helps when the number of interested participants far exceeds the number needed, but it also provides important information concerning group process. The follow-up interview provides an opportunity to explore in depth with the potential participant issues of reliving traumatic events, as in the case of some types of photovoice, and to explore concerns they may have about the project.

Administrative Functions

It is rare for a practitioner or academic to look forward to the administrative aspects of research or a project of any type. Yet poor administration will doom a project. The saying "failing to plan means planning to fail" is closely tied to administration. Photovoice brings added administrative responsibilities because of the nature of this research, which is community-focused, and the technical dimensions associated with photographs and exhibits, including establishment of procedures to safeguard data.

Obtaining informed consent (see Chapter 7) represents an important ethical challenge in research when using research methods such as photovoice (Buchanan, Miller, & Wallerstein, 2007; Leitch, 2008). It can be a challenging process, particularly in cross-cultural situations (McDonnell, 2009). Pink (2007), for example, raises this important point regarding informed consent: "It cannot be assumed that people have consented to . . . have large images of themselves exhibited in a gallery simply because they have allowed the images to be taken or have responded to the camera" (p. 551).

Fortunately, there are a number of field manuals that have been made available by organizations with experiences in carrying out photovoice projects involving youth. The issue of informed consent, as result, cannot be taken lightly. Washtenaw County Public Health (2009), Michigan, has samples of consent forms, for example, that can be modified to take local circumstances into account. The Asian Health Center (n.d.), too, has a detailed manual on the how facets related to photovoice can be implemented. Powers, Freedman, and Pitner (2012) have published a facilitator's manual to help organizations thinking about using photovoice that outlines procedures and considerations for this method.

How to distribute research resources, which is often the case with photovoice, is an administrative task with ethical implications (Buchanan et al., 2007). Where a project buys supplies, food, and equipment, for example, represents an opportunity to distribute scarce resources in communities with high levels of poverty. Further, buying these services and products from establishments with positive reputations is essential to maintain good will. This translates into making sure that participation does not result in harm—they are willing participants, and they are aware of the options they have to leave the project prior to completion. In addition, they must be aware of their bill of rights (See Chapter 7).

In the case of groups and communities where English is not the primary language, all forms must be translated into the most appropriate language. This adds another layer to the process, but it is crucial in helping to inform parents or legal guardians of youth participants. In addition, materials describing the project must be made available in multiple languages as deemed necessary. It is recommended that project personal, preferably co-leaders, make home visits and explain the project in person to the appropriate adult. This provides a "human face" that these adults can associate with the project, and it opens up lines of communication that may lead to other projects and potential community benefits.

TRAINING AND ONGOING SUPPORT (ADVISORY COMMITTEE AND PARTICIPANTS)

The provision of training, ongoing consultation, and support will vary in intensity from project to project, depending upon the experiences that co-facilitators and participants bring to the endeavor. Nevertheless, the basic concept of training and ongoing support is an essential aspect of a research project of this type (Rice, Primak, & Girvin, 2013). Before proceeding, it is important to pause and note that training and support for youth must not be accomplished in a manner that does not dramatically alter the very qualities that made them attractive as researchers. In other words, avoid "adultering" them (Lolichen, Shetty, Shenoy, & Nash, 2007).

The allocation of resources to these activities conveys to participants the importance of the endeavor and the difficulties or challenges associated with conducting a photovoice project. Further, resources will be needed to support youth participants: "Youth researchers represent diverse socioeconomic backgrounds. They do not enter the field with steady employment, expendable resources, transportation, and travel or professional development budgets. Youth-led research will always require the economic and logistical support of parents, organizations, institutions, agencies, and benefactors" (White, Shoffner, Johnson, Knowles, &

Mills 2012). There is no question that youth photovoice projects require resources that adult projects do not.

The training expectations that participants bring to the project must be explored and addressed. For example, youth expectations of what constitutes "training" may differ substantially from what we as photovoice researchers consider "appropriate." A participatory approach, which is the preferred method, may encounter resistance from youth expecting a prescriptive approach (Brown & Powell, 2012). A multi-method approach is recommended, using didactics, exercise, discussions, role play, homework, and visual aids to address different learning styles and make training participatory and exciting—and thus significantly different from what youth are used to in formal school settings.

Training and support should consist of much more than the necessary management and care of equipment and approaches towards photography. They will also involve team building (Horowitz, Robinson, & Seifer, 2009) and ethics (Shimshock, 2008; Wang & Redwood-Jones, 2001), because youth photovoice is both about individual participants and the group as an entity. Helping participants better understand group process will serve them well while they are involved in the project and in other spheres of their lives.

There will be a need to provide food and, depending upon sites, transportation (Chen, Weiss, & Nicholson, 2010). These two items facilitate the engagement of youth. It is also highly recommended that certificates be given at the end of the training portion of the project as a means of celebrating a major accomplishment. For many urban youth and their families, formal accomplishments may be few and far between. Any opportunity that presents itself for a celebration should not be passed up, including obtaining media coverage of the graduation.

Special attention must be paid to ethical conduct, preferably in the first two sessions, and this topic should be revisited throughout the project's existence (Shimshock, 2008). This topic must be seen as important and not relegated to a late training session as if it were an afterthought. There will be instances where participants will encounter situations that have ethical dimensions, requiring that time and space be set aside for discussions. In essence, these situations become teachable moments for all participants, including the co-facilitators.

ASSESSMENT NEEDS AND ASSETS AND GOALS

Photovoice provides viewers with a prodigious amount of encoded information (Grady, 2004). The nexus between visual content and the interpretation of the content brings an added dimension that only has meaning within a grounded context. The events leading up to the photography, the person taking the photo, and the expressed intent of the photographer all combine to provide a contextual meaning. Further, how the photo is mounted and placed in the exhibition is also part of this contextual grounding (Richardson & Nuru-Jeter, 2012).

Photovoice can be used to assess youth needs as well as assets. A focus on needs and issues is not counter to the basic philosophy and principles of photovoice (Henry, Ramdoth, White, & Mangroo, 2013). A deficit perspective will focus on the problems, needs, issues, and so forth, without regard to positive aspects of life for youth. A shift towards assets brings an opportunity for even more innovative photovoice uses. In Baltimore, Maryland, for example, one youth photovoice project focused on what "love" meant to the participants. They selected this focus because they were tired of all the news and attention on their problems while other aspects of their lives were ignored (Downing, Sonenstein, & Davis, 2006). In essence, a focus on daily living can have important outcomes.

The analysis of the data, which consists of actual photographs and responses (narratives that can be individual and group in nature), can take various forms depending upon the depth of analysis required. Typically, photovoice projects initiated by community agencies may not entail in-depth analysis of data, themes, and so on. Academy-initiated photovoice projects need to bring a level of analysis associated with highly competitive external funding. This depth of analysis, including the relationship of results to theories, is not high in priority in most cases of community organization–initiated photovoice projects. Chapter 6 addresses data analysis in greater detail.

PLANNING, SCHEDULING, AND IMPLEMENTATION

It is highly advisable that project participants play an active role in the planning and scheduling of the photovoice project. The degree to which they participate may vary according to time, interests, and competencies. At minimum, they must be aware of how decisions on tasks and scheduling have been made, along with the rationale that went into the decisions. Demystifying the process helps ensure that there is transparency, with decisions being opened for scrutiny and discussion.

Lorenz (n.d.) strongly recommends the development of a publicity campaign:

Develop a dissemination strategy right from the start. What local newspapers or radio stations might want to publicize the project when it is completed? Where can you hold the exhibit? What are the potential benefits to you, your organization, your school, or your participants from this project— new funding, new community partnerships, enhanced self-esteem, and new projects in the future? Answering this last question will help you to determine what types of dissemination activities and outlets are appropriate for your project.

Media should be expected to play a prominent role in facilitating implementation of the public-focused activities of the project. Local circumstances will dictate the most appropriate way of getting the word out. In some communities, for example, a public service announcement will be very effective. In others, this will yield minimal results.

As the saying goes, "to plan is human; to implement is divine." This saying captures the reality that even the best laid plans can go astray. The implementation stage incorporates a wide variety of major activities associated with photovoice, as addressed in the previous sections (the taking of photographs, discussion, analysis, and mounting an exhibition, for example). An ability to rebound when plans do not go according to schedule or intent provides an opportunity for lessons learned—an added bonus, so to speak.

SELECTION OF IMAGES AND NARRATIVES

The selection of the photographs and narratives that will be part of an exhibition is far from a straightforward process. This should not be surprising, since the photographs that were taken symbolize a great deal to the participants. This selection process may cause a great deal of anguish and insecurity, because the process is no longer focused on the group but has shifted toward an outside audience. Fears and insecurity are bound to emerge during discussions, and, to be quite frank, this is part of the transformational process that images can evoke.

Laverick (2010) described a situation and presents a number of provocative, yet critical, questions that will emerge in the photo selection process:

> Editing decisions regarding how much of the graphic detail of the accounts was to be included in the dissemination process brought up further dilemmas. Would the inclusion of descriptive accounts of sexual and physical abuse risk a degree of voyeurism on the part of the audience? How would it be received . . . could inclusion be conceived as faithful representation or exploitation in the furtherance of career aspirations? (p. 86)

Group process during the discussion and selection of photographs may take on aspects of mutual aid groups, with participants helping each other articulate and validate feelings, and thus bringing therapeutic outcomes to their experience (Barlow & Hurlock, 2013). Photovoice calls for realistic expectations (Schubotz, 2012). This activity can necessitate allocation of sufficient time and support opportunities that go far beyond what typically occurred during group discussion sessions in the past.

Time must be set aside for the selection of photographs and the development of narratives. Nevertheless, not every youth member will be able to adhere to an allotted time schedule for these tasks. Some can be quick and insightful; others may experience difficulty in selecting images and creating narratives. How much time should be devoted to these activities? One approach is to do a trial run for group members, with an understanding that time will vary, and that is perfectly fine. At the conclusion of this trial run, an average time will be determined. Simply take the longest and the fastest to arrive at the most likely scenario.

It is important to pause, reinforce, and be prepared to encounter the emotional upheaval that this phase of a photovoice project will engender when the focus of the project is on highly emotionally painful experiences. Obviously, this will not be the first time that emotionally laden and painful experiences will be discussed in the course of a project, since one of the goals of photovoice is transformative, and the growth that results often emanates from confronting painful experiences. The selection of the central focus of the project is emotionally demanding. The concentrated nature of this phase means that an enormous amount of time is devoted to reviewing the experiences and feelings captured by individual and collective photographs.

Mixed emotions will emerge. On the positive side, there will be a realization of the incredible journey the individuals and the group have undertaken, in carrying out a photovoice project and of the valuable insights they have obtained. There will also be a downside. Participants may express doubts about the success of the exhibition and the reactions that it may cause, with ramifications beyond the exhibit itself. Doubts will be expressed about the wisdom of sharing the photographs and narratives with the "outside world." Concerns about being misunderstood or even ridiculed are not uncommon. These reactions are not restricted to any particular age group. Nevertheless, youth, by the very nature of the age, may express greater mixed feelings and fears.

Laverick (2010) talks about qualitative research and emotional fatigue, and why it is so challenging for everyone involved, for participants as well as for the facilitators and researcher. One of the appealing aspects of photovoice is that is gives license to participants to share their stories to a group, which may be quite painful for those sharing publicly for the first time. Facilitators, too, are faced with a culmination of exposure to these stories over an extended period of time. They must put aside their own feelings and facilitate a purposeful process and create a climate that allows this sharing to transpire for participants. They must put aside their own reactions for the sake of the group. Nevertheless, facilitators also enter a phase that will tax them, raising questions about their role in the project, particularly if facilitators share similar histories and backgrounds as those of the youth participants.

CULTURAL FINAL PORTRAIT/EXHIBITION

Exhibitions, first and foremost, tell individual and collective stories in a public space. The exhibition of the photographs may represent the culmination of a photovoice project for participants and their family and friends (Wilkins & Liamputtong, 2010). Having their photographs in a community exhibition may have been one of the primary motivations for participating in a photovoice project (Larson, Mitchell, & Gilles, 2001). An exhibition can be thought of as a group narrative or story (Leitch, 2008). The setting and ambiance (place and space) takes on significance, as does the storyline.

Guillemin and Drew (2010) pose important questions regarding audiences that require considerable thought before arriving at a satisfactory answer: "The notion of the 'audience' requires more consideration. Questions such as: Who is the intended audience in the process of image production? What is their role? and How does this shape the image produced? are all important to explore" (p. 185). Not surprisingly, numerous considerations must go into how the exhibition will unfold. Barone and Eisner (2012) note that art "can be inviting and challenging without being-off putting or alienating. Creating a 'lay friendly' work might require that arts based researchers enter into the comfort zones of members of an intended audience, enabling them to identify with facets of the work . . . [and] manage to pull the lay onlooker into the world of the work, coaxing him or her to participate in a reconstruction of its meaning" (p. 69). Devoting time and resources to an exhibition is highly advisable.

Levy and Weber (2011) address an aspect of the exhibition that often is not sufficiently highlighted in the research literature, but that illustrates the power of the exhibit for youth participants: "The exhibit that culminated the workshops was highly effective in many ways. Seeing your work framed and on display is not the same as sharing it in workshops. It was a source of pride and achievement for the participants. Some of them dressed up for the event, indicating that it was special to them" (p. 306). The dynamics associated with interacting with a "live" audience interjects excitement and anxiety because so much can go wrong.

Another aspect of the exhibition needs attention, and that is the title of the exhibition. The title selected for an exhibition takes on importance and can be quite challenging. It should not be too long, but it needs to provide sufficient information to be catchy and draw attention and curiosity about the exhibit (Ollerton & Kelshaw, 2011). Arriving at a title can be framed as a "fun" activity, but one with very serious implications.

Bryce (2013) refers to photovoice exhibitions as co-curation: "Co-curation is the process of collecting artefacts to produce an exhibition together which represents a shared aspect of life. In this instance photography is the chosen medium to facilitate co-curation" (p. 33). Essentially, a curator can be considered the keeper and framer of culture. Some would argue that photovoice exhibitions can be thought of as "visual essays" conveying a series of themes that can best be appreciated as cogent and coherent interconnection of themes as found in an essay (Kay, 2013).

Photovoice, like other visual ethnographic methods, seeks to "capture the ways in which young people, as experts on, and researchers of, their own lives, can be facilitated through visual methodologies in curating their experiences of beholding, embodying, and performing physical culture" (Enright, 2013, p. 199). The ordering, or syntagm, of the images and narratives, must be carefully crafted or orchestrated, to achieve maximum impact on an audience (Spencer, 2011).

This entails a group decision regarding how best to achieve this goal. This conversation, it is important to note, may not be as simple as it first appears, because of differences within the group on how to arrange the photographs. The ordering must not be left to chance. It is very similar to a book: chapters are presented in a particular order, and content within chapters, too, face a similar ordering. A reader, like a photovoice audience, must be led through the material in a purposeful manner to achieve maximum impact or results.

Every effort should be made to record the reaction of audience participants. This can be accomplished in a variety of ways, including having (1) note cards next to each photograph for individual responses, (2) a short questionnaire at the end of the exhibit, (3) random interviews throughout the event, and (4) follow-up after a period of time to assess reactions. How this form of evaluation takes shape is dependent upon the needs of the project and the availability of funding. It can be very "sophisticated" or rather "simple" in form.

A photovoice exhibitions shares many similarities with major event openings: media contacts, press releases, invitations, date and time, location, traveling show schedule, development of sign-in book, contact information, and so on. A preliminary exhibition can occur with the parents, followed by a public exhibition (Kaplan, 2013). One innovative way of inviting the public and announcing the exhibition is to send out postcards with images from the exhibition. A variety of images can be used to entice the public. Posters, too, can be created with these images and placed at strategic places within the community. Banners represent another form of public art that have a history of community participation and bring sufficient flexibility (cost, level of participation, and type of banner) to take local circumstances into account.

There are two approaches towards attribution: (1) anonymity and (2) recognition. The former will have a caption under the photograph with a statement by the photographer; the latter will have the same statement but will also have the photographer's name (Larson, Mitchell, & Gilles, 2001). The nature of the topic the photovoice project is focused on will be a key determining factor in whether the photographer or artist wishes to be identified. Obviously, exhibitions that not only recognize the artist but also have them standing next to their photographs to answer questions, are the most rewarding for both artists and audiences.

A photovoice exhibition can occur in a variety of ways and combinations (Yonas, Burke, & Miller, 2013). It typically transpires through the printing and exhibition of photos, with accompanying narratives, which are displayed throughout a room. Photovoice exhibits also can transpire through slides and computer screens, or this can be done in combination with the typical showing. How the exhibit is conceptualized is dependent upon the goals of the project, particularly the size of the anticipated audience and the nature of interaction between photographer and audience.

Photovoice exhibitions create social spaces for discussion and reflection (Andreouh, Skovdal, & Campbell, 2013). These spaces are not your typical types, since they must be conducive for discussion of topics that are generally not discussed in public and are often relegated to private conversations at best. Exhibitions must be thought of from a two-dimensional perspective: (1) structure and (2) climate. "Structure" refers to the physical space and how the photos and narratives are displayed, and to areas where attendees can congregate and talk about their impressions and experiences, both with each other and with youth participants. "Climate," in turn, refers to the nonphysical surroundings and how conducive is it to engage in conversations. It thus includes elements such as noise, acoustics, music, and food, for example.

Group sharing of reflections, as opposed to individual responses, can be quite powerful. An opportunity and the provision of physical space for this to occur are an essential element of photovoice. Examples can be found of photographs being part of a traveling exhibit with accompanying journal vignettes (Hunter, Langdon, Caesar, Rhodes, & Estes, 2011). Kessi (2011) reports on photographs and narratives being published in local newspapers and magazines as an added dimension to the exhibit. Smith-Cavos and Eisenhauer (2013) show how it was used at local events, including health fairs. Gupta et al. (2013), in turn, show how photovoice can generate images that can be part of a public service announcement. Websites, too, are a viable vehicle to share photos (Levy & Weber, 2011; Papson, Goldman, & Kersey, 2007).

Youth can develop scrapbooks, media diaries, or photo diaries, consisting of photographs and narratives (video diaries also exist [Holliday, 2007]). These scrapbooks and diaries can be personal or meant to be shared (Allen, 2011; Bragg & Buckingham, 2008). In addition, these diaries and scrapbooks can include material beyond photographs and narratives, such as drawings, cutouts, newspaper clippings from news coverage of the exhibition, the program, and photographs from the exhibition. The content is determined by the individual, and no two scrapbooks or photo diaries will be similar in construction and content. Participation in a photovoice project and the exhibition are monumental moments in the lives of participants, and a scrapbook becomes a vehicle for capturing that moment.

A word of caution about the final portrait is in order:

> Whilst not denying the value and power of imagery produced through such means, one should perhaps question the authorship of the final work (the balance between "facilitator" and "participant") and examine exactly whose thoughts and opinions are being conveyed and whose voice is actually being heard. Such work often suggests that we are being shown a relatively unmediated, authentic "insider" view rather than that of an outside observer (photographer or researcher) and the crucial roles of devising, briefing, editing and presentation (often undertaken by the facilitator) can be minimized, overlooked or even ignored in favour of a focus on the contribution of the participants.
>
> —ROBINSON, 2011, p. 131

Robsinson's cautionary comment illustrates the many potential pitfalls that can await an outsider.

Unofficial and official openings can be considered (Erickson, 2012). Unofficial openings provide participants with an opportunity to do a trial run in a smaller venue and try different ways of presenting their work. The lessons learned at the initial "unofficial" opening can then be addressed before the grand opening. The parallels with film can be quite striking. Potential drawbacks to an official opening take on greater significance when local media are invited to record and cover the occasion, just like Hollywood produced film openings, but at a community scale.

Finally, a graduation ceremony with a presentation of certificates is highly advisable:

> Linda Good has stressed the capacity of digital photography to build a sense of community, especially when photos are exhibited publicly (Good, 2005). This was certainly the case in the workshop that I oversaw. The day of the exhibit, parents, students and teachers helped to prepare the seats, refreshments, and the exhibit itself. Then everyone celebrated together the success of the participating students and took time to admire and discuss the photos displayed.
>
> —ERICKSON, 2012

There is no denying that the official opening of an exhibit represents an accomplishment, and for many young people it is one of few with public recognition. It is highly recommended that a ceremony marking this accomplishment take place, with the appropriate invitations sent out family, friends, and community leaders. This event, too, should be covered by local media and advertised throughout the community in local radio programming, cable shows, and appropriate community venues. This type of publicity elevates youth participants as role models and may counter popular negative narratives often associated with urban youth of color.

PROJECT EVALUATION

A meaningful evaluation of a photovoice project will not occur at the end of the project, although that phase is extremely important. Evaluation must talk place throughout all phases of a project and not be limited to the end. Process evaluation can be informal or highly formal and structured (Garcia et al., 2013). The evaluation of a photovoice project will entail examining process, products, and outcomes. Participatory evaluation involving youth has a relatively long and distinguished history (White et al., 2012), and much can be learned from these efforts and applied to youth photovoice evaluation.

Youth participants are expected to play an active and meaningful role in carrying out an evaluation of their photovoice experience, and the literature highlights how youth have played significant and leadership roles in carrying out evaluation (Delgado, 2006; Heath, Brooks, Cleaver, & Ireland, 2009; Heath

& Walker, 2012b). This active involvement will necessitate instituting training on evaluation, and although the topic can be covered in the training phase of the project, it will need to be revisited again during this stage.

The end of a photovoice project brings forth an evaluation, but it does not mean the termination of relationships or the end of an opportunity to advance the career of participants. There will be possibilities for career counseling and referrals to be made to appropriate sources for further training, for example. These next steps will be facilitated if the values embraced in Chapter 4 were embraced and bridges established between youth participants and key institutions are maintained.

SOCIAL CHANGE ACTION

Not surprisingly, the shift from research to a social action project is not a typical transition for research projects, but it can be greatly facilitated when the participants in the research have a decision-making role in selecting the social change action, and when the research was firmly grounded within a community context (Smits & Champagne, 2008). In thinking about the next step in photovoice and focusing on a change effort, it can be easy to think about this effort being a group-led project. Action to achieve change can be done by individuals, or by a combination of members, or by the group as a whole. This flexibility in who and how many undertake a change effort allows the group to make decisions in a manner that is not one project or another.

Some would categorize photovoice as a form of social action research because of how it emphasizes the importance of change resulting from the findings. Huang (2010) provides a definition of action research that brings forth the need for photovoice to result in purposeful social action:

> Action research is an orientation to knowledge creation that arises in a context of practice and requires researchers to work with practitioners. Unlike conventional social science, its purpose is not primarily or solely to understand social arrangements, but also to effect desired change as a path to generating knowledge and empowering stakeholders. We may therefore say that action research represents a transformative orientation to knowledge creation in that action researchers seek to take knowledge production beyond the gate-keeping of professional knowledge makers. (p. 93)

Youth action research, in this case involving CBPR, in turn, has been found to increase efficacy and empowerment among urban youth (Berg, Coman, & Schensul, 2009; Ozar, Ritterman, & Wanis, 2010).

Prior to the actual transition to an action project, a decision will need to be made concerning release of a report on the findings and recommendations of the project. Dissemination of publicity and reports on photovoice will undoubtedly involve institutional and community gatekeepers. Ideally, these gatekeepers should have been consulted earlier in the project and can be tapped at this stage. Gatekeepers can be conceptualized as playing influential roles throughout a youth research project and helping to negotiate power relationships (Leonard, 2007). A well-planned publicity campaign must consider stakeholders for advice and possible active players in such a plan.

Photovoice has been found to be a qualitative method that facilitates transition from findings to specific social action steps among youth when compared to other qualitative methods (Downey, Ireson, & Scutchfield, 2008). This transition may prove to be challenging (Amsden and VanWynsberghe, 2005). Griffith et al. (2008) found that the organization sponsoring the youth photovoice project, in this case one focused on violence, wields tremendous influence in the change effort and the results flowing from the photovoice findings. The authors found that intra-organizational infrastructure; inter-organizational membership practices and networking; and extra-organizational research, training, and organizing activities facilitate positive social change.

Photovoice can also be used to raise funds for causes related to the subject of the project (Levy & Weber, 2011). The visual nature of this project lends itself to portraying conditions that may not generate the enthusiasm usually associated with written reports. A picture is worth a thousand words, so to speak. The very nature of how photovoice lends itself to new insights, knowledge, and actions can also be a key factor in generating funds for social change projects. Images have wide appeal in this society, particularly when they capture social situations that are difficult to talk about and lend themselves to new ways of thinking about the subject matter.

Innovation and Photovoice

The topics of innovation and research are not often associated with each other because of an academic emphasis on the tried and true. Although photovoice and other forms of visual-focused research fall under the innovative category, there is still debate about these forms of research. Marín and Roldán (2010) identify a common set of critical arguments concerning visual-based research:

> Despite the large quantity of research using photographs problems persist, especially as regards issues of validity and objectivity and the narrative and persuasive functions of images. These are evident in art education and other research disciplines that have traditionally used photographs, such as visual anthropology, visual ethnography and visual sociology. Furthermore, there is an abundance of terms related to the various uses of photographs. Some of these, like photo elicitation, photojournalism, photo montage and photo story have existed for some time; others like photo activism, photo dialogue, photo interview, photo inventory, photo poem, photo questionnaire, photo voice or photo writing are newer. (p. 9)

The expansion of the field of photographic research can only be expected to continue, and with this expansion, definitional issues will emerge, particularly as the number of academic fields and helping professions adopt visual research. This expansion is not all bad news, because it reflects the attractiveness of a method, as in the case of this book with photovoice, which has found a receptive audience, for many of the reasons identified in this book. It can be argued that this definitional issue is inherent from an evolutionary perspective and will eventually result in a universal definition, but that will take time. Efforts to bring together how photovoice is conceptualized and carried out in multiple fields of practice, as represented in this book, is a step in that direction.

Photovoice is an exciting research method, not only because it brings an innovative dimension to community-based research, but also because it brings the potential for innovative changes in how this method gets conceptualized to take local goals and circumstances into account. Nykiforuk, Valianatos, and Nieuwendyk (2011) predict that the evolution of photovoice will provide even more nuanced details on community life as this method gets wider use in different settings and population groups. A review of Chapter 5 will bring this realization to life.

The introduction of new methods, such as the "going-along," which has community residents pairing up with project staff to take photographs, is an example of how this method has evolved over the past several years (Capriano, 2009). Garcia, Auguilera-Guzman et al. (2013), report on pairing adults and youth and finding that the benefits go beyond what is typically found in photovoice projects, with improvements in intergenerational relations resulting. Ohmer and Owens (2013) undertook a crime prevention photovoice project that paired youth and adults to create collective efficacy, and in this case it resulted in conversion of a vacant lot into an art and garden space. This method has also paired students and teachers (Warne, Snyder, & Gadin, 2013).

A going-along method opens up photovoice to individuals and groups with certain types of disabilities, such as those with blindness or visual impairment. The joining together of the walking interview with photovoice adds a qualitative dimension that has only recently started to get attention, and that has the potential of presenting a multidimensional picture of how photographs get grounded and contextualized in urban settings (Evans & Jones, 2011; Fink & Keynes, 2012; Miaux et al., 2010). Loebach and Gilliland (2010) report on child-led tours, photovoice, and the use of GPS to convey perceptions of the children's neighborhood to the external community. Photovoice as a technological tool can be combined with other technological tools. Gupta et al. (2013), for example, used photovoice as the basis for developing informational videos on asthma.

Combining photovoice with other participatory methods, such as the use of the arts, for example, also has much promise and is starting to find its way in a number of educational and helping professions (Fenge, Hodges, & Cutts, 2011; Moxley, Feen-Calligan, & Washington, 2012; Osei-Kofi, 2013). The potential of photovoice projects using photo novella (picture stories) as a method for reaching marginalized groups with histories of using this method, too, has great potential, particularly in cultures where the photo novella has a long and strong tradition (Burke & Evans, 2011; Purcell, 2009), as in the case of low-acculturated Latinos in the United States (Delgado, 2006).

Photographs and photovoice can be used with various types of groups. Skowdal and Oguto (2012) describe a project focused on friendships and children with HIV in Kenya. Families can undertake a photovoice project as a means of capturing and convening insights about their lives and how these experiences shape their perceptions and interactions as family members (Garcia et al., 2013; Hampton, 2011; Janhonen-Abruquah & Holm, 2008; Valentine & Knibb, 2011). Subunits of families can also use photovoice. Children and youth can undertake a project and share their results with parents or legal guardians. Intergenerational family projects can open the door for exploration of how age and other factors influence social navigation for those who are undocumented.

Photofriend, for example, brings visual ethnography as a tool to capture everyday life and does not have to focus on painful events or memories (Oh, 2012). Similar approaches to capturing everyday life have been reported in the literature (D'Alonzo & Sharma, 2010; Janhonen-Abruquah & Holm, 2008; Morgan et al., 2010; Tijm, Cornielje, & Edusei, 2011; Warne, Snyder, & Gadin, 2013; Woodgate, Edwards, & Ripat, 2012; Yi & Zebrack, 2010). The case study of Camp CAMERA (Chapter 8) serves as an example of how photovoice can be a useful method to capture nonstigmatizing and stigmatizing experiences.

Cartoons and drawings, too, can be supplements to photographs (Guillemin & Drew, 2010; Hinthorne, 2012; Skowdal & Ogutu, 2012), bringing an arts dimension that may appeal to younger children. Photographs can also be used to create calendars and posters that can be distributed throughout the community and bring an added perspective to the exhibit (Necheles et al. 2007), allowing the exhibit to reach far beyond its boundaries into other spheres. The creation of a children's book with photographic images illustrates the possible reach of photovoice (Sanchez, 2009). In addition, music can bring an audio dimension to visual research exhibitions (Garcia-Vera, 2012; Laughey, 2006). The addition of music does introduce potential complications in the selection of the music, however. Finally, photovoice projects can be used to capture community art and the role it plays in shaping a community's perceptions of itself.

Urban communities often have art displayed throughout in the form of murals, sculptures, and other public art forms (Buckley, 2013). Public spaces are excellent venues for engaging residents in various forms of art-based social justice (Duncan, 2011). A photovoice project can bring an added dimension to these art representations (Berman, 2013; Schuermans, Loopmans, & Vandenabeele, 2012). A search of the literature did not uncover such a photovoice project (Delgado, 1999). This type of art photovoice project could be used to identify community assets as opposed to deficits. Other approaches will be addressed in the next few chapters (Russell, 2009). Special attention has been paid to the role of facilitator or co-facilitator in the case of collaboration between professional and resident participants in the use of visual methods in combination with other approaches.

Personal Qualities and Skill Sets

It is fitting to end this chapter by laying out the "nuts" and "bolts" of carrying out a youth photovoice project, with attention being paid to the key personal qualities and skill sets needed to undertake a project of this type. The following lists will hopefully aid practitioners and researchers seeking to embrace photovoice in their approaches for reaching urban youth.

Personal Qualities: At this point, readers may be wondering out loud whether or not photovoice is the "right" method for them. Obviously, only the reader can answer this question. Nevertheless, I can safely say that my "artistic" abilities are far from exemplary, and that certainly applies to cameras and photographs, and I am being kind to myself when I say that. The subject of skill set and photovoice must be discussed. It is best to address this topic from the point of view of what qualities would be needed to be a good community practitioner working with urban youth. Eleven different qualities come to mind:

1. An ability to tolerate ambiguity is important, because no two situations will be similar, and we cannot have all the details and information we want.
2. Creativity is a quality that is always in great demand.
3. Flexibility in allowing local circumstances to dictate what is needed.
4. Resiliency, or an ability to bounce back from failure.
5. A good sense of humor, because we will find ourselves in situations no one could have foreseen, and a sense of humor, particularly being able to laugh at ourselves, will go a long way.
6. A willingness to be tested by youth.
7. A thirst for new experiences and challenges.
8. A desire to learn about other cultures, not just ethnic or racial, but also youth.
9. A willingness to be a part of a group effort is important, though not all practitioners do well in group undertakings, particularly ones in which they are not leaders but co-facilitators.
10. Patience is a virtue, and it surely will be tested when plans simply do not unfold in the time frame they were planned for; remember that no two work days or work weeks will ever be the same.
11. Empathy is the final quality, and probably the most important one (Lenz & Sangganjanavanich, 2013). A person can be an outstanding

technician, but without empathy, one is just a merchant, in the crudest sense of the word, because youth can be very forgiving of mistakes but unforgiving of those who cannot relate to their circumstances.

Skill Sets: I can approach this topic from the conventional point of view of the importance of organizing, planning, management, and research skills. I will not do so, however, but will instead highlight certain skill sets that could be lost when taking a broad overview. I have identified ten skills that stand out because of their importance.

1. Group work skills stand out in importance because of the nature of collective learning and memory and how it transpires within groups (Molloy, 2007).
2. Listening skills take on significance because they may represent one of the few times that youth can open up with adults (Mitchell, DeLange, Moletsane, Stuart, & Buthelezi, 2005).
3. Communication skills are clearly important, particularly being able to communicate with youth and understanding the role of language and slang in their lives (Strawn & Monama, 2012).
4. Language skills are very helpful in the case of youth who are bilingual or primarily monolingual in a language other than English, since work with parents is necessary (Scacciaferro, Goode, & Frausto, 2009; Segars, 2007).
5. Advocacy skills take center stage upon completion of the analysis phase, and youth should be able to translate their findings into social change projects (Strack, Magill, & McDonagh, 2004; Wang & Redwood-Jones, 2001).
6. Skills in working with both youth and adults are important, since practitioners working with youth often prefer not to deal with adults, based upon my experiences.
7. Counseling skills are integral to photovoice, even though that may not be part of the job description (Osseck, Hartman & Cox, 2010; Smith, Bratini & Appio, 2012).
8. An ability to organize and bring structure during periods that may appear chaotic will generate reassurance for those youth who are concerned about what the process will uncover for them and their loved ones (Dixon & Hadjialexiou, 2005; Steyn & Kamper, 2011).
9. Photovoice co-facilitators are first and foremost teachers, and the ability to impart knowledge is a skill that is necessary, because there are so many moments that represent teachable opportunities (Schell, Ferguson, Hamoline, Shea, & Thomas-Maclean, 2009; Strack, Magill & McDonagh, 2004).

10. Problem-solving skills must be imparted as part of the photovoice transformative process (Sharma, 2010).

The above two lists no doubt have some items that will not come as any great surprise, and others that will cause a moment of pause and reflection. These are not meant to intimidate but to help in determining areas of strengths and areas for improvement, and that includes the author of this book.

Conclusion

Photovoice is certainly an exciting research method that brings an innovative dimension to the field of research with undervalued groups. It is certainly not a research method that is immune from the pitfalls often associated with community-based participatory research. Yet the rewards certainly far outweigh the challenges. This chapter has sought to ground the reader with the key elements and considerations needed in planning and implementing a photovoice research project, and to not romanticize this method in the process. In addition, an effort was made to highlight areas for innovation and moving this method forward.

A photovoice research project centered on youth brings added considerations that a project focused on adults does not include. Nevertheless, the long-term rewards of investing in youth will bring significant payouts in the future for communities and the youth that participate in this type of endeavor. Practitioners and academics must be prepared to be challenged throughout all facets of a photovoice project; further, there will be facets and activities that will appeal to them and those that will not, and this is to be expected. Nevertheless, this research method will only increase in importance in the foreseeable future.

6

Approaches and Challenges for Analyzing Results

Introduction

It is relatively easy to get caught up in the excitement of implementing a photovoice project, forgetting the role and importance of data analysis. It is almost as if data analysis can be an afterthought, with researchers getting wrapped up in the moment and looking forward to the change effort that will emanate from the insights gathered through the participant exchanges. These insights can be conceptualized as *data analysis*, although they go by many other terms that may be less intimidating to participants.

Visual research has the potential to greatly expand the nature, quantity, and quality of data within a short period of time (Patton, Higgs, & Smith, 2011). An abundance of quality data is both a researcher's dream and nightmare, and when discussing photovoice, the question of what constitutes "data" is certainly open to debate, adding both excitement and tensions to the process of analysis.

Youth participation in a photovoice project is a unique experience, and the dynamics of carrying out a project by having young people actively engaged in taking photographs and sharing their reasons for doing so can generate "rich" and "nuanced" data that can stand alone or work in combination with other methods. It is also a unique type of experience for adult researchers. Nevertheless, we cannot lose sight of the fact that photovoice is both a research and intervention method, and that it is research with a social purpose. The depth of analysis will be greatly dependent upon the goals and the competencies of participants in the project. An intervention focus relies on data analysis to direct the focus of the change effort; a research focus, in turn, results in a focus on depth of meaning, without losing sight of the importance of a change effort.

Qualitative data are only as good as the time and effort that has gone into the initial question(s) and the analysis. Furthermore, data are only as good as the degree of participation and social change resulting from the research. Both dimensions of photovoice involve gathering data, and therein we find tension between engaging in a transformative experience, bringing about change, and engendering new knowledge. This tension is not unique to youth, but it is more pronounced when compared with adults. This greater sense of injustice translates into a greater need to achieve social change.

The worldwide popularity of photovoice lends itself to a meta-analysis and an established database for practitioners and researchers to draw upon. A review of this literature will show an emphasis on the process of establishing and running a photovoice project, and on the many benefits resulting from participation for both individuals and their communities. Unfortunately, the literature, with some notable exceptions, has not emphasized any depth of detail in how analyses were conducted. As more books get written on the subject, this absence in the literature will surely be rectified.

This chapter is organized into five sections to provide a requisite grounding on the various dimensions on the process and structure of data analyses: (1) Word of Warning, (2) Photovoice and Mixed Methods, (3) Youth Participation in Data Analysis, (4) Types and Levels of Analyses, and (5) Framework for Analysis and Considerations. Special attention will be paid to group process to highlight how peer interactions influence all facets of data analysis, and bring an important dimension to this phase of a photovoice project.

WORD OF WARNING

It is appropriate, if not wise, to pause at this juncture and state the obvious, and that is that regardless of how diligent and conscientious a researcher is, there will be criticism of the "quality" of the analysis of visual data. A major criticism of arts-based qualitative research methods such as photovoice is that photographs lend themselves to a manipulation of images and cannot be considered "objective," and thereby have very limited appeal and consequences beyond the individual taking the photograph. Research that is not "generalizable" to groups is often considered "interesting" or "preliminary," but certainly cannot be categorized as "real" research. The discussions on ontology and epistemology in Chapter 2 get at the root of the question of what constitutes "data," or "evidence," and at the most appropriate ways of analyzing and sharing this information.

Nothing puts more fear in the hearts of researchers than being accused of manipulating data or lacking objectivity. There is recognition that researching that is tacit and instinctual, for example, necessitates an expansion of what conventionally goes for "evidence" in social research (Prior, 2013). Goldstein (2007), in an article titled "All Photos Lie: Images as Data," argues that a camera cannot replicate human vision, since it is a two-dimensional rather than a three-dimensional representation. Perspectives or fields of vision, for example, bring a different perspective. The use of awide-angle lens, for example, can capture an image, but it also distorts it (Goldstein, 2007): "Falling back on our language of images or data, we might expect the viewers to have little tolerance for error in the production of photo journalism. However, little criticism is heard of manipulation of the truth by a wide-angle lens. This may simply be due to the fact that most viewers are unaware of the photograph's ability to manipulate perspective" (p. 65).

Photovoice captures the world through the eyes of one individual, and it is that person's view that counts. Subjectivity is not only embraced but celebrated (Potash, 2013). Arts-based researchers would view this perspective as authentic; those who subscribe to positivism would label it as biased and of limited value under the best of circumstances. Researchers can help record this view, and, in combination with the views of others in the photovoice project, they can identify themes that cut across these individual views, setting a backdrop for the story, and the telling of the story itself.

Arts-based research is predicated upon a practical and experiential history of understanding (Prior, 2013). Experiential knowledge and meaning is open to varied approaches being captured and is not dependent on words or the written language. Prosser and Burke (2008), for example, speak to how words fall within the spheres, or domains, of adult researchers and are disempowering to youth. Words alone cannot capture the lived experience (Rappaport, 2013). Refining and uncovering new ways of learning becomes a goal of arts-based inquiry, and photovoice fills this gap.

PHOTOVOICE AND MIXED METHODS

Photovoice lends itself to the use of mixed-method approaches (Johansen, 2012). This is particularly the case with other qualitative methods, although there is an increasing number of projects involving quantitative and GIS methods (Dennis, 2006). Uncovering unexpected forms of knowledge (Kendall, Marshall, & Barlow, 2013; McNaughton, 2009), particularly when nuanced, increases the importance of using mixed research methods, including the use of photovoice (Lopez, 2006) and video, for example, as an evaluation tool (Fitzgerald, Hackling, & Dawson, 2013). Mixed methods, particularly the use of focus groups and key informants, will be highlighted when appropriate because of how often these two approaches have been used in the field.

Mixed methods and youth research have increased in popularity, enhancing the use of creative approaches that take the age and interests of participants into account as a means of making research more youth-friendly and relevant (Hannay, Dudley, Milan, & Leibovitz, 2013). Bagnoli (2012), for example, addresses the value of using a mixed-method approach to obtain a holistic portrait of youth identities. Telling stories through visual, verbal, and written formats allows youth a strength in recalling and sharing their stories in a manner that one method could not do justice to (Henderson, Holland, McGrellis, & Thomson, 2007). The flexibility that comes with using mixed methods brings with it challenges in data analysis because of the variety of qualitative data that are generated.

Visual research, as in the case of photovoice, relies heavily upon the individual taking or making the image for interpretation. Photovoice can be used alone or with other qualitative methods that are also participant-driven, depending upon the goals of a project, local circumstances, budget, and the comfort level of youth participants (Cooper & Yarbrough, 2010; Hannay et al., 2013; Nitsch et al., 2013; Rudkin & Davis, 2007). Gibson et al. (2013), for example, illustrate how audio diaries, photovoice, and interviews can be combined for use with young men with disabilities. Linzmayer and Halpenny (2013), in turn, used sand tray pictures as a visual research method for use with children.

Using mixed methods, although complicating the research process and making analysis more arduous, but adding a greater variety of data facilitates the engagement of youth who may not naturally gravitate towards photovoice but would prefer other arts-based methods (Gold, 2007; Gubrium & Torres, 2013; Hannay et al., 2013; Richardson & Nuru-Jeter, 2012). For the purposes of this book, the focus will be on photovoice as either the sole or primary method of inquiry.

Cameras, not surprisingly, can capture and represent the subjective and the objective simultaneously (Kalmanowitz, 2013). Photos can help solidify messages in a way that few mediums can. These messages can be enhanced through accompanying narratives. K. McNiff (2013), although referring specifically to creative writing, discusses narratives and how they provide an avenue for the expression of human experience, and this has relevance to photographic narratives. Narratives, in the case of photovoice accompanying photos or as part of reflexive journals, contribute to individual and collective memories.

Having participants maintain reflexive journals, for example, brings an added dimension to an analysis, although not all youth will be prone to using this method, and it is suggested that it not be required but optional. This type of journal takes on added significance in the case of youth participants who face challenges in the recall of memories or who find that writing enhances their experiences (Genoe & Dupuis, 2013). Having a reflexive journal takes away the anxiety of being able to recall on the spot. The level of detail and structure of this journal can be flexible enough to take into account local circumstances and goals, becoming another point of analysis, and adding an even greater nuanced perspective on photos and narratives, but also complicating the data analyzing process.

YOUTH PARTICIPATION IN DATA ANALYSIS

Before proceeding to conducting an analysis, we need to stop and acknowledge the participatory nature of photovoice analysis, which is one of the key elements in making this arts-based method appeal to groups that are marginalized. It is important to note that although participatory action research is increasingly popular with youth (Jardine & James, 2012), their involvement has not included data analysis, a critical element in any form of research, but particularly in CBPR (Foster-Fishman et al., 2010).

This absence of youth involved in data analysis is particularly perplexing and disturbing. It may be the result of adults thinking that youth would not be interested, or that their involvement would prove to be too labor intensive. Highly detailed descriptions of youth engaging in data analysis are missing from the literature, limiting our understanding of the process and issues faced.

Not surprisingly, participatory research necessitates that participatory analysis be integral to the process (Nind, 2011; Shilton & Srinivasan, 2008). Special attention is needed in the case of youth, for example, who have disabilities to ensure that their voices are not lost in the hectic and fast pace of data analysis (Teachman & Gibson, 2012). In the case of urban youth photovoice, all youth are central actors in the analysis with adults acting as facilitators of the process.

Photovoice enabled participants to be powerful actors in the research process as they generated and interpreted data about their own lived experiences and aspirations. In using photography, the participants distance themselves somewhat from embodied experience, taking on the role of contemplative "quasi-outsider," which in turn, invites deeper reflection and more meaningful interpretation. . . . This deep reflection is indicative of the innovative approach of Photovoice upon which its validity in research with young people rests (Brown & Powell, 2012, p. 139).

It can be argued that youth empowerment cannot be turned on and off during various phases of the research process, as if it were a faucet.

Youth photovoice participants bring an interpretative capacity unencumbered by theoretical biases (Schubotz, 2012). This ability takes on greater prominence since it is their research and views that count in photovoice (Gubrium & Torres, 2013). In essence, they are center stage in this process. Furthermore, their ability to create narrative should not be devalued. Piper and Frankham (2007) argue that it should "be subject to the same processes of deconstruction as other texts produced under the aegis of voice activities" (p. 373). Nevertheless, researchers must be prepared to struggle with how to reduce the length of narratives without losing sight of their valuable message and disrespecting the owners of those narratives. Mair and Kieran (2007), for example, raise a series of provocative questions concerning how images must be weighed against narratives, since these interpretations are integral to arts-based visual research methods such as photovoice.

TYPES AND LEVELS OF ANALYSES

Photovoice provides a high level of flexibility regarding the types and levels of analyses that can be used to arrive at key themes and insights into experiences and worldviews. This flexibility can easily be either a blessing or a curse, depending upon the perspective that is taken by researchers, the goals of the project, and the funding source requirements. This section will highlight a range of approaches and considerations to assist in developing an overview before focusing on one approach that, I believe, is simple and the most prevalent in youth photovoice projects.

The use of constant comparison methods of a grounded theory facilitates photovoice analysis (Saimon, Choo, & Bulgiba, 2013; Torres, Meetz, & Smithwick-Leone, 2013). There is little question that pile-sorting, grounded theory, and thematic analysis, a deductive template analytical technique, are very popular approaches towards organizing and analyzing photovoice data (Bharmal et al., 2012; Cabassa, Nicasio, & Whitley, 2013; Harley, 2011; Lichty, 2013). Qualitative research in general, and the arts-based methods in particular, such as photovoice, necessitate both critical and creative thinking and interpretation (Patton et al., 2011; Skinner & Masuda, 2013).

Provision of a detailed map of the process used to make determinations and decisions takes on great significance in helping other researchers and organizations wishing to undertake photovoice. Fortunately, a few researchers have provided detailed maps tied to stages in the analysis of data. Three examples, in particular, will be selected as illustrative of an analysis approach. This detailed map can be conceptualized as process evaluation, making it easier to justify for external funders.

Woodgate & Kreklewetz (2012) propose a three-stage approach to analysis that is quite prevalent in the professional literature:

> Data analysis followed multi-level analytic coding procedures congruent with interpretive qualitative analysis and ethnography. . . . First-level analysis involved isolating concepts or patterns referred to as domains. Second-level analysis involved organizing domains. Through processes of comparing, contrasting, and integrating, items were organized, associated with other items, and linked into higher order patterns. The third level of analysis involved identifying attributes in each domain, and the last level involved discovering relationships among the domains to create themes. Various strategies were used to enhance the rigor of the research process including prolonged engagement with participants and data, careful line-by-line transcript analysis, and detailed memo writing throughout the research process. The researchers independently identified theme areas then jointly refined and linked analytic themes and categories. Discussion of initial interpretations with the youth themselves occurred during the second interviews, which also helped reveal new data and support emerging themes.

Leipert & Anderson (2012), too, propose a three-level approach to analysis, although it differs from that of Woodgate and Kreklewetz (2012):

> Participants' photographs were analyzed using a three-part procedure based on the work of Oliffe et al. In the first stage of analysis, preview, the

researcher views the photographs alongside their titles and narratives about each picture to understand intended representations. The second stage of analysis, cross-photo comparison, is where researchers develop themes that are reflected in the entire photograph collection. The final stage, theorizing, allows researchers to develop abstract understandings by linking themes to the purpose of the study, in this case, identification of challenges and facilitators of rural nursing practice.

Finally, Walsh, Rutherford, and Kuzmak (2010) used a multi-method research approach and utilized ATLAS.ti 5.0, a qualitative data analysis package, to analyze transcribed texts, which consisted of various qualitative data: digital story text, recorded discussion in photovoice, photovoice texts, creative writing discussion, creative writing texts, and recorded discussion during the design charrette session. Bibeau et al. (2012) also used ATLAS to identify common and disparate group themes. Most community organization–sponsored photovoice project data analysis efforts will not be as complicated as that addressed by Walsh, Rutherford, and Kuzmak, or the other two examples above. The following section provides a framework that enjoys widespread popularity because of its ease of use.

FRAMEWORK FOR ANALYSIS AND CONSIDERATIONS

The use of a framework, or guide, to analyze results provides youth photovoice researchers with a "tool" that they can use and follow through all of the stages usually associated with data analysis, visual-based or otherwise. A number of frameworks do exist that have shown positive results because of their ease of use and their ability to highlight key themes and considerations that need to be taken. Rose (2012), for example, recommends a four-step process for content analysis: (1) finding your images; (2) devising your categories for coding; (3) coding the images; and (4) analyzing the results.

Metropolitan Area Planning Council (n.d.), in turn, offered a very popular five-step guide (SHOWeD) that is illustrative of how youth participants can be guided in articulating their thoughts and reactions concerning the photographs that were taken:

S: What do you **See** here?
H: What's really **Happening** here?
O: How does this relate to **Our** lives?
We: **Why** does this situation **Exist**?
D: What can we **Do** about it?

Each of these questions guides participants in a process that is highly ambiguous with no easy "right" and "wrong" answers. Participant ability to tolerate ambiguity is one of the factors that were identified as critical in the selection process. This framework brings into discussion the element of social action, which is essential in urban youth photovoice.

Five aspects of data analysis will be addressed in this section because of their particular significance in youth photovoice: (A) coding of data/group process, (B) relevance and facilitating ease of use, (C) identification of crosscutting themes; (D) contextualization (telling the story); and (E) determination of the social change effort. The reader will see the interrelationship between these five aspects, and how one sets the stage for the following. Each of these considerations and dimensions to photovoice brings inherent rewards and challenges. An urban youth focus adds a geographical context and age factor into these rewards and challenges.

Coding of Data/Group Process

The goal of achieving methodological congruency is very familiar to qualitative researchers, and it certainly applies to photovoice (Plunkett, Leipert, & Ray, 2013). The coding of data, in the case of photovoice, entails working with images and narratives, and represents the initial step in the process of analysis.

An initial preview of the photographs and narratives is recommended as a way of introducing the group to the analysis process. There is no pressure on participants to develop codes or code books during this facet of the analysis process. Familiarizing the group with the data will facilitate the tasks that follow. The coding process assists youth in organizing and interpreting data, with the development of a code book that helps participants categorize reactions and impressions of photographs.

The group, in turn, plays a critical role in separating images and narratives into groupings or themes (Morgan et al., 2010; Padgett, Smith, Derejko, Henwood, & Tiderington, 2013). Green and Kloos (2009) point out that photovoice is essentially an individual-focused and individual-driven method, where individual participants are the center of the research process. Relative frequencies of codes can be calculated to arrive at major themes (Gupta et al., 2013). A voting process is recommended to help facilitate this sorting into themes, and it may be essential in cases where some photos and narratives can easily fall into multiple categories. It is essential that the meaning of the whole is not lost while categorizing these images and narratives. These themes become important in the development of the exhibition and determination of the social change to follow.

A group participatory process wields prodigious influence in the ultimate success of a project through group meaning-making. A goal of analyzing group interpretation of photographs and narratives must be built into the analysis process. Data integration helps bring into focus contextual factors that may either be totally overlooked or minimally attended to in an analysis (Patton, Higgs, & Smith, 2011). Narratives, incidentally, take on added significance in photovoice and serve to help youth researchers to organize, structure, and elicit much needed contextual meaning from data (van Lieshout & Cardiff, 2011). Meaning, it should be emphasized, can be grounded in many different ways (Prior, 2013). Finally, participant reactions to reviewing photographs and narratives will elicit both verbal and nonverbal reactions, and the latter must not be lost during this analysis data phase of the research.

Barlow and Hurlock (2013) specifically address the role and process of the group, for example, which shares many similarities with mutual aid groups in the emphasis on member helping member in sharing reflections. The themes that emerge will wield significant influence in shaping social action/advocacy efforts emanating from the photovoice data. Finally, participants must evaluate how they benefited from the project, and the group, too, must do so from a group perspective. Project analysis involves multiple perspectives and approaches because photovoice necessitates an embrace of a nuanced understanding. Life is not black or white.

Relevance and Facilitating Ease of Use

There are numerous practical considerations and decisions that must be made by the group if data analysis is to be productive and relatively painless. It is important to remember that the written narratives can only cover so much material. In circumstances where the photographer stands with the photograph and narrative during an exhibition, allowing them to answer questions and amplify content as needed, provides greater flexibility in the selection of content. It also introduces other potential issues because facilitators cannot monitor these interactions, and we do not want participants to be hurt when the audience is insensitive, if not cruel. Further, the nature and context of these interactions represent a further form of data that should be captured, if at all possible.

The question of whether, and when, to debrief must be considered. Youth participants may be debriefed at the end of an exhibition. Experience will show that it may be necessary to schedule a specific session sometime shortly afterward, because youth will not be in a mood to be "debriefed" after an exciting evening. This can also transpire during the evaluation of the project, though this may not capture information that is best tapped immediately after an event. Thus, mixed (yes and no) responses to debriefing are to be expected. This phase, too, can be captured by photographs or videos.

Schaefer (2012) addresses another aspect of youth photovoice and draws attention to the importance of knowing how, and why, youth researchers prefer or eschew specific visual methods, and its implications for future developments: "Analyzing young people's motives for using or not using specific visual methods provides an insight into young people's methodological sensitivity and might provide future youth research with valuable insights into young people's everyday lives" (p. 159). A willingness to engage in a highly detailed analysis of data will also vary considerably among young people. Some will gladly see the value and enjoy spending considerable time doing an analysis; others will view this depth of attention as an excuse for action. This tension is not endemic to youth and can be found with other age groups, including university graduate students!

Each participant should be provided with an agreed-upon allotted time period in which to share their thoughts and feelings related to a photograph that they have taken and selected for discussion. This time period can vary depending upon how much time has been scheduled. Facilitators must be flexible, because some of the images may elect a wide response and emotionality. Cutting these discussions short is not recommended. These sessions may even take on the appearance of a "group therapy" session for the uninitiated. There may be situations where some participants would benefit from speaking with someone with mental health qualifications, necessitating that a referral be made (Erdner & Magnusson, 2011). The following chapter delves into this topic in much greater detail and highlights the tensions and key decisions that await the group, with corresponding ethical considerations.

Walker and Early (2010) describe one approach that typifies how this process can unfold:

> Participants presented their chosen photographs and interpretations to the primary researcher by way of individual interviews and follow-up discussions. Data was transcribed by the researchers and analyzed by participants and researchers using the constant-comparative method to identify the significant themes and patterns that emerged. Emergent themes were categorized as impeding or promoting factors or as an action item.

Walker and Early's description is facilitated as long as the number of photographs and narratives are not too numerous. It is not unusual to have well over 200 photographs and narratives, making the categorizing process challenging and time-intensive, as in the case of several youth participants in the Camp CAMERA case presented later on in this book. One effective strategy is to have youth select their top five or six photographs and narratives to be discussed by the group. This number, in turn, can be reduced to two or three per youth participants for an exhibition. The photographs and narratives that are not selected can still be part of an analysis.

Where should analysis transpire? This is a topic that is rarely discussed in the professional literature, and it may seem like an inane question. This may be because it is assumed that this task should transpire in a setting that is conducive to this activity, and in a place that participants feel safe. It is worth taking a moment on this. Yes, it should be in a setting that is accessible (culturally, psychologically, geographically, and operationally). In all likelihood, this will be in a community setting. It can also occur in a more formalized setting such as a university or college.

My experience has been that when the group wants such a setting, it conveys to participants that it is a serious undertaking. It is wise to ask participants their preference, but we must be prepared to review the advantages and disadvantages of various settings and not assume that it must be in the community. Community settings can be loud and home to a tremendous amount of activities and distractions, and they may not be safe from a psychological perspective.

Identification of Crosscutting Themes

The identification of crosscutting themes represents a stage in a long process, and one that rarely results in surprises if there has been active and meaningful participation on the part of youth. Themes will relate to the central purpose of the photovoice project. Invariably, these will highlight obstacles and resistance youth have encountered in their lives. Further, these themes will also identify particularly unresponsive systems and adults in positions of authority. Themes also can be asset-focused, with several examples of this focus being found in the Camp CAMERA case study.

Regardless of how painful the topics, situations and individuals will standout because of the good that transpired. Pride, resilience, hope, and even dreams can also emerge as themes with corresponding images and narratives. This dimension will rarely surprise me. It is important to keep in mind that youth, regardless of their dire life experiences and circumstances, still harbor aspirations, and this manages to emerge under the right circumstances. It becomes important that fears, hurt, and sorrow are accompanied by hopes, aspirations, and dreams, and that the individuals who have had perpetuated on them not stand alone. Those individuals and situations that inspired them, too, must find the light of the spotlight. Crosscutting themes can cover a wide variety of subjects, and these will emerge in the course of data analysis.

Contextualization (Telling the Story)

The themes that emerge during photo discussions and reviews of written materials can be tied together to tell a coherent story (Watson & Douglas, 2012). These discussions can be audiotaped or videotaped, or both, and then transcribed for further in-depth analysis and future reference. Major constructs or themes will emerge that will capture key findings or powerful messages (Freedman et al., 2012). Secondary or minor themes, too, can emerge, and these can help the group connect the major portions of the story. The process of constructing and telling a story increases youth critical thinking skills, empowers them, and makes the act of storytelling that much more meaningful and powerful (Chonody, Ferman, Amitrani-Welsh, & Martin, 2013).

The generation of many themes is an ultimate goal. It is not out of the question to have a photovoice project generate over 30 themes (Zenkov et al., 2013). This generation of themes can be quite overwhelming for all parties, researchers as well as participants, and articulating a clear process and possessing the requite competencies to reduce the number of themes, including the will to do so, facilitates storytelling and the mounting of an exhibition. There are a variety of ways to group the photographs and narratives. One popular way is to set aside a number of tables on which the participants can place their photographs and accompanying narratives. As the process unfolds, each table will start taking on a particular meaning or theme (Taiapa, Barnes, & McCreamor, 2013).

Photovoice data lend themselves to being reused, recoded, and remixed (De Lange & Mitchell, 2012). As discussed in the next chapter on ethics, this does raise ethical issues as to who ultimately owns these data, and in the case of those who argue that participants are the owners, and not the researcher, do they give permission for the photos to be reanalyzed? Contextual grounding plays such an influential role in giving meaning to an image. Taking this image out of historical context to a present-day context can render the image less meaningful. If the original photographers are not present, their voices are limited to the images and narratives. Would they still select the same images? Would they have the same reactions or narratives? The subject of reusing images and narrative data has profound ethical implications and warrants attention in the next chapter on ethics.

Determination of the Social Change Effort

Finally, the determination of the change effort that can result from data analysis makes this research project particularly important. This determination will not be a great surprise, since themes emerging and being discussed throughout the analysis process will lend themselves to several projects or targets of social change. The nature and extent of this change effort will vary across photovoice projects. Individual change efforts, of course, can be undertaken. Bringing to the fore a group-focused project adds an important collective dimension to this effort, stressing collective youth empowerment (Catalini & Minkler, 2010; Wilson et al., 2007).

The social change effort that is selected can be limited in scope or quite ambitious, and it will be determined in large part by the amount of support that can be garnered by the group. There may even be a series of change efforts, each relatively small in scope and time-limited, that will eventually lead to more challenging efforts. These types of efforts help a youth group build competencies and confidence (Quintero-Gonzalez & Stewart, 2014; Watson & Douglas, 2012).

Conclusion

This chapter on data analysis has attempted to provide an appreciation of the breadth of approaches available to researchers in categorizing and interpreting image-related data. Further, the quality of the analysis of the findings rests with youth participants as individuals and members of a group, and this makes youth photovoice participatory, empowering, and transformative. Youth, not surprisingly, are rarely interested in theory validation or theory construction; they are interested in gaining awareness and sharing this with interested parties, and then doing something about the causes of pain and sorrow.

Actions rest on the results and the interpretation that youth have. That being said, it is equally important to stress that there is no "standard" way of interpreting and assessing photovoice images and narratives. Some readers may argue that this is a serious limitation, and that it will undermine efforts at widening the acceptance of this method in academic circles, which, in turn, will limit funding possibilities. I would argue that this "flexibility" facilitates, or even encourages, the introduction of new methods that are attuned to cultural nuances, allowing for the results to reflect local circumstances and priorities. This flexibility facilitates implementation of this phase and translation of findings.

The nature of the analysis will be shaped by the goals of the photovoice project, and the role of researcher, co- and otherwise, will be dictated by these goals. This role, at least as how it is conceptualized in this book, it will be facilitative in character. Researchers will no doubt encounter ethical dilemmas in the process of doing analysis and selecting a social change. This issue is dealt with in the next chapter.

7

Ethical Considerations

Introduction

It is appropriate to start this chapter on ethical considerations in the use of photovoice with urban youth with a provocative question that Helen Jones (2010) posed regarding research and ethical intentions: "Is it possible to be aware of our intentions, our interpretations and our relations of power and still act in a way that might be harmful and unethical?" (p. 30). The answer, the reader may be surprised to learn, is a resounding yes. Intentions, although noble, are no guarantee that we will, or can, act in an ethical manner, or think beyond our own self-interests (consciously or unconsciously), making the subject of ethics and youth photovoice of paramount importance.

This chapter will review some of the most important ethical considerations and dilemmas of using photovoice with youth within an urban context, both nationally and internationally. Particular attention will be paid to how age and culture wield a prodigious influence in decision-making, increasing the likelihood of harm and misconduct being perpetrated in the name of good intentions and participatory democracy. Some research dilemmas are related to all phases of a photovoice project, while others may be phase-specific.

The subject of ethics lends itself to very erudite discussions that have appeal for an academic audience but no appeal to a lay audience. Further, Alderson and Morrow (2011) rightly point out the challenges associated with ethical standards: "Much ethics guidance sets high standards, but says little about how the complicated and often messy day-to-day conduct of research can fit these standards" (p. 63). Riele and Brooks (2013) stress the need for using field and real life examples to guide discussions at both the academic and community levels, and for addressing three crosscutting themes: (1) power and agency, (2) protection and harm reduction, and (3) trust and respect. Not surprisingly, their book only scratches the surface of this subject, which will no doubt lead to countless other books on this important topic.

Bridges and McGee (2011) note that "ethics is central to all research" (p. 214). The position that researchers are only as good as their ethical stance and the competence that they bring to research, rather than the technical proficiency they possess, may seem like a radical stance. I would argue that having a clear stance on ethical conduct cannot be taught; research skills, in turn, can be taught. The ethical core of a researcher is something that one brings to a research undertaking such youth photovoice. The moral compass, so to speak, is the core that helps keep us on a clear and purposeful path.

Tolich (2010) warns that research can be compromised if the researcher is reactive rather than proactive in anticipating ethical issues. There will be situations that will prove particularly problematic and totally unexpected in carrying out an urban youth photovoice project, making preparations difficult. Transparency and openness with participants is a goal throughout the research process, and achieving this goal will go a long way toward minimizing ethical misconduct (Leadbeater, Riecken, et al., 2006). This stance then facilitates having transparency and authenticity with the community, which is critical in trusting collaborative partnerships.

We cannot eschew all ethical situations, regardless of how transparent and open we are; when they occur, we can attempt to minimize the potential consequences for youth, their communities, and researchers, and we can have mechanisms in place to help us address them (Anderson & Morrow, 2011). Further, not all ethically compromising situations are of equal importance, further introducing the need for careful and nuanced deliberation into any discussion of ethical issues and misconduct (New Zealand Ministry of Health, 2012).

If a color must be assigned to the subject of ethics and youth photovoice, it would be gray and not black or white. A nuanced interpretation is missing in a black/white dichotomy (Potash, 2013). Nevertheless, Hammersley and Traianou (2012) argue that the primary goal of research is to ensure that it answers important or worthwhile questions, and this goal must not be lost in any discussion of ethics and photovoice, or any other form of research. Addressing important and worthwhile questions will go a long way towards helping all those involved in research to ensure that the process is not ethically compromised (Alderson & Morrow, 2011; Brydon-Miller, 2012).

There are tensions to be expected when methodological innovations are introduced into social research, making ethical considerations that much more challenging (Nind, Wiles, Bengry-Howell, & Crow, 2013). Methodological innovations necessitate pushing boundaries and creating spaces for experimentation to occur, and for taking nuances into account (Horsfall & Higgs, 2013; McNiff, 2013a). Those of us who have undertaken photovoice projects have done so with the best of intentions of addressing the ills caused by a society that is callous at best, or complicit at worst, about marginalized groups in society.

Yet these intentions have not guaranteed that we have successfully navigated turbulent ethical waters, or prevented us from causing unintended harm.

The concept of "harm," in similar fashion to risk, is far from explicit. Many researchers would consider it to be elusive and invisible (Alderson & Morrow, 2011). It becomes a matter of necessity that the subject of ethics be broached in a prominent and systematic manner in the context of youth photovoice, and that integrity and adequacy of ethical conduct be placed front and center (Fisher & Masty, 2006).

Qualitative research, particularly when it is part of a CBPR effort, relies heavily upon engendering trust between researcher and the participant. Photovoice, if ethically compromised, is at best but a shell of its potential. Aluwihare-Samaranaya (2012), for example, addresses the question of the role of the qualitative researcher and its ethical implications: "Certain ethical challenges in qualitative research necessitate sustained attention of two interconnected worlds: the world of the researcher and the world of the participant. A critical view of some of the ethical challenges in the participants' and researchers' world reveals that how we examine both these worlds' effects [sic] how we design our research" (p. 64). Each of these worlds brings complications for youth photovoice. In interactions with each other, these complications are exponentially increased.

Ross et al. (2010b) address nine functions of the ethical conduct of Community-Engaged Research (CEnR), which requires an integrated and comprehensive human subjects protection (HSP) program that addresses concerns that may be prevalent in research where community residents have dual roles as partners and participants. The nine functions are: (1) minimize psychological, safety, and harm risks; (2) reasonable benefit-risk ratio; (3) fair subject selection; (4) adequate monitoring; (5) informed consent; (6) privacy and confidentiality; (7) conflicts of interest; (8) address vulnerabilities; and (9) HSP training. These nine functions get manifested in a variety of ways, and one size does not fit all types of research and circumstances, putting arts-based visual researchers in the difficult situation of having to explain to institutional review boards (IRBs) why their research is "different."

The potential of photovoice to achieve positive change is matched by its potential to compromise human rights, necessitating that a subject that normally is considered "important" take on even greater significance, as in the case of ethical conduct. The subject of ethics and participatory arts-based research, such as visual and digital methods, for example, have started to get increased attention and have raised concerns such as boundaries, recruitment and consent to participate, power of shaping the nature of representation, potential for harm, confidentiality, and release of materials, which will be addressed later on in this chapter (Gubrium, Hill, & Flicker, 2013; Wiles, 2013).

The values and principles outlined in Chapter 4 established a foundation for examining a range of potential ethical conflicts and dilemmas, setting the stage for this chapter's focus on ethics. Some of these ethical challenges will be obvious and therefore will not be of any great surprise. Others will be new and totally unexpected, highlighting the challenges inherent in urban youth photovoice.

Levine (2013) speaks to expecting the unexpected in arts-based research and the importance of improvisation. The same need for improvisation can be seen in youth photovoice ethics.

This chapter includes 11 sections, with each section addressing a specific set of ethical challenges or questions that must be successfully addressed in the course of a photovoice project. Following a section titled "Cautions," the following 11 topics will be addressed: (1) the popularity of youth research and ethical conduct books, (2) the United Nations Convention on the Rights of the Child, (3) the national emphasis on ethics and social research, (4) ethics and arts-based qualitative research, (5) unique ethical challenges in urban youth photovoice, (6) areas of potential ethical conflicts, (7) inclusion/exclusion dilemmas, (8) a participant bill of rights, (9) community rights, (10) the institutional review board (IRB), and (11) the community advisory committee.

Caution

The reader is warned about three issues. First, although each of the following sections addresses a specific set of ethical challenges or sets a historical context, there is considerable overlap between the various sections and challenges, and this may prove confusing at times. Ethics does not lend itself to easy categorization. The emphasis of the ethical topic dictates the category it is put into. That is a judgment call on the part of the author of this book, and it is open to being challenged.

The second issue addresses the language used in ethical discussions and deliberations. Presenting ethical matters as being either "ethical" or "unethical" is a dichotomy that presents this subject as an "either/or" proposition (Jansson, Mitic, Hulten, & Dhami, 2006). A comparable point is the saying: "Are you part of the problem or part of the solution?" Such a frame always finds me as being part of the problem, and negates the multilayered and nuanced nature of the topic, particularly when ethics is grounded within the cultural context of youth and their families.

Finally, the reader must be prepared to enter uncharted waters, and accept the ambiguity and anxiety associated with unclear boundaries or demarcation lines. Arts-based research has the potential to unsettle established ways of thinking, feeling, and acting (Innis, 2013). Kalmanowitz (2013) eloquently speaks to the potential of art to uplift new ways of thinking and informing practice: "Indeed, there are so many ways of knowing but if we want to know through art we try to make manifest through the arts that which is still unsaid. It is through our imagination and creativity combined with the making that something new is formed, and that which is between the words is represented" (p. 150). Having an mind open to all kinds of knowledge and experiences will continue to set fertile grounds for advancement of arts-based methods such as photovoice (Higgs & Titchen, 2011). Ethical subjects and processes, too, may be uncharted, and endemic to any new research method.

Popularity of Youth Research and Ethical Conduct Books

An excellent indicator of the popularity an issue or topic is the number of books that have been written on it, particularly when done over a relatively short period of time. This is certainly not to take away from the influence of scholarly articles. Books on a particular subject get written when there is a sufficient body of knowledge (scholarly articles) and widening interest, causing a demand for a major synthesis of the subject, as well as the advances that emerge from a topic receiving concentrated attention and space.

Fortunately, the growing significance of ethics and youth research has spurred increased scholarly attention on this topic, and this bodes well for future scholarship and research, as evidenced by the increasing number of outstanding books on the subject. The following list and overview of eight books on youth and ethics represents a variety of points of view, and all highlight the unique aspects and challenges of children and youth involvement in research, and thus require focused and specialized treatment.

Riele and Brooks's *Negotiating Ethical Challenges in Youth Research* (2013) is an excellent example of how ethics and youth research is drawing critical attention across academic disciplines and internationally, drawing upon numerous case illustrations to highlight the importance of a nuanced perspective on the subject. Leadbeater and colleagues' *Ethical Issues in Community-Based Research With Children and Youth* (2006) provides researchers with specific guidance in conducting research with children and youth, with an emphasis on how community context must be taken into consideration. Alderson and Morrow's *Ethics of Research With Children and Young People: A Practical Handbook* (2011) provides a comprehensive perspective of the multifaceted aspects of ethics and research with youth, including highly detailed practical advice.

Freeman and Mathison's *Researching Children's Experiences* (2008) stresses a social constructivist methodological perspective, emphasizing the lived experiences and importance of this perspective on research with children. Ross's *Children in Medical Research: Access Versus Protection* (2008) traces the evolution of children involvement in medical research up to the present, contextualizing advances and rights, and providing concrete recommendations and considerations for including children in research while protecting them in the process. Clark's *In a Younger Voice: Doing Child-Centered Qualitative Research* (2010) provides a variety of qualitative child-centered methods, including the use of photography, artwork, and metaphors, and integrating ethical considerations.

Heath and Walker's *Innovations in Youth Research* (2012), although not specifically focused on youth research and ethics, has a theme of ethics that cuts across the contributions of the authors in the book. Sargeant and Harcourt's *Doing Ethical Research With Children* (2012) provides a guide and reflection mechanism from which to view this topic from a variety of perspectives, including youth as equal partners in the research.

The topic of youth work and ethics, too, has emerged to address practice and research with youth (Banks, 2010; Sercombe, 2010), expanding the subject into other arenas that are youth-focused, and highlighting how age becomes a critical factor in the formulation of ethical standards and procedures. Heath and Walker's edited book, *Innovations in Youth Research* (2012), devotes considerable attention to ethical concerns. This and other books on youth work emphasize activities and strategies, with ethics also being addressed.

These books provide countless field-based case examples of ethical dilemmas that were unexpected and required researchers to think and act on the spot to address unexpected situations. Not surprisingly, the focus of these books is mostly on qualitative forms of research, including those that are arts-based and visually based. Needless to say, there is no book specifically focused on ethics and photovoice, let alone ethics and youth photovoice, although it is just a question of time before one is written.

United Nations Convention on the Rights of the Child

Any search for one monumental act that spurred dramatic advances in a field or discipline is bound to create controversies. Clearly, singling out an event that changed the course of ethics and youth research is certainly not an exception. Still, it is important to acknowledge the role of the United Nations Convention on the Rights of the Child (1989), which embraced the rights of children to form and express their views on what matters in their lives and their lived experiences (Alderson & Morrow, 2011; Freeman & Mathison, 2008). It is the most widely ratified human rights convention. Unfortunately, the United States is one of two nations, with Somalia being the other nation, that did not ratify the convention.

Even though the United States did not ratify this convention, the existence of this human rights document set the stage for why children and youth cannot be considered extensions of adults. Elevating their rights to the status of inalienable human rights, including valuing their perspectives and opinions, necessitates that social research intended to better their circumstances must find a way of empowering them and not suppressing their rights in the process. The role and influence of this UN convention may not be at the top of everyone's list, but there is no denying that it will appear near the top on everyone's list.

National Emphasis on Ethics and Social Research

National and international attention on ethics and social research signifies this topic is gaining in importance. It is important to pause and acknowledge that ethical conduct and research assumed greater prominence with the issuing of the report of the National Commission for the Protection of Human Subjects of Biomedical and Behavioral Research in 1978, commonly referred to as the Belmont Report. This historic report is widely credited with establishing principles that have served as a foundation for ethical conduct and research. Concepts such as informed consent, respect for persons, beneficence, and justice, for example, were part of this reports' recommendations, helping to provide a framework from which to address ethical decision-making.

Yet, although the Belmont Report highlighted and affirmed the importance of ethical standards and conduct, it did not adequately address a number of key dimensions, such as communities, or provide guidelines for engaging communities, or address the role of participants as co-researchers (Flicker, Travers, Guta, McDonald, & Meagher, 2007; Hacker, 2013; Williams et al., 2010). Advances that have occurred in social research since the report was issued, particularly in arts-based qualitative research, have significant relevance to highly vulnerable population groups, and have set the need for a major national effort at updating this report (Cerulli, 2011).

In 2012, New Zealand's Ministry of Health issued a report titled *Ethical Guidelines for Observational Studies: Observational Research, Audits and Related Activities*, which represents an important, if not seminal, contribution to moving this form of qualitative research forward by acknowledging its uniqueness, and why conventional scientific approaches to ethical review must be modified to take this into account in reviews. A comparable report issued by the United States on photovoice and other forms of arts-based qualitative research would represent a major step forward in helping to advance research in this realm internationally (Alderson & Morrow, 2011).

Lafrenière, Hurlimann, Menuz, & Godard (2013) specifically address arts-based research and the absence of literature on this form of research and ethics:

> No doubt, any research involving human beings is framed by national and international ethical guidelines that should apply in any case, including in arts-based research. Yet, it remains to be seen whether such guidelines that do not focus on or even consider the potential particularities of arts-based methods may always be appropriate or practicable given the many different contexts in which such methods may be used. The lack of resources and literature addressing ethical issues associated with arts-based methods may be problematic for researchers. It is thus important for them to add to the current knowledge and feed the debate on this topic, by explicitly addressing and documenting the ethical issues that they may encounter when conducting their study.

This absence of scholarly attention will no doubt change in the near future. Nevertheless, this is an important "hole" that has profound implications for the field.

Photovoice provides researchers with a powerful tool for achieving a wide range of social goals in a manner that is participatory and affirming. Photovoice, by its very nature, introduces situations and tensions that can compromise its potential for achieving noble intentions. These tensions or challenges can be called by many different names (Boote, Baird, & Beecroft, 2010). Attaching an ethical label to them increases their significance and the urgency of not overlooking or undervaluing them, and also puts the researcher on notice, so to speak (H. Jones, 2010). It is important to emphasize that generic responses are minimally helpful in addressing ethical dilemmas that necessitate specific deliberations and responses (Leadbeater, Barrister, Benoit, Jansson, Marshall, & Riecken, 2006).

Ethics and Arts-Based Qualitative Research

Any discussion concerning ethical behavior and youth photovoice must first be grounded within ethical considerations regarding qualitative and arts-based research, including CBPR. How best to conceptualize and address areas of potential ethical conflicts is not new to qualitative research, resulting in probing questions and discussions.

There are various ways of looking at ethical dilemmas and conduct, with the posing of key questions and development of frameworks being two popular ways. Creswell (2013a), for example, advocates for thinking and addressing potential ethical issues from a research phase perspective to ensure that they not be overlooked. Separating the research processes into phases forces researchers to focus on the particular tasks and goals for each phase, including the potential ethical dilemmas associated with that particular phase (Banister & Daly, 2006). Carrying out the technical aspects of research projects is sufficiently challenging, making it easier to overlook ethical considerations.

Although this grounding makes coverage of ethics that much more challenging, it also signals to researchers the need to acknowledge the interrelationship between researchers, participants, and community context (Hacker, 2013). This interrelationship makes photovoice powerful as a method, but it also blurs boundaries between these three arenas, introducing tension and possible conflicts. Youth photovoice is an excellent example of how tensions and potential conflicts are integral to using this arts-based qualitative method.

Qualitative research has made significant strides in focusing on the importance of ethical decision-making (Creswell, 2013b). Hammersley and Traianou (2012), for example, specifically focus their attention on ethical behavior and qualitative research, and they pose four questions that help guide qualitative researchers: (1) What is ethical and unethical in qualitative research? (2) What does it mean to be ethical or unethical? (3) Who should judge whether or not qualitative researchers are being ethical? (4) How is this to be done? These four questions do not have definitive answers, but they highlight the prevalence of ambiguities and the role of context and culture in shaping nuanced responses to these complex questions.

Pink's (2007) comments regarding ethnography are also applicable to photovoice: "The issue of ethics in ethnography work refers to more than simply the ethical conduct of the researcher. Rather, it demands that ethnographers develop an understanding of the ethical context(s) in which they work a reflexive approach to their own ethical beliefs, and a critical approach to the idea that *one* ethical code of conduct be hierarchically superior to all others" (p. 37). The subject of context has permeated all of the previous chapters, and it stands to reason that it will in this and the following chapters. This attention and prominence given to context makes ethical behavior in conducting photovoice inquiry extremely challenging for all parties involved in this endeavor.

Wang and Redwood-Jones (2011), in a rare and pioneering article specifically focused on ethics and photovoice, identified four distinct areas of potential conflict for researchers that must be a part of any serious discussion on youth photovoice ethics: (1) intrusion into one's private space, (2) disclosure of embarrassing facts about individuals, (3) being placed in false light by images, and (4) protection against the use of a person's likeness for commercial benefit. There are ways of minimizing the potential for ethical breaches, however. One popular way is to engage in co-investigation, or collaborative inquiry, with participants.

Collaborative inquiry is a concept that the research community uses to describe forms of research that stress participatory principles, with mutually beneficial benefits, including minimizing potential ethical dilemmas, as espoused in this book (Bridges & McGee, 2011). This approach to knowledge creation is antithetical to the central arguments used by positivist researchers. Wiersma (2011), for example, sees tremendous value in using photovoice as a method for undertaking research "with" and not "for" or "on" people with early stage Alzheimer's disease, with implications for minimizing ethical dilemmas often associated with research and highly marginalized groups.

There are an endless number of topics that warrant closer attention regarding youth photovoice. One such topic is monetary payment. Why is that not surprising? Monetary payment, as initially discussed in Chapter 5, may raise ethical dilemmas (Head, 2009). It is necessary to differentiate between four types of payments (Wendler, Rackoff, Emanuel, & Grady, 2002): (1) reimbursement, (2) compensation, (3) appreciation, and (4) incentive. Wendler et al. (2002) provide eleven safeguards to avoid ethical conflicts when involving children and youth in research, although they can also be applied to adults:

(1) Develop guidelines for all four types of payment;
(2) Adopt an explicit policy on advertising payment to children;
(3) Require explicit justification for all incentives;
(4) Allow that children are paid less than adults in identical studies;
(5) Ensure payment to subjects who withdraw;

    (6) Consider carefully any cases when there is concern that people are consenting because of payment and not because they wish to take part;

    (7) Develop a general policy on describing payments in consent and asset forms;

    (8) Make direct payments to the proper party;

    (9) Avoid lump sum payments;

   (10) Consider deferred payments;

   (11) Consider non-cash payments. (pp. 169–170)

A review of the above guidelines will surely raise questions or concerns about some, and that is to be expected. For example, youth advocates will take issue with paying youth less than adults. Why must non-cash payments be emphasized over cash payments? Would adults prefer non-cash over cash? I seriously doubt it. So why should we consider it for youth?

Budgeting and contracting bring ethical considerations and dilemmas, particularly the fair distribution of resources (Alderson & Morrow, 2011). Paying participants a fair wage falls within this realm. Some researchers may fear paying youth as a form of manipulation and therefore breaching an ethical standard, for example. How youth spend this money, too, brings up other possible concerns.

Youth may spend their money on alcohol and cigarettes, for example, compromising their health status. These and other "vices" may not raise concerns if we were discussing adults, but they do when discussing youth. Yet if the photovoice project is addressing marginalized youth, then finances are a major issue or challenge in their lives. My philosophy is that I am being paid for this work, and why shouldn't youth get paid, too? Their time, what little they have discretion over, is very limited, and this needs to be recognized monetarily. In light of the emphasis of money in our society, it also sends an important message to their parents and legal guardians that the work that they are doing is very important.

There are a variety of ways that monetary payments can be handled. I have, for example, written funding for youth participants into grants, with half of their weekly stipend being set aside in a bank account, and half being provided to them to spend as they wish. At the completion of the project, the bank accounts are "officially" turned over to participants. One of the goals of this strategy is to encourage youth to save money, but it also acknowledges that they have daily expenses. A discussion related to payment provides all participants with an opportunity to address the subject of money and possible ways that it can compromise decision-making.

Job titles are another way in which ethical dilemmas can occur. Researchers must be careful not to create jobs and job titles that mask significant power differentials, nor should they label youth co-researchers as "junior" researchers (Greene, 2013). There is a potential ethical trap in giving the community the impression that residents are playing decision-making roles in the research when they are not. We would not think of doing this with adults, and we should not consider it with youth. Further, youth are not to assume menial jobs that have "fancy" titles attached to the job descriptions.

Hatch (2002) identifies the need for reciprocity (giving back to the community) to be considered an ethical issue in qualitative research projects, although this argument can also be made for quantitative research. Photovoice is certainly not an exception, and giving back to a community is a key value and component guiding this research method. As addressed in Chapter 4, photovoice is community-centered and intended to improve the life of a particular segment of the community, and thereby the community in general. Failure to have direct and immediate benefits can be viewed as a breach of ethics.

Unique Ethical Challenges in Urban Youth Photovoice

The role and importance of ethical standards and widely accepted decision-making processes for resolving ethical conflicts, and in informing all facets of community research, are indisputable. The promulgation of standards and procedures related to ethics serves to bring distinct fields of practice together under one roof, so to speak. All forms of research pose ethical challenges (Randall & Rouncefield, 2010). There is a common understanding that the intensity of ethical scrutiny must be proportional to the level of risk of the intervention (New Zealand Ministry of Health, 2012).

Ross (2006) reminds us that, historically, medical research largely eschewed women and children ("women and children last"). Traditionally, adult white males were the focus of attention, which brought with it the benefits of this knowledge through improved medicine and health procedures. There is a tension between access and protection, and nowhere is this more strongly experienced than with low-income children and youth of color. It can certainly be argued that all population subgroups bring inherent ethical challenges because of their unique circumstances, including all other forms of qualitative research, which also bring unique challenges (Patton, Higgs, & Smith, 2011).

Community-based participatory research (CBPR), sometimes referred to as youth participatory action research (YPAR) (Batsleer, 2010) with youth brings added challenges (Coser et al., 2014; Leadbeater, Barrister, et al., 2006), as in the case of photovoice. Adult power and authority are a "core" concern when researchers "study down," rather than "study with" youth (Best, 2007), resulting in exploitation of youth (Joanou, 2009). Bringing a participatory stance, in turn, serves to minimize, but not totally eliminate, this potential power differential and ethical issue associated with this status (Patton, Higgs, & Smith, 2011).

Langman and Pick (2013) address research photography ethics from a dignity-in-context perspective, which has implications for photovoice projects because of the emphasis this perspective puts on respect:

The first, dignity-in-outcome, assists deciding what and whether to photograph by drawing attention to the need for those being researched to benefit from the research, to present an authentic view of the situation and to ensure that participants are not demeaned or reduced. The second is dignity-in-process that helps researchers decide why and how to photograph in terms of involving those being researched in the way an image is captured, choosing the right angle for the image and the impression the image will give if and when it is published.

Youth benefit from Langman and Pick's framework because of how they often are disrespected by adults due to their age. Emphasizing authenticity places youth in decision-making roles, so that their perceptions must be considered.

Morrow (2012) comments on the universal aspects of research and the existence of variations that have direct applicability to youth photovoice: "Research ethics exist to ensure that the principles of justice, respect, and the avoidance of harm are upheld, by using agreed standards. These principles are universal, though there many subtleties and diversities, and how principles are understood, interpreted, and practised can vary from place to place" (p. 24). The subtleties and diversities Morrow makes reference to can have a significant influence on how ethical behavior is anticipated, judged, and acted upon.

Youth-involved/focused community participatory research brings an added dimension to ethical conduct that must be spotlighted if urban youth photovoice is to make significant contributions to the practice of this method and the lives it seeks to alter, and not compromise youth participants in the process. Youth as equal partners in a research endeavor brings with it all of the tensions associated with any collaborative venture, and also some additional ones resulting from the disparities in age between adults and youth (Sargeant & Harcourt, 2012). Youth agency (competence and ability to act independently) emerges as a potential area of difference, for example.

Yates (2010) observes that the good intentions associated with participatory visual research methods also bring potential for conflict:

> The decision to use participatory visual methods with young people in education, health or public policy research is linked to a desire to allow them to have some greater voice in the research and the professional activities that impact on their lives. But how that 'voice' is produced, whose voice it represents, and how the product of that research is used and interpreted are all contentious issues for researchers. (p. 280)

Attention to ethics helps increase the likelihood of a youth photovoice project achieving success and paving the way for future research projects by establishing a foundation based on mutual trust and benefits.

There is agreement that age of consent brings with it added responsibilities, and that there are aspects of ethical conduct that get complicated when cultural factors enter into the decision-making process. As it is with any other age group, undertaking research with youth is fraught with challenges, some obvious and others less obvious. The difference in age between youth photovoice participants and adult co-facilitators, in the case where one is an academic or professional and the other is a youth member, can be both a barrier as well as a facilitating factor for building trust: "Furthermore, the fact that children have the undivided attention of an adult who values and respects their perspectives can give them the space and confidence to disclose more than what is immediately apparent in the photograph" (Graham & Kilpatrick, 2010, p. 103). Trust is a two-way street, and this needs to be acknowledged openly. This trust must be authentic for youth photovoice to be in a position to maximize its potential.

The reader may question this last statement and ask why trust is considered an ethical issue in youth photovoice. Leonard (2007) addresses the subject of gatekeepers and the role and importance of presentation of one-self as a "quasi-adult" in order for researchers to negotiate systems that may feel uncomfortable with youth as researchers and "quasi-child or youth" in interactions and negotiations with youth. This shifting in roles and appearance management is viewed as essential in order to carry out youth research projects. This shifting is not unique to arts-based qualitative research, however, and this perspective can be found in the world of practice. In social work, for example, it brings to mind the concept of "conscious use of self," which captures this element in addition to others. It does raise questions of authenticity, with no easy answers.

Mockler (2011) addresses the subject of authenticity from a research design perspective, discussing the role and importance of congruence between the researcher and how research is carried out. Lack of authenticity results in a series of disconnects that can compromise the quality of a study in a variety of ways, including ethically. Youth photovoice will create an atmosphere or climate that will break down barriers between adult and youth researchers, allowing all parties to know each other in ways that transcends research roles. Lack of authenticity on the part of adult researchers will quickly become known to youth, who can then question the motivation of researchers and what they say they believe in.

Initiating youth research, such as photovoice, within systems dominated by adults requires researchers to navigate their way through multiple gatekeepers: "There are no easy solutions to the difficulties associated with achieving a balance between these sometimes contradictory aims, but childhood researchers need to engage in an ongoing process of reflection and make public the rationales that underlie the compromises they subsequently make" (Leonard, 2007, p. 154). Gatekeepers also can be found in all communities, posing similar challenges and requiring the need to assess in depth what they bring to a photovoice and what the tradeoffs are. Gatekeepers, as discussed in Chapter 7, can pose ethical dilemmas.

CBPR (or YBPR), as highlighted throughout this book, for example, is exciting and has immense potential to significantly and positively alter the lives of urban marginalized youth (Jeanes & Kay, 2013). Nevertheless, this form of research is also fraught with potential tensions and conflicts for researchers, particularly when this research is firmly grounded within a community context and the views of community participants are counter to those of authorities in power (Bessant, Emslie, & Watts, 2013).

Photovoice as a form of CBPR adds another layer of potential ethical dilemmas that complicates a process that is difficult to begin with. Ethnography stresses the importance of ethics, politics, and representation, while also introducing another layer of challenges (H. Jones, 2010). Mikesell, Bromley, & Khodyakov (2013) reviewed the literature on ethics and CBPR and concluded that the rights and well-being of communities requires additional ethical considerations focused beyond the individual, and specifically on communities. Unfortunately, these considerations, although discussed in the literature, have not benefitted from the synthesis and analysis that is required to move discussion and have recommendations evolve.

Riele (2013) maps out an ethical terrain for youth-focused/involved research that is challenging and highlights the explicit and implicit role of values and principles: "The ethical conduct of youth research requires deliberation on values and principles, the exercise of judgment, and appreciation of context" (p. 3). Heath and Walker (2012a), too, raise the specter of ethical dilemmas with CBPR and youth: "A commitment to participatory approaches represents a very specific ethical stance in relation to youth research . . . 'youth-friendly' methods are frequently deployed within participatory research, yet their very 'friendliness' can sometimes be a source of ethical concern" (pp. 10–11). An ethical minefield may be a more graphic analogy to use in describing these challenges. If researchers are adverse to crossing minefields, then they should stop being researchers. Helping professional practitioners, too, encounter ethical challenges on a daily basis in the course of their work.

As with any community-based participatory research method, there is serious consideration given to ethical behavior on the part of both the leadership and participants. Photovoice is certainly no exception (Clark, Prosser, & Wiles, 2010; Harper, 2003). Pope, De Luca, and Tolich (2010, p. 33) describe a research process that is anything but lineal and neat: "Qualitative research, especially visual ethnography, is an iterative not a linear process, replete with good intentions, false starts, mistaken assumptions, miscommunication and a continually revised statement of the problem. That the camera freezes everything and everyone in the frame only complicates ethical considerations."

I am always very fond of saying that research is messy; and good research is even messier. "Good" research requires that careful thought be given to participant rights and community rights, as addressed later on in this chapter. Ethical conduct takes on even greater significance in the case of research involving youth (Riele & Brooks, 2013). The question of ethical conduct is not restricted to the researcher but is also applicable to participants (Mitchell, 2011).

Martinez, Carter-Pokras, and Brown (2009) argue that the first principle of any community-based participatory research is to arrive at a locally defined definition of "community." Different population groups may define community differently because of their unique experiences and vantage points within this ecological context (Kegler, Rigler, & Honeycutt, 2011). This takes on added significance when a photovoice project seeks to convey an image of a community as opposed to that of a select group. This takes on great significance because it is arduous, and some would argue, impossible, since communities consist of many different subgroups.

The influence of context permeates qualitative research, and it is prominent in shaping how youth view their surroundings, as evidenced in Ritterbusch's (2011) study. Ritterbusch, based upon participatory action research with Colombian street girls, shows how context also influences key ethical concepts, resulting in discrepancies between human subject concepts such as definitions of childhood, vulnerability, protection, and consent. How these concepts get contextualized is influenced by places, spaces, culture, age, and local circumstances. This need to contextualize ethical concepts takes on even greater significance when photovoice is used in non-Western cultures without the safeguards usually associated with IRBs, which have serious limitations, as addressed later on in this chapter.

Youth are an excellent example of a highly vulnerable and marginalized group, since they live in communities where they have been disenfranchised from decision-making roles (Evans, 2007). Their use of photovoice to capture their definition of community will differ significantly from that of adults in the same community, for example, and that should come as any great surprise to the reader. Cultural and local circumstances may thrust youth into adult roles, even though from an age-chronological standpoint they still are youth (Brooks, 2013). Last, safety becomes a consideration in how photovoice projects get conceptualized and implemented, particularly in social-ecological contexts where violence (physical and psychological) is a common occurrence, which will be addressed later in this chapter (Graham et al., 2013).

Tunnell (2012), in a rare article focused specifically on the "challenges" of undertaking visual research, touches upon the dangers of this form of research:

> As I am learning, qualitative researchers should not go blindly into the field no matter the research strategy or instrument. From observation to participant observation, from interviewing to photographing, the research setting seems littered with one potential risk after another. Despite my assumption that photographing a statue or a defunct business was absent of any risk, I learned otherwise and now realize that visual research, like any qualitative research, has both its rewards and its risks. Just as we try and consider the potential risks of raising questions to our participants, we should likewise consider the same when raising a camera to the eye. (p. 350)

Visual research has little meaning without a contextual grounding or background to help the person taking the photograph, (and the viewer) understand and appreciate how images relate to the surroundings. This places the power to shape the central message in the hands of the individual who should have this power. Empowerment transpires when this occurs, and it requires reintroducing an urban context to any discussion of youth photovoice before proceeding with areas of potential ethical conflicts.

Photovoice is a method that places tremendous emphasis on context, and it stands to reason that geographical context, too, must enter into any reasoned discussion of "urban youth photovoice." Factors related to population density, lack of privacy, safety, police scrutiny, access to quality health care, negative publicity by news media, and negative overall reputation within the broader context all come together to shape a context that is not facilitative of empowerment and youth. These factors or forces must be taken into account in discussing urban youth photovoice ethics.

AREAS OF POTENTIAL ETHICAL CONFLICTS

This section addresses six major topic areas of potential conflict in urban youth photovoice: (A) private issues/confidentiality, (B) protection of participants, (C) ownership of photographs/narratives, (D) distortion of images/reinforcement of negative stereotypes, (E) consent agreements, and (F) inclusion/exclusion dilemmas. This list is far from exhaustive and meant to be illustrative. Further, these topics are not presented in any order of importance and are not mutually exclusive of each other. Nevertheless, the following categories are typically found in the literature on ethical conduct and qualitative research, particularly that which is arts-based.

Private Issues/Confidentiality

Confidentiality is a considered a cornerstone of ethics. Privacy and confidentiality are on every researcher's list of topics in any discussion of ethical conduct and research, qualitative or quantitative. Youth photovoice participants have every expectation that what is shared in the group stays in the group, unless there is an explicit agreement to share information regarding discussions outside of the group. There are accidental breaches of confidentiality when participants discuss their experiences in a photovoice project with outsiders, or when researchers to do the same with peers (Wiles, 2013). Individual rights must be weighed against group rights in decision-making and ethical deliberations (Marshall & Shepard, 2006).

There are complications regarding youth photovoice. For example, how are youth to respond to situations where parents demand to know what transpired in group sessions? What if youth refuse to share as per their agreement, even though parents are aware that youth would violate their agreement in doing so? Facilitators must be prepared to address situations such as these as part of their meetings with participants and their parents or legal guardians. Breach of this confidentiality can have a profound impact on trust within the group and compromise a project.

Protection of Participants

The challenge of engaging in research on a topic that is laden with emotions because of injustices that have been perpetrated on the youth participants is a powerful motivator, and a cause of considerable tension.

Kirshner, Pozzoboni, and Jones (2011) address this factor as it relates to activism and research when they are closely tied together: "This combination of activism and inquiry can pose a cognitive challenge for participants, who must coordinate their emotional investment in a specific outcome with openness to unexpected or disconfirming evidence. We call this process managing bias" (p. 140).

The ability of youth participants to manage their emotions to create positive change puts the team involved in a research project in a precarious position—on one level, the emotional investment in engaging in the research and activism is a powerful motivator that can be channeled into a positive outcome; on another level, too much emotion can cloud judgment and engender reactions that are counterproductive to the social change goal (Wood, 2010).

The psychological and physical safety of the participants is always on the mind of a researcher or practitioner. Cheon (2011), for example, addresses the ethical challenge of positive youth development ensuring that youth are safe from harm. Harm can be invisible and elusive, and it is highly dependent upon who is being asked (Alderson & Morrow, 2011). All social research brings with it an element of risk of harm (Wiles, 2013): "Despite some researchers' claims that social research is relatively risk-free, there is evidence that it poses a range of potential risks for both research participants and researchers" (p. 67). Youth research brings with it a heightened awareness of how participation in photovoice must not result in harming the youth participants.

Graham and Kilpatrick (2010) address the impact of emotionality in the use of photography with children, and the potential for harming them:

> Photographs are powerful images that enhance the credibility and authenticity of children's stories. They communicate meaning to audiences by liberating children's stilted and often disjointed dialogue, and provide visual impact and emotional intensity to the voices of the least heard. However, it is the intensity of the stories that emerge that leads to the need for caution when using photographs, or other creative visual methods, especially with children. (p. 99)

Graham and Kilpatrick's cautions are validated by many other scholars undertaking arts-based research.

Emotionally laden content may precipitate participants having to spend additional time and energy addressing the pain caused by traumatic events in their lives. This can occur throughout all phases of a photovoice project. For example, these memories may be heightened when the group begins the selection of photographs and narratives for the exhibit. The exhibition, too, may present difficult situations because the audience may not respond in the manner that youth wanted them to respond, and thus not affirm their experiences. Youth options for getting help are very much dependent upon adult authorities saying that they can. Photovoice sessions may prove to be an attractive outlet for sharing pain that they have been reluctant to share in the past.

Developing mechanisms to help ensure that youth undergoing these intense emotional situations have a protocol that they can follow to get assistance is highly recommended. It may be a buddy system, whereby they have a contact person within the group, or access to co-facilitators. It should be stressed that facilitators can "normalize" these reactions by raising the topic during the contracting with participants and throughout various parts of the project. Seeking assistance should not be viewed as a "pathological" response. Co-facilitators, for example, may be able to share experiences they may have had during a research project that elicited a revisiting of a painful experience.

When photovoice projects focus on a population group facing a situation that is stigmatizing, extra care must be taken to ensure that they are not further stigmatize and hurt (Ballermini, 1997; Walsh, Hewson, Shier, & Morales, 2008). Photovoice participants may re-experience traumatic events that necessitate professional follow-up (Leicher, Lagarde, & Lemaire, 2013; Palibroada, Krieg, Murdock, & Havelock, 2009; Ruiz-Casares, 2013). Precautionary measures or protocols must be in place to help ensure that youth participants are not harmed physically or psychologically (Yuile, Pepler, Craig, & Connolly, 2006). In addition, careful screening must take place to ensure that participants are able to engage in a project that may cause them to confront unresolved feelings.

McAreavey and Das (2013) raise issues about how interactions with community gatekeepers can present ethical dilemmas, which are often not discussed in the literature, even though gatekeepers are often integral to most forms of community research. Photovoice and other visual-focused methods are certainly no exception to involvement of gatekeepers (Eglinton, 2013; Gubrium, Hill, & Flicker, 2013; Harley, 2012). Youth may encounter community residents who do not take them, or their project, seriously, and who still view youth from a marginalized position (Alderson & Morrow, 2011). Their telephone calls and efforts to meet to take photographs, for example, may be ignored or demeaned. The psychological harm resulting from these experiences can be quite profound and long-lasting, and can seriously compromise a photovoice research project.

In turning to physical safety, there is a need to differentiate between situational safety threats, which can occur at any place and time and are therefore arduous to predict, from locational safety threats, which refers to settings and geographical areas that have a high likelihood of activities that can lead to physical harm (Wiles, 2013). Physical violence can often be an integral part of the daily existence of urban youth. Undertaking a photovoice project does not magically protect participants from the potential of physical violence or even death. Photovoice projects must be prepared to address how to help increase the likelihood that participants are not physically harmed. This may entail undertaking conflict resolution training as a means of reducing the likelihood of physical encounters.

Metropolitan Area Planning Council (n.d.) identified a series of strategies that can help minimize physical safety concerns: (1) do not take unnecessary risks; (2) only go into areas where you feel confident; (3) if in doubt about an area, partner with another participant; and (4) always be aware of your environment. The Asian Health Center (n.d.) also notes that when someone is aggressive, it is important to stay calm. Further, if someone wants the camera, for example, it is important not to resist.

Protocols, as addressed earlier, can be developed specifically to address the population group that is the focus of photovoice, as in the case of women and intimate partner violence (Ponic & Jategaonker, 2012), or in the case of communities (Wilhelm & Cheecham, 2013). Debriefing sessions can be structured into each session, for example, and be part of a protocol. Involving interested parties in developing these protocols helps to ensure ownership of these protocols, and that they respect and incorporate cultural factors unique to the area and population group involved (Boote, Baird, & Beecroft, 2010).

It is appropriate to end this section on risk with a quote from Wiles (2013) concerning assessment of risk: "Assessment of risk, harm and benefits are far from straightforward. It is not possible to identify all risks that an individual might encounter from participating in research" (p. 57). This statement may not be reassuring to those researchers who feel the need to anticipate and control situations so that there are no risks to youth participants. Yet that is the reality. The best we can do is be as prepared as possible. Otherwise, youth photovoice will be relegated to the world of privileged youth, living in privileged surroundings, where the odds of physical and emotional harm are minimal.

Ownership of Photographs/Narratives

Wood and Kidman (2013) discuss the ethical borders of visual research with youth and raise a topic that is rarely addressed in the literature on photovoice: Who has ultimate ownership of intellectual property? Interestingly, it seems like the central focus of ethical reviews tends to fall on the data collection phase, with minimal attention being paid to the dissemination phase that usually consists of scholarly publications and conference presentations (Anderson & Morrow, 2011).

In the case of photovoice, ownership of images and the accompanying narrative represent potential ethical conflicts that are not typically encountered in other forms of qualitative research. This question, incidentally, is not restricted to youth but is applicable to any photovoice participant (Patton, Higgs, & Smith, 2011).

The initial response, in all likelihood, will be that the participants, or creative producers, own the photographs and narratives (Riecken & Strong-Wilson, 2006). In essence, it is their lived experiences and labor that has created this work of art. They, and only they, could have produced this work. The answer to this question is much more complex, however, and deserving of its own section in this book (Thomson, 2008a).

Since the participants are youth, do their parents or legal guardians who gave permission for their participation have this ultimate ownership right? Some may argue that youth participants are the owners, and that if they do not have the ultimate say, it represents a continuation of adult betrayal. It was their project and narratives that shaped the process and outcome, and images and narratives are the artifacts of this experience. Among some ethnic and racial groups, parental power over these photos and narrative would be paramount (Delgado, Jones, & Rohani, 2005). This discussion on ownership must transpire at the beginning of a project, BUT researchers should be aware that it can emerge throughout all phases of the research.

Guillemin and Drew (2010) address the subject of ownership and recommend the use of a structured deliberation process prior to commencement of the act of photography:

> In order to further establish research ownership, participants were also informed during recruitment that a detailed authorisation document would be incorporated into the conclusion of the research interview process. In this document, participants were asked to indicate whether or not they were comfortable for the images they had produced to be used in particular contexts, including academic publications, research reports and a variety of visual presentations such as those at conferences and in public photographic displays. Once photographs containing the faces of participants and other individuals form part of the research data, it is necessary to think even more carefully about aspects of permissions around image generation and use. These issues were also discussed with participants prior to them taking photographs. (p. 180)

The reproduction of photovoice material must be discussed and agreed upon by the researcher, participants, and their families, since it involves youth, and it should be accomplished before photography commences. This negotiation adds another layer to the research process. One recommendation is for adult researchers to negotiate a renewable one-year agreement. This agreement must cover professional presentations, use of content in the classroom for instructional purposes, and scholarly publications. This may seem excessively burdensome for some, but it does highlight how images can exist for an extended period of time, particularly if they are digital.

Wiles (2013) raises an often overlooked aspect of ownership related to visual data over an extended period of years, if not decades: "While an individual may be happy for a specific image or expressed view to be made public at one point in their lives they may be less so in the future as their circumstances change, yet once something enters the public domain it may be difficult or impossible to remove it" (p. 54). Mitchell (2011) also addresses this topic, but within a cultural context: "Although researchers ask permission to show images in their publications, how is this understood by the participants? Do the girls living in Swaziland who produced the images of the toilets have an understanding of what it means to have these images projected onto a movie screen as part of a PowerPoint presentation?" (p. 198). The contextual grounding of this subject illustrates how a nuanced perspective is needed, rather than taking a blanket approach that misses key elements.

Castleden, Morgan, and Neimanis (2010) address the importance of recognizing the intellectual and practical contributions of participants and communities, with one possibility being to negotiate co-authorship of scholarly publication rights as one means of acknowledging their rights and publically commending the intellectual contributions of participants. This step towards recognition brings the acknowledgement into the academic world and legitimizes co-authorship within this realm.

Distortion of Images/Reinforcement of Negative Stereotypes

It certainly would be critical that the voices, or central messages, of participants are actually those that they selected for themselves, rather than what the researcher thinks they should be (Fawcett & Hearn, 2004; Goldring, 2010; Oleson, 2008). Empowerment is not possible otherwise. Furthermore, it is unethical. Control over the images and messages represents a critical element of youth photovoice. Hammersley and Traianou (2012) note that the use of new technologies has introduced distinctive qualitative problems, such as misuse of images involving children.

There are multiple risks associated with representation resulting in serious ethical dilemmas or breaches (Rumbold, Fenner, & Brophy-Dixon, 2012; Phelan & Kinsella, 2011). This is particularly the case when projects involve children and youth, since they can be considered "vulnerable subjects" (Graham & Kilpatrick, 2010; Morris, Hegarty, & Humphreys, 2012; Powell & Smith, 2009). From an ontological perspective, photovoice and other visual forms of research do raise questions about perceptions and interpretations of what constitutes operative reality (Spencer, 2011). The answer to these questions are found in the intentions of the photographer.

It is important to raise potential concerns about photographs concerning young children, in particular. Nutbrown (2011), for example, raises a cautionary flag concerning the use of photographs of young children and how their images may be distorted once they leave their control and the control of those creating the initial image. Maud (2012) raises concerns about how the exercise of power between researcher and young children can compromise how participants share parts of themselves. In addition, there remains a need to develop research methods that are participatory of children and youth that do not lump together age groups in a fashion that blurs critical distinctions. Children and youth can cover a wide range of ages and developmental stages. Finally, Robinson and Gillies

(2012) stress the contradictions and instabilities inherent in performance participation involving youth.

Insuring that photovoice research does not reinforce negative stereotypes presents researchers with a potential ethical conflict. Researchers must endeavor to make sure that the findings of the research, in this case photovoice, do not reinforce negative views of youth while still advocating for their cause (Walsh, Black, & Berman, 2013). It may be tempting to reinforce the most negative images and narrative to rally support and funding for their cause. That tendency to reinforce stereotypes must be guarded against.

Consent Agreements

Finally, consent agreements, touched upon earlier, and participant rights need to be addressed in greater detail because of their importance in helping to ensure that participants are well aware of what is expected of them. Assessment of the adequacy of the consent process takes on even greater significance when it involves children and youth and in cases where the participants do not have English as their primary language.

In the case of youth photovoice, there are at least three possible levels of consent: (1) youth participants; (2) their parents or legal guardians; and (3) appropriate authorities, as in the case of school settings (Jansson et al., 2006; Sippola, 2006). This may seem typical. In cases where multiple languages are necessary, it takes on great significance, as in the case of youth who are bilingual and parents who may be monolingual in languages other than English or illiterate in their native language and English, for example.

A typical consent agreement requires participants to sign a written statement that addresses their willingness to participate, and enumerates what will happen to the photographs and stories shared (anonymously or acknowledged). The Rights of the Participants developed by TB Voices (n.d.) for their Snohomish and King County, Washington, project, titled *tb.tuberculosis:pv photovoice,* is a very good example that can serve as a basis for a participant statement, with the necessary modifications to take into account local circumstances, including language preference of participants, and, in the case of minors, signature of the parent or adult guardian.

In the case of minors, it is recommended that an active, rather than passive approach (sending a letter and project-related correspondence home for a signature) be taken, as a means of both grounding the research project to the appropriate adult(s), and establishing a relationship between the researcher and the participant's family (Fisher & Masty, 2006). The relationships that youth develop during their participation in photovoice are anything but superfluous, as can be found in other forms of qualitative research (Horsfall & Higgs, 2011). So, too, are the relationships that researchers establish with youth and their families.

It is possible to have youth participants develop a consent agreement. They can modify an existing agreement in cases where they signed them in order to participate in a project. An addendum can incorporate issues and considerations not covered in the original agreement, for example. Although an active approach is time-consuming, it is an excellent opportunity to bridge the divide the normally exists between researcher and community. Riecken and Strong-Wilson (2006) use the term "edge of consent" to capture the myriad of layers of consent that need to be navigated (different types of participation necessitate different protocols) in CBPR involving youth, and photovoice is not an exception. Researchers must be prepared to explain all facets of the research, and consent should not be viewed as a "blanket" statement (Alderson & Morrow, 2011).

INCLUSION/EXCLUSION DILEMMAS

One of the great appeals of photovoice is its universal appeal and flexibility to be adapted to a wide variety of circumstances and population groups (Ollerton & Kelshaw, 2011). The systematic exclusion of youth groups because of their abilities must be viewed from an ethical perspective. Those who resist including youth with physical and intellectual challenges may be quick to point out that doing so will necessitate extra time and resources, but they rarely mention the ethical implications of not including them. The emergence of the concept of inclusive participatory research, otherwise referred to as inclusive research (IR), is a response to how discrimination according to abilities is so pervasive (Ollerton & Kelshaw, 2011).

The exclusion of youth because of disabilities represents a breach of ethics, particularly if their absence is considered to facilitate implementation of a research project (Bigby & Frawley, 2010). A civil rights–based interpretation of ethical principles increases the likelihood of including co-investigators with disabilities (McDonald & Patka, 2012). Just as importantly, including these youth provides information on a community sector that we know very little about, yet these youth constitute a part of the community. A more comprehensive picture of the community is not possible without their participation. It is, after all, possible to balance inclusion, respect, and protection (Alderson & Morrow, 2011). Boxall and Ralph (2009) address exclusion from a different perspective by raising concerns that tighter regulation of social research regarding visual research may discourage involvement of participants with disabilities in this emerging field of research.

Using photovoice with individuals who are facing a host of cognitive or mobility challenges is possible if the researcher is flexible and able to accommodate participants in their use of cameras and narratives (Dupuis et al., 2012; Genoe & Dupuis, 2013; Rush, Murphy, & Kozak, 2012; Newman, 2010). For example, narratives are an essential component of photovoice. In the case of people with Alzheimer's disease, they may take a photograph and have a particular reason for doing so. When it comes time to reflect on the reasons for taking the photograph, they may simply forget why they did so. Scheduling discussion sessions soon after the taking of a picture increases the likelihood of the participant remembering why they selected that particular image (Wiersma, 2011).

The use of digital cameras has advantages over disposable cameras when youth with disabilities are involved in a project (Phelan & Kinsella, 2011). Digital cameras provide immediate feedback and allow youth to confirm the photographs taken through the use of the LCD. Further, these photos can be loaded onto computers, facilitating viewing and distribution of images among project participants. There are a variety of ways of maximizing the participation of co-researchers with memory challenges. The use of voice recording devices allows researchers to record their impressions and can be retrieved later on. Maintaining journals that allow participants to record their reasons for taking a particular photograph can also aid in helping participants maximize the benefits of participation (Genoe & Dupuis, 2013). Having challenges can be addressed if inclusion is a major principle. "If there is a will, there is a way."

PARTICIPANT BILL OF RIGHTS

A focus on the rights of participants brings an important dimension to participation by helping to reduce the likelihood of ethical dilemmas occurring because of a lack of understanding of a photovoice project. TB Voices (n.d.) identified 12 specific participant rights:

1. By participating in this project, you are choosing to share with the public your tuberculosis (TB) story either: (1) anonymously, including your county of residence, or (2) using your first name and county of residence.
2. Why is this project being done?
3. What do you have to do in the project?
4. What are the risks and discomforts to you?
5. What will happen if you are injured during your participation?
6. Are there benefits for you taking part in this project?
7. Who is paying for this project?
8. What are your costs?
9. Will you be paid to participate in this project?
10. What if you want to withdraw from the project?
11. Who to call if you have questions or problems?
12. What about confidentiality of information?

A review of the 12 rights, or questions, identified above highlights the complexities of sharing personal information for the good of the participants and others who share the same conditions and circumstances. Each of these questions defies a simple response, and a violation of the rights has profound ethical consequences. Yet concerted effort must be made to address each of these rights in a manner that takes into account local circumstance and cultural backgrounds in order for nuances to surface.

Marshall and Sheppard (2006) focus their attention on an aspect of youth (adolescents) that often gets overlooked in discussions of research ethics—namely, ethics within a group setting or context. Youth spend much of their lives as members of groups, whether in school, sports, or friendships, for example. Groups are a natural venue for important work to occur. There is individual consent, which researchers are well familiar with, yet group consent introduces new elements to this process. Group process and dynamics, including decision-making and conflicts, are an integral part of photovoice. Personality differences, for example, can carry over into group discussions and deliberations, thereby causing "camps" to emerge, gossip to transpire, and acting out behavior to occur, which can undermine photovoice goals.

COMMUNITY RIGHTS

The rights covered in the previous section focused on individuals, and on groups to a certain extent, and few readers would be surprised by the appearance of community rights in this chapter. Addressing community rights is not a far stretch, since photovoice projects are community projects, and communities must therefore also be addressed. It is important to emphasize that youth photovoice falls within a CBPR paradigm. A community bill of rights is in order, as a way of minimizing potential ethical breaches, although it brings into the forefront potential tensions and challenges. There are a variety of perspectives that can be taken.

Cordner, Ciplet, Brown, & Morello-Frosch (2012), for example, argue that community-engaged research has had a profound impact on researcher-participant relationships, academic-community interaction, and the potential role of a community partner's involvement in human subject protection and ethical oversight. The community is not only the focus of research but also an active participant in the process, bringing with participation an entrance into the world of ethical conduct (Kono, 2012).

Although no one individual or organization is expected to sign off for the community, promulgating a community bill of rights in publications will the public the message of the central importance of communities in photovoice. A community rights perspective will generally cover many of the same topics covered in an individual bill of rights, which generally address ethical issues related to privacy, representation, the decision-making process, and procedures for raising ethical concerns, for example. Some readers may view a community bill of rights as extraneous or a publicity stunt. That is far from being the case. It is important to emphasize that communities have historically been viewed as a place to do research and not as potential partners in research. Having a community bill of rights is not only appropriate but essential.

INSTITUTIONAL REVIEW BOARD (IRB)

The subject of the institutional review board (IRB) review and qualitative research is bound to elicit a visceral response, and for very good reasons (Alderson & Morrow, 2011; Dyer & Demeritt, 2008). Amon, Baral, Beyrer, and Kass (2012) note that researchers may even go so far as to see these ethical reviews as counterproductive and compromising of the research goals. The number of IRB horror stories that circulate at professional meetings and conferences are legendary, particularly when the research is participatory and involves youth under the age of 18.

This is not to say that IRBs should not take the age of the participant into special consideration to avoid ethical abuses. Schrag (2011) identified six major types of complaints that social scientists have against IRBs: "1) ethics committees impose silly restrictions, 2) ethics review is a solution in search of a problem, 3) ethics committees lack expertise, 4) ethics committees apply inappropriate principles, 5) ethics review harms the innocent, and 6) better options exist." (p. 128). The experienced reader can no doubt add a few additional categories to Schrag's list (Heimer & Petty, 2010). Silberman and Kahn (2011) note that although there is evidence that these bodies impose burdens on researchers, more research is needed to be validated with data as to the extent of these burdens and how IRBs need to be reformed. McMurphy, Lewis, and Boulos's (2013) well-titled article "Extending the Olive Branch: Enhancing Communication and Trust Between Research Ethics and Qualitative Research," in turn, addresses the absence of trust and the need for greater dialogue and collaboration between qualitative researcher and IRBs.

IRB's are not fail safe systems, thereby increasing the need for, and importance of, community advisory committees: "Institutional review boards (IRBs), designed to protect individual study participants, do not routinely assess community consent, risks, and benefits. Community groups are establishing ethics review processes to determine whether and how research is conducted in their communities. To strengthen the ethics review of community-engaged research, we sought to identify and describe these processes" (Shore et al., 2004, p. S359). Chalmers (2011), for example, argues that research ethics committees (IRBs in the United States) have not kept up with advances in science and research. The inability of IRBs to keep up with advances in research represents a serious obstacle for advances to occur, such as those embodied in photovoice. IRBs reviewing research involving those who use sign language, for example, are deficient when discussing this population group (Harris, Holmes, & Mertens, 2009).

The challenges faced by those undertaking photovoice projects provide an example. Guta et al. (2010) argue that scientific reviewing boards, in this case related to those in Canada, but also applicable to the United States, have a long tradition of reviewing biomedical research but are at a disadvantage when reviewing ethical considerations in CBPR proposals.

Burr and Reyonds (2010) pose the question of IRBs imposing a paradigm designed for medical research on social science. Sieber and Tolich (2013), and Dyer and Demeritt (2008), too, echo the concern that these deliberative bodies lack an informed understanding and are unable to address the unique research techniques, venues, and ethical challenges and needs of researchers using emerging research methodologies, particularly those that are qualitative in approach, such as photovoice. In essence, this deliberative body has the potential to be counterproductive and outdated.

From an institutional point of view, it is essential that IRBs have representation of faculty and staff members who do ethnographic, arts-based, research. Their presence will provide the board with an opportunity to have an informed discussion of projects such as youth photovoice, including how they conform and are different from more conventional forms of research, qualitative and otherwise (DuBois et al., 2011). It is also recommended that training and consultation be made available to increase the competencies of members to review methodologies that are emerging (Beskow, Grady, Iltis, Sadler, & Wilfond, 2009; Harvard, Cho, & Magnus, 2012; Sirotin, Wolff, Catania, Dolcini, & Lo, 2010). Trudeau (2012), although specifically addressing geographers, suggests that graduate students be included in IRBs as a means of increasing their competence in addressing ethical issues.

Tolich and Tumilty's (2013) novel approach to fostering and improving qualitative research, particularly those that are emerging, by helping researchers navigate IRBs, attempts to help fellow researchers with ethical review boards by making examples available for review. The Ethics Application Repository (http://tear.otago.ac.nz/) solicits applications and makes them available free of charge:

> TEAR is long overdue. Few novice IRB (ethics committee) applications are approved on their first reading leading to multiple resubmissions delaying the commencement of research. Novices forced to reinvent the ethics wheel from scratch, creates, at best, a fear of dealing with the processes around ethics rather than engaging in thinking about ethical principles. At worst, many supervisors get students to avoid IRB review and conduct secondary analysis. The latter students fail to learn how to think ethically. What they do learn is ethical cynicism: IRBs are to be avoided if possible. TEAR sets out to break this cycle of fear and avoidance facilitating better relationships between researchers and their IRBs in the short and long term. Current practice sees IRBs as a singular compliance moment in a linear process. TEAR promotes a new role for IRBs: they can become part of an iterative ethics review cycle but only if the IRB approval process is less daunting.

Efforts such as TEAR reflect a growing concern about the power and influence of IRBs in discouraging the use of qualitative research methods in the social sciences. It will no doubt take a multifaceted strategy involving training, consultation, increasing membership of qualitative researchers on IRBs, to make these deliberative bodies receptive to photovoice and other arts-based research methods. Efforts such as this hold much promise and can be relatively inexpensive to undertake. Institutions sponsoring these websites also benefit from increased exposure and the development of a reputation in areas that are innovative and have the potential to dramatically influence an emerging field such as photovoice.

COMMUNITY ADVISORY COMMITTEE

It is noteworthy that this chapter on ethics ends with the role of community advisory committees as a mechanism to help increase the chances that youth photovoice is conducted to the highest ethical standards. As addressed in Chapter 5, advisory committees can fulfill many important roles and functions in helping to implement urban youth photovoice. One of those important functions is related to helping to ensure that ethical conduct is central to the planning and implementation of youth photovoice. Nevertheless, advisory committees can also be sources of ethical misconduct, bringing an added set of challenges for researchers who must contend with ensuring that photovoice activities are not interrupted or compromised.

IRBs are not the only place where ethics are or can get reviewed (Sieber & Tolich, 2013). It can be argued that a review by an IRB does not guarantee that a research project will be ethical. A national shift towards emphasizing translational research has resulted in researchers turning to communities as partners in the research to breakdown translational barriers and increase the likelihood that results can influence practice (Hacker, 2013; Ross et al., 2010a). This shift has increased the relevance of the research findings, but it has also brought into question risks to communities.

Ross et al. (2010a) developed a three-by-three framework to facilitate viewing risks: ". . . (risks to well-being secondary to process, risks to well-being secondary to outcome and risks to agency) must be evaluated against the 3 distinct agents: individuals as individual participants, individuals as members of a group (both as participants and as non-participants) and to communities as a whole" (p. 5). This framework breaks down ethical risks starting from the individual and working their way out to groups and the community at large.

Community advisory committees can play an important role in helping to ensure ethical conduct in youth photovoice projects. IRBs cannot bear the total responsibility for addressing ethics. Quinn (2004), for example, advocates the use of community advisory boards, or committees, as a way of helping to ensure that ethical research is conducted, and to minimize the potential transgressions that can harm the community and compromise the research:

> Increasingly, researchers grapple with meaningful efforts to involve communities in research, recognizing that communities are distinct from individuals. We also struggle to ensure that individual participants in research

are fully protected. Community advisory boards (CABs) offer an opportunity to adopt a relationships paradigm that enables researchers to anticipate and address the context in which communities understand risks and benefits, and individuals give consent. CABs provide a mechanism for community consultation that contributes to protecting communities and fostering meaningful research. Furthermore, CABs can help us to re-create informed consent as a process. It is critical that we conduct research to understand the role of CABs in the informed consent process. (p. 918)

Actively engaging a community in a research process is one of the key values underpinning photovoice, as addressed in Chapter 4 and other sections of this book (Kelley, Belcourt-Dittloff, Belcourt, & Belcourt, 2013). Yet such an action sets in motion countless number of situations that can present unanticipated ethical dilemmas for a researcher. For example, Simon and Mosavel (2010) discuss the ethics of having community residents actively recruit other residents to participate in community participatory research. Engaging the community in this task empowers them and also increases the likelihood that the recommendations will help ensure that participants are well respected and regarded within the community, thereby increasing the community legitimacy of those involved in the research. This, in turn, increases the potential for the results of the photovoice to be accepted by the community. Clearly, the benefit of community participation in recruitment is full of impressive gains for those involved and their respective communities.

There are potential ethical dilemmas inherent in actively soliciting input from the community in suggesting potential participants. For example, there is potential for suggesting those youth who share similar politics and perspectives and views. Further, there is potential for coercion and increased likelihood of breaching confidentiality. Some of us may have a propensity to romanticize communities as consisting of nothing but pure and good. Communities consist of human beings, with all of the tendencies and foibles of being human. Breaches of ethical conduct are not restricted to professionals! Therefore, researchers may weigh the advantages and disadvantages of involving an advisory committee in recruitment and other aspects of a project, and they may conclude that the advantages far outweigh the disadvantages. I certainly fall into that category. However, it is not all smooth sailing.

CBPR is predicated upon researchers entering into partnerships with community-based organizations, and these partnerships represent a potential benefit that can be derived in photovoice. These relationships can also be the cause of major conflicts, some of which may be classified as ethical (Ross et al., 2010c). In similar fashion to any collaborative agreement, it is necessary to outline potential areas of disagreement, but, most importantly, the process that will be used to resolve these disagreements are to be resolved. It is recommended that formal written agreements be made about the nature of the relationship, and that the process and participants who will be part of the problem-solving process be articulated, should a problem arise (Resnik & Kennedy, 2010).

Conclusion

The promise of visual qualitative methods such as photovoice is matched by the challenges this method faces in ensuring that the rights of youth, their families, and their communities are not violated in the process of carrying out a project, and that harm (physical, emotional, and political) does not occur as a result of participation. All forms of research bring inherent challenges. Nevertheless, visual arts–based qualitative research must confront additional challenges because of the goals it sets for itself, and because of the age group that it seeks to engage. Arts-based qualitative research seeks to generate new knowledge, empower participants, and bring about significant social change. Each of these goals is significant. Together, they are quite formidable in significance.

This chapter has touched upon several general and some very unique key ethical issues or challenges inherent in urban youth photovoice, and it has alerted the researcher to potential pitfalls in using this research method. In addition, an effort has been made to ground the subject matter historically and contextually. The importance of ethical conduct is heightened when addressing marginalized groups and communities, since they have a history of being exploited and have limited access to authorities and power structures that can redress these harms. Youth definitely fall into this group.

SECTION THREE

Voices from the Field

One of the axiomatic truths in cognitive psychology is that the frame of reference through which one peers at the world shapes what one learns from that world. To the carpenter, the world is made of wood. To the psychometrician, the world is made of quantity. Pluralism and diversity are virtues not only in race relations but they can be extremely important virtues in getting multiple perspectives on states of affairs. Without support of the conception of such diversity, it is not likely to be provided.

—BARONE & EISNER, 2012, p. 4

8

Camp CAMERA Case Study

Introduction

Barone and Eisner's (2012) quote at the top of Section 3 stresses the viewpoint that the context participants find themselves embedded in shapes their world-view, which has been a major theme of this book. Although numerous examples of youth photovoice have been provided throughout this book, this chapter will focus on providing greater depth of context and practice regarding the use of photovoice with urban youth by utilizing a case example to illustrate how urban youth photovoice has been conceptualized and implemented by one program.

Every effort was made to select case examples from throughout the country to tap potential regional differences and contexts. An opportunity was presented to do a more in-depth case study of one program that illustrates many of the values and principles outlined in this book. Access to youth participants, and their willingness to share their work and experiences, is necessary for a case study to unfold in a manner that helps the readers appreciate urban youth photovoice. The case study of Camp CAMERA was ideal for this book, and that is why this chapter focuses on one case example as opposed to multiple case studies, which would necessarily have more limited depth.

Gaining access necessitated an extensive process of contacting appropriate individuals, making chapters of this book available, and answering numerous questions pertaining to the central thrust of this book and the perspective that the author brings to work with youth, particularly those who are undervalued in this society. This case study of Camp CAMERA will provide (1) a contextual description and history of setting, (2) details on photovoice conceptualized, (3) a description of how the project(s) unfolded, (4) an account of the dilemmas encountered and addressed, (5) photographs, (6) narratives, (7) key findings and themes, (8) the change that resulted, and (9) lessons learned and recommendations. Sufficient details will be provided on each of these nine categories to bring theory and practice together.

Role and Purpose of a Case Study Method

Research encompasses many different methods and approaches, which are usually classified as to whether or not they are quantitatively or qualitatively focused. The arguments put forth earlier in this book, particularly Chapters 3 and 5, provide detailed reasoning as to why qualitative studies bring a great deal of elucidation on the lives of the marginalized in this society. This does not mean that quantitative studies do not enlighten. The picture they provide is very limited, however, and they do not provide practitioners with nuanced and detailed perspectives on the lives of urban youth.

Case studies provide researchers with a way to compose a portrait that draws from many different research perspectives, qualitative as well as quantitative. If done well, it brings the lives of marginalized youth to life in a way that a strict qualitative or quantitative approach cannot. The case study that follows attempts to provide an in-depth picture or context in the hopes of facilitating the consideration and eventual adaptation of photovoice as a viable and attractive research method for urban youth.

Case studies are never meant to take the "easy" way out for researchers, since a successful case study entails presenting a picture from a multifaceted perspective: "Doing case study research remains one of the most challenging of all social science endeavors. . . . Do not underestimate the extent of the challenge" (Yin, 2013, p. 3). Spencer (2011) also comments on the challenge:

> There is considerable controversy around the case study; it is a broad strategy or a specific method. . . . By its very nature the case study is a unique instance; an integrated and usually well-defined and bounded system. . . . Therefore, the criticism of a case study research, namely that the results are not widely applicable in real life, can be refuted because analytical generalisations are appropriate and make good use of the in-depth specificity of the case study. (p. 50)

Camp CAMERA embodies many of the values and principles exposed in Chapter 4, and it illustrates the power of photovoice to transform lives in ways that go beyond conventional measures, and to do so in a manner that transforms all parties to these ventures. Further, in the case of Camp CAMERA, we witness how co-facilitators who are relatively close in age can effectively work together in a manner that is empowering and affirming, opening up the possibilities of youth of different age groupings working together in a photovoice project.

Camp CAMERA, Minneapolis, Minnesota

CONTEXTUAL DESCRIPTION OF SETTING

The importance of context in the use of photovoice has been strongly emphasized throughout the previous chapters and sections of this book. Arts-based qualitative research, and the lived experience, must be firmly based in the daily life and surroundings of those participating in this form of inquiry. This context, and in this case it is urban youth, serves as a backdrop to images, as well as a guide for understanding why they are meaningful to urban youth. Youth photovoice is best appreciated and understood when adult researchers have a solid grounding in the forces shaping the daily life of young people. This grounding can be conceptualized in a variety of ways. A sociocultural-socioecological perspective is often recommended as a way to capture nuanced information that often gets overlooked if relying upon a narrow perspective or interpretation.

There are multitudes of ways that this grounding can transpire from a practical point of view. For the purposes of this case study of Camp CAMERA, four dimensions will be focused on: (A) a demographic profile of Minneapolis–St. Paul, Minnesota, (B) a history of Camp CAMERA, (C) organizational descriptions, and (D) program leadership. Each of these contextual aspects provides details that can aid in developing an appreciation of how these forces set a foundation for Camp CAMERA's conceptualization of photovoice. Due to limited space, these dimensions will include only the most pertinent facts and information.

Camp Camera has a website where the reader can obtain more information (www.campcamera.org/). This site also has numerous photographs covering each of the project collaboration sites. Websites are increasingly being used to broaden the potential audience for images and narratives. A quick search of the Internet will uncover numerous sites representing a range of program models and goals reinforcing the flexibility that photovoice brings to take into account local circumstances and advances in communication technologies.

Internet sites provide a way for youth interested in the arts to learn about other programs and to take pride in their work before a broader audience. These sites also open up potential contacts for collaboration and contributions from a wide variety of community sources. Websites, incidentally, can also be used for recruitment of youth participants, advisory committee members, fundraising, and specific requests for pertinent studies and evaluation tools, examples of activities, and assistance with particular questions or challenges. In essence, there are endless possibilities

Demographic Profile of Minneapolis–St. Paul, Minnesota

Demographic data provide a picture of communities that many critics would argue is one-dimensional and static because it captures a point in time. Furthermore, demographics often miss hidden population groups, such as those who are undocumented, which really impacts communities of color who are newcomers to this country. Yet demographics help fill in a picture of a community that can be supplemented with qualitative information that adds depth and nuance, and it brings a community to life in a manner that is not possible without combining quantitative and qualitative information.

The Twin Cities of Minneapolis and St. Paul are closely matched in size and have sizable communities of color and youth populations, yet there are differences between these twins. They are not identical. According to estimates by the U.S. Census Bureau, Minneapolis had a population of 392,880 in 2012, with 20 percent of the total under the age of 18. The population of color represented 36.7 percent, and was distributed as follows: African American/black, 18.6 percent; Latino, 10.5 percent; Asian, 5.6 percent; and American Indian/Alaska Native, 2.0 percent. St. Paul's 2012 estimated population was 290,770, with 25.1 percent under the age of 18. The population of color represented 41.4 percent of the total, with the following distribution: African American/black, 15.7 percent; Asian, 15.0 percent; Latino, 9.6 percent; and American Indian/Alaska Native, 1.1 percent. These "official" counts do not capture those who are undocumented, which will be highly prevalent in the Asian and Latino communities.

History of Camp CAMERA

Programs and initiatives often have a "start date" that everyone can look to as the official beginning. However, the true start date is often very hard to trace because it starts with an idea or interest on the part of the founder, which will, in all likelihood, go back many years. The "official" Camp CAMERA start date is 2011, making its history relatively short. Camp CAMERA is a semester-long program that completed its eighth session of existence in the spring of 2014, and it represents a photovoice example of a medium-length project, as discussed in Chapter 5.

The program is intended to provide arts and photography programming for high school youth and leadership, and for youth development training for students from Macalester College. Nevertheless, its short period of existence does not take away from the impact of its reach in the St. Paul and Minneapolis youth community, which has been accomplished through strategic collaborative partnerships involving a college (Macalester College) and community-based organizations (YouthCARE and the Al Lenzmeier West Side Boys & Girls Club), as addressed later on in this case study.

Organizational Descriptions

Camp CAMERA has been embedded, and is ongoing, in two nonprofit youth development organizations in the Twin Cities, YouthCARE (established in 1974) and the Al Lenzmeier West Side Boys & Girls Club (origins traced to 1926). In addition, there was one semester where Camp CAMERA adapted the program to be implemented in a public school in downtown St. Paul, the Open World Learning Community School (established in 1971). The program is anticipated to continue at the Al Lenzmeier West Side Boys & Girls Club in the fall of 2014. The program bridges multiple communities and contexts involving major community-based institutions with substantial histories.

For the 2013–2014 school year, Camp CAMERA worked with the Al Lenzmeier West Side Boys & Girls Club. In addition, during the first semester of implementation, Camp CAMERA collaborated with the Hennes Art Company to host an exhibition celebration, and since then it has partnered each year with Gallery 13, a local gallery in Minneapolis, for the photography show. Wing Young Huie, a local artist, has been a guest speaker and usually works with the program once every semester for one session as a way to inspire youth to think of the arts from a multifaceted perspective, including possible careers. He also discusses with the youth the intersection of one's own identity with the subject/environment being captured.

Macalester College (established in 1874) is located in St. Paul and is the institution where the program began and continues to be hosted. Each semester, high school youth (approximately 11) come to campus and participate alongside Macalester student volunteers (ranging from 4 to 7) in an experience of self-exploration and photography. Macalester College is a small liberal arts school with students from all over the country and abroad. It is a liberal arts college known for its high standards for scholarship and its special emphasis on internationalism, multiculturalism, and service to society. These institutions have provided the right "climate" for a that is arts-based project such as Camp CAMERA.

Program Leadership

The subject of leadership and leadership development was addressed earlier in this book. The perspective was heavily focused from a participant point of view, necessitating a different perspective focused on facilitators. Youth photovoice projects get shaped by the vision and leadership qualities of facilitators, and Camp CAMERA is certainly no exception. It is important to look at the driving force behind Camp CAMERA.

Organizational founders are a unique breed, as the professional literature has shown, because of how personal qualities interact with environmental factors and circumstances. In this instance, a college student was instrumental in conceptualizing and implementing this program. It should be noted that Leah Krieble had no formal training in photography other than a course in high school, so a formal education or specialized training in photography is not a prerequisite for engaging in photovoice. An interest in this medium is sufficient.

Camp CAMERA began through an Action Fund Grant, written by Leah Krieble, a senior Macalester student, in 2011. She brought forth a passion for bringing people together and a deep and profound interest in photography as an art form. Krieble along with Lauryn Gutierrez, another Macalester senior, created a pilot program bridging Macalester College and YouthCARE. The pilot program proved so successful that it spurred a commitment to permanently establish Camp CAMERA.

Krieble had worked for YouthCARE for the previous two years and was involved in direct service with the youth and programming, and this history of involvement facilitated the initiation of this project. In addition, Krieble and Gutierrez rechartered MacPICS, the photography student organization at Macalester College, which was widely considered to be a languishing student organization prior to its reorganization and its embrace of a youth photovoice project. Institutions of higher learning have tremendous potential to draw upon their resources (expertise, students, and financial support) to create programs that reach out to communities, and this was the case with Macalester College.

In working within these two communities, YouthCARE and MacPics, at Macalester College, Krieble realized that both groups shared a similar passion and enthusiasm for social change and would benefit from learning from each other. Youth photovoice is an excellent mechanism for enhancing social capital (bonding and bridging). Photovoice projects must actively seek to develop relationships with key community institutions as a means of enhancing the possibilities that these relationships can be brokered to create other opportunities in the future.

Growing up in Brooklyn, New York, Krieble initially struggled with the transition from a major city to a small liberal arts college and wished there had been more avenues for a wider and more diverse representation in both academic and informal discussions on campus. Camp CAMERA was a program designed to bring people together for inspiring conversation within a more diverse group of students (age, ethnicity, economic background, etc.), and to break down stereotypes.

As a senior majoring in psychology and education, Krieble created her own internship to lead this pilot program focusing on the principles of youth development under the guidance of Dr. Tina Kruse, her Macalester professor in educational studies. Kruse, too, has a scholarly interest in youth and positive youth development. It is important to pause and note that Professor Kruse played an instrumental role in brokering contacts between Krieble and the author of this book, and, as addressed in the Epilogue, the creation of a community of researchers and practitioners with an interest in photovoice is an important step in the direction of widening the use of photovoice with youth and other population groups. Interestingly, many Camp CAMERA high school and college alumni still maintain contact through Facebook, representing a medium that can be used by a community of scholars (youth and adults).

Programs such as Camp CAMERA rely upon the good intentions and competencies of many individuals. Lauryn Gutierrez and Alex Bendtz (Macalester College students), and John Hardeman (Boys & Girls Club branch director) played an instrumental role in the implementation and sustainability of this program. Since its pilot year, the program has continued to be offered each semester to high school and college students.

CAMP CAMERA PROGRAM

Youth photovoice can be conceptualized in a variety of ways. There are two primary approaches—as a research project or as an intervention project. This does not mean that an intervention approach cannot involve undertaking research or that a research approach cannot involve undertaking an intervention. One approach is foreground and the other is background. It is important that regardless of how it gets conceptualized, it must not stigmatize or further marginalized urban youth. The language used to capture the purpose of a photovoice project plays a determining role in how the project is perceived by participants and the outside world. The name Camp CAMERA is nonstigmatizing.

Camp CAMERA is best conceptualized as an after-school program structured to be both a fun interactive photography program for high school students and a service learning and leadership development program for college students. After-school programs have a reputation of being places that are fun, educational, and safe environments where the arts are valued. As is often the case with arts-based youth programs, there is a strong explicit and implicit reliance on youth development principles, which enhances youth competencies and provides a vehicle for helping them voice their concerns and aspirations.

Camp CAMERA embraces a curriculum that strives to address technical aspects related to photography, artistic principles, and communication/interpersonal relationship-building. Each week, college students plan presentations, workshops, field trips, darkroom and studio workshops, team-building activities, and critiques for the high school students. Activities play an important role in generating excitement and discussions. The Macalester students are volunteers who meet weekly to plan the program. During this program, high school youth are given the opportunity to take cameras home and take their own photographs for two weeks. Their photographs are then displayed in a gallery exhibition at the end of the program, and at the end of the academic year. In the April 2014 exhibition, for example, there were approximately 70 guests, which included families, friends, sponsors, teachers, college students, and the principal of a partnering school.

There is a distinct set of values and principles guiding Camp CAMERA's conceptualization. Values such as the embrace of diversity, experiential and incidental learning, community investment, leadership development, utilization of local and self-knowledge, cultural competency/cultural humility, and social justice combine to set a stage for operating principles to guide how youth photovoice unfolds, along with the priorities that the program places on achieving change in participants and their respective communities. These values are an essential element of Camp CAMERA and facilitate the engagement of urban youth. They affirm and convey to the community where the program stands, which is critical in enlisting necessary support.

This description of Camp CAMERA will address the following contextual perspectives, which will help the reader understand better how the program was conceptualized and implemented, including the rewards and challenges associated with a youth photovoice project: (A) mission and philosophical underpinnings, (B) program objectives, (C) recruitment and retention, (D) composition of artists, (E) structure and scheduling of activities, (F) exhibitions, (G) funding, (H) evaluation, (I) key findings and the change that resulted, (J) donations, (K) local media coverage, and (L) retention.

Mission and Philosophical Underpinnings

It is certainly appropriate to start with Camp CAMERA's mission. An organization's mission statement seeks to capture the heart and soul of a program and represents its DNA, so to speak. Some nonprofits have mission statements that have long lost their original meanings and are little more than words printed on a paper, with staff and consumers being unaware of the organization's mission. These organizations, I believe, may have lost their original reason for existence and just exist. This may seem like a very harsh statement to make. Nonprofits get established because of a profound sense of purpose, and when this gets undermined, or totally forgotten, in the search for any kind of funding, then a missed opportunity for significant transformation results.

Camp CAMERA's mission is to engage students from different sociodemographic backgrounds, experiences, and levels of education, in an exploration of photography and self-expression. The program exposes the belief that through photography we—youth and adults—are able to explore cultural diversity and multiple perspectives, which are often overlooked. Camp CAMERA's focus is on utilizing positive youth development and building of positive relationships between high school and college students through collaboration, creativity, and mutual respect. Photography, in turn, is used to illuminate life narratives, promote creative expression, and celebrate diversity.

Camp CAMERA's underpinning philosophy stresses collaboration and the transformative power that results from the reciprocity that comes from teaching and learning. Staff works to provide an environment where both high school and college students understand their responsibility to learn and teach each other through a photographic dialogue. The program uses an asset-based framework, both in the trainings with the college students, when preparing weekly sessions, and in the workshops that are offered. The youth gain a unique voice through photography as a venue for their contributions, perspectives, and talents.

Program Objectives

Camp CAMERA believes that through learning about photography, students will gain a deeper understanding of how art can strengthen communities. The benefits of this project to youth are multifaceted and include college access, exposure to the arts, understanding diversity and cooperation, exploring identity and culture through artistic expression, and building positive relationships with older role models. For example, one youth said, *"Through this program I got the chance to meet a famous photographer, work in the darkroom and build stronger relationships with my peers. Also, I got the chance to learn the basics of photography. My favorite part was seeing the results of my pictures. I was surprised by my creativity in taking photos.*" This quote does a wonderful job of capturing the obvious, and not so obvious, ways that youth can have takeaways from participating in an arts-based program.

Providing artistic outlets in high school through building relationships with caring college students can help with dropout prevention and youth motivation. Not only will this program have an impact on our youth, but the college students will also benefit, as they will develop leadership and community organizational skills. Communities, too, will benefit from having a cadre of well-trained artistic photographers in their midst. A comprehensive perspective on benefits is essential for an understanding that is nuanced. The reach of photovoice projects can unfold in very important but not so obvious ways. For example, youth visiting a college campus for photovoice activities are exposed to surroundings that helo dispel any preconceived biases they may have about institutions of higher learning, and this was the case with Camp CAMERA.

Camp CAMERA believes that the impact of this program will go beyond just the high school and college students directly involved, as the photographs will be displayed in a gallery show open to the public. Through the exhibition, Camp CAMERA is able to illuminate the power and perspectives of the youth and young adults to a larger audience of students, friends, families, and artists. This reach to a broader audience beyond their social network helps to dispel myths and stereotypes.

A total of six objectives were created to capture the multidimensional experience of Camp CAMERA artists:

1. Provide opportunities for high school youth to learn more about the history, techniques, and power of photography (both in terms of skill development and in terms of utilizing it as a tool to create social change).
2. Provide consistent weekly workshops for high school youth who have had little prior exposure to the arts.
3. Teach students about the agency they have in representing and sharing their own background, while also learning about other cultures and communities.
4. Provide opportunities for high school youth and college students to build positive connections through creative expression.
5. Provide opportunities and structure for college students to implement positive youth development practices, learn about community organizing, and develop leadership skills through weekly planning sessions.
6. Explore and share narratives through the means of visual art, both as individuals and as a community.

The importance of providing a structured and safe environment facilitates the development of relationships and the exploration of creative mechanisms for expressing feelings, hopes, and concerns. In addition, these program objectives highlight the importance of empowerment and democratic principles shaping of youth participation and their decision-making powers.

Recruitment and Retention

Participation in youth photovoice projects is best conceptualized along two important dimensions: recruitment and retention. Camp CAMERA relies heavily upon the organizational structure of the host organizations for recruitment. In the case of the Boys & Girls Club, participants must be a member of the organization. Participation in Camp CAMERA represents one of many program options open to members. YouthCARE, too, draws upon participants in their program.

Retention has not been a major issue for the program. There have been several participants that have been members for several years. These individuals go through the same structured participation every year, and each year the experiences and depth and quality of their work shows progression and further development. There are many members who have successfully sold their photographs, ranging in price from $15 to $400. Participation in a photovoice project does not guarantee that youth will be able to generate money for their art.

The program has found that retention increases in cases where sizeable numbers of participants attend the same schools. In instances where a youth participant is not part of a group and lives in a shelter, for example, that individual will not have the benefit of a group reinforcing his or her participation. Many students take the school bus after school to arrive at the Boys and Girls Club for this program, but if a student does not regularly attend school, he or she may not have transportation at the end of the day. It is important to emphasize that transportation home after the program is provided to help ensure participation, and, when possible, transportation to the program may also be provided. Also, weekly reminder texts are sent, and youth send project staff texts to confirm meetings.

Composition of Youth Artists

A total of 80 youth artists have enrolled in Camp CAMERA over the past four years (eight semesters). In addition, 27 college students were participants in the project. The high school youth in the Camp CAMERA program are urban youth who face a high probability of leaving school before graduation and possibly engaging in negative or unsafe behavior. These low numbers of high school and college students in the program facilitates relationship-building, which will be addressed again later in this chapter.

The majority of Camp CAMERA's artists must contend with navigating neighborhood gang-related violence, drug abuse, homelessness, and/or inequitable educational opportunities. Many of the program participants come from families with household incomes at or below the federal poverty guidelines.

Many of the high school youth served have not had prior access to formal programs using the arts, and they will be the first in their family to attend college, for those who consider this a goal. Their neighborhood environment makes participation in a safe and constructive after-school program that much more meaningful from a safety and intellectual perspective. When this participation involves an arts-based curriculum, it brings an exciting and much-needed dimension to their participation.

The ethnic/racial and gender composition differs according to the semester. Camp CAMERA partnered with the Open World Learning Community School for its first fall semester in 2011. Following the first year, the program partnered with the Al Lenzmeier West Side Boys & Girls Club for the fall semesters. The Boy and Girls Club serves youth 13 to 18 years old and works only with females, as the organization requested gender-specific programming to help address the need for equity and engagement for adolescent women in their community.

The ethnic backgrounds of youth attending the Boys & Girls Clubs of the Twin Cities are as follows: African American (49 percent), Asian American (10 percent), Caucasian (20 percent), Latino (10 percent), Native American (3 percent) and multiracial (8 percent). There is a larger representation of Latino youth and families at the Al Lenzmeier West Side Branch, for St. Paul's West Side has historically been a Mexican and Latino neighborhood. Camp CAMERA's groups of young women from the two fall semesters at the West Side Branch were predominantly Latina. The Boys & Girls Club's mission is to enable all young people, especially those who are most in need, to reach their full potential as productive, caring, responsible citizens.

For the spring semesters of 2011, 2012 and 2013, Camp CAMERA partnered with YouthLEAD (Youth Leadership, Education, and Diversity), which is a yearlong after-school program run by YouthCARE. This program serves adolescents ages 13–18 from Minneapolis and St. Paul. The ethnic backgrounds of youth attending programming in YouthLEAD are as follows: African American (40 percent), Asian American (31 percent), Native American (4 percent), Chicano/Latino (7 percent), white, non-Latinos (6 percent), and African (5 percent). YouthLEAD's mission is to develop youth leadership and employment skills while building multicultural friendships among youth, through positive after school and weekend activities. Their mission paralleled closely that of Camp CAMERA, which helped facilitate a collaborative partnership. However, it was not sustainable, and Camp CAMERA then strengthened its partnership with the Boys & Girls Club, where the program lives on each semester.

Structure and Scheduling of Activities

Camp CAMERA is a structured program covering a total of ten weeks, with each session lasting approximately two hours (4:45 to 6:45). The following outline typifies the structure and scheduling of the activities, including the pedagogical philosophy and learning objectives:

Week	Activity	Pedagogical Philosophy/Learning Targets
1	Ice breakers, intro to program, & scavenger hunt	Providing a basic framework of photography and giving students the opportunity to meet each other and get to know each other.
2	Presentations and practicum	Learn about digital and black-and-white photography, the history of photography, and guidelines of framing, lighting and composition. Also, learn about careers in the media and photojournalism.
3	Gallery field trip— Wing Young Huie	Discuss identity development, capturing community's realities and self-expression. Engage with a professional photographer to learn how art can mobilize individuals and communities. Chalkboard activity.
4, 5	Darkroom & studio workshops	Develop photographs and learn the chemical and technical process of darkroom procedures. Think about the narratives and messages behind photographs through working in a studio space. Build pinhole cameras and learn light writing.
6	Camera time	Experiment with photographing and apply what they have learned to their photography.
7	Critiques	Receive input from their peers and the college students and practice giving constructive criticism and learning different perspectives and stories through photographs.
8	Editing & artist statement	Practice articulating their own artistic process and the narratives behind the photographs.
9	Gallery exhibition & A cappella group for opening night	Celebrate and share their hard work with the company of family, friends, and community members. Show is accompanied by musical performances.
10	Evaluation	Reflect individually and collectively on the success and challenges of the program and of their own personal development.

The chart outlining the 10-week structure of the program touches upon the key elements associated with photovoice covered in the previous seven chapters, and illustrates a wide range of ways that photovoice can be implemented. Each of these sessions can involve bringing in youth consultants, or they can be self-contained, depending upon the goals and budget of a project.

Exhibitions

As addressed in Chapter 5, photo exhibitions represent a major activity in the life of a photovoice project, and every effort must be made to ensure the likelihood of success for this phase of a project. Camp CAMERA's photovoice exhibitions are carefully planned and are multifaceted in how they are conceptualized, reflecting the importance of this event in the lives of youth artists. Regardless of how they are conceptualized, and the budget and resources devoted to them, there is no question of their importance, because they represent a culminating event in a project's history.

Due to the semester structure of the program, there is but one annual photo exhibition involving both groups. The Boys & Girls Club group finishes their project at the end of the fall semester. They are provided with a copy of a photo album book and have a small exhibition at Macalester College. The photobook and exhibition help to anchor the group until the annual exhibition in the spring, which highlights both semesters of work from the year.

Camp CAMERA has endeavored to have its gallery shows catered to increase attendance and introduce a celebratory atmosphere. In the spring of 2013, one of the youth photographers broke out into singing and playing the guitar, adding a nice arts-dimensional and participatory feel to the event. Usually, the program invites students in the Macalester College choir to come join the evening pro-gramming. A special effort is also made to reach out and be inviting to parents of Camp CAMERA participants. Their presence represents an opportunity for them to join in a celebration with their children.

Camp CAMERA's exhibition illustrates professionalism and pride, and this is clearly conveyed to the audience. The setting for the exhibition must be acces-sible geographically, psychologically, culturally, and operationally, and this is the case with Camp CAMERA's exhibitions, which are held at a local gallery.

Very few youths will experience the joys and anxieties associated with being part of a public art exhibit. Photovoice provides them with such an experience, and with an opportunity to bask in the glory of a major accomplishment. This is both an individual and group–based accomplishment. The photographs taken during an exhibition become part of this experience and allow them to share the event to others. This set of artifacts will always remain to reassure them that they have artistic talent and stories to tell the world.

Funding

External funding through grants is a viable and common way of sponsoring a youth photovoice project. Provision of funds specifically targeting a photovoice project brings with it flexibility to engage and pay participants, for example. External fund-ing can also serve as a constraint to the evolution of a project. In-kind resources, too, bring with them facilitating and hindering forces. For example, the Boys & Girls Club program is focused on adolescent females. There were males who wanted to be a part of the program but could not participate because of funding restrictions.

As will be addressed later on under the category of "Challenges," funding of Camp CAMERA has been in-kind and closely tied to grants funded through host-collaborative organizations. The established nature of these organizations has facilitated the development of programming, although these grants have shaped the nature of the projects. Camp CAMERA has been funded by a variety of sources, including the Metropolitan Regional Arts Council, as well as the organizations them-selves (Boys & Girls Club of the Twin Cities, YouthCARE, and Macalester College).

Camp CAMERA originally started with $500.00 in funding. An anonymous funder met the director of the program and was impressed with her energy and vision and donated ten cameras. Catering for the annual gallery shows is usually donated. It is truly collaborative in its funding—a local school allows the youth to borrow cameras for the program at the Boys & Girls Club. Broadening donations necessitates a systematically planned effort, and ideally a point person who does this as a major activity. Because Camp CAMERA is a small program, the director wears many different hats, making specialization impossible. Ideally, there would be a staff member in charge of donations, who would also be the person in charge of publicity, since the two functions often go hand-in-hand. Funding is the greatest challenge in sustainability of this program.

Evaluation

It is often said that it is arduous to demonstrate competence, but it is easy to demonstrate a lack of competence. The building of markers that are widely accepted as indicating competence is important in photovoice. These markers cannot be imposed on youth. Instead, the participants must play an active and meaningful role in determining them.

Depending on funding sources, each semester has its own evaluation structure, including both a written and oral component for all students to complete. Camp CAMERA often has surveys at the end of the program. The evaluation instruments and process are structured in a manner than facilitates youth sharing their experiences and opinions, with questions relevant to their participation. Furthermore, evaluation results shape how the program gets modified for future participants.

The following findings were reported on Camp CAMERA's Metropolitan Regional Art Council's grant with YouthCARE in spring 2012. In addition to oral and written evaluations, the program was also evaluated by the advisory board, and by alumni staff of the program. In addition, the program used the comment book to provide insight from the gallery audience (the public). The audience aspect of evaluation brings a different and much needed perspective to the project. These comments supplement verbal comments made throughout the exhibition.

Camp CAMERA employs a variety of scavenger hunt activities to help the youth put their new knowledge into practice. There are also different tutorials and workshops to help them develop and explore composition and specific photographic techniques. In the evaluations, the high school youth report that they learned a lot about lighting, portraits, how to use a professional camera, how cameras function, the aperture, light writing, pinhole cameras, how to develop photographs in the darkroom, and long-exposure motion manipulation. In addition to providing youth with workshops that help them develop their photographic skills and techniques, they are taught about the agency they have in representing their own lives through photography, which becomes apparent in their artist statements and in their evaluations.

Below are examples of excerpts and interpretations taken from the 2012 evaluations that provide a range of experiences and responses, and that bring to life what Camp CAMERA meant to these young artists. These excerpts touch upon key themes related to arts-based practice, and to the transformative potential it has in the life of urban youth.

One youth writes, "*I learned I like photography. It captures a moment in time that only a certain person sees and makes it into something everyone can see and interpret.*" Another youth states, "*I think photography can help you express yourself because you can capture moments forever.. . . It can show how different people live and how things work.*" The importance of exploring self-expression also became apparent through another youth, who wrote, "*I do think photography helps me express myself because I take pictures of my life and how I feel and what I see.*"

Also, both the college students and the high school students shared that getting to know new people was their favorite part of the program. A youth writes, "*My favorite part was the people! Everybody was so awesome!*" A college student writes, "*One of the great things about this program is that it brings people together with a diversity of backgrounds but with a common interest.*"

While the majority of Camp CAMERA students involved did feel like they got to know each other, some high school and college students disagreed and wished they could have developed stronger connections by having the program be longer. Many of the high school and college students also seemed to agree that they wanted it to be a longer experience, as they all wanted to continue to get to know each other and felt that they were just beginning that journey after eight weeks. Some high school students suggested meeting twice a week, and others wanted the Camp CAMERA program to be a yearlong experience.

The youth and the larger college art community were both very moved by the gallery show and this project. The gallery show gave high school youth an opportunity to see their work valued and professionally presented, which for many was very powerful and inspiring. One of the youth in the program referred to her experience at the gallery show as "*really different and new. It's like it's out of a movie. . .*"

The gallery show brought an immense amount of pride and honor to the youths' work and perspectives. Everyone who signed our gallery comment book as well as the gallery owner and curator himself was very impressed with the event and the quality of the youths' work. The gallery show also provided the larger audience of middle school, high school and college-aged students to come together to celebrate and explore the diversity in experiences displayed through the photographs. In writing the artist statements and biographies, one youth writes her favorite part as being "*the opportunity to show people what I see around my community. . . . I tried to portray diversity and unity—'everyone is connected some how.*'"

The youth have also been changed by the opportunity they have had to build positive relationships with older college students through this project. From this experience, they now feel more comfortable in a postsecondary educational setting, since they have all gotten to know college students and made friends with many of their peers through weekly team-building activities, icebreakers, and workshops on campus. All of the students have been asked in some form to step out of their comfort zone and join a community of trust centered on photography. They have experienced breaking out of their comfort zones and building relationships with people they would not otherwise have met. This can cause situations that are painful and produce tension, but that is part of the learning experience and prepares them for future encounters that expose them to new relationship experiences.

A youth reflects on the Camp CAMERA experience by saying, "*I feel like by the end of the program I was close with everyone.*" Another youth says, "*I mean really college is just like high school but with big kids, a little older.*" Beginning to identify with higher education is an important part of the experience. In addition, many of the college students were changed through their participation in the program and gained an immense amount from this experience, as they were challenged to take on leadership positions and facilitate workshops, critiques, and many weeks of programming. In the college students' written evaluations, many of them voiced their development of leadership and photographic knowledge as well as their interest in pursuing teaching and youth development work. One student writes, "*It's opened my eyes to the importance of nonprofits and youth engagement, something I will surely pursue in the future.*" Another student writes, "*It made me realize that even our smallest interactions with people can have such a profound impact.*"

The quotes provided by Camp CAMERA participants provide insights into the various ways they were transformed, with some being obvious and expected and others totally unexpected. Development of an evaluation process that welcomes a nuanced approach towards transformation is greatly encouraged. This qualitative approach humanizes their experiences. But as the reader can no doubt see, capturing voices is essential in photovoice evaluation. Youth photovoice is about capturing youth voices, and evaluation must do so as well.

Key Findings and Change That Resulted

Camp CAMERA has resulted in many positive outcomes, and the following list of six is illustrative of the potential of photovoice to transform lives of all those who are part of this type of undertaking. The program led to (1) a more positive connection to college for high school students, who felt that college was less intimidating; (2) a development of positive relationships for both high school and college students; (3) a better understanding of how art can strengthen communities and be used to promote self-expression and identity; (4) the high school students gaining photographic techniques and skills; (5) the college students learning about youth development practices and philosophies; and (6) students recognizing their own agency and ability to share their own life narratives and perspectives through photography.

Urban youth rarely have the opportunity to venture out of their prescribed social circles and meet and relate to students, particularly those who are white, non-Latino, and in college. Urban youth have talents, dreams, fears, and life stories that are worth sharing, and the arts provide a viable vehicle for doing this. Opportunities to do so, unfortunately, are very limited. The same can be said about those who have privileged backgrounds. This divide is never easy to close. Photography, and more specifically photovoice, has unlimited potential for bridging these worlds. Arts-based methods, as addressed throughout this book, provide alternative ways of arriving at lived experiences.

Donations

Successful youth photovoice projects require various forms of funding, and donation of supplies, equipment, food, and transportation, for example. When donations are made by community organizations, ownership of the project increases, and this translates into engendering community pride in their youth.

Local Media Coverage

Publicity related to the exhibition must be carefully thought through, because it needs to target the specific audience that the project wishes to reach. Camp CAMERA's exhibitions rely heavily upon the galleries sponsoring the exhibition. They handle the publicity for the event through websites and the issuing of invitations. Camp CAMERA has not undertaken a media campaign. If the program wishes to expand in the future, such a campaign will be essential, particularly if the funding base is to expand. They did successfully complete a kickstarter campaign, which increased their visibility and media exposure.

Retention

Urban youth photovoice projects are very much needed to help these youth develop competencies and be empowered. It is important to note that retention is not a serious concern for Camp CAMERA. Typically, a project might start with 13 participants and one or two may not finish. Reliability and consistency are qualities that are assessed to help ensure that those who start will finish.

Those who can benefit the most from this arts-based method also tend to be living in highly under-organized neighborhoods. Photovice projects can be viewed as an anchor in their lives, and retention becomes an important challenge. Camp CAMERA provides transportation, which is a critical service to ensure participation. When youth participants are clustered in local schools, they reinforce attending the program for each other. Those who live far away, or are not in daily contact with other members, find it harder to attend and are more likely to drop out.

FUTURE LEADERSHIP PLANS

All good things endure change and are subject to new directions. After Leah Krieble and Lauryn Gutierrez founded the program, Alex Bendz moved forward and took over the program's leadership, maintaining the partnership with YouthCare through the spring of 2013 and then strengthening the partnership with the Boys & Girls Club, where the program still continues. While the leadership of Camp CAMERA program has been taken over by Alex Bendz, a Macalester student who started with the program during his freshman year, he is now a senior and is looking for a current Macalester student to step forward. The plans for fall 2014 are for a current student to assume leadership as an intern for credit under the supervision of Professor Tina Kruse. The post-2014 plans have not yet been determined as this book goes to press.

LESSONS LEARNED AND RECOMMENDATIONS

Summarizing lessons and recommendations in a limited amount of space is always a challenge, and it certainly is in this instance. Nine lessons stand out and address a variety of results that show the power of photography to be an affirming and liberating method. None of the lessons learned and recommendations will come as a surprise.

Photovoice is a very powerful and instrumental tool for sharing identities and narratives. Chapters 2 and 3 ground photovoice within a rich tradition of arts-based interventions that actively seek to help youth gain a greater awareness of their identities. Although narratives play an active role in helping youth to construct messages, in combination with images these narratives give voice to identities that are difficult to convey, and they do so in a manner that is "youth-friendly."

This program is run best by a college student who currently has access to all resources, spaces, and tools made available by the institution. Thus, it is important to inspire loyalty and commitment within your cohort of college volunteers. Youth photovoice can be undertaken with a wide range of resources. There is no denying that resources, financial or in-kind, are necessary to maximize participation and assist with telling of a story. Age, in turn, becomes a resource or a form of capital that can be considered invisible but wields considerable influence on relationship development and outcomes.

It is important to give college students agency in order for them to be personally invested in the program's sustainability. Good will is necessary for

co-researchers to be effective. Financial, technical, administrative, and psychological support are essential to aid youth in maximizing their potential and achieving positive transformations in their lives. Empowerment that results from participation in an urban youth photovoice projects can also occur among those collaborating with youth. In the case of Camp Camera, college students, too, are young.

Camp CAMERA asks for a strong level of commitment, and when choosing and recruiting both high school and college students for this program, commitment is a key to success. Thus, it is best to be very explicit in describing how much the program will ask of the individual, sharing the timeline with the student and, in the case of the high school student, with a guardian or parent as well. Clear expectations and explanations of the program is standard procedure in youth photovoice projects (see Chapter 5). Actively seeking the consent and support of parents or legal guardians represents an opportunity for photovoice projects to dispel suspicions and misunderstandings regarding what a project consists of and what is expected of participants. This support, needless to say, is essential.

The time and effort expended during the recruitment period can be a foundation for future support. For example, the project requires parental or legal guardian consent because participants are under the age of 18. This consent sometimes involves telephone contact or in-person meetings.

The ideal ratio of college students to high school students is 1:2. This ratio allows each youth participant to get individualized attention, making it easier to establish and maintain a relationship. The subject of photovoice ratio is obviously very important. Unfortunately, it is rare for a program to advocate for, or suggest, a particular ratio. A small participant-to-facilitator ratio helps ensure that relationship-building can transpire, and also facilitates sharing of expectations and communication.

Transportation is often a barrier for program youth, so providing rides to and from the program is critical. Geographical access must not be a hindering factor for participation in an urban photovoice project. Offering transportation conveys to youth that a project values their participation and creates opportunities to share and engage in development of trust and relationship-building while traveling from home to site.

Many of our youth have a variety of responsibilities and changes in housing during the course of the program, so checking in with them and sending them reminders increases consistency in weekly attendance. Lives that can be classified as chaotic require structure and consistency. Developing routines in these lives becomes a major goal in helping urban youth navigate troubling environments. This grounding also serves to reinforce the importance of planning daily and weekly schedules.

Focusing on process and experience instead of product is important, and focusing on building relationships with each other is a large part of the program's success. Indeed, all the students involved listed this as one of their

favorite aspects of the program. A focus on the lived experience and ensuring that all youth are actively engaged in the process increases the likelihood that the photos and narratives capture the meaning and potential for transformation. This emphasis places project staff in the difficult position of addressing a multiple of expressive and instrumental needs that will emerge in the course of carrying out a photovoice project.

While the program's focus is on the experience of building positive relationships and feeling celebrated, Camp CAMERA also provides youth with a tangible takeaway. This can vary depending on capacity and funding, but it might be a personal thank you from one of their college mentors, two prints of their two favorite photographs, a photobook, a certificate of completion, or a t-shirt with their logo on it. Camp CAMERA has found that these "takeaways" help reinforce the youth's positive experience and help them take their experience (their lessons learned and skills developed) with them post-program. Concrete takeaways will remain constant reminders of their accomplishments, and reinforce that they were part of a positive group experience. These artifacts may be relatively inexpensive. For some youth, and possibly many, this may be a rare experience.

The lessons learned fall into experiential, instrumental, and information realms, highlighting how much work goes into a youth photovoice program. It would be simplistic to think about how this program has impacted youth without taking a comprehensive perspective, and it is fair to say that all participants, including staff, have benefitted from their involvement in this program.

CHALLENGES AND DILEMMAS

Camp CAMERA has encountered a number of dilemmas, which should not come as any great surprise to anyone who has carried out a youth photovoice project. Over the course of designing and working to sustain this program, three main dilemmas were encountered: (A) funding and organizational needs can shift over time, (B) sustaining the tools (competencies) developed in the program is a challenge, and (C) an understanding of reciprocity is critical to the program's goals.

Funding and Organizational Needs

Instead of creating its own independent organization (501c3 status), Camp CAMERA currently works within existing organizations (Boys & Girls Club of the Twin Cities and YouthCARE) because this has been most effective in terms of writing grants, ensuring program sustainability, and having a strong relationship with the youth. The leaders of Camp CAMERA sometimes wonder if they could be more effective as a separate nonprofit that partners with other organizations rather than existing solely within them.

The program has been able to adapt to fit within the needs of the Boys & Girls Club's different grant requirements by including additional themes in the programming. This has, however, shifted the program's structure and content, creating additional successes and challenges. One of the main changes is that the Al Lenzmeier West Side Boys & Girls Club asked for gender-specific programming, primarily for adolescent women, because they wanted to address this specific population and the need to engage young women in programming. Thus, one year, for a workforce development grant, Camp CAMERA focused on "Careers in the Media for Young Women," which provided an additional theme and focus on photojournalism and job readiness. This was a very engaging and powerful theme for participating youth to consider, and they enjoyed this additional level of depth.

Another year, Camp CAMERA focused on the theme of "Capturing Inspiring Women." This theme reflected the United Way grant the Boys & Girls Club had received to run young women's empowerment programming. While the college students in the program enjoyed this theme, the youth felt overly confined and voiced their distaste for this lens. Many of the young women felt they didn't have role models (particularly women) who inspired them in their lives, and they wanted to focus on other content. To address this issue, the youth were asked to consider the theme as a guide but not to let it limit them, and to continue to capture anything they felt worth exploring.

One of the youth said she would have enjoyed the theme of "Family" but didn't like the idea of focusing solely on women role models. The issue of an additional imposed theme due to organizational needs or grant requirements has both its plusses and minuses for program development. Being cognizant of the differences between communities (our youth) and funders (grants & organizations) is critical in finding a theme that does not inhibit youth creativity while also recognizes the grant's motives and objectives.

Sustainability of Tools (Competencies) Developed

One of the other dilemmas in this program is sustaining the tools and skills the high school youth develop, since they do not regularly have access to digital cameras, darkrooms, and photography post-program. As phone technology continues to improve, there has been an increase in the continuation of photography post-program as youth use their iPhones and camera phones to take photographs. However, it is still important to recognize that after improving their technical and stylistic skills in this program, the high school students do not get to keep the camera they used.

During the program, there is usually a two-week period where the youth get to borrow a camera and do their own "field study" research. This is where the majority of the photographs begin to develop and where the youth begin to truly understand and engage with photography. Camp CAMERA struggled with this structure initially, because it was not clear how giving a youth a camera and then taking it away could create a sustainable experience.

To address this issue, the program has stressed that the importance of Camp CAMERA is in the understanding of how to share one's story, narrative, values, and culture, as much as it is about the specific photographic skills developed. Camp CAMERA hopes that in the future the participants will continue with digital photography, either in college or in another program. The primary focus is in gaining pride and confidence in one's own identity and story, and recognizing one's own agency and talents. Camp CAMERA has also sought to reinforce the experience of sharing stories and celebrating each other through the large gallery show exhibition at the end of the program. There are very few instances and places where such sharing can transpire in this society. Using photography, and the corresponding narratives, is one vehicle for achieving this transformation.

Understanding Reciprocity, Race, Privilege, and Power

The subject of racial and ethnic relations is endemic to any serious discuss of urban youth photovoice. Some researchers would go so far as to argue that the value, learning, and transformation that occur because of these discussions are at the heart or urban-based photovoice. The dilemma of bridging a liberal arts college community and a high school youth group is making sure to ensure reciprocity and the principle that we are all here to learn and teach each other.

Quite often, college students initially take teaching roles in administering activities, and they need to be reminded that we are all participants being led by each other. While the program is structured for individual college students to create and lead the activities, everyone participates (both the other college students and the high school students).

High school youth often recognize the lack of racial diversity in the college student group, because the college campus is predominantly white, non-Latino, while the youth groups are mostly of color. Usually this conversation happens once the youth are back at YouthCARE or the Boys & Girls Club, or when riding home in the van after the program, so the college students are not present. The youth's observations lead to productive conversations about the achievement gap as well as the history and impacts of oppression in the United States.

Also, during the college trainings and planning sessions, a similar background is provided to the college students so they can understand diversity and their own position within the student body and the larger community, opening up the space for conversations about racism, inequities, diversity, privilege, and power.

PHOTOS AND NARRATIVES

There is no question that youth photovoice is all about photos and narratives. The reader, I would dare guess, has faithfully read the material related to setting the context and describing the program. Each photograph will have information regarding the artist, the photo and corresponding narrative, and additional information when provided to help further contextualize the experience. Typically, Camp CAMERA creates themes to be used for each session, and leaves them open-ended. The following are examples of the various frameworks and instructions: "take what you feel should be shared with the world"; "what inspires you" or "what are you thankful for"; "what is valuable to you"; "use your camera to tell your story." The photographs selected for inclusion in this chapter represent examples of these themes.

A total of eight youths agreed to share their work in this book, and that involved fifteen photographs with corresponding narratives. Each of the artists selected brings a unique perspective on photovoice, yet there are prevailing themes that emerge related to identity, hopes and dreams, painful episodes, and perspectives on life. Several artists wanted more than one photograph to be included in this book. Some of the artists provided great detail on the photographs, while others were content in using few words. One artist (Dianna Gadea-Rodrigues) elected to provide a detailed background of who she was.

Photo Image and Narrative #1

Name: Dianna

School: Open World Learning Community School

Background of artist: *"I am a Mexican American girl that takes pride in my education and my community. Born in Saint Paul, MN, and raised everywhere my family could find work. My heart will always be on the West Side of Saint Paul as it is the only place I have memories from all different stages of my life. I have moved many times, created new friends and had to adjust to different new situations, but between each place, my family always moves back to the West Side. I've lived in Oregon, Utah, and Mexico.*

Living in Mexico, I learned that life isn't always easy. I always could afford glasses and shoes and that's why other kids from the neighborhood would pick on me. Because I got picked on, I learned how to not take everything to heart and to treat others with the respect and consideration I knew I deserved. Everyone deserves the opportunity to be supported and to be themselves. In Mexico, I saw a lot of poverty and watched my family be creative in making new businesses to keep our family going. I would always help my mother with the store and the house. I remember when the living room turned into my mom's shoe store and the garage was where my dad fixed the neighborhood's cars.

I am one of seven children from both my mom and my dad's families. I represent the future."

Narrative of why she is sharing the photograph, titled *A Walk of Life*: *"I am sharing this photograph because I believe it represents nature and city life, as the bottom half is taken by the Mississippi River and the top half is showing downtown buildings, including my school. The pathway leading towards the city is representing where I may go on my journey through life. I have framed this image so the path cuts off and leaves us wondering and in a mystery."*

Photo Image and Narrative #2

Monica (Three Photographs of the Same Rose)

Title: *La Rosa de Guadalupe*

Description of Photograph: *"This flower makes miracles. It is important part of the tradition of remembering miracles happen and anything is possible."*

Photo Image and Narrative #3

Name: Jennifer

Title: *Beautiful*

Description of photograph: *"I chose this photograph because there are different stages represented by the green and brown leaves and white and green tree bark. I like how the different colors show different stages life goes through and each stage is beautiful. I also liked this photograph because I liked the angle I was able to capture it all from, and I felt the picture tells a story."*

Photo Image and Narrative #4

Name: Blanca

Title: *Stressin*

Description of Photograph: *"Thinking of the if's of life. Worrying about the future. Struggling with high grades and gossip. Confused and stressed about what the future holds for this high school teen?"*

Photo Image and Narrative #5

Name: Brenda (Two Photographs)

Title 1: *Yellow House*

Description of Photograph: *"What may seem small to you may be huge to someone else."*

Title 2: *Man in the woods*

Description of Photograph: *"Watch your back—you never know who's following you."*

Photo Images and Narratives #6

Name: Corrina (Three Photographs)

Title 1: *Other Side of the Fence*

Description of Photograph: *"I was after school one day and I decided to look over the river. I walked all the way to the end of the street and hopped a fence. I sat there for a while taking in the beautiful view and I just decided to capture it."*

Title 2: *Blue Rust*

Description of Photograph: *"This city has been through a lot and been here a long time but through all of this roughness, it is still strong and beautiful."*

Title 3: *The Last Leaf*

Description of Photograph: *"This photo captures the end of fall and the beginning of winter, with the last leaf of fall and first frost of winter."*

Photo Image and Narrative #7

Name: Maricella (YouthCare Participant) (Two Photographs)

Title 1: *Connections*

Description of Photograph: *"As a student who has a dream to become a marine biologist, a lot of people tell me 'It's not about what you know, but who you know'. This photo exemplifies that the relationships that one makes can benefit them in the long run. It could be as simple as making wise choices among the group of friends one choses to be around, or it can be as easy as introducing yourself to different people. Having a relationship and connection with positive people will benefit the individual in his/her future. This photo focuses on the web of people holding each other up. Connections and positive relations will build a better, healthier community."*

Title 2: *The New Girl*

Description of Photograph:"*A Pancake Breakfast event with YouthCARE introduced me to this beautiful brick wall. My friends and I were cleaning up the aftermath and were told to throw trash bags off of a balcony to a trash can below us. On my way back in the building I stopped at the doorway and took this photo, not thinking much of it, I focused on the blue bricks and took the photo. When looking back at my photos, the red door on the brown brick building stood out to me, as if it was the new girl in a school where everyone knows each other. The red door looks exposed, different, and new. Though the photo focuses on the rustic blue brick wall, the red door calls with vulnerability. It is radiant in it's color and exposure."*

Photo Image and Narrative #8

Name: Brittany (Two Photographs)

Title 1: *Defying Gravity*

Description of Photograph: *"I took this photograph at the sculpture garden and I thought it was cool and different."*

Title 2: *Music in the Sky*

Description of Photograph: *"Rules are made to be broken. Set yourself free."*

PHOTOGRAPHS/NARRATIVES OBSERVATION THEMES

There are a number of themes that can be found in the reading of this case study of Camp CAMERA. It shows off one model for youth photovoice in which the program uses photovoice as the central mechanism for reaching out to urban youth. Photovoice, in this arts-based example, showcases this method as a form of intervention or practice rather than as a research mechanism. Participation in an after-school program is nonstigmatizing, thereby allowing photovoice projects to address a variety of themes or issues with minimal concerns about negative reactions. Having a photovoice based in community institutions with positive relationships further grounds this method within the community. Photovoice's flexibility allows local circumstances to dictate how this method unfolds, whether as an intervention or research project.

The premise that every youth is an artist waiting for an opportunity to express himself or herself is certainly true in the case of Camp CAMERA. Every community, regardless of economic level, has a cadre of poets, authors, painters, and photographers. The youth photographs and narratives are evidence of this premise. Some youth will continue and pursue advanced studies in photography, while others will use photography as a hobby. Their homes and communities will be beneficiaries of their artistic talents.

Finally, it is important to comment on what happens when an organization's founder decides to leave and a program or organization must contend with a new leader. That will be the case When Leah Krieble leaves her leadership position to pursue graduate social work study in New York City. How this transition is planned will go a long way towards dictating whether, and how, Camp CAMERA evolves, or if it will stop operating.

Conclusion

Case studies can be viewed from a storytelling perspective, in very similar fashion to photovoice. The perspective of the storyteller/photographer brings a lens, and bias, to what he or she thinks is what is important to share, and how it is best shared. This chapter has provided an in-depth view of how an urban youth photovoice project can be initiated by stressing the importance of community collaborative partnerships. Camp CAMERA's collaborative arrangements allowed for this program to emerge with minimal external funding. Such a model brings with it challenges in how photovoice themes are selected.

The voices of youth participants bring to life the potential of this arts-based method of inquiry to capture voices and transform lives. Camp CAMERA's youth artists, and their college counterparts, opened up worlds for each that rarely get crossed. Achievements in these areas are often very arduous to measure. When they occur, everyone is able to identify this accomplishment and the profound meaning it has for their lives. This discovery of newfound knowledge and insight often represents the cornerstone of any photovoice outcome. Personal transformation is not possible without this knowledge.

As programs and organizations using photovoice continue to evolve, there will be opportunities to develop organizational ladders for participants to continue their involvement in programming and eventually assume leadership. This is critical, since such a ladder increases the likelihood that a photovoice project can be community-owned, and can provide an opportunity for youth who age-out to continue work in this field. In essence, the investment in this generation will secure future success and strength within the next generation and the community at large.

SECTION FOUR

Lessons Learned and Future Directions

It is important, however, to not lose sight of why we do the work we do. If we think that change is always about someone else, or about some divisions of policy-making **out there**, we fail to recognize that all of us who engage in research, visual or otherwise, are already in positions to affect some change or some social action somewhere. We can do this most effectively when we attend to the details of both production and display. Let us, then, be haunted by images, and work with communities in ways that ensure that others are similarly haunted.

—MITCHELL, 2011, p. 200

Epilogue

Any reader familiar with my writing would know that I have an affinity for epilogues. An epilogue provides me with a final opportunity to highlight current and emerging issues that were encountered in the process of writing this book. In many ways, it is also an opportunity to pontificate, if you wish, under the guise of scholarship, and to draw attention to topics that I believe are salient, but it will necessitate a considerable and concerted effort to address them. Identifying them is the first step in solving them, although "solving" them in the near future, or even at all, may just be wishful thinking on my part.

There is no one way of conducting photovoice, which should not come as any great surprise, and therein lies the beauty and attractiveness of this method. This "flexibility" is both a strength and challenge for this method. Flexibility allows local circumstances to dictate the best approach, and there is no "litmus test" that must be passed in order to officially call a research project "photovoice worthy." This flexibility brings with it profound theoretical and practical challenges in achieving a high degree of conformity on the elements and process that are essential in order for research to be photovoice.

The goal of achieving conceptual clarity and consistency is still in its infancy, so to speak. Photovoice, I believe, is best conceptualized as an expanding universe that will eventual pause and solidify. Before that happens, photovoice will encompass everything labeled "photography." This is natural and it sets the stage for the issues that follow. Youth photovoice gets shaped by a thirst for creativity and innovation, care of people, and curiosity interacting together, resulting in living practice research (Croker & Tooth, 2013). These aspects are endemic to arts-based research (Learmonth & Huckvale, 2013).

The following eleven themes or topics are particularly challenging and have received insufficient attention in the literature, or been completely overlooked. In either case, they need to benefit from attention and debate if urban youth photovoice, or photovoice in general, as a research method is to advance theoretically or empirically in the near future. These topics are not presented in any order of importance. Rather, they are presented as they emerged in the course of writing this book.

Is Photovoice a Research Panacea?

I would love to answer yes to this question. Unfortunately, I cannot. In all fairness, no research method is a panacea, as noted by Patton, Higgs, and Smith (2011): "Visual data will not solve all problems or answer all questions and there may be times when use of photographs would be inappropriate, intrusive and unethical" (p. 121). This does not mean that photovoice does not have tremendous potential for helping those on the margins of society find their voices and seeking redress by undertaking social change projects.

Hernandez-Albujar (2007) acknowledges that there are other research approaches, and that the research questions and goals will dictate whether or not photovoice is the preferred method: "It is not my intention to sustain that visual methodologies are the only approach to explore human experiences, but is my experience, visual work is decisively one of the best for conveying the lived experiential components of social life" (p. 304). Photovoice, with necessary modifications to make it a more inclusive research method, can be used to reach out to undervalued groups in a manner that resonates with their preferences for telling their stories.

Visual methodologies bring technical challenges and cost considerations to a research process, as addressed later in this epilogue. Although photovoice can be a standalone method, there is little dispute that it can be an attractive method within a constellation of mixed methods, although it is primarily qualitative in nature. It may also be the case that as this method finds wider acceptance and use it will lose its appeal as innovative. Nevertheless, the potential for photovoice to transform in response to changing circumstances and changes in society means that this method has longevity appeal. Nevertheless, it is not a panacea.

Photovoice, it must be remembered, is a research method that emphasizes action throughout all facets, including a change project at the end. Although this method has been grounded as an arts-based and qualitative method, it also can be grounded as action research. My experience with youth has shown that if I can use activities that are youth-friendly, and that tap their lived experiences, this will facilitates discussions.

These activities represent a nonthreatening way to facilitate mutual trust-building and create an atmosphere of sharing. Further, it is also important to note that photovoice is not a method that lends itself to use by all types of groups and political circumstances, such as those found in totalitarian regimes, for example. Oppressive and reactionary governments represent a sociopolitical context that undermines human rights, severely limiting empowerment and the exercise of freedom of speech. Photovoice would be viewed as a spying technique rather than a transformative method in such circumstances.

In more democratic and less reactionary sociopolitical contexts, photovoice is particularly appealing for youth because of its technical aspects and group-focused activity. It should not be expected to be used by all groups regardless of their social and political circumstances. This is not to say that arts-based visual research approaches do not have universal appeal. Visual approaches to research can be modified, and they are able to be used in a wide variety of circumstances and goals.

Youth-Led or Youth Co-Led

Deciding whether youth photovoice is youth-led or co-led with adults, versus youth participation, strikes at the heart of power and decision-making. The discussion in Chapter 3 concerning the differences between positive and youth-led development has tremendous relevance for youth photovoice projects. That discussion highlighted two very different sociopolitical visions for youth participation, with profound implications for how photovoice unfolds. Each perspective brings certain sociopolitical advantages and disadvantages in the carrying out of a photovoice project, with implications for the type and amount of external funding that can be tapped in carrying out a project; this is not an insignificant a topic in the lives of academics who may be facing pressure to bring in grants, particularly federal grants with high overheads.

Having youth play influential and participatory roles within a positive youth development view of photovoice may make these types of projects more politically and socially acceptable by institutions and funding sources, and that fact should not be minimized. Having youth co-lead or lead, which is preferable from a capacity-enhancement and empowerment perspective, brings a host of political concerns and considerations. Youth photovoice does not operate in a political vacuum. Whether we chose to call this context sociopolitical or socioecological, social change actions by urban youth will get attention, and possibly an adverse reaction, from authorities, depending upon the focus of the photovoice project (Conchas & Virgil, 2010).

There is tension between youth being research leaders or co-leaders with adults. It would be foolhardy to ignore this, even under the best of intentions and circumstances. It is ideal to have youth lead photovoice projects, including membership and leadership of advisory committees, for example, because it removes any doubt about who owns the final product, making the results of photovoice much more meaningful when compared to youth playing secondary roles in this form of research. There is always tension in community research, but this tension is heightened when discussing youth roles in this research.

Technology and Photovoice: Inherent Tensions?

Advances in technology will bring with them opportunities and challenges, with implications for costs and ease of use. Three-dimensional images and web technology, for example, will bring photovoice and digital storytelling closer than ever before, and forever shape both approaches in ways that we can only imagine. These and other forms of advances will challenge the field to keep abreast of innovations. As addressed earlier in this epilogue, these advances present practitioners with ever-increasing options regarding this visual method. These advances also bring with them ever-increasing ethical challenges and dilemmas (Wiles, 2013). Visual research advances not related to technology, too, can be expected to continue to evolve in the near future (Patton, Higgs, & Smith, 2011).

There is little dispute that technological advances have made photovoice both easier and harder to use. Cruz and Meyer (2012), for example, specifically address the technological and telecommunication advances in the production of photography, and how practice is influenced by these devices. It is safe to say that advances will continue, and will bring an additional set of elements and considerations for photovoice, not to mention ethical conduct dilemmas.

On one hand, technology has made it less expensive to take and display photographs, and it has introduced new ways of modifying pictures to enhance certain desirable elements, and to reduce or eliminate undesirable aspects. Prior to these digital advances, processing photographs was very expensive and provided limited options for photographers. I can remember having youth take "air-photos," or pictures without film, as a way of practicing and getting use to a camera. Obviously, that was not ideal, but it was necessary based upon the available technology and costs at the time.

Advances in digital media have opened up visual image-making, and it is now more available to the general public (Franklin, 2013). This has made photovoice that much more widely acceptable, because there is a wider potential audience for this form of research. Digital images can be loaded onto computers and lend themselves to being distributed quite easily, facilitating access for the group.

Advances in technology, too, have made cameras that much more advanced and sophisticated, and the costs have been reduced in the process. There is so much more that can be done with photographs as a result. At the same time, however, this has introduced a level of "sophistication" that can be off-putting to youth, who may not be inclined to using cameras. The reader may argue that it is possible to use different types of cameras during a project. That approach may introduce elements of "senior" and "junior" photographers, however, thereby creating the potential for discord into the group process.

Should Youth Weigh In on Ethics?

This question, I hope, proves provocative, since youth play a central role in youth photovoice. The subject of ethics, or more commonly fairness, is an integral part of urban youth life. Discussions on ethics and research are dominated and discussed among academics, with very erudite arguments made that have appeal in academic circles. Community or youth opinions on what constitutes ethics bring to mind my work with youth in getting their opinions on what constitutes "youth development," for example (Delgado, 2002). Efforts to tap youth thoughts or opinions on what constitutes unethical behavior as it relates to photovoice, as in the case of this book but not restricted to this method, offers much appeal.

Once tapped, their opinions and thoughts can bring a more nuanced approach to established ethical principles, as well as add new ones pertaining to fairness, for example. They will introduce vocabulary that engages them in a manner that is not possible from a professional language perspective. I have found the concept of fairness to be sufficiently specific to elicit youth views of moral behavior, for example, and to do so in a way that addresses many of the aspects associated with social justice. Youth-friendly language, including the use of slang, which is often very alien to adult researchers, minimizes distance between those carrying a research project and those who are the focus of the research.

The arts-based literature is replete with pleas and encouragement pertaining to community participation and its role in gaining insight into the lived experience. Interestingly, youth participation in establishing criteria for determining ethical conduct has not received similar attention. It is only when this occurs that arts-based research, with its CBPR (community-based participatory research) propensity, can bring an important dimension that is missing. It may be that specific aspects of ethical conduct are more appealing for youth to address. It is advisable that youth have input into designing or refining ethical decision-making. Their input will have a positive impact on their ultimate ownership of these standards and decision-making processes.

Urban Youth as Artists

Values and principles related to indigenous community assets and viewing youth as a national resource set the stage for viewing urban youth as assets. Photovoice is both an art form and a research method. Youth engagement with photovoice casts them as artists and researchers. In their role as artists, this art form may open up new vistas or opportunities for them to assume a new way of thinking about themselves. "Artist" as part of a social identity, serves to broaden potential youth contributions to their community, and also open up avenues for youth to pursue careers.

It certainly is not out of the ordinary to see artistic representation in the nation's inner cities. Murals, graffiti, or community-built sculptures, for example, are created by indigenous artists. Unfortunately, these artists have not been labeled as such by outside authorities. Instead, they have been labeled "lawbreakers." Efforts to impose this label and social identity on youth artists has necessitated that they go underground.

I am of saying that urban communities consist of authors, painters, poets, and other artists. There are very few formal outlets for their talents. Youth with gifts of cartooning, for example, get in trouble if this is done during school time. Yet there are very limited after-school outlets that allow them to advance their talents and show their community their gifts. Having youths assume the label of "artist" shows the community that it, too, has these gifted residents.

New Challenges for Urban Youth Photovoice

There are numerous challenges for photovoice, youth-focused or otherwise. One challenge is to find new topics of particular relevance to urban youth, and to do so without being exploitive or sensational. Although photovoice has seen an explosion in its use under a wide variety of circumstances, this method is still in its infancy. It may be tempting to find projects that are "exotic" to attract external funding (Spencer, 2011). It is our role to take our marching orders, so to speak, from youth and their community, and to "frame" or "package" them in a way that does justice to them and their community, and that attracts funding in the process.

A second challenge will be to find new styles and approaches to photovoice, including combining it with other research methods, particularly those that are qualitative and arts-based. If photovoice is able to continue to evolve, it has a very bright future, particularly if the energy and inspiration for this evolution comes from community participants. Our role as researchers then becomes bridging the worlds of community and academia to foster greater acceptance of photovoice in wider academic and policy circles. Lofus, Higgs, and Trede (2001) speak to the role that qualitative researchers can play in opening up new intellectual spaces: "One of the exciting things about being involved in qualitative research is that we can give ourselves permission to open up new intellectual spaces and be creative . . ." (p. 10).

Community of Practice/Scholars

There is a tremendous need to tap the experiences and expertise of youth photo-voice researchers, in a similar vain to Sanberg and Copes's (2012) study of eth-nographers who do research on drug dealers and offenders. Although a study focused on those who undertake photovoice in general is worthwhile, I believe that a study of those who undertake research with urban youth can be very fruit-ful for the field in general, too. There is no mistake that a call for a community of arts-based research scholars is meant to solidify this partnership (Higgs & Cherry, 2011; Rumbold, Fenner, & Brophy-Dixon, 2012).

Tapping these researchers' knowledge would be invaluable, in that it would allow us to delve deeper into decision-making processes that do not work them-selves into published scholarship, and to find out how undertaking photovoice research has changed the lives of researchers for better or worse. Scholarly published articles rarely discuss issues that are considered "messy" or require researchers to respond in ways that may be considered "unprofessional." The insights these situations generate can be quite helpful in moving the field of photovoice forward.

There is a need to connect youth researchers with each other, in similar fashion to what occurs with their adult counterparts, if youth photovoice is to make significant strides:

> Finally, adult researchers gain recognition of scholarly achievement through journals, books, and conferences. Without adult support, these venues are economically and logistically out of reach or uninviting to youth researchers. If youth are to demonstrate competence and confidence as researchers, more will need to be done to connect them with their adult counterparts. Scholarships that support conference registrations, travel, and lodging will be required. The use of electronic media (e.g., Polycom, Adobe Connect, or GoToMeeting) can connect youth researchers from remote locations. Failure to accommodate the needs of young researchers marginalizes their contributions and hinders the development of youth-led research as a field, practice, and subject of study.
> —WHITE, SHOFFNER, JOHNSON, KNOWLES, & MILLS, 2012

Efforts to bring photovoice researchers together, including co-researchers, as a community of scholars will encourage collaborative projects across communities and nations, providing important insights into how context shapes this research, as well as strategic thinking on how this research method can be advanced. These meetings and collaborative partnerships can also serve as training grounds for those interested in becoming photovoice researchers, including inviting youth. There is a desperate need for new thinking regarding youth as researchers and co-researchers. Youth will no doubt be central players in creating these new ideas on photovoice.

Each One, Teach One

Capacity enhancement is not a concept restricted to geographical or identity communities. This concept can also be applied to communities of practitioners, scholars, and other groups (Lincoln, 2010; Riggs, 2011). Expanding a cadre of researchers is a goal that can be accomplished through a variety of means, including the use of mentoring (Moon, 2012), workshops, internships, and active research collaboration (Titchen & Horsfall, 2011). Photovoice must find its way into school curriculums at all levels of formal education. Social science programs are using photovoice for the purpose of teaching student specific course content such as sociology, anthropology and psychology, for example. This method can also be used to teach a wide variety of topics in adult-education programs that are not higher-learning associated.

Taking this charge and applying it to urban youth taps the values and principles addressed in Chapter 4, and helps to ensure that future generations are well versed in this method. This bodes well for the introduction of innovations that will need to take into account changing demographics and a country that will be facing increased economic challenges, the continued expansion of marginalized groups, and the continued urbanization of its population. This increased urbanization is not restricted to the United States, of course; it is a worldwide phenomenon that shows no sign of slowing down.

We as Adults Are Visitors in the World of Urban Youth

There is a dramatic difference between interviewing youth and "existing" in their world, including addressing researchers' own subjectivities, an all too common occurrence in ethnographic research (Pascoe, 2007). We as adults cannot exist in their world. It is, after all, their world. The best we can do is to visit with a temporary visa, so to speak. We are, in essence, visitors who have been allowed to enter their world for a brief period of time. We had our turn at being young, and the time we now spend in their world must be efficiently used. It is important to remember that their world is not static (the world of adults is not static, either, of course).

Photovoice provides all age groups with an opportunity to bear witness to their joys, sorrows, and aspirations. Their photographs and stories can best be appreciated against a dynamic socioecological background. Their stories, in essence, become tools for change, and we as adults can be allies in these efforts (Morgan et al., 2010). This realization is important to emphasize, though it is frustrating for adult researchers to do so. It must be remembered that, regardless of our abilities to "connect" with urban youth, it is their world and culture. We, at best, are guests. This does not mean that youth can be unwelcoming hosts. But we as adults must be grateful guests.

Researchers Know Yourself

If there is a prevailing theme related to photovoice researchers, it is the importance of reflexive knowledge (Boomer & Frost, 2011; Higgs & Titchen, 2011). Reflexive knowledge refers to self- knowledge and self-awareness. It would be profoundly sad if reflexive knowledge were thought of as being youth-centered, and if adults therefore considered themselves above this form of learning.

The journey of self-awareness is one that should never stop. Unfortunately, we often think of knowledge acquisition as being stage-related in life, and as we grow older there is less and less emphasis on reflexive knowledge. These are not the principles photovoice is predicated upon. Youth and adult photovoice partnerships are enhanced when it is understood that it is a learning journey for all those involved and not just youth. This may seem simplistic. However, the joy of learning is not age-specific.

Limits of Photovoice

Although it would certainly be tempting to complete this book on a positive note about the value and importance of photovoice as a method for addressing social justice themes in the lives of urban youth, I cannot do so. No practice or research method is perfect, and that certainly applies to photovoice, regardless of the population group using it and its focus (Sass, 2008). It is necessary to pause and address what can be considered important limitations, although the advantages far outweigh the limitations. The epilogue is arguably the best place to do so.

The following discussion of limitations is far from being exhaustive and can best be considered illustrative. It also goes beyond the typical debate about the generalizability of the results many in qualitative research are so used to addressing (Stegenga & Burks, 2013). This discussion of limitations is long and I ask the readers' indulgence.

Sass (2008) specifically addresses photovoice and youth empowerment efforts. Research methods, in this case one that is qualitative, provide important insights into social justice issues, and they do so through a participatory process that emphasizes participant voices. Although the process of discovery is immensely important, change must be attempted because of this insight. Thus, at least in the way photovoice has been conceptualized in this book, social change must be attempted. Castleden, Gaucin and First Nation (2008), in turn, in reviewing their experience in using photovoice, see a need for an iterative process as being a key element to the methodological success of their project.

Gant et al. (2009) found that the age of youth using photovoice may be a key factor in determining its potential transformative power. Those youth over the age of 18 benefited more than their younger colleagues. Although all age groups may benefit from photovoice, there may have to be significant modifications to this method in order to take into account developmental stages.

Ponic and Jategaonkar (2012), in their article on balancing safety and action with women who have experienced violence, raise ethical limitations regarding the use of photovoice with women who have experienced intimate partner violence. The subject matter brings with it inherent ethical and safety tensions, placing participants and researchers in the difficult position of creating deleterious consequences when, how, and if reporting to authorities.

Not all experiences and social phenomenon are observable and subject to being photographed (Wilkin & Liamputtong, 2010), and the subject or topic being addressed must lend itself to being photographed. Conversely, discussions can be limited to the photographs being taken, missing important aspects because they were not part of the photos (Bibeau et al., 2012). Sounds, for example, are not captured, and sounds are often part of an experience in an urban setting.

Establishing limits as to how many photographs are taken or considered sufficient becomes a challenge in photovoice, because photographs are a means to an end and not an end in itself (Nykiforuk, Vallianatos, & Nieuwendyk, 2011). Finally, photovoice lends itself to being used to identify social justice issues in the lives of youth, and to identify their assets and strengths. It is critical that practitioners and academics do not focus exclusively on deficits and challenges (Snow, 2007). Such an approach limits the power of photovoice for discovery of community assets. This takes on prominence because marginalized urban youth have very few opportunities to undertake this form of discovery, limiting its potential for transformation.

Conclusion

This epilogue, as the reader certainly noticed, was very therapeutic for me. There is such much that has been accomplished with youth photovoice within an urban context. However, much remains to be accomplished, too. This book is focused on urban youth, and I cannot help but wonder how a book on rural or suburban youth will share similarities and also bring significant differences to how photovoice unfolds. The role and influence of context is heightened with photovoice, and imagery helps to bring this context to life, so to speak.

It is appropriate to end this epilogue and book with a quote by Higgs and Titchen (2011) on the future of qualitative research that also can be applied to photovoice: "Our vision for the future of qualitative research is that it can contribute to the creation of healthy people spaces and conditions for the growth of individuals, teams, organizations, communities and societies that are respectful of all peoples, the land and nature. Qualitative research, we contend, can contribute to the transformation of researchers and practices both through its means—emancipation, liberation and shared action—and its research products" (p. 309).

REFERENCES

Adams, D., & Goldbard, A. (2005). *Creative community: The art of cultural development.* Updated ed. Lulu.com. Available from http://www.lulu.com/shop/adams-donald-goldbard-arlene-and/creative-community-the-art-of-cultural-development/paperback/product-168174.html

Affleck, W., Glass, K. C., & Macdonald, M. E. (2012). The limitations of language: Male participants, stoicism, and the qualitative research interview. *American Journal of Mental Health, 7*(2), 155–162.

Ahmed, S. M., & Palermo, A-G. S. (2010). Community engagement in research: Frameworks for education and peer review. *American Journal of Public Health, 100*(8), 1380–1387.

Alcock, C. L., Camic, P. M., Barker, C., Haridi, C., & Raven, R. (2011). Intergenerational practice in the community: A focused ethnographic evaluation. *Journal of Community & Applied Social Psychology, 21*(5), 419–432.

Alderson, P., & Morrow, V. (2011). *The ethics of research with children and young people: A practical guide handbook.* London: Sage.

Aldridge, J. (2012). Working with vulnerable groups in social research: Dilemmas by default and design. *Qualitative Research, 14*(1): 112–130.

Allen, J. O., Alaimo, K., Elam, D., & Perry, E. (2008). Growing vegetables and values: Benefits of neighborhood-based community gardening for youth development and nutrition. *Journal of Hunger & Environmental Nutrition, 3*(4), 418–439.

Allen, L. (2011). The camera never lies?: Analysing photographs in research on sexuality and schooling. *Discourse: Studies in the Cultural Politics of Education, 32*(5), 761–777.

Allen, Q. (2012). Photographs and stories: ethics, benefits and dilemmas of using participant photography with Black middle-class male youth. *Qualitative Research, 12*(4), 443–458.

Allett, N. (2012).Unraveling attachments to extreme metal music with "music elicitation." In S. Heath & C. Walker (Eds.), *Innovations in youth research* (pp. 21–36). London: Sage.

Allmark, P. (2011).Towards a photographic feminine: Photography of the city. In S. Spencer (Ed.), *Visual research methods in the social sciences: Awakening visions* (pp. 171–183). London: Routledge.

Aluwihare-Samaranayake, D. (2012). Ethics in qualitative research: A view of the participants' and researchers' world from a critical standpoint. *International Journal of Qualitative Research, 11*(2), 64–81.

Ahmed, S. M., & Palermo, A-G., S. (2010). Community engagement in research: Frameworks for education and peer review. *American Journal of Public Health, 100*(8), 1380–1387.

Amon J. J., Baral S. D., Beyrer C., & Kass, N. (2012). Human Rights Research and Ethics Review: Protecting Individuals or Protecting the State? *PLoS Med, 9*(10). e1001325. doi:10.1371/journal.pmed.1001325

Amsden, J., & VanWynesberhe, R. (2005). Community mapping as a research tool with youth. *Action Research*, 3(4), 357–381.

Anderson, P., & Morrow, V. (2011). *The ethics of research with children and young people: A practical handbook* (2nd ed.). London: Sage.

Andreouh, E., Skovdal, M., & Campbell, C. (2013). "It made me realize that I am lucky for what I got": British young carers encountering the realities of their African peers. *Journal of Youth Studies*, 16(8): 1038–1053.

Antal, A. B. (2013). Art-based research for engaging not knowing to organizations. In S. McNiff (Ed.), *Art as research: Opportunities and challenges* (pp. 171–180). Bristol, England: Intellect.

Arches, J. (2013). Social action, service learning, and youth development. *Journal of Community Education and Higher Education*, 3(1).

Ardoin, N. M., Castrechin, S., & Hofstedt, M. R. (2013). Youth-community-university partnerships and sense of place: Two case studies of youth participatory action research. *Children's Geographies*. Advance online publication. doi:10.1080/14733285.2013.827872

Arredondo, E., Mueller, K., Mejia, E., Rovira-Oswalder, T., Richardson, D., & Hoos, T. (2013). Advocating for Environmental Changes to Increase Access to Park Engaging Promotoras and Youth Leaders. *Health Promotion Practice*, 14(3), 759–766.

Asian Health Center. (n.d.). *Photovoice*. Chicago, IL: Author.

Aslam, A. Pearson-Beck, M., Boots, R., Mayton, H., Link, S., & Elzey, D. (2013). Effective community listening: A case study on photovoice in rural Nicaragua. *International Journal for Service Learning in Engineering*, 8(1): 36–47. Retrieved from http://library.queensu.ca/ojs/index.php/ijsle/article/view/4535

Aspy, C. B., Oman, R. E., Vesely, S. K., McLeroy, K., Rodine, S., & Marshall, L. (2004). Adolescent violence: The protective effects of youth assets. *Journal of Counseling & Development*, 32(3), 268–276.

Bagley, C., & Castro-Salazar, R. (2012). Critical arts-based research in education: Performing undocumented historias. *British Educational Research Journal*, 38(2), 239–260.

Bagnoli, A. (2009). Beyond the standard interview: The use of graphic elicitation and arts-based methodology. *Qualitative Research*, 9(5), 547–570.

Bagnoli, A. (2012). Making sense of mixed methods narratives: Young people's identities, life-plans, and time orientations. In S. Heath & C. Walker (Eds.). *Innovations in youth research* (pp. 77–100). London: Sage.

Baird, G. L., Scott, W. D., Dearing, E., & Hamill, S. K. (2009). Cognitive self-regulation in youth with and without learning disabilities: Academic self-efficacy, theories of intelligence, learning versus performance and goal preference, and effort attributions. *Journal of Social and Clinical Psychology*, 28(7), 881–908.

Ballermini, J. (1997). Photography as a charitable weapon: Poor kids and self- representation. *Radical History Review*, 69(2), 160–188.

Balsano, A. B. (2005). Youth civic engagement in the United States: Understanding and addressing the impact of social impediments on positive youth and community development. *Applied Developmental Science*, 9(4), 188–201.

Baker, K. (2005). Assessment in youth justice: Professional discretion and the use of asset. *Youth Justice*, 5(2), 106–122.

Baker, T. A., & Wang, C. C. (2006). Photovoice: Use of a participatory action research method to explore the chronic pain experience in older adults. *Qualitative Health Research, 16*(10), 1405–1413.

Baldridge, B. J., Hill, M. L., & Davis, J. E. (2011). New possibilities: (Re)engaging Black male youth within community-based educational spaces. *Race Ethnicity and Education, 14*(1), 121–136.

Banister, E., & Daly, K. (2006). Walking a fine line: Negotiating dual roles in a study of adolescent girls. In B. Leadbeater, E. Banister, C. Benoit, M. Jansson, A. Marshall & T. Riecken (Eds.), *Ethical issues in community-based research with children and youth* (pp. 157–172). Toronto, Canada: University of Toronto Press.

Banks, S. (Ed.). (2010). *Ethical issues in youth work.* New York, NY: Routledge.

Barbour, K.N. (2006). Embodied engagement in arts research. *International Journal of the Arts in Society, 1*(2), 85–91.

Barlow, C. A., & Hurlock, D. (2013). Group meeting dynamics in a community-participatory research photovoice project with exited sex trade workers. *International Journal of Qualitative Research, 12*(1), 132–151.

Barnes, D. B., Taylor-Brown, S., & Wiener, L. (1997). "I didn't leave y'all on purpose": HIV-infected mothers' videotaped legacies for their children. *Qualitative Research, 20*(1): 7–32.

Barnidge, E., Baker, E. A., Motton, F., Rose, F., & Fitzgerald, T. (2010). A Participatory method to identify root determinants of Health: The heart of the matter. *Progress in Community Health Partnerships: Research, Education, and Action, 4*(1), 55–63.

Barniskis, S.C. (2013). Teaching art to teens in public libraries. *Teaching Artist Journal, 11*(2), 81–96.

Barone, T. E., & Eisner, E. W. (2012). *Arts based research.* Thousand Oaks, CA: Sage.

Basto, E. Warren, E., & Barbour, S. (2012). Exploring American Indian adolescents' needs through a community-driven study. *The Arts in Psychology, 39*(2), 134–142.

Baszile, D. (2009). Deal with it we must: Education, social justice, and the curriculum of hip hop culture. *Equity & Excellence in Education, 42*(1), 6–19.

Bates, D. (2010). The memory of photography. *Photographies, 3*(2), 243–257.

Batsleer, J. (2010). Youth workers as researchers. Ethical issues in practitioner and participatory research. In S. Banks (Ed.), *Ethical issues in youth work* (pp. 178–191). New York, NY: Routledge.

Batsleer, J. (2011). Voices from an edge. Unsettling the practices of youth voice and participation: Arts-based practice in The Blue Room, Manchester. *Pedagogy, Culture & Society, 19*(3), 419–434.

Beh, A., Bruyere, B. L., & Lolosoli, S. (2013). Legitimizing local perspectives in conservation through community-based research: A photovoice study in Samburu, Kenya. *Society & Natural Resources: An International Journal, 26*(10), 1390–1406.

Bell, L. A., & Desai, D. (2011). Imaging otherwise: Connecting the arts and social justice to envision and act for change [Special issue introduction]. *Equity & Excellence in Education, 44*(3), 287–295.

Bell, S., & Menec, V. (2013). "You don't want to ask for the help" The imperative of independence: Is it related to social exclusion. *Journal of Applied Gerontology.* Advance online publication. doi:10.1177/0733464812469292

Bell, S. E. (2008). Photovoice as strategy for community organizing in the central Appalachian coalfields. *Journal of Appalachian Studies, 14*(1–2), 34–48.

Bennett, N., & Dearden, P. (2013). A picture of change: using photovoice to explore social and environmental change in coastal communities on the Andaman Coast of Thailand. *Local Environment: The International Journal of Justice and Sustainability, 18*(9), 983–1001.

Benson, P.L., Leffert, N., Scales, P. C., & Blyth, D. A. (2012). Beyond the "village" rhetoric: Creating healthy communities for children and adolescents. *Applied Developmental Science, 16*(1), 3–23.

Berg, M., Coman, E., & Schensul, J. J. (2009). Youth action research for prevention: A multi-level intervention designed to increase efficacy and empowerment among urban youth. *American Journal of Community Psychology, 43*(4), 345–359.

Berlinger, D. C. (2013). Inequality, poverty, and the socialization of America's youth for the responsibilities of citizenship. *Theory into Practice, 52*(3), 203–209.

Berman, K. (2013). Students as agents of change: Engagement between university- based art students and alternative spaces. *Third Text, 27*(3), 387–399.

Bers, M. V. (2012). *Designing digital experiences for positive youth development: From playpen to playground.* New York, NY: Oxford University Press.

Beskow, L.M., Grady, C., Iltis, A. S., Sadler, J. Z., & Wilfond, B. S. (2009). Points to consider: The Research Ethics Consultation Services and the IRB. *IRB, 31*(6), 1–9.

Bessant, J., Emslie, M., & Watts, R. (2013). When things go wrong: A reflection on students in youth researchers. R. Brooks (Eds.), *Negotiating ethical challenges in youth research* (pp. 31–42). New York, NY: Routledge.

Bessell, A. G., Deese, W. B., & Medina, A. L. (2007). Photolanguage: How a picture can inspire a thousand words. *American Journal of Evaluation, 28*(4), 558–569.

Best, A. (2007). Introduction. In A. Best (Ed.), *Representing youth: Methodological issues in critical youth studies* (pp.1–36). New York, NY: New York University Press.

Best, A. (2011). Youth identity formation: Contemporary identity work. *Sociology Compass, 5*(10), 908–922.

Bharmal, N., Kennedy, D., Jones, L., Lee-Johnson, C., Morris, D. A., Caldwell, B., Brown, A., Houston, T., Meeks, C., Vargas, R., Franco, I., Razzak, A. R., & Brown, A.F. (2012). Through our eyes: Exploring African-American men's perspective on factors affecting transition to manhood. *Journal of General Internal Medicine, 27*(2), 153–169.

Bibeau, W. S., Saksvig, B. I., Gittelsohn, J., Williams, S., Jones, L., & Young, D.R. (2012). Perceptions of the food marketing environment among African American teen girls and adults. *Appetite, 58*(1), 396–399.

Bigby, C., & Frawley, P. (2010). Reflections on doing inclusive research in the "Making Life Good in the Community" study. *Journal of Intellectual and Developmental Disability, 35*(2), 53–61.

Biklen, S.K. (2007). Trouble on memory lane: Adults and self-retrospection in researching youth. In A. Best (Ed.), *Representing youth: Methodological issues in critical youth studies* (pp. 251–268). New York, NY: New York University Press.

Blackman, S., & Commane, G. (2012). Double flexivity: The politics of friendship, fieldwork and representation within ethnographic studies of young people. In S. Heath & C. Walker (Eds.), *Innovations in youth research* (pp. 229–247). London: Sage.

Bogart, L. M., & Vyeda, K. (2009). Community-based participatory research: Partnering with community for effective and sustainable behavioral health interventions. *Health Psychology, 28*(4), 391–393.

Boote, J., Baird, W., & Beecroft, C. (2010). Public involvement at the design of primary health research: A narrative review of case examples. *Health Policy, 96*(1), 10–23.

Boomer, C., & Frost, D. (2011). Our journeys of becoming authentic researchers. In J. Higgs, A. Titchen, D. Horsfall, & D. Bridges (Eds.). *Creative spaces for qualitative research: Living research* (pp. 281–290). Rotterdam, The Netherlands: Sense Publishers.

Booth, T., & Booth, W. (2002). Photovoice and mothers with learning disabilities. *Disability Society, 18*(4), 431–442.

Borgdorff, H. (2005). *The debate on research in the arts*. Retrieved from http://www.ips. gu.se/digitalAssets/1322/1322713_the_debate_on_research_in_the_arts.pdf

Boydell, K. M. (2011). Making sense of collective events: The co-creation of a research-based dance. *Forum: Qualitative Social Research, 12*(1). Retrieved from http://www. qualitative-research.net/index.php/fqs/article/view/1525/3143

Boydell, K. M., Gladstone, B. M., Volpe, T., Allemang, B., & Stasiulls, E. (2012). The production and dissemination of knowledge: A scoping review of arts-based health research. *Forum: Qualitative Social Research, 13*(1). Retrieved from http://www. qualitative-research.net/index.php/fqs/article/view/1711

Boxall, K., & Ralph, S. (2009). Research ethics and the use of visual images in research with people with intellectual disability. *Journal of Intellectual and Developmental Disability, 34*(1), 45–54.

Brader, A., & Luke, A. (2013). Re-engaging marginalized youth through digital music production: performance, audience and evaluation. *Pedagogies: An International Journal, 8*(3), 197–214.

Bragg, S., & Buckingham, D. (2008). "Scrapbooks" as a resource in media research with young people. In P. Thomson (Ed.), *Doing visual research with children and young people* (pp. 114–131). London: Routledge.

Brann-Barrett, M. T. (2009). We're here, you just don't know how to reach us: A reflective examination of research with citizens on the socio-economic margins. *Canadian Journal for the Study of Adult Education, 21*(2), 53–66.

Brazg, T., Bekemeier, B., Spigner, C., & Huebner, C. E. (2010). Our Community in Focus: The use of photovoice for youth-driven substance abuse assessment and health promotion. *Health Promotion Practice, 12*(4), 502–511.

Bredeson, J. A., & Stevens, M. S. (2013). Using photovoice methodology to give voice to health care needs of homeless families. *American International Journal of Contemporary Research, 3*(3), 1–12.

Bresler, L. (2011). Arts-based education and drama education. In S. Shammann (Ed.), *Key concepts in theartre and drama education* (pp. 321–326). New York, NY: Springer.

Bridges, D., & McGee, S. (2011). Collaborative inquiry: Reciprocity and authenticity. In J. Higgs, A. Titchen, D. Horsfall, D. & D. Bridges (Eds.), *Creative spaces for qualitative research: Living research* (pp. 213–222). Rotterdam, The Netherlands: Sense Publishers.

Britzman, D. (1989). Who has the floor? Curriculum teaching and the English student teacher's struggle for voice. *Curriculum Inquiry, 19*(2), 143–162.

Brooks, R. (2013). Ethical challenges of youth research: Themes and issues. In K. Riele & R. Brooks (Eds.). *Negotiating ethical challenges in youth research* (pp. 179–190). New York, NY: Routledge.

Brown, A., & Powell, S. (2012). Multiple facets of people and place: Exploring youth identity and aspirations in Madurai, South India. In S. Heath & C. Walker (Eds.), *Innovations in youth research* (pp.121–142). London: Sage.

Brown, C. (2013). Capturing the transient. In S. McNiff (Ed.), *Art as research: Opportunities and challenges* (pp. 221–228). Bristol, England: Intellect.

Brueggemann, W. G. (2013). *The practice of macro social work* (4th ed.). Belmont, CA: Brooks/Cole.

Bryce, H. (2013). Navigating multiple roles as a researcher in a photovoice project. *Groupwork, 22*(3), 33–48.

Brydon-Miller, M. (2012). Addressing the ethical challenges of community-based-research. *Teaching Ethics, 12*(2), 157–162.

Brydon-Miller, M., Greenwood, D. D., & Maguire, P. (2003). Why action research? *Action Research, 1*(1), 9–28.

Buchanan, D. R., Miller, F. G., & Wallerstein, N. (2007). Ethical issues in community-based participatory research: Balancing rigorous research with community participation in community intervention studies. *Progress in Community Health Partnerships: Research, Education, and Action, 1*(2), 153–160.

Buckingham, D. (2009). "Creative" visual methods in media research: possibilities, problems and proposals. *Media, Culture & Society, 31*(4), 633–652.

Buckley, C. (2013, October 29). Artist's work pops up daily. Reviews vary by boroughs. *The New York Times*, p. A20.

Buffington, M. L., & Muth, W. (2011). Visual arts and literacy: The potential of interdisciplinary coalitions for social justice. *The Journal of Social Theory in Art Education, 31*, 1–22. Retrieved from http://www.jstae.org/index.php/jstae/issue/view/2

Bungay, H., & Clift, S. (2010). Arts on prescription: A review of practice in the UK. *Perspectives in Public Health, 130*(6), 277–281.

Burghardt, S. (2013). *Macro practice in social work for the 21st century* (2nd ed.). Thousand Oaks, CA: Sage.

Burke, C. (2008). "Play in focus": Children's visual voice in participative research. In P. Thomson (Ed.), *Doing visual research with children and young people* (pp. 23–36). London: Routledge.

Burke, D., & Evans, J. (2011). Embracing the creative: The role of photo novella in qualitative nursing research. *International Journal of Qualitative Research, 10*(2), 164–177.

Burles, M. (2010). *Negotiating serious illness: Understanding young women's experiences through photovoice.* Saskatchewan, Canada: University of Saskatchewan.

Burr, J., & Reynolds, P. (2010). The wrong paradigm? Social research and the predicates of ethical scrutiny. *Research Ethics, 6*(4), 128–133.

Cabassa, L.J., Nicasio, A., & Whitley, R. (2013). Picturing recovery: A exploration of recovery dimensions among people with serious mental illness. *Psychiatric Services, 64*(9), 837–842.

Calvert, M., Emery, M., & Kinsey, S. (Eds.). (2013). *Youth programs as builders of social capital.* San Francisco, CA: Jossey-Bass.

Cameron, C.A., & Theron, L. (2011). With pictures and words I can show you: Cartoons portray resilient migrant teenagers' journey. In L. Theron, C. Mitchell, & A. Smith (Eds.), *Picturing research* (pp. 205–217). Rotterdam, The Netherlands: Sense Publishers.

Cameron, M., Crane, N., Inge, R., & Taylor, K. (2012). Promoting well-being through creativity: How arts and public health can learn from each other. *Perspectives on Public Health, 133*(1), 52–59.

Cammarota, J. (2011). From hopelessness to hope: Social justice pedagogy in urban education and youth development. *Urban Education, 46*(4), 828–844.

Cannuscio, C. C., Weiss, E. E., Fruchtman, H., Schroader, J., Weiner, J., & Asch, D. A. (2009). Visual ethnography: Photographs as tools for probing street-level etiologies. *Social Science & Medicine, 69*(4), 553–564.

Capriano, R. M. (2009). Come take a walk with me: The "Go-Along" interview as a novel method for studying the implications of place for health and well-being. *Health and Place, 13*(3), 263–272.

Carlson, E. D., Engebretson, J., & Chamberlain, R. M. (2006). Photovoice as a social process of critical consciousness. *Qualitative Research, 16*(6), 836–852.

Carnegie Council on Adolescent Development. (1989). *Turning points: Preparing American youth for the 21st century.* New York, NY: Carnegie Corporation of New York.

Castleden, H., Gacuin, T., & First Nation, H. (2008). Modifying photovoice for community-based-participatory indigenous research. *Social Science & Medicine, 66*(6), 1393–1405.

Castleden, H., Morgan, V. S., & Neimanis, A. (2010). Researchers' perspectives on collective/community co-authorship in community-based participatory indigenous research. *Journal of Empirical Research on Human Research Ethics: An International Journal, 5*(4), 23–32.

Catalini, C., & Minkler, M. (2010). Photovoice: A review of the literature in health and public health. *Health Education & Behavior, 37*(3), 424–451.

Celedonia, K. L., & Rosenthal, A. T. (2011). Combining art and eco-literacy to reconnect urban communities in nature. *Ecopsychology, 3*(4), 249–255.

Cerecer, D. A. Q., Cahill, C., & Bradley, M. (2013). Toward a critical youth policy praxis: Critical youth studies and participatory action research. *Theory into Practice, 52*(3), 216–223.

Cerulli, C. (2011). Research ethics in victimization studies: Widening the lens: A response and alternative view. *Violence Against Women, 17*(12), 1529–1535.

Chalmers, D. (2011). Viewpoint: Are the research ethics committees working in the best interests of participants in an increasingly globalized research environment? *Journal of Internal Medicine, 269*(4), 392–395.

Chaskin, R. J. (2013). Theories of community. In M. Weil (Ed.), *Handbook of community practice* (pp. 105–121). Thousand Oaks, CA: Sage.

Chavez, V., Israel, B., Allen, A. J., III, DeCarlo, M. F., Lichtenstein, R., Schulz, A., Bayer, I. S., & McGranaghan, R. (2004). A bridge between communities: Video-making using principles of community-based participatory research. *Health Promotion Practice, 5*(4), 395–403.

Chauke, A. (2009, May 3). Finding healing in a camera lens. *Sunday Times* (Reef Metro Edition, Social Issues) (South Africa), p. 4.

Checkoway, B. (2011). What is youth participation? *Children and Youth Services Review, 33*(2), 340–345.

Checkoway, B. (2013). Social justice approaches to community development. *Journal of Community Practice, 21*(4), 472–486.

Checkoway, B., & Aldana, A. (2013). Four forms of youth civic engagement for a diverse society. *Children and Youth Services Research, 35*(11), 1894–1899.

Checkoway, B., & Goodyear, L. (Eds.). (2002). *Youth participation in community evaluation research*. Ann Arbor: University of Michigan, Center for Community Change.

Checkoway, B., & Richards-Schuster, K. (2004). Youth participation in evaluation and research as a way of lifting new voices. *Children, Youth and Environments, 14*(2), 84–89.

Checkoway, B., & Richards-Schuster, K. (2012). Youth participation in community research for racial justice. In P.W. Nyden, L.A. Hossfield, & G.N. Nyden (Eds.), *Public sociology: Research, action, and change* (pp. 169–175). Thousand Oaks, CA: Sage.

Chen, P-Y, Weiss, F. L., & Nicholson, H.J. (2010). Girls Study Girls Inc.: Engaging girls in evaluation through participatory action research. *American Journal of Community Psychology, 46*(1–2), 228–237.

Cheon, J.W. (2011). *Positive youth development and youth-professional relationships: Exploring the nature of strengths-based practices with children and youth from professionals' perspectives*. ProQuest, UMI Dissertation Publishing.

Chew, A. (2009, March 17). A new voice for indigenous people. *New Straits Times* (Malaysia), p. 12.

Children's Defense Fund. (2007). *America's cradle to prison pipeline report*. Washington, D.C.: Author.

Chin, E. (2007). Power-puff ethnography/guerilla research: Children as native anthropologists. In A. Best (Ed.), *Representing youth: Methodological issues in critical youth studies* (pp. 269–283). New York, NY: New York University Press.

Chio, V. C., & Fandt, P. M. (2007). Photovoice in the diversity classroom: Engagement, voice, and the "Eye/I" of the camera. *Journal of Management Education, 31*(4), 484–504.

Chonody, J., Ferman, B., Amitrani-Welsh, J., & Martin, T. (2013). Violence through the eyes of youth: A photovoice exploration. *Journal of Community Psychology, 41*(1), 84–101.

Chouinard, J. A., & Cousins, J. B. (2009). A review and synthesis of current research on cross-cultural evaluation. *American Journal of Evaluation, 30*(4), 457–494.

Christens, B. D., & Dolan, T. (2010). Interweaving youth development, community development, and social change through youth organizing. *Youth & Society, 43*(2), 528–548.

Christens, B. D., Peterson, N. A., & Speer, P.W. (2011). Community participation and psychological empowerment: Testing reciprocal causality using a cross-lagged panel design and latent constructs. *Health Education & Behavior, 38*(4), 339–347.

Clark, A. (2010). Young children as protagonists and the role of participatory, visual methods in engaging in multiple perspectives. *American Journal of Community Psychology, 46*(1–2), 115–123.

Clark, A., Prosser, J., & Wiles, R. (2010). Ethical issues in image-based research. *Art & Health: An International Journal for Research, Policy and Practice, 2*(1), 81–93.

Clark, C. D. (2010). *In a younger voice: Doing child-centered qualitative research*. New York, NY: Oxford University Press.

Clark-Ibanez, M. (2008). Gender and being "bad": Inner-city students' photographs. In P. Thomson (Ed.), *Doing visual research with children and young people* (pp. 95–113). London: Routledge.

Clary, E. G., & Rhodes, J. E. (Eds.). (2006). *Mobilizing adults for positive youth development: Strategies for closing the gap between beliefs and behaviors*. New York, NY: Springer.

Clements, K. (2012). Participatory action research and photovoice in a psychiatric nursing/clubhouse collaboration exploring recovery narrative. *Journal of Psychiatric and Mental Health Nursing, 19*(9), 785–791.

Cleveland, W. (2011). *Arts-based community development: Mapping the terrain*. Washington, DC: Americans for the Arts. Retrieved from http://www.lacounty-arts.org/UserFiles/File/CivicArt/Civic%20Engagment%20Arts%20Based%20 Community%20Develop%20BCleveland%20Paper1%20Key.pdf

Cnaan, R.A., & Boehm, A. (2012). Towards a practice-based model for community practice: Linking theory and practice. *Journal of Sociology & Social Welfare, 39*(1), 141–168. Retrieved from http://www.wmich.edu/hhs/newsletters_journals/jssw_institutional/institutional_subscribers/39.1.Boehm.pdf

Coakley, J. (2011). Youth sports: What counts as "positive development." *Sport & Social Issues, 35*(3), 306–324.

Colucci, E. (2013). Arts-based research in cultural mental health. In Y. Kashima, M.S. Kashima & R. Beaton (Eds.). *Steering the cultural dynamics: Selected papers from the 2010 Congress of the International Association for Cross-Cultural Psychology* (pp. 41–48). Melbourne, Australia: International Association for Cross-Cultural Psychology.

Conchas, G. Q., & Virgil. J. D. (2010). Multiple marginality and urban education: Community and school socialization among low-income Mexican-descent youth. *Journal of Education for Students Placed At-Risk, 15*(1), 51–65.

Conner, J., Zaino, K., & Scarola, E. (2013). "Very powerful voices": The influence of youth organizing on educational policy in Philadelphia. *Educational Policy, 27*(3), 560–588.

Conrad, D. (2004). Exploring risky experiences: Popular theatre as a participatory, performance research method. *International Journal of Qualitative Methods, 3*(1). Retrieved from http://www.ualberta.ca/~iiqm/backissues/3_1/html/conrad.html

Cooper, A., Nazzari, V., King, J. K. K., & Pettigrew, A. (2013). Speaking rights: Youth empowerment theory through a participatory approach. *International Journal of Child, Youth & Family Studies, 4*(3.1), 489–501. Retrieved from http://journals.uvic. ca/index.php/ijcyfs/issue/view/707

Cooper, C. M., & Yarbrough, S. P. (2010). Tell Me–Show Me: Using combined focus groups and photovoice methods to gain understanding of health issues in Guatemala. *Qualitative Health Research, 20*(5), 644–653.

Cordner, A., Ciplet, D., Brown, P., & Morello-Frosch, R. (2012). Reflexive research ethics for environmental health and justice: Academics and movement building. *Social Movement Studies: Journal of Social, Cultural and Political Protest, 11*(2), 161–176.

Cornwall, A., Capibaribe, F., & Gonçalves, T. (2010). Revealed cities: A photovoice project with domestic workers in Salvador, Brazil. *Development, 53*(2), 299–300.

Coronel, J., & Pascual, I. R. (2013). Let me put it another way: Methodological considerations on the use of participatory photography based on an experiment with teenagers in secondary schools. *Qualitative Research in Education, 2*(2). Retrieved from http://www.hipatiapress.info/hpjournals/index.php/qre/article/view/519

Coser, L.R., Tozar, K., Borek, N. V., Tzemis, D., Taylor, D., & Saewyc, E. (2014). Finding a voice: Participatory research with street-involved youth in the Youth Injection Prevention Project. *Health Promotion Practice, 15*(5),732–738.

Cosgrove, L., & McHugh, M. (2010). A post Newtonian, postmodern approach to science. In S. N. Hesse-Biber & P. Leavy (Eds.), *Handbook of emergent methods* (pp. 73–86). New York, NY: The Guilford Press.

Coyle, J., & Olsen, A. M. (2011). Learning to be a researcher: Bridging the gap between research and creativity. In J. Higgs, A. Titchen, D. Horsfall, & D. Bridges (Eds.), *Creative spaces for qualitative research: Living research* (pp.169–178). Rotterdam, The Netherlands: Sense Publishers.

Creswell, J. W. (2013a). *Qualitative inquiry and research design: Choosing among five approaches* (3rd ed.). Thousand Oaks, CA: Sage.

Creswell, J. W. (2013b). *Research design: Qualitative, quantitative, and mixed methods approaches* (4th ed.). Thousand Oaks, CA: Sage.

Croker, A., & Tooth, J.A. (2013). Creating spaces to bring research into practice. In J. Higgs, A. Titchen, D. Horsfall, D. & D. Bridges (Eds.), *Creative spaces for qualitative research: Living research* (pp. 23–32). Rotterdam, The Netherlands: Sense Publishers.

Cruz, E. G., & Meyer, E. T. (2012). Creation and Control in the Photographic Process: iPhones and the emerging fifth moment of photography. *Photographies, 5*(2), 203–221.

Curry-Stevens, A. (2012). The end of the honeymoon: CBPR, positional privilege and working with community coalitions. *American International Journal of Contemporary Research, 2*(7), 92–107.

D'Alonzo, K. T. (2010). Getting started in CBPR: Lessons in building community partnerships for new researchers. *Nursing Inquiry, 17*(4), 282–288.

D'Alonzo, K. T., & Sharma, M.L. (2010). The influence of *marianismo* beliefs on physical activity of mid-ife immigrant Latinas: A photovoice study. *Qualitative Research in Sport and Exercise, 2*(2), 229–289.

Datoo, A., & Chagani, Z. M. (2011). Street theatre: Critical pedagogy for social studies education. *Social Studies Research and Practice, 6*(2), 21–30.

Davies, C. R., Rosenberg, M., Kruiman, M., Ferguson, R., Pikora, T., & Slatter, N. (2011). Defining arts engagement for population-based health research: Art forms, activities and level of engagement. *Arts & Health: An International Journal for Research, Policy and Practice, 4*(3), 203–216.

Davey, G. (2010). Visual anthropology: Strengths, weaknesses, opportunities, threats. *Visual Anthropology, 23*(4), 344–352.

Day, P. (2011). Community-based learning: A model for higher education and a community partnership. *The Journal of Community Informatics, 7*(3). Retrieved from http://ci-journal.net/index.php/ciej/article/view/805/786

De Lange, N., & Mitchell, C. (2007). *Putting people in the picture: Visual methodologies for social change.* Rotterdam, The Netherlands: Sense Publishers.

De Lange, N., & Mitchell, C. (2012). Community health workers working the digital archive: A case for looking at participatory archiving in studying stigma in the context of HIV and AIDS. *Sociological Research Online, 17*(1), 7. Retrieved from http://www.socresonline.org.uk/17/1/7.html

De la Nueces, D., Hacker, K., DiGirolamo, A., & Hicks, L. S. (2012). A systemic review of community-based participatory research to enhance clinical trials in racial and ethnic minority groups. *Health Services Research, 47*(3pt2), 1363–1386.

Decoster, V. A., & Dickerson, J.W. (2014). The therapeutic use of photographs in clinical social work: Evidence-based best practices. *Social Work in Mental Health, 12*(1), 12–19.

Degarrod, L. (2013). Making the unfamiliar personal: Arts-based ethnographies as public engaged ethnographies. *Qualitative Research, 13*(4), 402–413.

Delanty, G. (2003). *Community.* London: Routledge.

Delgado, M. (1999). *Community social work practice within an urban context: The potential of a community capacity enhancement perspective.* New York, NY: Oxford University Press.

Delgado, M. (2002). *New directions for youth development in the twenty-first century: Revitalizing and broadening youth development.* New York, NY: Columbia University Press.

Delgado, M. (2006). *Designs and methods for youth-led research.* Thousand Oaks, CA: Sage.

Delgado, M. (2013). *Social justice and the urban obesity crisis: Implications for social work.* New York, NY: Columbia University Press.

Delgado, M. (2014). *Baby boomers of color: Rewards and challenges for the nation.* New York, NY: Columbia University Press.

Delgado, M., & Humm-Delgado, D. (2013). *Asset assessments and community practice.* New York, NY: Oxford University Press.

Delgado, M., Jones, K., & Rohani, M. (2005). *Social work practice with refugees and immigrant youth in the United States.* Boston, MA: Allyn & Bacon.

Delgado, M., & Staples, L. (2007). *Youth-led community organizing: Theory and practice.* New York, NY: Oxford University Press.

Delgado, M., & Staples, L. (2013). Youth-led organizing, community engagement, and opportunity creation. In M. Weir, M. Reisch & M.L. Ohmer (Eds.), *The handbook of community practice* (2nd ed.), (pp. 547–565). Thousand Oaks, CA: Sage.

Delgado, M., & Zhou, H. (2008). *Youth-led health promotion in urban communities: A community capacity-enhancement perspective.* Lanham, MD: Rowman & Littlefield.

Dempster, N. C., Stevens, E. M., & Keeffe, M. (2011). Student and youth leadership: A focused literature review. *Leading and Managing, 17*(2), 1–20.

Dennis, S. F., Jr. (2006). Prospects for qualitative GIS at the intersection of youth development and participatory urban planning. *Environment and Planning, 38*(11), 2039–2054.

Dennis, S. F., Jr., Gaulocher, S., Carpiano, R. M., & Brown, D. (2009). Participatory photo mapping (PPM): Exploring an integral method for health and place research with young people. *Health & Place, 15*(2), 466–473.

Denoi, M., Doucet, D., & Kamara, A. (2012). Engaging war affected youth through photography: Photovoice with former child soldiers in Sierra Leone. *Intervention, 10*(2), 117–133.

Derr, V., Chawler, L., Mintzer, M., Cushing, D. F., & Van Vliet, W. (2013). A city for all citizens: Integrating children and youth from marginalized populations into city planning. *Buildings, 3*(4), 482–505.

Desyllas, M. C. (2013). Using photovoice with sex workers: The power of art, agency and resistance. *Qualitative Social Work,13*(4), 477–501.

Deuchar, R. (2010). "It's Just Pure Harassment . . . As if it's a crime to walk in the street": Anti-social behaviour, youth justice and citizenship—The reality for young men in the East End of Glasgow. *Youth Justice, 10*(3), 258–274.

Dewhurst, M. (2011). Where is the action? Three lenses to analyze social justice art education. *Equity and Excellence in Education, 44*(3), 364–378.

Diemer, M. A., & Cheng-Hsien, L. (2011). Critical consciousness development and political participation among marginalized youth. *Child Development, 82*(6), 1815–1833.

Diemer, M. A., Voight, A. M., & Mark, C. (2010). Youth development in traditional and transformational service-learning programs. In T. Stewart & N. Webster (Eds.), *Problemitizing service-learning: Critical reflecting for development and action* (pp. 155–173). Charlotte, NC: Information Age.

Dixon, M., & Hadjialexiou, M. (2005). Photovoice: Promising practice in engaging young people who are homeless. *Youth Studies Australia, 24*(2), 52.

Dooley, T. P., & Schreckhise, W. D. (2013). Evaluating social cognitive theory in action: An assessment of the youth development program's impact on secondary student retention in selected Mississippi Delta communities. *Youth & Society.* Advance online publication. doi:10.1177/0044118X13493445

Downey, L. H., & Anyaegbunam, C. (2010). Your lives through your eyes: Rural Appalachian youth identify community needs and assets through the use of photovoice. *Journal of Appalachian Studies, 16*(1–2), 42–60.

Downey, L. H., Ireson, C. L., & Scutchfield, F. D. (2009). The use of photovoice as a method of facilitating deliberation. *Health Promotion Practice, 10*(3), 419–427.

Downing, R., Sonenstein, F., & Davis, N. (2006). Love through the eyes of Baltimore youth: Photovoice as a youth empowerment tool. Paper presented at the 134th Annual Meeting and Exposition of the American Public Health Association, November 4–8, 2006.

Drew, S. E., Duncan, R. E., & Sawyer, S.M. (2010). Visual storytelling: A beneficial but challenging method for health research with young people. *Qualitative Health Research, 20*(12), 1677–1688.

Dreyfus, E.A. (1972). *Youth: Search for meaning.* Columbus, OH: Merrill.

Driver, S. (2007). Beyond "straight" interpretations: Researching queer youth digital video. In A. Best (Ed.), *Representing youth: Methodological issues in critical youth studies* (pp.1–36). New York, NY: New York University Press.

DuBois, J., Bailey-Burch, B., Bustillos, D., Campbell, J., Cottler, L., Fisher, C. B., . . . Stevenson, R.D. (2011). Ethical issues in mental health research: The case for community engagement. *Current Opinion in Psychiatry, 24*(3), 208–214.

Duckett, P., Kagan, C., & Sixsmith, J. (2010). Consultation and participation with children in healthy schools: Choice, conflict and context. *American Journal of Community Psychology, 46*(1–2), 167–178.

Duffy, L. R. (2010). Hidden heroines: Lone mothers assessing community health using photovoice. *Health Promotion Practice, 11*(6), 788–797.

Duncan, P. (2011). Engaging public space: Art education pedagogies for social justice. *Equity & Excellence in Education, 44*(3), 348–363.

Dupuis, J., & Mann-Feder, V. (2013). Moving towards emancipatory practice: Conditions for meaningful youth empowerment in child welfare. *International Journal of Child, Youth & Family Studies, 4*(3). Retrieved from http://journals.uvic.ca/index.php/ijcyfs/article/view/12436

Dupuis, S. L., Whyte, C., Carson, J., Genoe, R., Meshino, L., & Sadler, L. (2012). Just dance with me: An authentic partnership approach to understanding leisure in the dementia context. *World Leisure Journal, 54*(3), 240–254.

Durand, T. M., & Lykes, M. B. (2006). Think globally, act locally: A global perspective on mobilizing adults for positive youth development. In E. G. Clary & J. L. Rhodes (Eds.), *Mobilizing adults for positive youth development* (pp. 233–254). New York, NY: Academic Press.

Dyer, S., & Demeritt, D. (2008). Un-ethical review? Why it is wrong to apply the medical model of research governance to human geography. *Human Geography, 33*(1), 46–64.

Eckholm, E. (2005, November 25). Villagers' visions of their own lives: Photovoice records what local eyes see. *The International Herald Tribune*, p. 22.

Eglinton, K. A. (2013). Between the personal and the professional: Ethical challenges when using visual ethnography to understand young people's use of popular visual material culture. *Young, 21*(3), 253–274.

Eisner, E. (2008). Art and knowledge. In J. G. Knowles & A. L. Cole (Eds.), *Handbook of the arts in qualitative research* (pp. 3–12). Thousand Oaks, CA: Sage.

Emery, M., & Flores, C. (2006). "Spiraling up": Mapping community transformation with community capitals framework. *Community Development, 37*(1), 19–35.

Enright, E. (2013). Young people as curators of physical culture. In L. Azzarito & D. Kirk (Eds.), *Pedagogies, physical culture, and visual methods* (pp. 198–211). New York: Routledge.

Erbstein, N. (2013). Engaging underrepresented youth populations in community youth development: Tapping social capital as a critical resource. *New Directions for Youth Development, 2013*(138), 109–124.

Erdner, A., & Magnusson, A. (2011). Photography as a method of data collection: Helping people with long-term mental illness to convey their life world. *Perspectives in Psychiatry, 47*(3), 145–150.

Erickson, J. (2012). Photography workshop in rural Paraguay. Retrieved from http://www.ipg.vt.edu/Students/Photography_in_Rural_Paraguay_Julie_Erickson.pdf

Escueta, M., & Butterwick, S. (2012). The power of popular education and visual arts for trauma survivors' critical consciousness and collective action. *International Journal of Lifelong Education, 31*(2), 325–340.

Estrada, E., & Hondagneu-Sotelo, P. (2010). Intersectional dignities: Latino immigrant street vendor youth in Los Angeles. *Journal of Contemporary Ethnography, 40*(1), 102–131.

Evans, J., & Jones, P. (2011). The walking interview: Methodology, mobility and place. *Applied Geography, 31*(2), 849–858.

Evans, K., & Lowery, D. (2008). The scholarship of elegance and significance: Expressive and aesthetic truth claim. *Administration & Society, 40*(1), 3–24.

Evans, S. D. (2007). Youth sense of community: Voice and power in community contexts. *Journal of Community Psychology, 35*(6), 693–709.

Farrugia, D. (2013). The possibility of symbolic violence in interviews with young people experiencing homelessness. In K. Riele & R. Brooks. (Eds.), *Negotiating ethical challenges in youth research* (pp. 109–121). New York, NY: Routledge.

Fawcett, B., & Hearn, J. (2004). Researching others: Epistemology, experience, standpoints and participation. *International Journal of Social Research Methodology: Theory and Practice, 72*(2), 201–218.

Fenge, L.-A., Hodges, C., & Cutts, W. (2011). Seen but seldom heard: Creative participatory methods in a study of youth at risk. *International Journal of Qualitative Research, 10*(4), 418–430.

Fielden, S. J., Chapman, G. E., & Cadell, S. (2011). Managing stigma in adolescent HIV: Silence, secrets and sanctioned spaces. *Culture, Health & Sexuality: An International Journal for Research, Intervention and Care, 13*(2), 267–281.

Findholt, N. E., Michael, Y. L., & Davis, M. M. (2011). Photovoice engages rural youth in childhood obesity prevention. *Public Health Nursing, 28*(2), 186–192.

Findholt, N. E., Michael, Y. L., Davis, M. M., & Brigotti, V. W. (2010). Environmental influences on children's physical activity and diets in rural Oregon: Results of a youth photovoice project. *Online Journal of Rural Nursing and Health Care, 10*(2). Retrieved from http://rnojournal.binghamton.edu/index.php/RNO/article/view/33

Fink, J., & Keynes, M. (2012). Walking the neighborhood, seeing the small details of community life: Reflections from a photographic walking tour. *Critical Social Policy, 32*(1), 31–50.

Finley, S. (2005). Arts-based inquiry: Performing revolutionary pedagogy. In N.K Denzin & Y.S. Lincoln (Eds.), *The Sage handbook of qualitative research* (pp. 681–694). Thousand Oaks, CA: Sage.

Finley, S. (2008). Arts-based research. In J. G. Knowles & A. L. Cole (Eds.), *Handbook of the arts in qualitative research, methodologies, examples, and issues* (pp. 71–82). Thousand Oaks, CA: Sage.

Finley, S. (2011). Ecoaesthetics: Green arts at the intersection of education and social transformation. *Cultural Studies–Critical Methodologies, 11*(3), 306–313.

Fisher, C., & Masty, J. (2006). Through the community looking glass: Participant consultation for adolescent risk research. In B. Leadbeater, E. Banister, C. Benoit, M. Jansson, A. Marshall, & T. Riecken (Eds.). *Ethical issues in community-based research with children and youth* (pp. 22–41). Toronto, Canada: University of Toronto Press.

Fisher, C. B., Busch-Rossnagel, N. A., Jopp, D. S., & Brown, J. L. (2012). Applied developmental science, social justice and socio-political well-being. *Applied Developmental Science, 16*(1), 54–64.

Fitzgerald, A., Hackling, M., & Dawson, V. (2013). Through the viewfinder: Reflecting on the collection and analysis of classroom video data. *International Journal of Qualitative Research, 12*(2), 52–61.

Fitzpatrick, A. L., Steinman, L. E., Tu, S-P, Ly, K. A., Ton, T. G. N., Yip, M-P, & Sin, M.K. (2012). Using photovoice to understand cardiovascular health awareness in Asian elders. *Health Promotion Practice, 13*(1), 48–54.

Flacks, M. (2007). "Label jars not people": How (not) to study youth civic engagement. In A. Best (Ed.), *Representing youth: Methodological issues in critical youth studies* (pp. 60–83). New York, NY: New York University Press.

Fleming, J., Mahoney, J., Carlson, E., & Engebretson, J. (2009). An ethnographic approach to interpreting a mental illness photovoice exhibition. *Archives of Psychiatric Nursing, 23*(1), 16–21.

Flicker, S., & Danforth, J. (2013). Decolonizing HIV research using arts-based methods: What Aboriginal youth in Canada had to say. Paper presented at the Annual Meeting of the American Public Health Association, Boston, Massachusetts, November 3, 2013.

Flicker, S., Travers, R., Guta, A., McDonald, S., & Meagher, A. (2007). Ethical dilemmas in community-based participatory research: Recommendations for institutional review boards. *Journal of Urban Health, 84*(4), 478–493.

Forum for Youth Investment. (2006). *Engaging young people in community change: The Youth Impact Approach.* Washington, D.C.: Author.

Foster, V. (2012a). The pleasure principle: Employing arts-based methods in social work. *European Journal of Social Work, 15*(4), 532–545.

Foster, V. (2012b). What if? The use of poetry to promote social justice. *Social Work Education: The International Journal, 31*(6), 742–755.

Foster-Fishman, P., Nowell, B., Deacon, Z., Nievar, M.A., & McNann, P. (2005). Using methods that matter: The impact of reflection, dialogue, and voice. *American Journal of Community Psychology, 36*(4), 275–291.

Foster-Fishman, P. G., Law, K. M., Lichty, L. F., & Aoun, C. (2010). Youth ReACT for Social Change: A method for youth participatory action research. *American Journal of Community Psychology, 46*(1–2), 67–83.

Fox, N. J. (2013). Creativity and health: An anti-humanistic reflection. *Health, 17*(5), 495–511.

Frank, K. I. (2006). The potential of youth participation in planning. *Journal of Planning Literature, 20*(4), 351–371.

Franklin, M. A. (2013), Know thyself: Awakening self-referential awareness through arts-based research. In S. McNiff (Ed.), *Art as research: Opportunities and challenges* (pp.85–94). Bristol, England: Intellect.

Fraser, K. D., & al Sayah, F. (2011). Arts-based methods in health research: A systematic review of the literature. *Arts & Health: An International Journal of Research, Policy and Practice, 3*(2), 110–145.

Fraser-Thomas, J. L., Cote, J., & Deakin, J. (2005). Youth sports programs: An avenue to foster positive youth development. *Physical Education & Sport Pedagogy, 10*(1), 19–40.

Fredricks, J. A., & Eccles, J. S. (2010). Breadth of extracurricular participation and adolescent adjustment among African-American and European-American youth. *Journal of Research on Adolescents, 20*(2), 307–333.

Freedman, D. A., Pitner, R. O., Powers, M. C. F., & Anderson, T. P. (2012). Using photovoice to develop a grounded theory of socio-environmental attributes influencing the health of community environments. *British Journal of Social Work.* Advance online publication. doi:10.1093/bjsw/bcs173

Freeman, M., & Mathison, S. (2008). *Researching children's experiences.* New York, NY: The Guilford Press.

Freire, P. (1982). Creating alternative research methods: Learning to do it by doing it. In B. Hall, A. Gillette, & R. Tandon (Eds), *Creating knowledge: A monopoly? Participatory research in development* (pp. 29–37). New Delhi, India: Society for Participatory Research in Asia.

Fresque-Baxter, J. A. (2013). Participatory photography as a means to explore young people's experiences of water resource change. *Indigenous Policy Journal, 23*(4). Retrieved from http://www.indigenouspolicy.org/index.php/ipj/article/view/147

Frohmann, L. (2005). The Framing Safety Project: Photographs and narratives by battered women. *Violence Against Women, 11*(11), 1396–1419.

Furman, G. (2012). Social justice leadership as praxis developing capacities through preparation programs. *Educational Administration Quarterly, 48*(2), 191–229.

Futch, V. A. (2011). (Re)presenting spaces of/for "At-Opportunity" urban youth. *Curriculum Inquiry, 41*(1), 98–109.

Gamble, G. N., & Weir, M. (2009). *Community practice skills: Local to global perspectives.* New York, NY: Columbia University Press.

Gant, L. M., Shimshock, K., Allen-Meares, P., Smith, L., Miller, P., Hollingsworth, L. A., & Shanks, T. (2009). Effects of Photovoice: Civic engagement among older youth in urban communities. *Journal of community practice, 17*(4), 358–376.

Garcia, A., & Morrell. E. (2013). City youth and the pedogagy of participatory media. *Media, Learning, Media and Technology, 38*(2), 123–127.

Garcia, A. P., Minkler, M. Cardenas, Z., Grills, C., & Porter, C. (2014). Engaging homeless youth in community-based participatory research: A case study from Skid Row, Los Angeles. *Health Promotion Practice, 15*(1), 18–27.

Garcia, C. M., Aguilera-Guzman, R. M., Lindgren, S., Gutierrez, R., Raniolo, B., Genis, T., Benitez, G.V., & Clausen, L. (2013). Intergenerational photovoice project: Optimizing the mechanism for influencing health promotion policies and strengthening relationships. *Health Promotion Practice, 14*(5), 695–705.

Garcia, C., Lindgren, S., & Pintor, J.K. (2011). Knowledge, skills, and qualities for effectively facilitating an adolescents' girls group. *The Journal of School Nursing, 27*(6), 424–433.

Garcia, L.-G. (2012). Making cultura count inside and out of the classroom: Public art and critical pedagogy in South Central Los Angeles. *Journal of Curriculum and Pedagogy, 9*(2), 104–114.

Garcia-Vera, A. B. (2012). Knowledge generated by audiovisual narrative action research loops. *Educational Action Research, 20*(3), 423–437.

Gardner, H. (1983). *Frames of mind.* New York, NY: Basic Books.

Garvin, M. (2003). Developing positive negatives: Youth on the edge capture images of their lives with help from photovoice. *Children, Youth and Environments, 13*(2), 254–259.

Genoe, M. R., & Dupuis, S. L. (2013). Picturing leisure: Using photovoice to understand the experience of leisure and dementia. *The Qualitative Report, 18*, Article 21, 1–21. Retrieved from http://www.nova.edu/ssss/QR/QR18/genoe21.pdf

Gerber, N., Templeton, E., Chilton, G., Liebman, M.C., Manders, E., & Shim, M. (2013). Art-based research as a pedagogical approach to studying intersubjectivity in the creative arts therapies. In S. McNiff (Ed.). *Art as research: Opportunities and challenges* (pp. 37–46). Bristol, England: Intellect.

Gertler, B. (2003). Selk-knowledge. In E.N.Zalta (Ed.). *Stanford encyclopedia of philosophy.* Retrieved June 15, 2004, (www.http://plato.stanford.edu/archives/spr2003/entries/selfknowledge)

Gibson, B. E., Mistry, B., Smith, B., Yoshida, K. K., Abbott, D., Lindsay, S., & Hamdani, Y. (2013). The integrated use of audio diaries, photography, and interviews in research with disabled young males. *International Journal of Qualitative Research, 12*(1), 382–402.

Ginwright, S., Noguera, P., & Cammarota, J. (2006). *Beyond resistance! Youth activism and community change.* New York, NY: Routledge.

Glover-Graf, N. M. (2000). Student-produced photography: A constructivist approach to teaching psychosocial aspects of disability. *Rehabilitation Education, 14*(3), 285–296.

Gold, S. (2007). Using photography in studies of immigrant communities: Reflecting across projects and populations. In G.C. Stanczak (Ed.), *Visual research methods: image, society, and representation* (pp. 141–166). Thousand Oaks, CA: Sage.

Goldring, J. F. (2010). Between partisan and fake, walking the path of the insider: Empowerment and voice in ethnology. In J. S. Jones & S. Watt (Eds.), *Ethnography in social science practice* (pp. 126–140). London: Routledge.

Goldstein, B. M. (2007). All photos lie: Images as data. In G.C. Stanczak (Ed.), *Visual research methods: Images, society, and representation* (pp. 61–81). Thousand Oaks, CA: Sage.

Good, L. (2005). Snap it up: using digital photography in early childhood. *Childhood Education, 82*(2), 79–85.

Gooden, M. A., & Dantley, M. (2012). Centering race in a framework for leadership development. *Journal of Research on Leadership Education, 7*(2), 237–253.

Goodman, P. S. (2003, September 16). Cultural revelation: In China, a picture of its people takes shape one snapshot at a time. *The Washington Post,* p. CO1.

Goodwin, S., & Young, A. (2013). Ensuring children and young people have a voice in neighbourhood community development. *Australian Social Work, 66*(3), 344–357.

Goffman, E. (1963). *Stigma: Notes on the management of spoiled identity.* New York, NY: Simon & Schuster.

Gordon, L. (2002, June 19). Society: Putting us in the picture: Refugees' photo exhibition aims to change negative image. *The Guardian* (London), p. 4.

Gosessling, K., & Doyle, C. (2009). Thru the lenz: Participatory action research, photography, and creative process in an urban high school. *Journal of Creativity in Mental Health, 4*(4), 343–365.

Grady, J. (2004). "Working with visible evidence: An invitation and some practical advice." In C. Knowles & J. Sweetman (Eds.), *Picturing the social landscape: Visual methods and the sociological imagination* (pp. 18–32). London: Routledge.

Graham, A., & Kilpatrick, R. (2010). Understanding children's educational experiences through image-based research. In J. S. Jones & S. Watts (Eds.). *Ethnography in social science practice* (pp. 89–106). London: Routledge.

Graham, L. F., Reyes, A. M., Lopez, W., Gracey, A. Snow, R. C., & Padilla, M. B. (2013). Addressing economic devastation and built environment degradation to prevent violence: A photovoice project of Detroit Youth Passages. *Community Literacy Journal, 8*(1). Retrieved from http://www.communityliteracy.org/index.php/clj/article/view/223

Grant, L. M., Shimshock, K., Allen-Meares, P., Smith, L., Miller, P. Hollingsworth, L. A., & Shanks, T. (2009). Effects of photovoice: Civic engagement among older youth in urban communities. *Journal of Community Psychology, 17*(4), 358–376.

Green, E., & Kloos, B. (2009). Facilitating youth participation in a context of forced migration: A photovoice project in Northern Uganda. *Journal of Refugee Studies, 22*(4), 460–482.

Greene, S. (2013). Peer research assistantships and the ethics of reciprocity in community-based research. *Journal of Empirical Research on Human Research Ethics: An International Journal, 8*(2), 141–152.

Greene, S., Burke, K., & McKenna, M. (2013). Forms of voice: Exploring the empowerment of youth at the intersection of art and action. *Urban Review, 45*(3), 311–334.

Grieb, S. M. D., Joseph, R. M., Pridget, A., Smith, H., Harris, R., & Ellen, J. M. (2013). Understanding housing and health through the lens of transitional housing members in a high-incarceration Baltimore City neighborhood: The GROUP Ministries Photovoice Project to promote community redevelopment. *Health & Place, 21*(1), 20–28.

Griebling, S., Vaughn, L. M., Howell, B., Ramstetter, C., & Dole, D. (2013). From passive to active voice: Using photography as a catalyst for social action. *International Journal of Humanities and Social Science, 3*(2), 16–28.

Griffith, D. M., Allen, J. O., Zimmerman, M. A., Morrel-Samuels, S. Reischi, T. M., Cohen, S. E., & Campbell, K. A. (2008). Organizational empowerment in community mobilization to address youth violence. *American Journal of Preventive Medicine, 34*(3) (Suppl), S89–S99.

Groundwater-Smith, S. (2011). Living ethical practice in qualitative research. In J. Higgs, A. Titchen, D. Horsfall, & D. Bridges (Eds.). *Creative spaces for qualitative research: Living research* (pp. 201–210). Rotterdam, The Netherlands: Sense Publishers.

Gubrium, A. C. (2009). Digital storytelling: An emergent method for health promotion research and practice. *Health Promotion Practice, 10*(2) 186–191.

Gubrium, A. C., & Difulvio, G. T. (2011). Girls in the world: Digital storytelling as a feminist public health approach. *Girlhood Studies, 4*(2), 28–46.

Gubrium, A. C., Hill, A. L., & Flicker, S. (2013). A situated practice of ethics for photographic visual and digital methods in public health research and practice: A focus on digital storytelling. *American Journal of Public Health, 104*(9), 1606–1614.

Gubrium, A. C., & Torres, M. I. (2013). The meaning is in the bottle: Latino youth communicating double standard ideologies through photovoice. *American Journal of Health Education, 44*(3), 146–155.

Guillemin, M., & Drews, S. (2010). Questions of process in participant-generated visual methodologies. *Visual Studies, 25*(2), 175–188.

Gupta, R. S., Lau, C. H., Springston, E. E., Warren, C. W., Mears, C. J., Dunford, C. M., Sharp, L. K., & Hott, J. L. (2013). Perceived factors affecting asthma among adolescents: Experiences and findings from the Student Asthma Research Team Pilot Study. *Journal of Asthma & Allergy Educators, 4*(5), 226–234.

Gupta, R. S., Lau, C. H., Warren, C. M., Lelchuk, A., Alencar, A., Springston, E. E., & Hull, J. L. (2013). The impact of student-directed videos on community asthma knowledge. *Journal of Community Health, 38*(3), 463–470.

Guta, A., Wilson, M. G., Flicker, S., Travers, R. Mason, C. Wenyeve, G., & O'Campo, P. (2010). Are we asking the right questions? A review of Canadian REB practices in relation to community-based participatory research. *Journal of Empirical Research on Human Research Ethics: An International Journal, 5*(2), 35–46.

Hacker, K. (2013). *Community-based participatory research.* Thousand Oaks, CA: Sage.

Hague, N., & Eng, B. (2011). Tackling inequity through a photovoice project on the social determinants of health: Translating photovoice evidence to community action. *Global Health Promotion, 18*(1), 16–19.

Haines, R. J., Oliffe, J. L., Bottorff, J. L., & Poland, B. D. (2010). "The missing picture": Tobacco use through the eyes of smokers. *Tobacco Control, 19*(3), 206–212.

Halifax, N. V. D., Meeks, J., & Khander, E. (2008). Photovoice in a Toronto community partnership: Exploring the social determinates of health with homeless people. *Progress in Community Health Partnerships: Research, Education, and Action, 2*(2), 129–136.

Hammersley, M. (1990). *Reading ethnographic research: A critical guide.* New York, NY: Longman.

Hammersley, M., & Traianou, A. (2012). *Ethics in qualitative research: Controversies and contexts.* London: Sage.

Hampton, R. (2011). *Family photos: Digital photography as emancipatory art education in Montreal's black community.* Portland, OR:Concordia University.

Hannay, J., Dudley, R., Milan, S., & Leibovitz, P. K. (2013). Combining photovoice and focus groups: Engaging Latina teens in a community assessment. *American Journal of Preventive Medicine, 44*(3) (Suppl. 3), S216–S224.

Hansen-Ketchum, P., & Myrick, F. (2008). Photo methods for qualitative research in nursing: An ontological and epistemological perspective. *Nursing Philosophy, 9*(3), 265–273.

Haque, N., & Eng, B. (2011). Tackling inequity through a photovoice project on the social determinants of health: Translating photovoice evidence to community action. *Global Health Promotion, 18*(1), 16–19.

Hardcastle, D. A., Powers, P. R., & Wenocur, S. (2011). *Community practice: Theories and skills for social work* (3rd ed.). New York, NY: Oxford University Press.

Harley, A. (2012). Picturing reality: Power, ethics, and politics in using photovoice. *International Journal of Qualitative Research, 11*(4), 103–124.

Harley, D. B. (2011). *Perceptions of hope and hopelessness among inner-city African American adolescents: A qualitative study utilizing grounded theory and photovoice methods.* Columbus, OH: Ohio State University School of Social Work.

Harper, D. (2003). Framing photographic ethnography: A case study. *Ethnography, 4*(2), 241–266.

Harper, K. (2009). New Directions in Participatory Visual Ethnography: Possibilities for Public Anthropology. Paper presented a the American Anthropological Association Annual Meeting, Philadelphia, December, 2009. Retrieved from http://scholarworks.umass.edu/anthro_faculty_pubs/79/

Harper, T. H. (2002). *Understanding youth popular culture and the hip-hop influence.* Clinton, MD: Youth Popular Culture Institute.

Harris, A., & Guillemin, M. (2012). Developing sensory awareness in qualitative interviewing: A portal into the otherwise unexplored. *Qualitative Health Research, 22*(5), 689–699.

Harris, A., Wyn, J., & Younes, S. (2010). Beyond apathetic or activist youth: "Ordinary" young people and contemporary forms of participation. *Young, 18*(1), 19–32.

Harris Interactive. (2011, October 26). $211 billion and so much to buy—American youths, the new big spenders. Retrieved from http://www.harrisinteractive.com/ NewsRoom/PressReleases/tabid/446/ctl/ReadCustom%20Default/mid/1506/ ArticleId/896/Default.aspx

Harris, R., Holmes, H. M., & Mertens, D. M. (2009). Research ethics in sign language communities. *Sign Language Studies, 9*(2), 104–131.

Hart, D. (1992). Ladder of participation, children's participation: From tokenism to citizenship. New York: UNICEF.

Harvard, M., Cho, M. K., & Magnus, D. (2012). Triggers for research ethic consultation. *Science Translation Medicine, 4*(118), 1–4.

Hatch, J. A. (2002). *Doing qualitative research in educational settings.* Albany, NY: State University of New York Press.

Hauge, M.-I. (2013). Research with young people on female circumcision: Negotiating cultural sensitivity, law and transparency. In K. Riele & R. Brooks (Eds.), *Negotiating ethical challenges in youth research* (pp. 137–149). New York, NY: Routledge.

Haw, K. (2008). "Voice" and video: Seen, heard and listened to? In P. Thomson (Ed.), *Doing visual research with children and young people* (pp. 192–207). London: Routledge.

Haywood, J. (2013). *Arts-based research primer.* New York, NY: Peter Lang.

Head, B. W. (2011). Why not ask them? Mapping and promoting youth participation. *Children and Youth Services Review, 33*(4), 541–547.

Head, E. (2009). The ethics and implications of paying participants in qualitative research. *International Journal of Social Research Methodology, 12*(4), 335–344.

Heath, S., Brooks, R., Cleaver, E., & Ireland, E. (2009). *Researching young people's lives.* London: Sage.

Heath, S., & Walker, C. (Eds.). (2012a). *Innovations in youth research.* New York, NY: Palgrave Macmillam.

Heath, S., & Walker, C. (2012b). Innovations in youth research: An introduction. In S. Heath & C. Walker (Eds.), *Innovations in youth research* (pp. 1–20). London: Sage.

Heath, S., & Walker, C. (2012c). Conclusion. In S. Heath & C. Walker (Eds.), *Innovations in youth research* (pp. 248–255). London: Sage.

Heery, G. H. M. (2013). Use of photovoice in addiction. *Nursing Centers of North America, 48*(3), 445–458.

Heimer, C. A., & Petty, J. (2010). Bureaucratic ethics: IRBs and the legal regulation of human subjects research. *Annual Review of Law and Social Science, 6*, 601–626.

Henderson, S. Holland, J., McGrellis, S., & Thomson, R. (2007). *Inventing adulthoods: A biographical approach to youth transitions.* London: Sage.

Henry, C., Ramdoth, D., White, J., & Mangroo, S. (2013). Engaging youth in creating a healthy school environment: A photovoice strategy. *Journal of International Educational Research, 9*(1), 97–106.

Hergenrather, K. C., Rhodes, S. D., Cowan, C. A., Bardhoshi, G., & Pula, S. (2009). Photovoice as community-based participatory research: A qualitative review. *American Journal of Health Behavior, 33*(6), 686–698.

Hernandez-Albujar, Y. (2007). The symbolism of video: Exploring migrant mothers' experiences. In G. C. Stanczak (Ed.), *Visual research methods: image, society, and representation* (pp. 255–279). Thousand Oaks, CA: Sage.

Heron, J. (1996). *Cooperative inquiry research into the human condition*. London: Sage.

Higgs, J., & Cherry, N. (2011). Creative partnerships in research degree programs. In J. Higgs, A. Titchen, D. Horsfall, & D. Bridges (Eds.), *Creative spaces for qualitative research: Living research* (pp.257–266). Rotterdam, The Netherlands: Sense Publishers.

Higgs, J., & Titchen, A. (2011). Journeys of meaning making. In J. Higgs, A. Titchen, D. Horsfall, & D. Bridges (Eds.), *Creative spaces for qualitative research: Living research* (pp.301–310). Rotterdam, The Netherlands: Sense Publishers.

Hill, J. (2013). Using participatory and visual methods to address power and identity in research with young people. *Graduate Journal of Social Sciences, 10*(2), 132–151.

Hinthorne, L. L. (2012). A picture is worth a thousand words: Using the visual interpretation narrative exercise elicit non-elite perceptions of democracy. *Field Notes, 24*(3), 348–364.

Ho, W-C, Rochelle, T. L., & Yuen, N-K. (2011). "We are not sad at all": Adolescents talk about their "City of Sadness" through photovoice. *Journal of Adolescent Research, 26*(6), 727–765.

Hoberecht, T., & Miller-Cribbs, J. (2011). Some health literacy aspects of a photovoice project. *Journal of Consumer Health on the Internet, 15*(4), 389–395.

Holliday, R. (2007). Performance, confessions, and identity: Using video diaries to research sexualities. In G.C. Stanczak (Ed.), *Visual research methods: Images, society, and representation* (pp. 255–279). Thousand Oaks, CA: Sage.

Holland, J. (2009). Young people and social capital. *Young, 17*(4), 331–350.

Horowitz, C. R., Robinson, M., & Seifer, S. (2009). Key issues in outcome research: Community-based participatory research from the margin to the mainstream. *Circulation, 119*, 2633–2642.

Horsfall, D., & Higgs, J. (2013). Boundary riding and shaping research spaces. In J. Higgs, A. Titchen, D. Horsfall, & D. Bridges (Eds.), *Creative spaces for qualitative research: Living research* (pp. 44–54). Rotterdam, The Netherlands: Sense Publishers.

Huang, H. H. (2010). What is good action research? Why the resurgent interest? *Action Research, 8*(1), 93–109.

Hunter, H., & Lewis, D. (2013, June 10). Helping young adults address grief through art [*Musings* blog post]. *Journal of the American Academy of Physician Assistants*. Retrieved from http://journals.lww.com/jaapa/blog/musings/pages/post.aspx?PostID=5

Hunter, J., Langdon, S., Caesar, D., Rhodes, S. D., & Estes, C. P. (2011). Voices of African American health: Stories of healing and health. *Arts & Health: An International Journal for Research, Policy and Practice, 3*(1), 84–93.

Hurd, N., & Zimmerman, M. (2010). Natural mentors, mental health, and risk behaviors: A longitudinal analysis of African American adolescents transitioning into adulthood. *American Journal of Community Psychology, 46*(1–2), 36–48.

Huss, E. (2012). What we see and what we say: Combining visual and verbal information within social work research. *The British Journal of Social Work, 42*(8), 1440–1459.

Innis, R. E. (2013). Frames of enquiry: Perplexity, self-integration, pregnant images. In S. McNiff (Ed.), *Art as research: Opportunities and challenges* (pp.117–123). Bristol, England: Intellect.

Irizarry, J. G. (2009). Representin': Drawing from hip-hop and urban youth culture to inform teacher education. *Education and Urban Society, 41*(4), 489–515.

Jacquez, F., Vaughn, L. M., & Wagner, E. (2013). Youth as partners, participants or passive recipients: A review of children and adolescents in community-based participatory research (CBPR). *American Journal of Community Psychology, 51*(1–2), 176–189.

Jain, S., & Cohen, A. K. (2013). Fostering resilience among urban youth exposed to violence: A promising area for interdisciplinary research and practice. *Health Education & Behavior, 40*(6), 651–662.

Janhonen-Abruquah, H., & Holm, G. (2008). Using photographs as a data collection method in family research. In I. Jarventie & H. Landa (Eds.). *Methodological challenges in childhood and family research* (pp. 72–80). Tempere, Finland: Tempere University Press.

Jansson, M., Mitic, W., Hulten, T., & Dhami, M. (2006). A youth population health survey. In B. Leadbeater, E. Banister, C. Benoit, M. Jansson, A. Marshall & T. Riecken (Eds.), *Ethical issues in community-based research with children and youth* (pp. 59–69). Toronto, Canada: University of Toronto Press.

Jardine, C. G., & James, A. (2012). Youth researching youth: Benefits, limitations and ethical considerations within a participatory research process. *International Journal of Circumpolar Health, 71*(10), 1–19.

Jeanes, R., & Kay, T. (2013). Conducting research with young people in the global south. In R. Brooks (Eds.), *Negotiating ethical challenges in youth research* (pp. 19–30). New York, NY: Routledge.

Jenson, J. M., & Alter, C.F. (2013). *Risk, resilience, and positive youth development.* New York, NY: Oxford University Press.

Joanou, J. P. (2009). The bad and the ugly: ethical concerns in participatory photographic methods with children living and working on the streets of Lima, Peru. *Visual Studies, 24*(3), 214–223.

Johansen, S., & Le, T. N. (2012). Youth perspectives on multiculturalism using photovoice methodology. *Youth & Society, 46*(4), 548–565.

Johnson, K. (2008). Teaching children to use visual research methods. In P. Thomson (Ed.), *Doing visual research with children and young people* (pp. 77–94). London: Routledge.

Jones, G. (2009). *Youth.* Cambridge, MA: Polity Press.

Jones, H. (2010). Being really there and really aware: Ethics, politics and representations. In J. S. Jones & S. Watt (Eds.), *Ethnography in social science practice* (pp. 28–41). London: Routledge.

Jones, J. S. (2010). Origins and ancestors: A brief history of ethnography. In J. S. Jones & S. Watt (Eds.), *Ethnography in social science practice* (pp. 13–27). London: Routledge.

Jones, K. R. (2009). Influences of youth leadership within a community-based context. *Journal of Leadership Education, 7*(3), 246–263.

Judd, B. (2006). *Incorporating youth development principles into adolescent health programs.* Washington, DC: The Forum for Youth Investment. Retrieved from http://www.state.nj.us/dcf/documents/behavioral/providers/IncorporatingYD.pdf

Jurokowski, J. M., & Paul-Ward, A. (2007). Photovoice with vulnerable populations: Addressing disparities in health promotion among people with intellectual disabilities. *Health Promotion Practice, 8*(4), 358–365.

Jurokowski, J. M., Rivera, Y., & Hammel, J. (2009). Health perceptions of Latinos with intellectual disabilities: The results of a qualitative pilot study. *Health Promotion Practice, 10*(1), 144–155.

Kalmanowitz, D. (2013). On the seam: Fiction as truth—what art can do? In S. McNiff (Ed.), *Art as research: Opportunities and challenges* (pp. 141–151). Bristol, England: Intellect.

Kankanan, P., & Bardy, M. (2013). Life stories and arts in child welfare: Enriching communication. *Nordic Social Work Research, 4*(1), 37–51.

Kaplan, E. B. (2013). *"We live in the SHADOW": Inner-city kids tell their stories through photographs.* Philadelphia, PA: Temple University Press.

Kaplan, I. (2008). Being "seen" being "heard": Engaging with students on the margins of education through participatory photography. In P. Thomson (Ed.), *Doing visual research with children and young people* (pp.175–191). London: Routledge.

Kay, L. (2013). Visual essays: A practice-led journey. *International Journal of Education Through Art, 9*(1), 131–138.

Kegler, M.C., Rigler, J., & Honeycutt, S. (2011). The role of community context in planning and implementing community-based health promotion projects. *Evaluation & Program Planning, 34*(3), 246–253.

Keller, C., Fleury, J., Perez, A., Ainsworth, B., & Vaughan, L. (2008). Using visual methods to uncover context. *Qualitative Health Research, 18*(3), 428–436.

Kellett, M. (2005). *How to develop children as researchers: A step by step guide to teaching the research process.* London: Paul Chapman.

Kellett, M. (2010). Small shoes, big steps: Empowering children as active researchers. *American Journal of Community Psychology, 46*(1–2), 195–203.

Kelley, A., Belcourt-Dittloff, C., Belcourt, A., & Belcourt, G. (2013). Research ethics and indigenous communities. *American Journal of Public Health, 103*(12), 2146–2152.

Kelly, C. M., Hoehner, C. M., Baker, E. A., Ramierez, L. K. B., & Brownson, R. C. (2006). Promoting physical activity in communities: Approaches for successful evaluation of programs and policies. *Evaluation and Program Planning, 29*(3), 280–292.

Kelly, P. (2007). The entrepreneurial self and "youth at-risk": Exploring the horizons of identity in the twenty-first century. *Journal of Youth Studies, 9*(1), 17–32.

Kendall, E., Marshall, C. A., & Barlow, L. (2013). Stories rather than methods: A journey of discovery and emancipation. *International Journal of Qualitative Research, 12*(1), 258–271.

Kessi, S. (2011). Photovoice as a practice of re-presentation and social solidarity: Experiences from a youth empowerment project in Dart es Salaam and Soweto. *Papers on Social Representation, 20*, 7.1–7.27. Retrieved from http://www.psych.lse.ac.uk/psr/PSR2011/20_07.pdf

Kia-Keating, M. (2009). Positive psychology and school/community-based youth participatory photography programs. In R. Gilman, E.S. Fuebner & M.J. Furlong (Eds.), *Handbook of positive psychology in schools* (pp. 383–398). New York, NY: Routledge.

Kim. J., & Sherman, R. F. (2006). Youth as important civic actors: From the margins to the center. *National Civic Review, 124*(1), 3–5.

Kirshner, B., & Ginwright, S. (2012). Youth organizing as a developmental context for African American and Latino adolescents. *Child Development Perspectives, 6*(3), 288–294.

Kirshner, B., & Pozzoboni, K., & Jones, H. (2011). Learning how to manage bias: A case study of youth participatory action research. *Applied Developmental Science, 15*(3), 140–155.

Kohfeldt, D., Chhun, L., Grace, S., & Langhout, R. D. (2011). Youth empowerment in context: Exploring tensions in school-based yPAR. *American Journal of Community Psychology, 47*(1), 28–45.

Kono, N. (2012). Ethics in research. In *The Encyclopedia of Applied Linguistics*. Hoboken, NJ: Wiley. Retrieved from http://onlinelibrary.wiley.com/doi/10.1002/9781405198431.wbeal0395/abstract

Kossak, M. (2013). Art-based enquiry: It is what we do! In S. McNiff (Ed.), *Art as research: Opportunities and challenges* (pp. 19–27). Bristol, England: Intellect.

Kramer, L., Schwartz, P., Cheadle, A., & Rauzon, S. (2012). Using photovoice as a participatory evaluation tool in Kaiser Permanente's Community Health Initiative. *Health Promotion Practice, 14*(5), 686–694.

Kubicek, K., Beyer, W., Weiss, G., & Kipke, M. D. (2012). Photovoice as a tool to adapt an HIV prevention interventions for African American young men who have sex with men. *Health Promotion Practice, 13*(4), 535–543.

Kuhn, A. (2007). Photography and cultural meaning: A methodological exploration. *Visual Studies, 22*(3), 283–292.

Kuratani, D. L., & Lai, E. (2011). Photovoice literature review. Los Angeles, CA: USC TEAM Lab. Retrieved from http://teamlab.usc.edu/Photovoice%20Literature%20Review%20%28FINAL%29.pdf

Lafrenière, D., & Cox, S. M. (2013). "If you can call it a poem": Towards a framework for the assessment of arts-based work. *Qualitative Research, 13*(3), 318–336.

"If you can call it a poem": Towards a framework for the assessment of arts-based work, D., Hurlimann, T., Menuz, V., & Godard, B. (2013). Health research: Ethics and the use of arts-based methods in knowledge translation processes. *The International Journal of the Creative Arts in Interdisciplinary Practice*. Retrieved from http://www.ijcaip.com/archives/IJCAIP-11-paper3.html

Lai, S., Jarus, T., & Suto, M. J. (2012). A scoping review of the photovoice method: Implications for occupational therapy research. *Canadian Journal of Occupational Therapy, 79*(3), 181–190.

Lally, V., & Sclater, M. (2013). The Inter-Life project: researching the potential of art, design and virtual worlds as a vehicle for assisting young people with key life changes and transitions. *British Journal of Guidance & Counseling, 41*(3), 318–338.

Lambert, J. (2013). *Digital storytelling: Capturing lives, creating community*. New York, NY: Routledge.

Langhout, R. D., & Thomas, E. (2010). Imagining participatory action research in collaboration with children: An introduction. *American Journal of Community Psychology, 46*(1-2), 60–66.

Langman, S., & Pick, D. (2013). Dignity and ethics in research photography. *International Journal of Social Research Methodology*. Advance online publication. doi:10.1080/13645579.2013.825473

Lapalme, J., Bisset, S., & Potvin, L. (2013). The role of context in evaluating neighbourhood interventions promoting positive youth development: A narrative review. *International Journal of Public Health, 59*(1), 31–42.

Larson, A., Mitchell, E., & Gilles, M. (2001). *Looking, listening and learning from young people through photographs: A photovoice project with young aboriginal people in*

Carnaron, Western Australia. Sixth National Rural Health Conference, Canberra, Australian Capital Territory, March 4–7, 2001.

Larson, R. (2011). Positive development in a disorderly world. *Journal of Research on Adolescence, 21*(2), 317–334.

Larson, R., Walker, K., & Pearce, N. (2005). A comparison of youth-driven and adult-driven youth programs: Balancing inputs from youth and adults. *Journal of Community Psychology, 33*(1), 57–74.

Laughey, D. (2006). *Music and youth culture.* Edinburgh: Edinburgh University Press.

Lavallée, L. F. (2009). Practical application of an indigenous research framework and two qualitative indigenous research methods: Sharing circles and anishnaabe symbol-based reflection. *International Journal of Qualitative Methods, 8*(1). Retrieved from http://www.ryerson.ca/asbr/projectsasbr_files/Indigenous%20Research%20Frame work%20and%20Methods.pdf

Laverick, W. (2010). Accessing inside: Ethical dilemmas and pragmatic compromises. In J. S. Jones and S. Watt (Eds.), *Ethnography in the social sciences* (pp. 73–88). London: Routledge.

Law, J. (2004). *After method: Mess in social science research.* London: Routledge.

Leavy, P. (Ed.). (2009). *Method meets art: Arts-based research practice.* New York, NY: The Guilford Press.

Leadbeater, B., Barrister, E., Benoit, C., Jansson, M., Marshall, A., & Riecken, T. (Eds.). (2006). *Ethical issues in community-based research with children and youth.* Toronto, Canada: University of Toronto Press.

Leadbeater, B., Riecken, T., Benoit, C., Barrister, E., Brunk, C., & Glass, K. (2006). Community-based research with vulnerable populations: Challenges for ethics and research guidelines. In B. Leadbeater, E. Banister, C. Benoit, M. Jansson, A. Marshall, & T. Riecken (Eds.), *Ethical issues in community-based research with children and youth* (pp.3–21). Toronto, Canada: University of Toronto Press.

Learmonth, M., & Huckvale, K. (2013). The feeling of what happens: A reciprocal investigation of inductive and deductive processes in an art experiment. In S. McNiff (Ed.), *Art as research: Opportunities and challenges* (pp. 95–106). Bristol, England: Intellect.

Ledwith, M., & Springett, J. (2010*). Participatory practice: Community-based action for transformative change.* Bristol, England: The Policy Press.

Leicher, P., Lagarde, E., & Lemaire, C. (2013). Windows to discover: A socially engaged arts project addressing isolation. *Arts & Health: An International Journal for Research, Policy and Practice,6*(1), 90–97.

Leipert, B., & Anderson, E. (2012). Rural nurisng education: A photovoice perspective. *Rural and Remote Health, 12*, 2061. Retrieved from http://www.rrh.org.au/articles/subviewnew.asp?ArticleID=2061

Leitch, R. (2008). Creatively researching children's narratives through images and drawings. In P. Thomson (Ed.), *Doing visual research with children and young people* (pp. 37–58). London: Routledge.

Lenz, A. S., & Sangganjanavanich, V.F. (2013). Evidence for the utility of a photovoice task as an empathic skill acquisition strategy among counselors-in-training. *The Journal of Humanistic Counseling, 52*(1), 39–53.

Leonard, M. (2007). With a capital "G": Gatekeepers and gatekeeping in research with children. In A. Best (Ed.), *Representing youth: Methodological issues in critical youth studies* (pp.133–156). New York, NY: New York University Press.

Leonard, M., & McKnight, M. (2013). Traditions and transitions: Teenagers' perceptions of parading in Belfast. *Children's Geographies.* Advance online publication. doi:10.1 080/14733285.2013.848740

Lerner, R., Alberts, A. E., Jelicic, H., & Smith, L.M. (2006). Young people are resources to be developed: Promoting positive youth development through adult-youth relations and community assets. In E. G. Clary & J. E. Rhodes (Eds.), *Mobilizing adults for positive youth development: Strategies for closing the gap between beliefs and behaviors* (pp.19–39). New York, NY: Springer.

Lerner, R., Lerner, J., Almerigi, J., Theokas, C., Naudeau, S., & Geststottir, S., . . . von Eye, A. (2005). Positive youth development, participation in community youth development programs, and community contributions of fifth grade adolescents: Findings from the first wave of the 4-H Study of Positive Youth Development. *Journal of Early Adolescence, 25*(1), 17–71.

Lerner, R., Lerner, J., & Benson, J. B. (Eds.). (2011). *Positive youth development.* New York, NY: Academic Press.

Lerner, R., Roeser, R. W., & Phelps, E. (Eds.). (2008*). Positive youth development & spirituality: From theory to research.* West Conshohocken, PA: Templeton Foundation Press.

Lesko, N. (2001). *Act your age! A cultural construction of adolescence.* London: Routledge Falmer.

Leung, M. W., Yen, I. H., & Minkler, M. (2004). Community based participatory research: A promising approach for increasing epidemiology's relevance in the 21st century. *The International Journal of Epidemiology, 33*(3), 499–506.

Levine, S. K. (2013). Expecting the unexpected: Improvisation in arts-based research. In S. McNiff (Ed.), *Art as research: Opportunities and challenges* (pp. 125–132). Bristol, England: Intellect.

Levy, L., & Weber, S. (2011). Teenmom.ca: Arts-based new media empowerment project for teenage mothers. *National Art Education Association Studies in Art Education: A Journal of Issues and Research, 52*(4), 292–309.

Lichty, L. F. (2013). Photovoice as a pedagogical tool in the community psychology classroom. *Journal of Prevention and Intervention in the Community, 41*(3), 89–96.

Lico, S., & Luttrell, W. (2011). An important part of me: A dialogue about difference. *Harvard Educational Review, 8*(4), 667–686.

Lincoln, Y.S. (2010). "What a Long, Strange Trip It's Been . . .": Twenty-five years of qualitative and new paradigm research. *Qualitative Inquiry, 16*(1), 3–9.

Linds W., Ritenburg, H., Goulet, L., Episkenew, J.-A., Schmidt, K., Ribeiro, N., & Witeman, A. (2013). Layering theatre's potential for change: Drama, education, and community in Aboriginal health research. *Canadian Theatre Review, 154*(154), 37–43.

Linzmayer, C. D., & Halpenny, E. A. (2013). "It was fun": An evaluation of sand tray pictures, an innovative visually expressive method for researching children's experience with nature. *International Journal of Qualitative Research, 12*(1), 310–327.

Literat, I. (2013). "A pencil for your thoughts": Participatory drawing as a visual research method with children and youth. *International Journal of Qualitative Methods, 12*(1), 84–98.

Loebach, J., & Gilliland, J. (2010). Child-led tours to uncover children's perceptions and use of neighborhood environments. *Children, Youth and Environments, 20*(1), 52–90.

Loftus, S., Higgs, J., & Trede, F. (2011). Researching living practices: Trends in creative qualitative research. In J. Higgs, A. Titchen, D. Horsfall, & D. Bridges (Eds.), *Creative spaces for qualitative research: Living research* (pp. 3–12). Rotterdam, The Netherlands: Sense Publishers.

Lolichen, P. Shetty, A., Shenoy, J., & Nash, C. (2007). Children in the driver's seat. *Participatory Learning and Action, 56*(1), 49–55.

Loopmans, M., Cowell, G., & Oosterlynck, S. (2012). Photography, public pedagogy and the politics of place-making in post-industrial areas. *Social & Cultural Geography, 13*(7), 699–718.

Lopez, E. D. S., Eng, E., Randall-David, E., & Robinson, N. (2005). Quality-of-life concerns of African American breast cancer survivors within rural North Carolina: Blending the techniques of photovoice and blended theory. *Qualitative Health Research, 15*(1), 99–115.

Lopez, K. K. (2006). *Youth-focused empowerment evaluation using photovoice* (Doctoral dissertation). Texas Medical Center Dissertations, Paper AA13241398. Austin, Texas: University of Texas School of Public Health.

Lorenz, L. S. (n.d.). *Photovoice: Giving Youth a Voice in Their Community.* Retrieved from http://www.photovoiceworldwide.org/photovoice_giving_youth_a_voice.htm

Lorenz, L. S., & Kolb, B. (2009). Involving the public through participatory visual research methods. *Health Expectations, 1*(3), 262–274.

Lunch, N., & Lunch, C. (2006). *Insights into Participatory Video: A Handbook for the Field.* Oxford, England: InsightShare. Retrieved from http://insightshare.org/resources/pv- handbook

Lundy, L. (2007). "Voice" is not enough: Article 12 of the United Nations Convention on the Rights of the Child. *British Educational Research Journal, 33*(6), 927–942.

Luttrell, W. (2010). "A camera is a big responsibility": A lens for analyzing children's visual voices. *Visual Studies, 25*(3), 224–237.

Luttrell, W., & Chalfen, R. (2010). Lifting up voices in participatory visual research. *Visual Studies, 25*(3), 197–200.

MacDonald, J. M., Gagnon, A. J., Mitchell, C., Di Meglio, G., Rennick, J. E., & Cox, J. (2011). Include them and they will tell you: Learnings from a participatory process with youth. *Qualitative Health Research, 21*(8), 1127–1135.

Mahalingam, R., & Rabelo, V. C. (2013). Theoretical, methodological, and ethical challenges to the study of immigrants: Perils and possibilities. *New Directions for Child and Adolescent Development, 141*(Fall), 25–41.

Mair, M., & Kieran, C. S. (2007). Descriptions as data: Developing techniques to elicit descriptive materials in social research. *Visual Studies, 22*(2), 120–136.

Majalhaes, L. (2010). *Other ways of knowing: How does photovoice work?* London, Ontario, Canada: University of Western Ontario, School of Occupational Therapy. Retrieved from http://www.ccqhr.utoronto.ca/sites/default/files/Other-ways-of-knowing-Magalhaes-Jan-2010.pdf

Malbon, B. (1999). *Clubbing: Dancing, ecstasy and vitality.* London, England: Routledge.

Mantoura, P., & Potvin, L. (2013). A realist-constructionist perspective on participatory research in health promotion. *Health Promotion International, 28*(1), 61–72.

Metropolitan Area Planning Council (n.d.). *Facilitator's guide to youth community safety photovoice.* Retrieved from http://www.mapc.org/sites/default/files/Photovoice%20 Facilitators%20Guide%20with%20Resources.pdf

Roldán Ramírez, J., & Marín Viadel, R. (2010). Photo essays and photographs in visual arts-based educational research. *International Journal of Education Through Art, 6*(1), 7–23.

Marn, R., & Roldn, J. (2010). Photo essays and photographs in visual arts-based educational research. *International Journal of Education through Art, 6*(1), 7–23.

Marshall, A., & Shepard, B. (2006). Youth on the margins: Qualitative research with adolescent groups. In B. Leadbeater, E. Banister, C. Benoit, M. Jansson, A. Marshall & T. Riecken (Eds.), *Ethical issues in community-based research with children and youth* (pp.139–156). Toronto, Canada: University of Toronto Press.

Martinez, I. L., Carter-Pokras, O., & Brown, P.B. (2009). Addressing the challenges of Latino health research: Participatory approaches in an emergent urban community. *Journal of the National Medical Association, 101*(9), 908–914.

Maton, K. I., & Domingo, M. R. Sto. (2006). Mobilizing adults for positive youth development: Lessons from religious congregations. In E. G. Clary & J. L. Rhodes (Eds.), *Mobilizing adults for positive youth development* (pp. 159–175). New York, NY: Academic Press.

Mattessich, P. W. (2012). Advisory committees in contract and grant-funded evaluation projects. *New Directions for Evaluation, 2012*(136), 31–48.

Maud, K. (2012). Giving children a "voice": arts-based participatory research activities and representation. *International Journal of Social Research Methodology, 15*(2), 149–160.

McAreavey, R., & Das, C. (2013). A delicate balancing act: Negotiating with gatekeepers for ethical research when researching minority communities. *International Journal of Qualitative Research, 12*(1), 113–131.

McAuliffe, C. (2012). Graffiti or street art? Negotiating the moral geographies of the creative city. *Journal of Urban Affairs, 34*(2), 189–206.

McDonnell, B. (2009). Ethical considerations in collaborative visual work. *Anthropology News, 7*(April), 7, 12.

McDonald, K., & Patka, M. (2012). "There is no black or white": Scientific community views on ethics in intellectual and developmental disability research. *Journal of Policy and Practice in Intellectual Disabilities, 9*(3), 206–214.

McGregor, C. (2012). Arts-influenced pedagogy: Tools for social transformation. *International Journal of Lifelong Education, 31*(3), 309–324.

McEwan, A., Crouch, A., Robertson, H., & Fagan, P. (2013). The Torres Indigenous Hip Hop Project: Evaluating the use of performing arts as a medium for sexual health promotion. *Health Promotion Journal of Australia, 24*(2), 132–136.

McIntyre, A. (2003). Through the eyes of women: photovoice and participatory research as tools for reimagining place. *Gender, Place and Culture: A Journal of Feminist Geography, 10*(1), 47–66.

McKenna, S. A., Iwasaki, P. G., Stewart, T., & Main, D. S. (2011). Key informants and community members in community-based participatory research: One is not like the other. *Progress in Community Health Partnerships: Research, Education, and Action, 5*(4), 387–397.

McMurphy, S., Lewis, J., & Boulos, P. (2013). Extending the olive branch: Enhancing communication and trust between research ethics and qualitative research. *Journal of Empirical Research on Human Research Ethics: An International Journal, 8*(4), 29–36.

McNiff, K. (2013). On creative writing and historical understanding. In S. McNiff (Ed.), *Art as research: Opportunities and challenges* (pp.109–116). Bristol, England: Intellect.

McNiff, S. (2008). Arts-based research. In J. G. Knowles & A. L. Cole (Eds.), *Handbook of the arts in qualitative research: Perspectives, methodologies, examples, and issues* (pp.29–40). Thousand Oaks, CA: Sage.

McNiff, S. (2013a). Opportunities and challenges in art-based research. In S. McNiff (Ed.), *Art as research: Opportunities and challenges* (pp. 3–9). Bristol, England: Intellect.

McNiff, S. (2013b). A central focus on art-based research. In S. McNiff (Ed.), *Art as research: Opportunities and challenges* (pp. 109–116). Bristol, England: Intellect.

McNaughton, M. J. (2009). Closing in on the picture: Analyzing interactions in video recordings. *International Journal of Qualitative Research, 8*(4), 27–44.

Meenai, Z. (2008). *Participatory community work.* New Dehi: Concept.

Mejia, A. P., Quiroz, O., Morales, Y., Ponce, R., Chavez, G. L., & y Torre, E. O. (2013). From *madres* to *mujeristas*: Latinas making change with Photovoice. *Action Research, 11*(4), 301–321.

Meo, A. I. (2010). Picturing students' habitus: The advantages and limitations of photo-elicitation interviewing in a qualitative study in the city of Buenos Aires. *International Journal of Qualitative Research, 9*(2), 149–171.

Merteus, D. (2010). Transformative mixed methods research. *Qualitative Inquiry, 16*(6), 469–474.

Metz, E. (2014). State of the field: Youth community service in the USA. In A. Ben- Arieh, F. Casas, J. Frones & J. E. Korbin (Eds.), *Handbook of child well-being: Theories, methods and policies in global perspective* (pp. 977–997). Amsterdam: Springer Netherlands.

Miaux, S., Drovin, L., Morency, P., Paquin, S., Gauvin, L., & Jacquemin, C. (2010). Making the narrative walk-in-real-time methodology relevant for public health towards an integrative approach. *Health & Place, 16*(6), 1166–1173.

Mikesell, L., Bromley, E., & Khodyakov, D. (2013). Ethical community-engaged research: A literature review. *American Journal of Public Health, 103*(12), e7–e14.

Mitchell, C. (2008). Getting the picture and changing the picture: Visual methodologies and educational research in South Africa. *South African Journal of Education, 28*(4), 365–383.

Mitchell, C. (2011). *Doing visual research.* Thousand Oaks, CA: Sage.

Mitchell, C., DeLange, N., Moletsane, R., Stuart, J., & Buthelezi, T. (2005). Giving a face to HIV and AIDS: On the uses of photo-voice by teachers and community health care workers working with youth in rural South Africa. *Qualitative Research in Psychology, 2*(3), 257–270.

Mitra, D., Serrierre, S., & Kirshner, B. (2013). Youth participation in U.S. contexts: Student voice without a national mandate. *Children & Society, 28*(4), 292–304.

Mockler, N. (2011). Being me: In search of authenticity. In J. Higgs, A. Titchen, D. Horsfall, & D. Bridges (Eds.), *Creative spaces for qualitative research: Living research* (pp. 159–168). Rotterdam, The Netherlands: Sense Publishers.

Mohajer, N., & Earnest, J. (2009) Youth empowerment for the most vulnerable: A model based on the pedagogy of Freire and experiences in the field. *Health Education*, 109(5), 424–438.

Mohammed, S., Sajum, S. Z., & Khan, F. S. (2013). Harnessing photovoice for tuberculosis advocacy in Karachi, Pakistan. *Health Promotion Journal*. Advance online publication.

Moloney, M. (2005, September 1). "Those who suffer write the songs": Remembering Frank Harte 1933–2005. *The Journal of Music*. Retrieved from http://journalofmusic.com/focus/those-who-suffer-write-songs.

Molloy, J. K. (2007). Photovoice as a tool for social justice workers. *Journal of Progressive Human Services*, 18(1), 39–55.

Montoya, M. J., & Kent, E. E. (2011). Dialogical action: Moving from community-based to community-driven participatory research. *Qualitative Health Research*, 21(7), 1000–1011.

Moon, B. L. (2012). Mentoring and other challenges in art-based enquiry: You will figure it out. In S. McNiff (Ed.), *Art as research: Opportunities and challenges* (pp. 29–36). Bristol, England: Intellect.

Morey, Y., Bengry-Howell, A., & Griffin, C. (2012). Public profiles, private parties: Digital ethnography, ethics and research in the context of Web 2.0. In S. Heath & C. Walker (Eds.), *Innovations in youth research* (pp. 195–209).

Morgan, M. Y., Vandell, R., Lower, J. K., Kinter-Duffy, V. L., Ibarra, L. C., & Cecil-Dyrkacz, J.E. (2010). Empowering women through photovoice: Women of La Carpin, C.R. *Journal of Ethnography & Qualitative Research*, 5(1), 31–44.

Morris, A., Hegarty, K., & Humphreys, C. (2012). Ethical and safe: Research with children about domestic violence. *Research Ethics*, 8(2), 125–139.

Morrison, M., & Arthur, L. (2013). Leadership for inter-service practice collaborative leadership lost in translation? An exploration. *Educational Management Administration & Leadership*, 41(4), 179–198.

Morrow, V. (2012). The ethics of social research with children and families in young lives: Practical experiences. In J. Boyden & M. Bourdillon (Eds.), *Childhood poverty: Multidisciplinary approaches* (pp. 24–42). New York, NY: Palgrave Macmillan.

Morton, M., & Montgomery, P. (2011). Youth empowerment programs for improving self-efficacy and self-esteem of adolescents. *Campbell Systematic Reviews*, 7(5). Retrieved from http://www.campbellcollaboration.org/lib/?go=monograph&year=2011

Mosher, H. (2013). A question of quality: The art/science of doing collaborative public ethnography. *Qualitative Research*, 13(4), 428–441.

Moss, J. (2008). Visual methods and policy research. In P. Thomson (Ed.), *Doing visual research with children and young people* (pp. 59–73). London: Routledge.

Moxley, D., Feen-Calligan, H., & Washington, O.G.M. (2012). Lessons learned from three projects linking social work, the arts, and humanities. *Social Work Education: An International Journal*, 31(6), 703–723.

Murray, M., & Crummett, A. (2010). "I don't think they knew we could do these sorts of things": Social representations of community and participation in community arts by older people. *Journal of Health Psychology*, 15(5), 777–785.

Naidus, B. (2009). *Arts for change: Teaching outside the frame*. Oakland, CA: New Village Press.

National Association of Social Workers. (2000). *Cultural competence.* Washington, D.C.: Author.

Nation, M., Collins, L., Nixon, C., Bess, K., Rogers, S., Williams, N., & Juarez, P. (2010). A community-based participatory approach to youth development and school climate change: The alignment enhanced services project. *Progress in Community Health Partnerships, 4*(3), 197–205.

Necheles, J. W., Hawes-Dawson, J., Ryan, G. W., Williams, L. B., Holmes, H. N., Wells, K. B., Valana, M. E., & Schuster, M. A. (2007). The Teen Photovoice Project: A pilot study to promote health through advocacy. *Progress in Community Health Partnerships: Research, Education, and Action, 1*(3), 2219–2229.

Neuman, W. L. (2007). *Basics of social research: Qualitative and quantitative approaches.* Boston, MA: Pearson, Allyn & Bacon.

Newbury, J., & Hoskins, M. (2012). Seeking solutions without centering problems: From research to practice. *Child, Youth & Family Studies, 3*(1), 20–45.

Newman, S. D. (2010). Evidence-based advocacy: Using photovoice to identify barriers and facilitators to community participation after spinal cord injury. *Rehabilitation Nursing, 35*(2), 47–59.

Newman, S. D., Andrews, J. O., Megwood, G. S., Jenkins, C., Cox, M. J., & Williamson, D.C. (2011). Community advisory boards in community-based participatory research: A synthesis of best practices. *Preventing Chronic Disease, 8*(3), A.70.

The New Times (Kigali, Africa). (2009, December 3). Women and gender: Girls' and women's strategies to eradicate poverty through visual communication. Author, p. 3.

New Zealand Ministry of Health. (2012). *Ethical guidelines for observational studies: Observational research, audits and related activities.* Wellington, New Zealand: Author. Retrieved from http://neac.health.govt.nz/system/files/documents/publications/ethical-guidelines-for-observational-studies-2012.pdf

Nind, M. (2011). Participatory data analysis: A step too far? *Qualitative Research, 11*(4), 349–363.

Nind, M., Wiles, R., Bengry-Howell, A., & Crow, G. (2013). Methodological innovation and research ethics: forces in tension or forces in harmony? *Qualitative Research, 13*(6), 349–363.

Ning, A. (2013). *Mobilities of Aboriginal youth: Exploring the impact on health and social support through photovoice.* Toronto, Canada: University of Toronto.

Nitsch, M., Waldheur, K., Denik, E., Grebler, U., Marent, B., & Foster, R. (2013). Participation by different stake holders in participatory evaluation of health promotion: A review of the literature. *Evaluation & Program Planning, 40*(1), 42–54.

Novak, D. R. (2010). Democratizing qualitative research: Photovoice and the study of human communication. *Communication methods and Measurement, 4*(4), 281–310.

Nutbrown, C. (2011). Naked by the pool? Blurring the image? Ethical issues in the portrayal of young children in arts-based educational research. *Qualitative Inquiry, 17*(1), 3–14.

Nygren, K. G., & Schmauch, V. (2011). Transcending subject-object dualism: Challenging normalized power relations in research power. In E. S. Fahlgren (Ed.), *Challenging gender: Normalization and beyond* (pp. 79–89). Mittuniversitetet: Mid Sweden University.

Nykiforuk, C. I. J., Valianatos, H. V., & Nieuwendyk, L. M. (2011). Photovoice as a method for revealing community perceptions of the built and social environment. *International Journal of Qualitative Research, 10*(2), 102–124.

O'Brien, J. (2011). Spoiled group identities and backstage work: A theory of stigma management rehearsals. *Social Psychology Quarterly, 74*(3), 291–309.

O'Donoghue, D. (2009). Are we asking the wrong questions in arts-based research? *Studies in Art Education: American Journal of Issues and Research, 50*(4), 352–368.

Oh, S.-A. (2012). Photofriend: Creating visual ethnography with refugee children. *Area, 44*(3), 382–388.

Ohmer, M. L., & Owens, J. (2013). Using photovoice to empower youth and adults to prevent crime. *Journal of Community Practice, 21*(4), 410–433.

Oliff, J. L., & Bottorff, J. L. (2007). Further than the eye can see?: Photo elicitation and research with men. *Qualitative Health Research, 17*(6), 850–858.

Oliffe, J. L., Bottorff, J. L., Kelly, M., & Halpin, M. (2008). Analyzing participant produced photographs from an ethnographic study of fatherhood and smoking. *Research in Nursing & Health, 31*(5), 529–539.

Oleson, V. L. (2008). Feminist qualitative research in the millennium's first decade: Developments, challenge, prospects. In N.K. Denzin & Y.S. Lincoln (Eds.), *The landscape of qualitative research* (pp.262–304). London, England: Sage.

Ollerton, J., & Kelshaw, C. (2011). Inclusive participatory action research. In J. Higgs, A. Titchen, D. Horsfall, & D. Bridges (Eds.), *Creative spaces for qualitative research: Living research* (pp.267–278). Rotterdam, The Netherlands: Sense Publishers.

Onwuegbuzie, A. J., Leech, N. L., & Collins, K. M. T. (2010). Innovative data collection strategies in qualitative research. *The Qualitative Report, 15*(3), 696–726.

Ortega-Alcázar, I., & Dyck, I. (2012). Migrant narratives of health and well-being: Challenging "other" process through photo-elicitation interview. *Critical Social Policy, 32*(1), 106–125.

Osei-Kofi, N. (2013). The emancipatory potential of arts-based research for social justice. *Equity & Excellence in Education, 46*(1), 135–149.

Osseck, J., Hartman, A., & Cox, C. C. (2010). Photovoice: Addressing Youths' Concerns in a Juvenile Detention Facility. *Children Youth and Environments, 20*(2), 200–218.

Owens, P. E., Nelson, A. A., Perry, A., & Montgomery-Block, K.F. (2010). *Youth Voice Matters: toward healthy youth environments.* Davis, CA: Center for Regional Change, University of California, Davis.

Ozar, E. J., & Douglas, L. (2012). The impact of participatory research on urban teens: An experiential evaluation. *American Journal of Community Practice, 51*(1–2), 66–75.

Ozar, E. J., Newlan, S., Douglas, L., & Hubbard, E. (2013). "Bounded" empowerment: Analyzing tensions in the practice of youth-led participatory research in urban public schools. *American Journal of Community Psychology, 52*(1–2), 13–26.

Ozar, E. J., Ritterman, M. L., & Wanis, M. G. (2010). Participatory action research (PAR) in middle school: Opportunities, constraints, and key processes. *American Journal of Community Psychology, 46*(1-2), 152–166.

Ozar, E. J., & Schotland, M. (2011). Psychological empowerment among urban youth measure development and relationship to psychosocial functioning. *Health Education & Behavior, 38*(4), 348–356.

Packard, J. (2008). "I'm gonna show you what it's really like out here": The power and limitations of participatory visual methods. *Visual Studies, 23*(1), 63–77.

Padgett, D. K., Smith, B. T., Derejko, K-S, Henwood, B. F., & Tiderington, E. (2013). *Qualitative Health Research, 23*(11), 1435–1444.

Palibroada, B., Krieg, B., Murdock, L., & Havelock, J. (2009). *A practical guide to photovoice: Sharing pictures, telling stories and changing communities.* Winnipeg, Manitoba, Canada: The Prairie Women's Health Centre of Excellence.

Pain, H. (2012). A literature review to evaluate the use of visual methods. *International Journal of Qualitative Research, 11*(4), 303–309.

Panazzola, P., & Leipert, B. (2013). Exploring mental health issues of rural women residing in southwestern Ontario, Canada: A secondary analysis photovoice study. *The International Electronic Journal of Rural and Remote Health, 13*: 2320.

Papson, S., Goldman, R., & Kersey, N. (2007). Website design: The precarious blend of narrative, aesthetic, and social theory. In G. C. Stanczak (Ed.), *Visual research methods: image, society, and representation* (pp. 307–344). Thousand Oaks, CA: Sage.

Parkins, J. R. (2010). The problem with trust: Insights from advisory committees in the forest sector of Alberta. *Society & Natural Resources: An International Journal, 23*(9), 822–836.

Paris, D. (2011). "A friend who understand fully": notes on humanizing research in a multiethnic youth community. *International Journal of Qualitative Studies in Education, 24*(2), 137–149.

Parrott, L. (2010). *Values and ethics in social work practice.* Exeter, England: Learning Matters.

Parson. J. A., & Boydell, K. M. (2012). Arts-based research and knowledge translation: Some key concerns for health-care professionals. *Journal of Interprofessional Care, 26*(3), 170–172.

Pascoe, C. J. (2007). "What if the guy hits on you?: Intersections of gender, sexuality and age in fieldwork with adolescents. In A. Best (Ed.), *Representing youth: Methodological issues in critical youth studies* (pp. 226–247). New York, NY: New York University Press.

Patton, N. Higgs, J., & Smith, M. (2011). Envisioning visual research strategies. In J. Higgs, A. Titchen, D. Horsfall, D. & D. Bridges (Eds.), *Creative spaces for qualitative research: Living research* (pp.115–124). Rotterdam, The Netherlands: Sense Publishers.

Peabody, C.G. (2013). Using photovoice as a tool to engage social work students in social justice. *Journal of Teaching in Social Work, 33*(3), 251–265.

Pedraza, J. E. A. (2010). *Assessment of "Community Stepping Stone," a community-based youth art education program.* Tampa, FL: University of South Florida.

Peterson, J. C., Antony, M. G., & Thomas, R.J. (2012). "This right here is all about living": Communicating the "common sense" about home stability through CBPR and photovoice. *Journal of Applied Communication Research, 40*(3), 247–270.

Phelan, S., & Kinsella, E.A. (2011). Photoelicitation interview methods and research with children. In J. Higgs, A. Titchen, D. Horsfall, & D. Bridges (Eds.), *Creative spaces for qualitative research: Living research* (pp. 125–134). Rotterdam, The Netherlands: Sense Publishers.

Phillips, E., Berg, M., Rodriguez, C., & Morgan, D. (2010). A case study of participatory action research in a public New England middle school: Empowerment, constraints and challenges. *American Journal of Community Psychology, 46*(1–2), 179–194.

Pink, S. (2007). *Doing visual ethnography* (2nd ed.). Thousand Oaks, CA: Sage Publications.

Pink, S., Hubbard, P., O'Neill, M., & Radley, A. (2010). Walking across disciplines: From ethnography to arts practice. *Visual Studies, 25*(1), 1–7.

Pinto, R.M., Spector, A. Rohman, R., & Gastolomendo, J.D. (2013). Research advisory board members' contributions and expectations in the USA. *Health Promotional International.* Advance online publication. doi:10.1093/heapro/dat042

Piper, H., & Frankham, J. (2007). Seeing voices and hearing pictures. Image as discourse and the framing of image-based research. *Discourse, 28*(3), 373–387.

Plunkett, R., Leipert, B. D., & Ray, S. L. (2013). Unspoken phenomena: Using the photovoice method to enrich phenomenological inquiry. *Nursing Inquiry, 20*(2), 156–164.

Ponic, P., & Jategaonkar, N. (2012). Balancing safety and action: Ethical protocols for photovoice research with women who have experienced violence. *Arts & Health: An International for Policy and Practice, 4*(3), 189–202.

Pope, C.V., De Luca, R., & Tolich, H. (2010). How an exchange of perspectives led to tentative ethical guidelines for visual ethnography. *International Journal of Research & Methods in Education, 33*(3), 301–315.

Porter, G., Hampshire, K., Bourdillion, M., Robson, E., Albane, A., & Mashiri, M. (2010). Children as research collaborators: Issues and reflections from a mobility study in sub-Saharan Africa. *American Journal of Community Psychology, 46*(1-2), 215–227.

Potash, J. (2013). A more complete knowing: The subjective objective partnership. In S. McNiff (Ed.), *Art as research: Opportunities and challenges* (pp.153–160). Bristol, England: Intellect.

Potash, J., & Ho, R. T. H. (2011). Drawing involves caring: Fostering relationship building through art therapy for social change. *Art Therapy: Journal of the American Art Therapy Association, 28*(2), 74–81.

Powell, M. A., & Smith, A. B. (2009). Children's participation rights in research. *Childhood, 16*(1), 124–142.

Power, F. C., Sheehan, K. K., McCarthy, K., & Carnevale, T. (2010). Champions for Children: reaching out to urban youth through sports. *Journal of Research in Character Education, 8*(2), 75–85.

Powers. M. C., & Freedman, D. A. (2012). Applying a social justice framework to photovoice research on environmental issues: A comprehensive literature review. *Critical Social Work, 13*(2). Retrieved from http://www1.uwindsor.ca/criticalsocialwork/applyingsocialjusticeframeworkphotovoiceresearch

Powers, M. C., Freedman, D. A., & Pitner, R. (2012). *Final snapshot to civic action: A photovoice facilitator's manual.* Columbia, SC: University of South Carolina School of Social Work.

Prag, H., & Vogel, G. (2013). Fostering posttraumatic growth in Shan adolescent refugees in northern Thailand. *Intervention, 11*(1), 37–51.

Prior, R. W. (2013). Knowing what is known: The subjective objective partnership. In S. McNiff (Ed.), *Art as research: Opportunities and challenges* (pp.161–169). Bristol, England: Intellect.

Prins, E. (2010). Participatory photography: A tool for empowerment or surveillance? *Action Research, 8*(4), 426–443.

Pritzker, S., LaChapelle, A., & Tatum, J. (2012). "We need their help": Encouraging and discouraging adolescent civic engagement through photovoice. *Children and Youth Services Review, 34*(11), 2247–2254.

Prosser, J., & Burke, C. (2008). Image-based educational research: Childlike perspectives. In J. G. Knowles & A. L. Cole (Eds.), *Handbook of the arts in qualitative research* (pp. 407–419). Thousand Oaks, CA: Sage.

Prosser, J., & Loxley, A. (2008). *Introducing visual methods.* ESRC National Centre for Research Methods Review Paper. Retrieved from http://eprints.ncrm.ac.uk/420/1/MethodsReviewPaperNCRM-010.pdf

Public Health England. (2009). Camden Alcohol Photo Voice Project. Retrieved from http://www.alcohollearningcentre.org.uk/LocalInitiatives/projects/projectDetail/?cid=6454

Purcell, R. (2009). Images for change: Community development, community arts and photographs. *Community Development Journal, 44*(1), 111–122.

Putland, C. (2008). Lost in translation: The question of evidence linking community-based arts and health promotion. *Journal of Health Psychology, 13*(2), 265–276.

Pyne, K. B., Scott, M. A., & Long, D. T. (2013) From structural inequalities to speaking out: Youth participatory action research in college access collaborations. *PRISM: A Journal of Regional Engagement, 2*(1), Article 4. Retrieved from http://encompass.eku.edu/prism/vol2/iss1/4/

Quinlan, M. M., Ruhl, S. M., Torrens, A., & Harter, L. M. (2013). Sensing gender by coupling visual and verbal storytelling. *Communication Teacher, 27*(1), 45–49.

Quinn, S. C. (2004). Ethics in public health research. *American Journal of Public Health, 94*(6), 918–922.

Quintero-Gonzalez, B., & Stewart, L.M. (2014). *Apoyos y obstaculos: Using photovoice to promote engagement and activism among at-risk Latino youth.* The Society for Social Work and Research 2014 Annual Conference, San Antonio, Texas.

Rabinowitz, P., & Holt, C. (2013). *The Community Toolbox.* Manhattan, KS: University of Kansas. Retrieved from http://ctb.ku.edu/en/table-of-contents/assessment/assessing-community-needs-and-resources/photovoice/checklist

Raby, R. (2007). Across a great gulf? Conducting research with adolescents. In A. Best (Ed.), *Representing youth: Methodological issues in critical youth studies* (pp.39–59). New York, NY: New York University Press.

Radcliffe, J., Doty, N., Hawkins, L. A., Gaskins, C. S., Beidas, R., & Rudy, B.J. (2010). Stigma and sexual health risk in HIV-Positive African American young men who have sex with men. *AIDS Patient Care and STDS, 24*(8), 493–499.

Radley, A. (2010). What people do with pictures. *Visual Studies, 25*(3), 268–279.

Randall, D., & Rouncefield, M. (2010). Sense and sensibility in interdisciplinary work: Designing and planning applied ethnography. In J. S. Jones & S. Watt (Eds.), *Ethnography in social science practice* (pp. 59–72). London: Routledge.

Rappaport, L. (2013). Trusting the felt sense in art-based research. In S. McNiff (Ed.), *Art as research: Opportunities and challenges* (pp.201–208). Bristol, England: Intellect.

Raw, A., Lewis, S. Russell, A., & Mcnaughton, J. (2012). A hole in the heart: Confronting the drive for evidence-based impact research in arts and health. *Arts & Health: An International Journal for Research, Policy and Practice, 4*(2), 97–108.

Reavey, P. (Ed.). (2011). *Visual methods in psychology: using and interpreting images in qualitative research.* New York, NY: Routledge.

Reed, B. (2005). Theorizing in community practice: Essential tools for building community, promoting social justice, and implementing social change. In M. Weil (Ed.), *The handbook of community practice* (pp. 84–102). Thousand Oaks, CA: Sage.

Rein, M. (1977). Planning by what authority? The search for legitimacy. In N. Gilbert & H. Specht (Eds.), *Planning for social welfare: issues, models, and tasks* (pp. 50–69). Englewood Cliffs, NJ: Prentice-Hall.

Reisch, M., Ife, J., & Weir, M. (2013). Social justice, human rights, values, and community practice. In M. Weir, M. Reisch & M. L. Ohmer (Eds.), *The handbook of community practice*(2nd ed.) (pp. 73–103). Thousand Oaks, CA: Sage.

Resnik, D. B., & Kennedy, C.E. (2010). Balancing scientific and community interests in community-based participatory research. *Accountability in Research: Policies and Quality Assurance, 17*(4), 198–210.

Rhodes, S. D., Hergenrather, K. C., Wilkins, A. A., & Jolly, C. (2008). Visions and voices: Indigent persons living with HIV in southern United States use photovoice to create knowledge, develop partnerships and take action. *Health Promotion Practice, 9*(2), 159–169.

Rice, K., Primak, S., & Girvin, H. (2013). Through their eyes: Using photography with youth experienced trauma. *The Qualitative Researcher, 18*, Article 52, 1–14. Retrieved from http://www.nova.edu/ssss/QR/QR18/rice52.pdf

Richardson, D. M., & Nuru-Jeter, A. M. (2012). Neighborhood contexts experienced by young Mexican-American women: Enhancing our understanding of risk for early childbearing. *Journal of Urban Health, 89*(1), 59–73.

Richardson, K., Sinclair, A. J., Reed, M. G., & Parkins, J. R. (2011). Constraints to participation in Canadian forestry advising committees: A gendered perspective. *Canadian Journal of Forest Research, 41*(3), 524–532.

Richter, P. (2011). Different lenses for studying local churches: A critical study of the uses of photographic research methods. *Journal of Contemporary Religion, 26*(2), 207–223.

Ridenour, A. (2012). *How to become a truly diverse organization: Organizational models of diversity.* Boston, MA: Boston University School of Social Work.

Riecken, T., & Strong-Wilson, T. (2006). At the edge of consent: Participatory research with student filmmakers. In B. Leadbeater, E. Banister, C. Benoit, M. Jansson, A. Marshall & T. Riecken (Eds.), *Ethical issues in community-based research with children and youth* (pp. 42–56). Toronto, Canada: University of Toronto Press.

Riele, K. (2005). Youth "at-risk": Further marginalizing the marginalized? *Journal of Educational Policy, 21*(2), 129–145.

Riele, K. (2010). Philosophy of hope: concepts and applications for working with marginalized youth. *Journal of Youth Studies, 13*(1), 35–46.

Riele, K. (2013). Formal frameworks as resources for ethical youth research. In K. Riele & R. Brooks (Eds.), *Negotiating ethical challenges in youth research* (pp. 3–15). New York, NY: Routledge.

Riele, K., & Brooks, R. (Eds.). (2013). *Negotiating ethical challenges in youth research.* New York, NY: Routledge.

Ries, A.V., Yau, A.F., & Voorhees, C.C. (2011). The neighborhood recreational environment and physical activity among urban youth: An examination of public and private recreational facilities. *Journal of Community Health, 36*(4), 640–649.

Riessman, C. K. (2008). *Narrative methods for human sciences.* Thousand Oaks, CA: Sage.

Riggs, J. (2011). Liberating research mentoring: Reflecting, re-visioning, re-creating. In J. Higgs, A. Titchen, D. Horsfall, & D. Bridges (Eds.), *Creative spaces for qualitative research: Living research* (pp. 191–200). Rotterdam, The Netherlands: Sense Publishers.

Ritterbusch, A. (2011). Bridging guidelines and practice: Toward a grounded care ethics in youth participatory action research. *The Professional geographer, 64*(1), 16–24.

Robinson, A. (2011). Giving voice and taking pictures: Participatory documentation and visual research. *People, Place and Policy Online, 5*(3), 115–134.

Robinson, N. (2012). *Picturing social inclusion: Photography and identity in Downtown Eastside Vancouver.* Birmingham, England: University of Birmingham.

Rodriguez, S. M. (2011). *Diversity revealed: Photovoice methodology as a means of understanding how teens construct a mosaic quilt.* Denton, TX: University of North Texas, Communications Study Department.

Rolling, J. H., Jr. (2013). *Arts-based research.* New York: Peter Lang.

Robinson, Y., & Gillies, V. (2012). Introduction: Developing creative methods with children and young people. *International Journal of Social Research Methodology, 15*(2), 87–89.

Roholt, R. V., & Mueller, M. (2013). Youth advisory structures: Listening to young people to support quality youth services. *New Directions for Youth Development, 139,* 79–100.

Rose, G. (2012). Visual methodologies: An introduction to researching with visual materials (3rd ed.). Thousand Oaks, CA: Sage.

Rosen, D., Goodkind, S., & Smith, M.L. (2011). Using photovoice to identify service needs of older African American methadone clients. *Journal of Social Service Research, 37*(5), 526–538.

Ross, L. (2011). Sustaining youth participating in a long-term tobacco control initiative: Consideration of a social justice perspective. *Youth & Society, 43*(2), 681–704.

Ross, L. F. (2008). *Children in medical research: Access versus protection.* New York, NY: Oxford University Press.

Ross, L. F., Loup, A. L., Nelson, R. M., Botkin, J. R., Kost, R., Smith, G. R., Jr., & Gehlert, S. (2010a). Human subject protection in community-engaged research: A research ethics framework. *Journal of Empirical Research on Human Research Ethics: An International Journal, 5*(1), 5–17.

Ross, L. F., Loup, A. L., Nelson, R. M., Botkin, J. R., Kost, R., Smith, G. R., Jr., & Gehlert, S. (2010b). Nine key functions for a human subjects protection program for community-engaged research: Points to consider. *Journal of Empirical Research on Human Research Ethics: An International Journal, 5*(1), 33–47.

Ross, L. F., Loup, A. L. Nelson, R. M., Botkin, J. R., Kost, R., Smith, G. R., Jr., & Gehlert, S. (2010c). The challenges of collaboration for academic and community partners in a research partnership: Points to consider. *Journal of Empirical Research on Human Research Ethics: An International Journal, 5*(1), 19–31.

Ross, M. (2013, December 23). Seeding university communities. *The Boston Globe*, p. A11.

Rudkin, J. K., & Davis, A. (2007). Photography as a tool for understanding youth connections to their neighborhood. *Children, Youth and Environment, 17*(4), 107–123.

Ruiz-Casares, M. (2013). Knowledge without harm?: What follow-up services are readily available. In K. Riele & R. Brooks (Eds.), *Negotiating ethical challenges in youth research* (pp. 3–15). New York, NY: Routledge.

Rumbold, J., Fenner, P., & Brophy-Dixon, J. (2012). The risks of representation: Dilemmas and opportunity in art-based research. *Journal of Applied Health, 3*(1), 67–78.

Rush, K. L., Murphy, M. A., & Kozak, J. F. (2012). A photovoice study of older adults' conceptualizations of risk. *Journal of Aging Studies, 26*(4), 448–458.

Russell, A. C., & Diaz, N. D. (2013). Photography in social work research: Using visual image to humanize findings. *Qualitative Social Work, 12*(4), 433–453.

Russell, R. (2009, January 17). Spread a little love—and create your own work of art. *The Daily Telegraph* (London), p. 10.

Russell, S. T., Muraco, A., Subramanian, A., & Laub, C.C. (2009). Youth empowerment and high school gay-straight alliance. *Journal of Youth and Adolescence, 38*(7), 891–903.

Sanberg, S., & Copes, H. (2012). Speaking with ethnographers: The challenges of researching drug dealers and offenders. *Journal of Drug Issues, 43*(2), 176–197.

Sanchez, P. (2009). Chicana feminist strategies in a participatory action research project with transnational Latina youth. *New Directions for Youth Development, 123*(Fall), 83–97.

Sands, C., Reed, L. E., Harper, K., & Shar, M. (2009). A photovoice participatory evaluation of a school gardening program through the eyes of fifth graders. *Practicing Anthropology, 31*(4), 15–20.

Saimon, R., Choo, W. Y., & Bulgiba, A. (2013). "Feeling unsafe": A photovoice analysis of factors influencing physical activity behavior among Malaysian adolescents. *Asia Pacific Journal of Public Health.* Advance online publication. Retrieved from http://www.ncbi.nlm.nih.gov/pubmed/23513006

Sajnani, N. (2012). Improvisation and art-based research. *Journal of Applied Arts & Health, 3*(1), 79–86.

Sandell, R., & Nightingale, E. (2012). *Museums, equality and social justice.* New York, NY: Routledge.

Santo, C. A., Ferguson, N., & Trippel, A. (2010). Engaging urban youth through technology: The Youth Neighborhood Mapping Initiative. *Journal of Planning Education and Research, 30*(1), 52–65.

Sargeant, J., & Harcourt, D. (2012). *Doing ethical research with children.* New York, NY: McGraw Hill Open University Press.

Sass, M. (2008). *Locating youth between power and marginality: The Limits of photovoice in youth empowerment* (Doctoral dissertation). Kalamazoo, MI: Kalamazoo College.

Scacciaferro, J., Goode, S., & Frausto, D. (2009). Using Photovoice as Participatory Needs Assessment with Youth at a Latino Youth Action Center. *Undergraduate Research Journal for the Human Sciences, 8*(1). Retrieved from http://www.kon.org/urc/v8/scacciaferro.html

Schaefer, N. (2012) Using video in a participatory multi-method project on young people's everyday lives in rural East Germany: A critical reflection. In S. Heath & C. Walker (Eds.), *Innovations in youth research* (pp. 143–160). London: Sage.

Schell, K., Ferguson, A., Hamoline, R., Shea, J., & Thomas-Maclean, R. (2009). Photovoice as a Teaching Tool: Learning by Doing with Visual Methods. *International Journal of Teaching and Learning in Higher Education, 21*(3), 340–352.

Schleien, S. J., Brake, L., Miller, K. D., & Walton, G. (2013). Using photovoice to listen to adults with intellectual disabilities on being part of the community. *Annals of Leisure Research, 16*(3), 212–229.

Schrag, Z. M. (2011). The case against ethics review in the social sciences. *Research Ethics, 7*(4), 128–131.

Schreider, B. (2012). Participatory action research, mental health service user research, and the Hearing (our) Voices Project. *International Journal of Qualitative Research, 11*(2), 132–151.

Schubotz, D. (2012). Involving young people as peer researchers in research on community relations in Northern Ireland. In S. Heath & C. Walker (Eds.), *Innovations in youth research* (pp. 101–120). London: Sage.

Schuermans, N., Loopmans, M. P. J., & Vandenabeele, J. (2012). Public space, public art and public pedagogy. *Social & Cultural Geography, 13*(7), 675–682.

Schwartz, L., Sable, M. R., Dannerbeck, A., & Campbell, J.D. (2007). Using photovoice to improve family planning services for immigrant Hispanics. *Journal of Health Care for the Poor and Underserved, 18*(4), 757–766.

Schwarzman, M., & Knight, K. (2005). *Beginner's guide to community-based arts*. Oakland, CA: New Village Press.

Segars, G. (2007). *Visible Rigths Conference Sequals: A participatory photography toolkit for practitioners and educators*. Compiled for the Cultural Agents Initiative, Spring 2007. Salt Lake City, UT: Kids with Cameras. Retrieved from http://www.kids-with-cameras.org/community/culturalagents-toolkit.pdf

Serido, J., Borden, L. M., & Perkins, D.F. (2009). Moving beyond youth voice. *Youth & Society, 43*(1), 44–63.

Seifer, S. D., & Sisco, S. (2006). Mining the challenges of CBPR for improvements in urban health. *Journal of Urban Health, 83*(6), 981–984.

Sercombe, H. (2010). *Youth work ethics*. Thousand Oaks, CA: Sage.

Shah, S. (2011). *Building transformative youth leadership: Data on the impacts of youth organizing*. New York: Funders' Collaborative on Youth Organizing.

Shapiro, D., Tomasa, L., & Koff, N. A.(2009). Patients as teachers, medical students as filmmakers: The video slam, a pilot study. *Academic Medicine, 84*(9), 1235–1243.

Sharma, M. (2010). Photovoice in alcohol and drug education. *Journal of Alcohol and Drug Education, 54*(1), 3–6.

Sharpe, D. (2012). Young people and policy research: Methodological challenges in CYP-led research. In S. Heath & C. Walker (Eds.), *Innovations in youth research* (pp. 161–177). London: Sage.

Shek, D. T. L., & Ma, C. M. S. (2010). Dimensionality of the Chinese Positive Youth Development Scale: Confirmatory factor analyses. *Social Indicators Research, 98*(1), 41–59.

Shell, K., Ferguson, A., Hamoline, R., Shea, J., & Thomas-Maclean, R. (2009). Photovoice as a teaching tool: Learning by doing with visual methods. *International Journal of Teaching and Learning on Higher Education, 21*(3), 340–352.

Sherman, R. F. (2004). The promise of youth is in the present. *National Civic Review, 93*(1), 50–55.

Shilton, K., & Srinivasan, R. (2008) *Participatory appraisal and arrangement for multicultural archival collections*. Los Angeles, CA: University of California, Graduate School of Education & Information Studies. Retrieved from http://rameshsrinivasan.org/wordpress/wp-content/uploads/2010/04/6-Shilton-Srinivasan-Multicultural-Archives-final.pdf

Shimshock, K. (2008). *Photovoice project organizer: and facilitator manual*. Ann Arbor, MI: University of Michigan School of Social Work, Good Neighbors Technical Assistance Center (TAC).

Shin, R. Q., Rogers, J., Stancin, A., Silas, M., Brown-Smythe, C., & Austin, B. (2010). Advancing social justice in urban schools through the implementation of transformative groups for youth of color. *The Journal for Specialists in Group Work*, 35(2), 230–235.

Shore, N., Brazauskas, R., Drew, E., Wong, K. A, Moy, L., Based, A. C., Cyr, K., Ulevicus, J., & Seifer, S.D. (2004). Understanding community-based processes for research ethics review: A national study. *American Journal of Public Health*, 101(51), S359–S364.

Sieber, J. E., & Tolich, M. B. (2013). *Planning ethical responsible research* (2nd ed.). Thousand Oaks, CA: Sage.

Silberman, G., & Kahn, K. L. (2011). Burdens on research imposed by institutional review boards: The state of the evidence and its implications for regulatory reform. *Milbank Quarterly*, 89(4), 599–627.

Simon, C., & Mosavel, M. (2010). Community members as recruiters of human subjects: Ethical consequences. *American Journal of Bioethics*, 10(3), 3–11.

Simons, H., & McCormack, B. (2007). Integrating arts-based inquiry in evaluation methodology: Opportunities and challenges. *Qualitative Inquiry*, 13(2), 292–311.

Sinding, C., Gray, R., Grassau, P., Damianakis, F., & Hampson, A. (2006). Audience responses to a research-based drama about life after breast cancer. *Psycho-Oncology*, 15(8), 694–700.

Singh, A. (2011). Visual artefacts as boundary objects in participatory research paradigm. *Journal of Visual Art Practice*, 10(1), 35–50.

Singhal, A., & Rattine-Flaherty, E. (2009). Pencils and Photos as Tools of Communicative Research and Praxis Analyzing Minga Perú's Quest for Social Justice in the Amazon. *International Communication Gazzette*, 68(4), 313–330.

Singhal, A., Rao, N., & Pant, S. (2006). Entertainment-education and processes for second-order social change. *Journal of Creative Communication*, 1(3), 267–283.

Sinner, A., Leggo, C., Irwin, R. L., Gouzouasis, P., & Grauer, K. (2006). Art-based educational research dissertations: Researching the practice of new scholars. *Canadian Journal of Education*, 29(4), 1223–1270.

Sippola, L. (2006). Ivory tower ethics: Potential conflict between community organizations and agents of the tri-council. In B. Leadbeater, E. Banister, C. Benoit, M. Jansson, A. Marshall, & T. Riecken (Eds.), *Ethical issues in community-based research with children and youth* (pp. 111–135). Toronto, Canada: University of Toronto Press.

Sirotin, N., Wolf, L. E., Catania, J. A., Dolcini, M. M., & Lo, B. (2010). IRBs and ethically challenging protocols: Views of IRB chairs about useful resources. *IRB*, 32(5), 10–19.

Sites, W., Chaskin, R. J., & Parks, V. (2007). Reframing community practice for the 21st century: Multiple traditions, multiple challenges. *Journal of Urban Affairs*, 29(5), 519–541.

Skinner, E., & Masuda, J. R. (2013). Right to a healthy city? Examining the relationship between urban space and health inequity by Aboriginal youth artist-activists in Winnipeg. *Social Science & Medicine*, 91(2), 210–218.

Skowdal, M., & Ogutu, V.O. (2012). Coping with hardship through friendship: The importance of peer social capital among children affected by HIV in Kenya. *African Journal of AIDS Research*, 11(3), 241–250.

Slade, M., Bird, V., Chandler, R., Fox, J., Larsen, J., Tew, J., & Learny, M. (2010). The contribution of advisory committees and public involvement to large scale studies: Case study. *BMC Health Services Research*, 10, 323. Retrieved from http://www.biomed-central.com/1472-6963/10/323

Smith, L. Bratini, L., & Appio, L.M. (2012). "Everybody's teaching and everybody's learning": Photovoice and youth counseling. *Journal of Counseling & Development, 90*(1), 3–12.

Smith, L., Chambers, D.-A., & Bratini, L. (2009). When oppression is the pathogen: The participatory development of social just mental health practice. *American Journal of Orthopsychiatry, 79*(2), 158–168.

Smith, S., & Blumenthal, D.S. (2012). Community health workers support community-based participatory research ethics: Lessons learned along the research-to-practice-to-community continuum. *Journal of Health Care of the Poor and Underserved, 23*(4 Suppl.), 77–87.

Smith, T. D. (2013). Shall I hide an art-based study within a recognized qualitative framework? Negotiating the spaces between research traditions at a research university. In S. McNiff (Ed.), *Art as research: Opportunities and challenges* (pp.191–199). Bristol, England: Intellect.

Smith-Cavos, E., & Eisenhauer, E. (2013). Overtown: Neighborhood, change, and "invironment." *Local Environment: The International Journal of Justice and Sustainability, 19*(4), 384–401.

Smits, P. A., & Champagne, F. (2008). An assessment of the theoretical underpinnings of practice participatory evaluation. *American Journal of Evaluation, 29*(4), 427–442.

Snow, M. M. (2007). Improving morale through photovoice technology. *Nursing Management, 38*(10), 50–52.

Springay, S., Irwin, R. L., & Kind, S.W. (2005). A/r/tography as living inquiry through art and text. *Qualitative Inquiry, 11*(6), 897–912.

Springett, J. (2010). Integrating values. Research and knowledge development through the use of participatory evaluation in community based health promotion. *Estudios sobre las Culturas contemporianeas, 16*(31), 277–297. Retrieved from http://www.redalyc.org/pdf/316/31613952011.pdf

Solomon, B. B. (1976). *Black empowerment: Social work in oppressed communities.* New York, NY: Columbia University Press.

Sommer, C. (2012, November 21). Purchase power of global teens tops $819 billion. *MasterCard Insights, Payments Perspecives Blog.* Retrieved from http://insights.mastercard.com/2012/11/21/purchase-power-of-global-teens-tops-819-billion/

South China Morning Post. (2004, August 4). Snapshots of isolation. Author, p. 6.

Spencer, S. (Ed.). (2011). *Visual research methods in the social sciences: Awakening visions.* London: Routledge.

Stanczak, G. C. (2007a). Images, methodologies, and generating social knowledge. In G.C. Stanczak (Ed.), *Visual research methods: Images and society* (pp. 1–22). London: Sage.

Stanczak, C. G. (2007b). Introduction: Images, methodologies, and generating social knowledge. In C. G. Stanczak (Ed.), *Visual research methods: Image, society, and representation* (pp.1–21). Thousand Oaks, CA: Sage.

Stanczak, C. G. (2007c). *Visual research methods: Image, society, and representation.* Thousand Oaks, CA: Sage.

Stanton-Salazar, R. D. (2011). A social capital framework for the study of institutional agents and their role in the empowerment of low-status students and youth. *Youth & Society, 43*(3), 1066–1109.

Stedman, M., McGovern, P. M., Peden-McAlpine, C. J., Kingery, L. R., & Draeger, K. J. (2012). Photovoice in the Red River Basin of the North: A systematic evaluation of a community-academic partnership. *Health Promotion Practice, 13*(5), 599–607.

Stegenga, K., & Burks, L. M. (2013). Using photovoice to explore the unique life perspectives of youth with sickle cell disease: A pilot study. *Journal of Pediatric Oncology Nursing, 30*(5), 269–274.

Stevens, C. A. (2010). Lessons from the field: Using photovoice with an ethnically diverse population in a HOPE VI evaluation. *Family & Community Health 33*(4), 275–284.

Stewart, S., Riecken, T., Scott, T., Tanaka, M., & Riecken, J. (2008). Expanding health literacy: Indigenous youth creating videos. *Journal of Health Psychology,13*(2), 180–189.

Stoecker, R. (2013). *Research methods for community change: A project-based approach* (2nd ed.). Thousand Oaks, CA: SAGE.

Strack, R. W., Lovelace, K. A., Jordan, T. D., & Holmes., A. P. (2010). Framing photovoice using a social-ecological model as a guide. *Health Promotion Practice, 11*(5), 629–636.

Strack, R. W., Magill, C., & McDonagh, K. (2004). Engaging youth through photovoice. *Health Promotion Practice, 5*(1), 49–58.

Strawn, C., & Monama, G. (2012). Making Soweto stories: photovoice meets the New Literacy Studies. *International Journal of Lifelong Education, 31*(5), 535–553.

Streng, J. M., Rhodes, S., Ayala, G., Eng, E., Arceo, R., & Phipps, S. (2004): Realidad Latina: Latino adolescents, their school, and a university use photovoice to examine and address the influence of immigration. *Journal of Interpersonal Care, 18*(4), 403–415.

Steyn, M. G., & Kamper, G. D. (2011). Barriers to learning in South African higher education: some photovoice perspectives. *Journal for New Generation Sciences, 9*(1), 116–136.

Stuckey, L. (2009). Creative expression as a way of knowing in diabetes adult health education: An action research study. *Adult Education Quarterly, 60*(1), 46–64.

Sutherland, C., & Cheng, Y. (2009). Participatory-action research with (Im)migrant women in two small Canadian cities using photovoice in Kingston and Peterborough, Ontario. *Journal of Immigrant & Refugee Studies, 7*(3), 290–327.

Swaans, K., Broerse, J., Meincke, M., Mudhara, M., & Bunders, J. (2009). Promoting food security and well-being among poor and HIV/AIDS affected households: Lessons from an interactive and integrated approach. *Evaluation and Program Planning, 32*(1), 31–42.

Sullivan, E. M., Sullivan, N. E., Cox, D. H., Butt, D., Dollemont, C., & Shallow, M. (2010). "You are taking who?! to a national conference on social policy?": A place for youth in the social policy life of their communities. *Community Development Journal, 46*(4), 511–525.

Sun, J. Buys, N. J., & Merrick, J. (2012). Community singing: What does that have to do with health? *International Journal of Adolescent Medicine & Health, 24*(4), 281–282.

Syson-Nibbs, L., Robinson, A., Cook, J., King, I. (2009) Young farmers' photographic mental health promotion programme: A case study. *Arts & Health 1*(2), 151–167.

Taft, J. K. (2007). Racing age: Reflections on antiracist research with teenage girls. In A. Best (Ed.), *Representing youth: Methodological issues in critical youth studies* (pp. 203–225). New York, NY: New York University Press.

Taiapa, K., Barnes, H. M., & McCreamor, T. (2013). "I don't want it to stop: I want it to keep going": Waimarino Youth Report. Wellesley St., Auckland, New Zealand: Massey University.

Tasker, D., McLeod-Boyle, A., & Bridges, D. (2011). From practice to research and back again. In J. Higgs, A. Titchen, D. Horsfall, D. & D. Bridges (Eds.), *Creative spaces for qualitative research: Living research* (pp.291–300). Rotterdam, The Netherlands: Sense Publishers.

Tay-Lim, J., & Lim, S. (2013). Privileging younger children's voices in research: Use of drawings and a co-construction. *International Journal of Qualitative Research, 12*(1), 65–83.

TB Voices. (n.d.). *TB Voices Project for Snohomish and King County, Washington.* Retrieved from http://www.tbphotovoice.org/index.php?option=com_content&view=article&id=41&Itemid=29

Teachman, G., & Gibson, B.E. (2012). Children and youth with disabilities: Innovative methods for single qualitative interviews. *Qualitative Health Research, 23*(2), 264–274.

Tervalon, M., & Murray-Garcia, J. (1998). Cultural humility versus cultural competence: A critical distinction in defining physician training outcomes in multicultural education. *Journal of Health Care for the Poor and Underserved, 9*(2), 117–125.

Teti, M., Pichon, L., Kabel, A., Farnan, R., & Benson, D. (2013). Taking pictures to take control: Photovoice as a tool to facilitate empowerment among poor and racial/ethnic minority women with HIV. *Journal of the Association of Nurses in AIDS Care. 24*(6), 539–553.

Thackeray, R., & Hunter, M. (2010). Empowering youth: use of technology in advocacy to affect social change. *Journal of Computer-Mediated Communication, 15*(4), 575–591.

Thomas, H. C., & Irwin, J. D. (2013). Using photovoice with at-risk youth in a community-based cooking program. *Canadian Journal of Dietetic Practice and Research, 74*(1), 14–20.

Thomson, P. (2008a). Children and young people: Voices in visual research. In P. Thomson (Ed.), *Doing visual research with children and young people* (pp.1–19). London: Routledge.

Thomson, P. (Ed.). (2008b). *Doing visual research with children and young people.* London: Routledge.

Thomson, P., & Hall, C. (2008). Dialogue with artists: Analyzing children's self-portraits. In P. Thomson (Ed.), *Doing visual research with children and young people* (pp.146–163). London: Routledge.

Tijm, M., Cornielje, H., & Edusei, A.K. (2011). "Welcome to my life!" Photovoice: Needs assessment of, and by, persons with physical disabilities with physical disabilities in the Kumasi Metropolis, Ghana. *Disability, CBR and Inclusive Development, 22*(1). Retrieved from http://dcidj.org/article/view/12

Tirri, K., & Quinn, B. (2010). Exploring the role of religion and spirituality in the development of purpose: case studies of purposeful youth. *British Journal of Religious Education, 32*(3), 201–214.

Titchen, A., & Horsfall, D. (2011). Creative research landscapes and gardens. *Creative Spaces for Qualitative Researching Practice, Education, Work and Society, 5*(1), 35–44.

Tobias, J. K., Richmond, C. A. M., & Luginaah, F. (2013). Community-based participatory research (CBPR) with indigenous communities: Providing respectful and reciprocal research. *Journal of Empirical Research on Human Research ethics: An International Journal, 8*(2), 128–140.

Tolich, M. (2010). A critique of current practice: Ten foundational guidelines for autoethnographers. *Qualitative Research, 20*(12), 1599–1610.

Tolich, M., & Tumilty, E. (2013). Making ethics review a learning institution: the Ethics Application Repository proof of concept. tear.otago.ac.nz. *Qualitative Research.* Advance online publication. doi:10.1177/1468794112468476

Torres, M. E., Meetz, E. G., & Smithwick-Leone, J. (2013). Latina voices in childhood obesity: A pilot study using photovoice in South Carolina. *American Journal of Preventive Medicine, 44*(3) (Suppl. 3), S2225–S231.

Travis, R., Jr., & Leech, T. G. J. (2014). Empowerment-based positive youth development: A new understanding of healthy development for African American youth. *Journal of Research on Adolescence, 24*(3), 411–550.

Trickett, E.J. (2009). Community psychology: Individuals and interventions in community context. *Annual Review of Psychology, 60*, 395–419.

Trauger, A., & Flur, J. (2014). Getting beyond the "God trick": Towards service research. *The Professional Geographer, 66*(1). 32–40.

Trudeau, D. (2012). IRBs as asset for education in geography. *The Professional Geographer, 64*(1), 25–33.

Tunnell, K. D. (2012). Reflections on Visual Field Research. *International Journal of Qualitative Methods, 11*(4), 340–351.

Underwood, M. K., Mayeux, L, Risser, S., & Harper, B. (2006). The ecstasy and the agony of collecting sociometric data in public school classrooms: Challenges, community concerns, and pragmatic solutions. In B. Leadbeater, E. Banister, C. Benoit, M. Jansson, A. Marshall, & T. Riecken (Eds.), *Ethical issues in community-based research with children and youth* (pp.93–110). Toronto, Canada: University of Toronto Press.

Ungar, M. (2007). Grow 'em strong: Conceptual challenges in researching childhood resilience. In A. Best (Ed.), *Representing youth: Methodological issues in critical youth studies* (pp.84–109). New York, NY: New York University Press.

Ungar, M. (2011). Community resilience for youth and families: Facilitative physical and social capital in contexts of adversity. *Children and Youth and Youth Services, 33*(9), 1742–1748.

Valaitis, R. (2005). Computers and the Internet: Tools for youth empowerment. *Journal of Medical Internet Research, 7*(5), 1–20.

Valera, P., Gallin, J., Schuk, D., & Davis, N. (2009). "Trying to eat healthy": A photovoice study about women's access to healthy food in New York City. *Affilia, 24*(3), 300–314.

Valentine, A. Z., & Knibb, R.C. (2011). Exploring quality of life in families of children living with and without a severe food allergy. *Appetite, 57*(2), 467–474.

van Lieshout, F., & Cardiff, S. (2011). Innovative ways of analyzing data with practitioners as co-researchers: Dancing outside the ballroom. In J. Higgs, A. Titchen, D. Horsfall, &D. Bridges (Eds.), *Creative spaces for qualitative research: Living research* (pp.223–234). Rotterdam, The Netherlands: Sense Publishers.

Vaughan, C. (2010). "When the road is full of potholes, I wonder why they are bringingcondoms?" Social spaces for understanding young Papua New Guineans' health-related knowledge and help-promoting action. *AIDS Care: Psychological and Socio-medical aspects of AIDS/HIV, 22*(2), 1644–1651.

Vaughan, C. (2014). Participatory research with youth: Idealising safe social spaces or building transformative links in difficult environments? *Journal of Health Psychology, 19*(1), 184–192.

Vaugh, L. M., Rojas-Guyler, L., & Howell, B. (2008). "Picturing" health: A photovoice pilot of Latina girls' perceptions of health. *Community Health: The Journal of Health Promotion and Maintenance, 31*(4), 305–316.

Villagran, M. (2011). Methodological diversity to reach patients along the margins, in the shadows, and on the cutting edge. *Patient Education & Counseling, 82*(3), 292–297.

Vissing, Y. (2007). A roof over their head: Applied research issues and dilemmas in the investigation of homeless children and youth. In A. Best (Ed.), *Representing youth: Methodological issues in critical youth studies* (pp. 110–130). New York, NY: New York University Press.

Walker, A., & Early, J. (2010). "We have to do something for ourselves": Using photovoice and participatory action research to assess the barriers to caregiving for abandoned and orphaned children in Sierra Leone. *International Electronic Journal of Health Education, 13*, 33–48. Retrieved from http://files.eric.ed.gov/fulltext/EJ895722.pdf

Walker, C. (2012). Positionality and difference in cross-cultural youth research: Being "other" in the former Soviet Union. In S. Heath & C. Walker (Eds.), *Innovations in youth research* (pp. 195–209). Sage: London.

Walker, R., Schratz, B., & Egg, P. (2008). Seeing beyond violence: Visual research applied to policy and practice. In P. Thomson (Ed.), *Doing visual research with children and young people* (pp. 164–174). London: Routledge.

Walsh, C. A., Hewson, J., Shier, M., & Morales, E. (2008). Unraveling ethics: Reflections from a community-based participatory research project with youth. *The Qualitative Researcher, 13*(3), 379–393.

Walsh, C. A., Rutherford, G., & Crough, M. (2013). Arts-based research: creating social change for incarcerated women. *Creative Approaches to Research, 6*(1), 119–139.

Walsh, L., Black, R., & Berman, N. (2013). Walking the talk: Youth research in hard times. In K. Riele & R. Brooks (Eds.), *Negotiating ethical challenges in youth research* (pp. 43–54). New York, NY: Routledge.

Wallerstein, N. B., & Duran, B. (2006). Using community-based participatory research to address health disparities. *Health Promotion Practice, 7*(3), 312–323.

Walsh, C.A., Rutherford, G., & Kuzmak, N. (2010). Engaging women who are homeless in community-based research using emerging qualitative data collection techniques. *International Journal of Multiple Research Approaches, 4*(3), 192–205.

Walters, K. L., Stately, A., Evans-Campbell, T., Simoni, J. M., Duran, B., Schultz, K., . . . Guerrero, D. (2009). "Indigenist" collaborative research efforts in Native American communities. In A. R. Stiffman (Ed.), *The field researcher survival guide* (pp. 146–173). New York: Oxford University Press.

Wang, C. C. (2006). Youth participation in photovoice as a strategy for community change. In B. Checkoway & L. M. Gutierrez (Eds.), *Youth participation and community change* (pp. 147–162). New York: Haworth Press.

Wang, C. C., & Burris, M. A. (1997). Photovoice: Concept, methodology, and use for participatory needs assessment. *Health Education & Behavior, 24*(3), 369–387.

Wang, C. C., Cash, J. L., & Powers, L. S. (2000). Who knows the streets well as the homeless? Promoting personal and community action through photovoice. *Health Promotion Practice, 1*(1), 81–89.

Wang, C. C., & Pies, C. A. (2004). Family, maternal, and child health through photovoice. *Maternal and Child Health, 8*(2), 95–102.

Wang, C. C., & Redwood-Jones, Y. A. (2001). Photovoice ethics: Perspectives from Flint Photovoice. *Health & Education Behavior, 28*(5), 560–572.

Warne, M., Synder, F., & Gillander Gådin, K. (2013). Photovoice: An opportunity and challenge for students' genuine participation. *Health Promotion International, 28*(3), 299–310.

Washington, G., & Johnson, T. (2012). Positive manhood development: A look at approaches and concerns from the frontline. *Journal of Human Behavior in the Social Environment, 22*(2), 172–187.

Washtenaw County Public Health. (2009). Youth photovoice: Implementation toolkit. Ypsilanti, NI: Author. Retrieved from http://www.ewashtenaw.org/government/departments/public_health/health-promotion/substance-abuse-prevention/pv_toolkit.pdf

Waasdrop. T. E., Baker, C. N., Paskewich, B. S., & Leff, S. S. (2013). The association between forms of aggression, leadership, and social status among urban youth. *Journal of Youth and Adolescence, 42*(2), 263–274.

Warne, M., Snyder, K., & Gadin, K.G. (2013). Photovoice: an opportunity and challenge for students' genuine participation. *Health Promotion International, 23*(10), 1354–1368.

Watson, M., & Douglas, F. (2012). *It's making us look disgusting . . . and it makes me feel like a mink . . . it makes me feel depressed!*: Using photovoice to help "see" and understand the perspectives of disadvantaged young people about the neighbourhood determinants of their mental well-being. *International Journal of Health Promotion and Education, 50*(6), 278–295.

Watts, S. (2010). "But it's got no tables or graphs in it. . .": A legacy of scientific dominance in psychology. In J.S. Jones & S. Watt (Eds.), *Ethnography in social science practice* (pp.42–56). London: Routledge.

Wearing, M. (2011). Strengthening youth citizenship and social inclusion practice—The Australian case: Towards rights based and inclusive practice in services for marginalized young people. *Children and Youth Services Review, 11*(4), 534–540.

Wee, B., DePierre, A., Anthanatten, P., & Barbour, B. (2013). Visual methodology as a pedagogical research tool in geography education. *Journal of Geography in Higher Education, 37*(2), 164–173.

Weil, M. (2004). Introduction: Contexts and challenges for 21st century communities. In M. Weil (Ed.), *Handbook of community practice* (pp.30–33). Thousand Oaks, CA: Sage.

Weis, L., & Fine, M. (Eds.). (2004). *Working method: Research and social justice.* New York, NY: Routledge.

Wendler, D., Rackoff, J., Emanuel, E., & Grady, G. (2002). Commentary: The ethics of paying for children's participation in research. *Journal of Pediatrics, 141*(2), 166–171.

Werne, M., Snyder, K., & Cadin, K.C. (2013). Photography: An opportunity and challenge for students' genuine participation. *Health Promotion International, 28*(3), 299–310.

Westphal, L. M., & Hirsch, J. L. (2010). Engaging Chicago residents in climate change action: Results from rapid ethnography inquiry. *Cities and the Environment, 3*(1), Article 13. Retrieved from http://digitalcommons.lmu.edu/cate/vol3/iss1/13/

Wexler, L, DiFluvio, G., & Burke, T.K. (2013). Resilience and marginalized youth: Making a case for personal and collective meaning-making as part of resilience research in public health. *Social Science & Medicine, 69*(4), 565–570.

Wexler, L., Gubrium, A., Griffin, M., & DiFulvio, G. (2013). Promoting positive youth development and highlighting reasons for living in Northwest Alaska through digital storytelling. *Health Promotion Practice, 14*(4), 617–623.

White, D. J., Shoffner, A., Johnson, K., Knowles, N., & Mills, M. (2012). Advancing positive youth development: Perspectives of youth as researchers and evaluators. *Journal of Extension, 50*(4). Retrieved from http://www.joe.org/joe/2012august/a4.php

White, R. J., & Green, A. E. (2012). The use of mental maps in youth research: Some evidence from research exploring young people's awareness of an attachment to place. In S. Heath & C. Walker (Eds.), *Innovations in youth research* (pp. 58–76). London: Sage.

White-Cooper, S. Dawkins, N.V., Kamin, S. L., & Anderson, L. A. (2007). Community-institutional partnerships: Understanding trust among partners. *Health education & Behavior, 36*(2), 234–237.

Wiersma, E. C. (2011). Using photovoice with people with early Alzheimer's disease: A discussion of methodology. *Dementia: The International Journal of Social Research and Practice, 10*(2), 203–216.

Wiles, R. (2013). *What are qualitative research ethics?* London: Bloomsbury Academics.

Wilhelm, A., & Cheecham, C. (2013). *Sharing worlds of knowledge: Research protocols for communities.* Manoa, Hawaii: University of Hawaii.

Wilkin, A., & Liamputtong, P. (2010). The photovoice method: researching the experiences of Aboriginal health workers through photographs. *Australian journal of primary health, 16*(3), 231–239.

Williams, R. L., Willging, C. E., Quintero, G., Kahishman, S., Sussman, A. L., & Freeman, W. L. (2010). Ethics of health research in communities: Perspectives from the Southwestern United States. *Annals of Family Medicine, 8*(5), 433–439.

Wilson, M. G., Lavis, J. N., Travers, R., & Rourke, S.B. (2010). Community-based knowledge transfer and exchange. Helping community-based organizations link research to action. *Implementation Science, 5*, 33. Retrieved from http://www.implementationscience.com/content/5/1/33

Wilson, N., Dasho, S., Martin, A. C., Wallerstein, N., Wang, C. C., & Minkler, M. (2007). Engaging young adolescents in social action through photovoice: The Youth Empowerment Strategies (YES!) Project. *The Journal of Early Adolescence, 27*(2), 241–261.

Wilson, N., Minkler, M., Dasho, S., Carrillo, R., Wallerstein, N., & Garcia, D. (2006). Training students as facilitators in the Youth Empowerment Strategies (YES!) Project. *Journal of Community Practice, 14*(1), 201–217.

Winskie, J., & Murray, J. (2013) Heirloom seed & story keepers: Growing community & sustainability through arts-based research. *Papers and Publications: Interdisciplinary Journal of Undergraduate Research, 2*(1), Article 10. Retrievded from http://digitalcommons.northgeorgia.edu/papersandpubs/vol2/iss1/10/

Wong, N., Zimmerman, M., & Parker, E. (2010). A typology of youth participation and empowerment for child and adolescent health promotion. *American Journal of Community Psychology, 46*(1–2), 100–114.

Woo, Y. Y. J. (2008). Engaging new audiences: Translating research into popular media. *Educational Researcher, 37*(6), 321–329.

Wood, B., & Kidman, J. (2013). Negotiating the ethical borders of visual research with young people. In K. Riele & R. Brooks (Eds.), *Negotiating ethical challenges in youth research* (pp. 149–162). New York, NY: Routledge.

Wood, J. (2010). Young people as activists: Ethical issues in promoting and supporting active citizenship. In S. Banks (Ed.), *Ethical issues in youth work* (pp. 192–205). New York, NY: Routledge.

Woodgate, R. L., Edwards, M., & Ripat, J. (2012). How families of children with complex care needs participate in everyday life. *Social Science & Medicine, 75*(10), 1912–1920.

Woodgate, R. L., & Kreklewetz, C. M. (2012). Youth's narratives about family members smoking: parenting the parent— it's not fair! *BMC Public Health, 12*: 965. Retrieved from http://www.biomedcentral.com/1471-2458/12/965

Woodgate, R. L., & Leach, J. (2010). Youth's perspectives on the determinants of health. *Qualitative Health Research, 20*(9), 1173–1182.

Woodson, S. E. (2007). Performing youth: Youth agency and the production of knowledge in community-based theater. Introduction. In A. Best (Ed.), *Representing youth: Methodological issues in critical youth studies* (pp. 284–303). New York, NY: New York University Press.

Wright, M. T., Roche, B., von Unger, H., Block, M., & Gardner, B. (2010). A call for international collaboration on participatory research for health. *Health Promotion International, 25*(1), 115–122.

Yankeelov, P. A., Faul, A. C., D'mbrosio, J. G., Collins, W. L., & Gordon, B. (2013). "Another Day in Paradise": A photovoice journey of rural older adults living with diabetes. *Journal of Applied Gerontology.* Advance online publication. doi:10.1177/0733464813493136

Yates, L. C. (2010). The story they want to tell, and the visual story as evidence: Young people, research authority and research purposes in the education and health domains. *Visual Studies, 25*(3), 280–291.

Yi, J., & Zebrack, B. (2010). Self-portraits of families with young adult cancer survivors: using photovoice. *Journal of Psychosocial Oncology, 28*(3), 219–243.

Yin, R. K. (2013). *Case study: Design and methods.* Thousand Oaks, CA: Sage.

Yonas, M. A., Burke, J. G., & Miller, E. (2). Visual voices: A participatory method for engaging adolescents in research and knowledge transfer. *Clinical and Translational Science, 6*(1), 72–77.

Yonas, M. A., Burke, J. G., Rak, K., Bennett, A., Kelly, V., & Gielen, A.C. (2009). A picture is worth a thousand words: Engaging youth in CBPR using creative arts. *Progress in Community Health Partnerships: Research, Education, and Action, 3*(4), 349–358.

Yoshida, S. C., Craypo, L., & Samuels, S. E. (2011). Engaging youth in improving their food and physical activity environments. *Journal of Adolescent Health, 48*(6), 641–643.

Yuile, A., Pepler, D., Craig, W., & Connolly, J. (2006). The ethics of peeking behind the fence: Issues related to studying children's aggression and victimization. In B. Leadbeater, E. Banister, C. Benoit, M. Jansson, A. Marshall, & T. Riecken (Eds.),

Ethical issues in community-based research with children and youth (pp. 70–89). Toronto, Canada: University of Toronto Press.

Zaff, J. F., & Lerner, R. M. (2010). Service learning promotes positive youth development in high school. *Phi Delta Kappan, 21*(5), 21–23.

Zenkov, K., & Harmon, J. (2009). Picturing a writing process: Photovoice and teaching writing to urban youth. *Journal of Adolescent & Adult Literacy, 52*(7), 575–584.

Zenkov, K., Pellegrino, A., Harmon, J., Ewaida, M., Bell, A., Lynch, M., & Sell, C. (2013). Picturing culturally literacy practices: Using photography to see how literacy curricula and pedagogies matter to urban youth. *International Journal of Multicultural Education, 15*(2), 1–20.

Zinn, H. (2005). *A people's history of the United States: 1491 to present.* New York, NY: Harper Perennial.

Zuch, M., Mathews, C. De Koker, P., Mtshizana, Y., & Mason-Jones, A. (2013). Evaluation of a photovoice pilot program for school safety in South Africa. *Children, Youth and Environments, 23*(1), 180–197.

INDEX

Page numbers followed by "f" and "t" indicate figures and tables.